The **Rough Guide** to

Belize

originally written and researched by

Peter Eltringham

with additional contributions by

Robert Coates and AnneLise Sorensen

www.roughguides.com

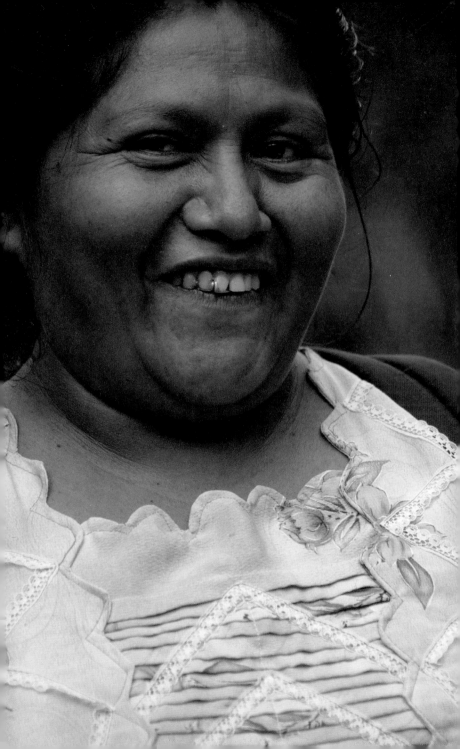

Contents

Underwater Belize
colour section
following p.88

The Maya world
colour section
following p.216

◀◀ Caye Caulker ◀ Maya woman, Toledo

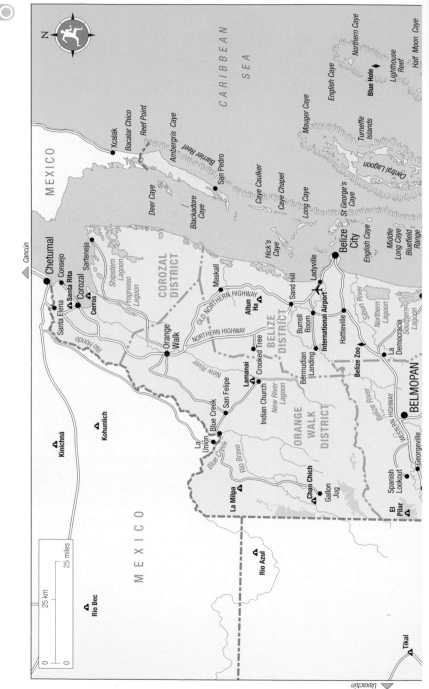

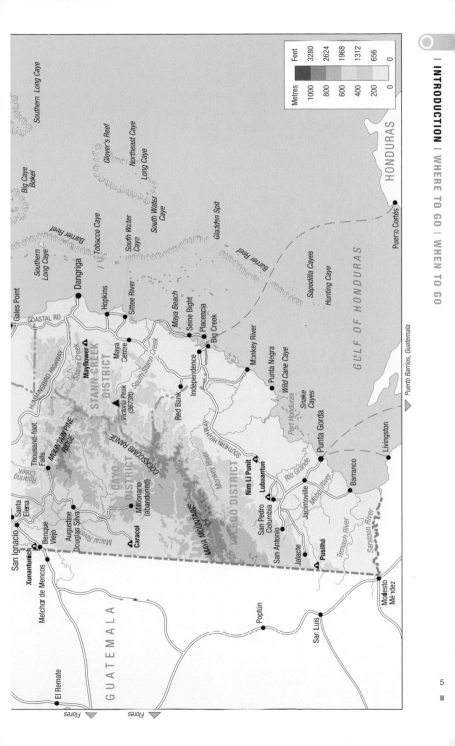

Introduction to
Belize

This Central American eco-pioneer may be petite, but it offers a huge range of extraordinary experiences: snorkel the longest Barrier Reef in the Americas; dive the inky depths of the Blue Hole; and embark on thigh-aching treks up soaring Maya pyramids. And, while geographically Belize is Central American, at heart it's Caribbean – offering a unique blend of both cultures.

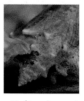

Belize is wedged into the northeastern corner of Central America, and features some of the most breathtaking coastal scenery – both above and below water – in the **Caribbean**. Throw in vast archeological sites and wildlife to rival that of any destination in the region, and it's easy to see why the number of visitors increases every year.

Belizean territory comprises marginally more sea than land, and for most visitors the sea is the main attraction. Lying just offshore is one of the country's, and the continent's, most astonishing natural wonders – the dazzling turquoise shallows and cobalt depths of the **barrier reef**. Beneath the surface, a brilliant technicolour world of fish and corals awaits divers and snorkellers, while a chain of islands known as cayes, scattered along the entire reef, protects the mainland from the ocean swell and holds more than a hint of tropical paradise. Beyond the reef lie the real jewels in Belize's natural crown – three of only four coral atolls in the Caribbean.

Belize has long been at the forefront of protecting its natural wonders and the country currently has the greatest proportion of protected land (over forty percent) in the hemisphere. As a result, the densely **forested interior** remains relatively untouched. The rich tropical forests support a tremendous range of **wildlife**, including howler and spider monkeys, tapirs and pumas, jabiru storks and scarlet macaws. Although it's the only Central American country without a volcano, Belize does have some rugged uplands – the **Maya Mountains**, situated in the south-central region and rising to over 3600ft. The country's main rivers start here, flowing north and east to the Caribbean, forming some of the largest **cave systems** in the Americas on the way.

In addition to these natural attractions, Belize boasts a wealth of archeological remains. Rising mysteriously out of the forests are the ruins of the **ancient cities**

of the **Maya**, the civilization that dominated the area from around 2000 BC until the arrival of the Spanish. Although only a few sites in Belize have been as extensively restored as the great Maya cities of Mexico's Yucatán Pensinsula, many are at least as large, and in their forest settings you'll see more wildlife and fewer tour buses.

Culturally, Belize is a unique blend of races and cultures that includes Caribbean, Central American, Maya, mestizo, African and European. English is the official language – Belize only gained full independence from Britain in 1981 – and Spanish is equally common, but it's the rich, lilting **Kriol**, based on English but essentially Caribbean, that's spoken and understood by almost every Belizean.

Where to go

Belize is an ideal place to explore independently; even on a short visit you'll be able to take in both the cayes and the heartland of the ancient Maya. Almost every visitor will have to spend at least some time in chaotic **Belize City**, even if only passing through, as it's the hub of the country's transport system. Nearby, the **Belize Zoo** is easily the best in Central America and well worth making a special effort to visit.

Northern Belize is relatively flat and often swampy, with a large proportion of agricultural land. **Lamanai**, near Orange Walk, is one of the most impressive Maya sites in Belize, while the lagoons, at **Shipstern Nature Reserve** on the northeast coast and inland at **Crooked Tree**, provide superb protected habitats for the country's abundant wildlife, particularly birds. In the northwest is the vast **Río Bravo Conservation and Management Area**, where you might have close encounters with the wildlife.

Fact file

- Belize shares a border with Mexico to the north and Guatemala to the west and south; to the east is the Caribbean Sea. Belize's 8666 square miles of land is roughly equal to that of Massachusetts or Wales, and it has a slightly greater area of territorial sea. Tourism is now the mainstay of the economy, but agriculture and fishing still play important roles.

- Belize has a bicameral National Assembly, consisting of a House of Representatives with 29 members and a twelve-member Senate. The government is headed by the Prime Minister but, as Belize is a constitutional monarchy, the head of state is Queen Elizabeth II, represented in Belize by the Governor-General, who is always a Belizean.

- Belize's national anthem is "Land of the Free by the Carib Sea", and a recording by schoolchildren is broadcast every morning at 6am on Love FM. The national animal is the Baird's tapir, the national bird is the keel-billed toucan, the national flower is the black orchid and the national tree is the mahogany tree; you can see all of these at the Belize Zoo (see p.63).

▼ Green Hills Butterfly Ranch

The mainland coast is almost entirely low-lying marsh – wonderful for wildlife, but for swimming and underwater activities you'll need to visit the **cayes**. The largest, **Ambergris Caye**, draws over half of all Belize's tourists, with the tiny resort town of **San Pedro** their main destination; **Caye Caulker**, to the south, is the most popular island for independent travellers. Organized diving and snorkelling day-trips are available to the wonderful atolls of the **Turneffe Islands** and **Lighthouse Reef**.

In the west, **San Ignacio** and its environs offer everything the eco-tourist could want: Maya ruins and rainforest, rivers and caves and excellent, low-impact accommodation in every price range. **Caracol**, the largest Maya site in Belize, is a routine day-trip from here, while the magnificent ruins of **Xunantunich** lie en route to the Guatemalan border. Cross the border and a few hours later you can be in **Tikal**, one of the greatest of all Maya cities.

Dangriga, the main town of the south-central region, is a jumping-off point for visitors to the central cayes and **Glover's Reef**, Belize's most remote atoll. Further south, on the coast, is the quiet Garifuna village of **Hopkins**, while the delightful, relaxed fishing village of **Placencia**, at the tip of a long, curving peninsula, has some of the country's best **beaches**. Inland, at

The Garifuna

One of Belize's most interesting ethnic groups is the **Garifuna** (or **Garinagu**), descendants of escaped African slaves and indigenous Caribbean islanders. Today they thrive along the southern coast, particularly in the villages of Dangriga, Hopkins, Seine Bight, Punta Gorda and Barranco. Most carry out a subsistence lifestyle, with women working the farms and preparing meals, men heading to sea before daybreak to fish and children helping with family chores.

Their culture is exuberantly displayed on November 19, **Garifuna Settlement Day**, a national holiday celebrating their historic arrival in Belize in the early nineteenth century. Many Garifuna re-enact their migration in dories loaded with drums, cassava, banana leaves, palm fronds and flags of yellow, white and black. This is also a great time to catch enthusiastic displays of the Garifuna's impressive musical heritage, including drumming and punta. Equally festive are **rituals** surrounding the deceased: the *beluria* is a nine-day devotional ceremony for the dead, and the *dugu* is a sacred rite involving ancestral spirit worship.

the village of **Maya Centre**, lies the road to **Cockscomb Basin Wildlife Sanctuary** (the **Jaguar Reserve**) and the trailhead to **Victoria Peak**, Belize's most majestic mountain. The majority of visitors to the coastal community of **Punta Gorda**, the main town of Toledo District, are on their way by boat to or from Puerto Barrios in Guatemala. Venture inland, however, and you'll come across the villages of the **Mopan** and **Kekchí Maya**, set in lovely countryside and surrounded by the country's only true **rainforest**. Here are yet more caves, rivers and Maya sites, including **Lubaantun**, source of the enigmatic Crystal Skull.

◀ Garifuna children, Dangriga

9

When to go

▼ Caye Caulker

Due to Belize's **subtropical** latitude, the weather is always warm by European standards, and often hot and very humid. The climate in any one place is largely determined by **altitude**: evenings in the forests of the Mountain Pine Ridge are generally pleasantly cool, while the lowland jungle is always steamy and humid. On the cayes, the sun's heat is tempered by near-constant ocean breezes.

Although Belize has its dry and rainy seasons, you'll find that the sun shines most of the year, and while rain can fall in any month, it's rarely persistent enough to ruin a holiday. The **dry season** runs roughly from February to May, and the last couple of months before the rains come can be stiflingly hot. During the **rainy season**, from around June to November, mornings are generally clear while afternoons can be drenched by an hour or two of downpours. During especially heavy rains, rural roads may be flooded and journeys delayed, particularly in the **south**. The worst of the rains fall in September and October, which is also the height of the **hurricane season**, though most severe storms follow a track well to the north of Belize. If you're out on the cayes or near the coast you'll need to leave, but rest assured that Belize has an efficient warning system and a network of shelters. The rain can continue into December, a time when **cold fronts**, known locally as **"northers"**, sometimes lower temperatures to 10°C for a couple of days.

With all this in mind, the **best time of year** to visit Belize is from late December to March, when the vegetation is still lush and the skies are generally clear. This is also the main tourist season and therefore the priciest time to visit. Plenty of people visit during the summer months, too – a period that's appropriately promoted by the tourism industry as the **"green season"**.

Average temperatures in Belize City

	Jan	Feb	Mar	Apr	May	Jun	Jul	Aug	Sep	Oct	Nov	Dec
Belize City												
Max/min (°C)	29/19	29/20	30/21	31/24	31/24	31/23	32/23	32/22	32/22	31/22	28/20	28/20
Max/min (°F)	84/66	84/68	86/70	88/75	88/75	88/73	90/73	90/72	90/72	88/72	82/68	82/68

things not to miss

It's not possible to see everything that Belize has to offer in one trip – and we don't suggest you try. What follows is a selective and subjective taste of the country's highlights: outstanding natural attractions, underwater wonders, Maya ruins and distinctive cultural traditions. They're arranged in five colour-coded categories to help you find the very best to see, do and experience. All entries have a page reference to take you straight into the Guide, where you can find out more.

01 The Belize Barrier Reef Page **97** • For spellbinding natural beauty, it's hard to beat a snorkelling or diving trip to the Belize Barrier Reef, the longest in the western hemisphere, and where you might see everything from turtles to tropical fish.

02 Toucans
Page **201** •
The unmistakable keel-billed toucan is the national bird of Belize and, though found almost anywhere, is best seen in the village of Sittee River.

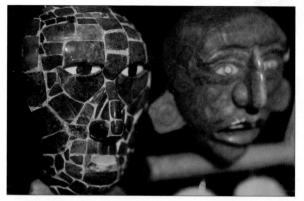

03 The Museum of Belize
Page **59** •
This museum features excellent collections of painted Maya ceramics and jade jewellery. A visit here is one of Belize City's highlights.

04 Caves
Page **135** • Belize has many spectacular caves, among them those at Barton Creek and Río Frio. Many are partly filled with water and hold Maya artefacts that haven't seen daylight for centuries.

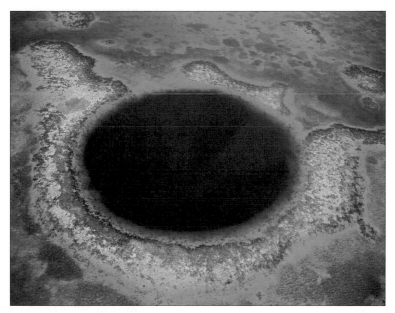

05 The Blue Hole Page **122** • On Lighthouse Reef, dive the inky depths of the coral-encrusted Blue Hole, an enormous circular cavern over 980ft across – or fly over it in a light plane or helicopter.

06 Caracol Page **142** • The greatest of Belize's ancient Maya cities is gradually revealing its history and attracting more visitors every year.

07  **The Belize Zoo** Page **63**
• Enjoy close encounters with the animals and birds of Central America at this charming and well-run little zoo.

08 Garifuna drumming Page **198** • Listen to the rhythms of Africa pulsing through the Caribbean as the drumbeats of the Garifuna proclaim their unique cultural heritage.

09 Lobster-Fest Page **113** • Ambergris Caye, Caye Caulker and Placencia celebrate the opening of the lobster season around June, with a festival featuring music and dancing – and of course sampling the catch.

10 Tikal Page **170** • Across the Guatemalan border is the monumental Maya city of Tikal, looming out of a magnificent protected rainforest.

11 Watersports on the cayes Page **107** • A supremely relaxing way to spend the day is to take one of many sailing trips available from the cayes; for an adrenaline-charged alternative, try windsurfing.

12 The Mountain Pine Ridge Page **170** • Hike the hills, peaks and gorges of this vast forest reserve, taking in the majesty of the tallest waterfall in Central America and perhaps staying in a luxurious riverside lodge.

13 Placencia Page **208** • This relaxed, southern fishing village is renowned for the beauty of its beaches.

14 Carnival Page **49** • The music and energy of Carnival in Belize City is the highlight of the "September Celebrations", which commemorate Independence Day and the Battle of St George's Caye.

15 Ambergris Caye Page 100 •
Enjoy sun and surf on Belize's largest and most popular island; come nightfall, hit the lively beach bars in San Pedro.

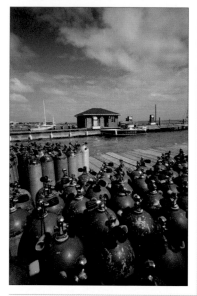

16 San Ignacio Page 145 • San
Ignacio, the adventure centre of western Belize, also has one of the best markets in the country.

17 Lamanai Page 83 •
More than two thousand years ago Lamanai was the largest city anywhere in the Maya world; today, take an exciting riverboat journey to see its massive temples rising out of the jungle.

Basics

Basics

Getting there

Although most visitors arrive by air at the international airport outside Belize City, it's also possible to reach Belize by bus or boat from neighbouring countries (see p.24). A pair of domestic airlines facilitate transport around the country once you arrive. An international airport is under construction in Placencia, with completion set for 2012.

Airfare prices from the US rise during the **high season** (December to early April, especially around Christmas and Easter) and also in July and August for flights originating in Europe. At these times seat availability can be a problem: flying mid-week and booking ahead are good ideas.

Flights from North America

Four US airlines fly **nonstop** directly to Belize: American Airlines, Continental, Delta and US Airways. El Salvador-based TACA also has nonstop flights from Houston. There are occasionally direct flights from Toronto, Canada; otherwise, you can generally get same- or next-day connections to the hubs above from Vancouver, Toronto and Montréal.

Typical **prices from the US** are around US$550 (low season)/600–900 (high season) from New York; US$550/900–1200 from Seattle; and US$500/800–900 from Houston. **From Canada** (Toronto, Montréal and Ottawa) expect to pay around Can$930 (low season)/1100 (high season) and from Vancouver, Can$850/940–1600.

Flights from the UK and Ireland

Visitors from the UK and Ireland have two options for getting to Belize, neither of which involves a direct flight (though several runways are being expanded at Belize International Airport to eventually facilitate direct flights from Europe). The first option is to fly to one of the US hubs and then take a connecting flight. Unfortunately, this invariably means passing through the officious **US immigration system**; you must have a machine-readable passport and leave ample time to obtain either a US visa-waiver online, or a US visa (see p.39).

Although **flying from London** gives you the widest choice of flights to the US and onwards to Belize, you can sometimes get flights from Manchester, Birmingham, Glasgow and other UK airports for the same price. A scheduled return flight to Belize City on American, Delta, Continental, US Airways or Virgin (in conjunction with TACA) will cost around £500–550 in low season (Feb & Nov to mid-Dec) and £700–1000 in high season (July, Aug, mid-Dec to Jan & Easter).

The second option is to fly to Mexico and continue **overland** (see p.20). Several European airlines fly directly to Mexico City or Cancún, often a considerably cheaper route than flying through the US. Many US airlines operating from the UK also have well-priced flights to Mexico via a US hub. From Mexico City, you can fly directly to Chetumal daily with Click Airways (☎52/55 5322 6262, ⓦwww.clickmx.com), for around £100, and continue by bus to Belize from there. Maya Island Air (ⓦwww.mayaregional.com) also has flights between Cancún and Belize City, while there are hourly buses from Cancún to Chetumal (5hr).

From Ireland, Continental and American Airlines fly direct from Belfast and Dublin to Houston, Newark or another US city requiring transit to one of the US hubs. You can also get flights from Belfast or Dublin to London and then connect with one of the transatlantic flights. Fares from Belfast to Belize (via the US) are similar to or sometimes lower than those from London, around £550 (low season)/850 (high season). From Dublin to Belize you can expect to pay around €770/1200. Alternatively, you can fly **direct from Ireland to Mexico** and continue overland; discount fares from Belfast to Cancún range from £500–680 return. The same airlines also often have good deals on flights from Dublin to Cancún from €800.

Flights from Australia, New Zealand and South Africa

With no direct flights from Australasia to Belize, you'll have to fly to the US first, generally and least expensively to Los Angeles. Flights via Asia are longer and cost more, but you often get a subsidized overnight stay in the carrier's home city. For most Australasian airlines, low season is mid-January to the end of February and October to the end of November; high season is mid-May to the end of August and December to mid-January.

From Australia, the cheapest fares (from Sydney and most of the eastern state capitals) via Los Angeles to Belize City (on Qantas and Delta, TACA via San Salvador or Continental via Houston) generally start at Aus$2900 (low season) and Aus$3700 (high season). Departing from Perth or Darwin can be Aus$400–650 higher. **From New** Zealand (Auckland) the cheapest flights to Belize City are via Los Angeles (on Air Tahiti Nui or Air New Zealand and Delta), around NZ$2800/3500. Flying to Cancún or Mexico City from any of these cities is several hundred dollars **cheaper** than flying into Belize.

From South Africa, you can fly to the US or to the UK and continue your journey from there. Flights from Johannesburg to Belize City (via Atlanta and London on Delta or South African Airways) start around R13,770 in the low season and R21,540 in the high season.

Overland from Mexico

Flying into Cancún or Mexico City from a non-US origin is an attractive option for travellers who don't want to tangle with US immigration. Click Airways (☎52/55 5322 6262, ⊛www.clickmx.com) runs **daily flights** from Mexico City to Chetumal, just north of the Belizean border. Maya Island Air (see opposite) offers flights between Cancún

Six steps to a better kind of travel

At Rough Guides we are passionately committed to travel. We feel strongly that only through travelling do we truly come to understand the world we live in and the people we share it with – plus tourism has brought a great deal of **benefit** to developing economies around the world over the last few decades. But the extraordinary growth in tourism has also damaged some places irreparably, and of course **climate change** is exacerbated by most forms of transport, especially flying. This means that now more than ever it's important to **travel thoughtfully** and **responsibly**, with respect for the cultures you're visiting – not only to derive the most benefit from your trip but also to preserve the best bits of the planet for everyone to enjoy. At Rough Guides we feel there are six main areas in which you can make a difference:

- Consider what you're contributing to the **local economy**, and how much the services you use do the same, whether it's through employing local workers and guides or sourcing locally grown produce and local services.
- Consider the **environment** on holiday as well as at home. Water is scarce in many developing destinations, and the biodiversity of local flora and fauna can be adversely affected by tourism. Try to patronize businesses that take account of this.
- Travel with a purpose, not just to tick off experiences. Consider **spending longer** in a place, and getting to know it and its people.
- Give thought to how often you **fly**. Try to avoid short hops by air and more harmful night flights.
- Consider **alternatives to flying**, travelling instead by bus, train, boat and even by bike or on foot where possible.
- Make your trips "**climate neutral**" via a reputable carbon offset scheme. All Rough Guide flights are offset, and every year we donate money to a variety of charities devoted to combating the effects of climate change.

and Belize City. Aside from this option, buses also shuttle between the two countries. **Buses** in Mexico are fairly fast, and there are regular connections between every Mexican city and the capital, and good connections from there to the town of **Chetumal** (around 22hr), close to the Belizean border. From Chetumal, several Belizean and Guatemalan bus companies depart for Orange Walk and onward to Belize City. Buses leave generally throughout the morning, with fewer in the afternoon. Note that if you've spent fewer than three days in Mexico, you shouldn't have to pay an exit fee.

Travelling **overland from the US** through Mexico is a long, two- to three-day haul, but allows you to see some of the country on the way. Greyhound buses (℡1-800/229-9424, ⓦwww.greyhound.com) run regularly to all major US-Mexico border crossings, and some even take you over the frontier and into the Mexican bus station.

Heading south **by car** gives you more freedom but involves a good deal of bureaucracy. You'll need a credit card to pay a bond to ensure you don't sell the car in Mexico, and separate **insurance** to cover your drive through the country; purchase it from Sanborns (℡1-800/222-0158, ⓦwww.sanbornsinsurance.com) at the US-Mexico border. Crossing the Belizean border with a car can entail large **customs charges** (payable in cash only), particularly if you plan to leave your vehicle in the country.

US, Canadian, EU, South African, Australian and New Zealand driving licences are valid in Mexico and Belize, but it's a good idea to arm yourself with an **International Driving Licence** as well; contact your local driving authority to obtain one. For details on driving in Belize, see p.25.

Airlines, agents and operators

Airlines

Aeroméxico ⓦwww.aeromexico.com.
Air New Zealand ⓦwww.airnz.com.
Air Tahiti Nui ⓦwww.airtahitinui-usa.com.
American Airlines ⓦwww.aa.com.
British Airways ⓦwww.ba.com.
Click Airways ⓦwww.clickmx.com.
Continental ⓦwww.continental.com.

Delta ⓦwww.delta.com.
JAL ⓦwww.japanair.com.
Maya Island Air ⓦwww.mayaregional.com.
Mexicana ⓦwww.mexicana.com.
TACA ⓦwww.taca.com.
Tropic Air ⓦwww.tropicair.com.
US Airways ⓦwww.usairways.com.
Qantas ⓦwww.qantas.com.
United Airlines ⓦwww.ual.com.

Agents and operators

Adventure Life ℡1-800/344-6118, ⓦwww.adventure-life.com. Specialists in small-group travel and customized itineraries to wilderness areas and nature reserves in Latin America.
Close Encounters ℡1-888/875-1822, ⓦwww.belizecloseencounters.com. Small company, experienced in arranging individual itineraries for all budgets to Belize.
Gap Adventures ℡1-800/708-7761, ⓦwww.gapadventures.com. Canadian company offering a wide range of group trips (some camping) with diving and kayaking in the Yucatán, Belize and throughout Central America.
Global Travel Club ℡01268/541 363, ⓦwww.global-travel.co.uk. Small company specializing in diving, adventure and cultural tours to Belize, Mexico and all of Central America.
International Expeditions ℡1-800/633-4734, ⓦwww.internationalexpeditions.com. Natural history tours and individual itineraries throughout Latin America, including Belize and Tikal.
Island Expeditions ℡1-800/667-1630, ⓦwww.islandexpeditions.com. Vancouver-based company, with sea and river kayaking expeditions to Belize and other destinations in Central America.
Journeys International ℡1-800/255-8735, ⓦwww.journeys.travel. Nature and cultural tours to Belize and the rest of Central America.
Journey Latin America UK ℡020/8747 8315, ⓦwww.journeylatinamerica.co.uk. One of the industry leaders for airfares and tours to Latin America, with good prices on high-season flights.
Latin American Escapes ℡1-800/510-5999, ⓦwww.latinamericanescapes.com. Adventure and diving holidays in Belize.
Naturetrek ℡01962/733 051, ⓦwww.naturetrek.co.uk. Superb birdwatching trips led by expert naturalists.
North South Travel UK ℡01245/608 291, ⓦwww.northsouthtravel.co.uk. Friendly, competitive travel agency, offering discounted fares worldwide. Profits are used to support projects in the developing world, especially the promotion of sustainable tourism.

Reef and Rainforest Tours ☎01803/866 965, ⓦwww.reefandrainforest.co.uk. Tours focusing on nature reserves, research projects and diving in Belize, Honduras and Costa Rica.
Slickrock Adventures ☎1-800/390-5715, ⓦwww.slickrock.com. One of the better adventure companies, offering sea kayaking and jungle and river (some whitewater) expeditions in Belize.
STA Travel US ☎1-800/781-4040, UK ☎0871/230 0040, Australia ☎134 782, New Zealand ☎0800/474 400, South Africa ☎0861/781 781; ⓦwww.statravel.com. Worldwide specialists in independent travel; also discount student fares.

USIT Ireland ☎01/602 1906, Northern Ireland ☎028/9032 7111; ⓦwww.usit.ie. Ireland's main student and youth travel specialists.
Travel CUTS Canada ☎1-866/246-9762, US ☎1-800/592-2887; ⓦwww.travelcuts.com. Canadian youth and student travel firm.
Trips Worldwide ☎0117/311 4400, ⓦwww.tripsworldwide.co.uk. Friendly, experienced company with a range of itineraries and tours to Belize, Mexico and all of Central America, among other global destinations.

Arrival

Most people will arrive in Belize City at Philip Goldson International Airport, about a twenty-minute drive from the centre. Those arriving by bus will pull in either at the Marine Terminal or the main bus terminal on Canal Street, where taxis are plentiful. Points of arrival in other towns are bus terminals and ports, from where it's simple to find your way around in a taxi or otherwise.

By air

From the international airport, most travellers either catch an onward flight to another Belizean destination; or go by taxi (Bz$50) to the centre. You can also take a bus from the airport to the centre, but this can be a tedious haul, as you'll need to walk to the Northern Highway (around 25min), and then flag down a local bus (which often run on irregular schedules, particularly in the evening) into the city.

By bus

All the Belizean companies arriving in Belize City will drop you at the main bus terminal on Canal Street. It's fairly central but in a not-so-desirable part of the city, so getting a taxi to or from here is a good idea. The **fare** to pretty much anywhere in town is around

Bz$8–10. If you arrive with a Guatemalan bus company, such as San Juan or Linea Dorada from Chetumal or Flores, you'll usually pull into the **Marine Terminal**, where you can catch a water taxi to the Northern Cayes (see p.97).

By car

There are only two land routes into Belize from outside the country, one from Mexico and the other from Guatemala. These points of entry merge, respectively, with the Northern and Western highways. If you arrive in the south by boat and rent a car in one of the southern towns, you'll travel north along the Southern Highway before turning onto the Western Highway for Belize City (east) or Belmopan and beyond (west). If you intend to bring your own car to Belize, watch out for heavy import taxes.

Getting around

Belize has a good public transport network and all main roads are paved. Buses on the three main highways (the Northern, Western and Southern) are cheap, generally frequent and fairly fast.

If you visit the cayes during your visit, you're likely to do some travelling by **boat**; water journeys to Guatemala and Honduras are also possible. River transport is popular in Belize, too – it's the most convenient way to reach some Maya ruins and isolated field stations.

Flying between Belizean destinations is the fastest way to get around, though it's not particularly cheap. In the south, however, where bus transport can be patchy, a short hop on a small plane can give superb views of the hills and the clear, blue sea. **Car rental** in Belize is not inexpensive, either: it generally costs US$60–120 per day, but it does enable you to visit more places in a shorter time than you could by bus.

By air

The main towns and tourist destinations in Belize are linked by domestic flights operated by the country's two chief carriers: Maya Island Air (☎223-1140, ⓦwww.maya regional.com) and Tropic Air (☎226-2012,

ⓦwww.tropicair.com). There are also several **charter airlines**. Together, Maya Island and Tropic Air provide up to eight to ten daily flights on each of the main routes – Belize City to Dangriga, Placencia and Punta Gorda – and dozens to San Pedro and Caye Caulker. Prices start at around Bz$67–85; note that they often offer seasonal deals and discounts. There are no direct flights from Belize City to Corozal, though you can fly there from San Pedro. Both airlines operate from Belize International Airport and the smaller, domestic Belize Municipal Airport (a few miles north of the city centre). Note that you'll usually pay around Bz$50 more to depart from the International Airport.

Flying is also the most convenient way to make **side trips** out of Belize to neighbouring countries. Both domestic airlines operate flights to Flores, Guatemala (for Tikal). Maya Island Air also offers flights to Cancún, Mexico; Guatemala City; and San Pedro Sula, Honduras. TACA also flies from Belize City to its main hub in San Salvador for connections throughout Central America.

By bus

The vast majority of buses in Belize are of the US school bus variety, brightly painted and managed by several different companies. They are well maintained and removed from service when they get too old, but still aren't that comfortable for lengthy journeys or long limbs. The faster **"express"** buses are occasionally the more comfortable coach type; they operate along all main highways, stopping only in terminals in the towns. The more common non-express or "regular" buses will stop anywhere along their route on request. Tell the driver or conductor where you're headed and they'll usually know where to let you off.

Distances from Belize City

Distances are based on transportation routes, not as the crow flies.

Belize City to	Distance
Belmopan	52 miles (84km)
Caye Caulker	21 miles (34km)
Chetumal, Mexico	93 miles (149km)
Corozal	84 miles (135km)
Dangriga	106 miles (171km)
Guatemalan border	81 miles (130km)
Orange Walk	54 miles (87km)
Placencia	161 miles (259km)
Punta Gorda	213 miles (343km)
San Ignacio	72 miles (116km)
San Pedro	32 miles (51km)
Tikal, Guatemala	149 miles (240km)

UNFORGETABLE

BELIZE

ADVENTURES

Sea Kayak & Snorkel
Remote Reefs
& Coral Atolls

Rainforest Rivers
Mayan Ruins
& Caves

EXPEDITIONS.COM
www.islandexpeditions.com
FREE ADVENTURE GUIDE
1-800-667-1630
FREEPHONE UK 0800-404-9535

Services usually begin in the very early morning and finish sometime in the evening. On Sundays and holidays, some services are reduced or, in the case of smaller, local ones, often non-existent. For details of the bus routes from Belize City, see p.69. Some bus schedules and further information is available at ⓦwww.nationaltransport belize.com and www.guidetobelize.info.

Over half of the buses that ply the Northern Highway cross the Mexican border to serve the town of Chetumal. Others terminate in Corozal town, nine miles south of the border. On the Western Highway, many buses terminate in Benque Viejo, so you'll need to take a *colectivo* (shared) taxi the remaining one mile to the **Guatemalan border**. Services along the Southern Highway are less frequent, particularly beyond Dangriga, although there are still several daily routes.

Heading away from the main highways, you'll rely mostly on **local buses** operated by small agencies, which rarely have backup plans when breakdowns occur. Travelling this way is a fairly slow business, as it caters primarily to the needs of villagers – taking produce to market, and so on – but it has its rewards: you're sharing a ride with people who know the area well, and by the time your ride's over you may have made friends eager to show you around.

Fares are a true bargain compared to the cost of most things in Belize. Regular buses start at around Bz$8–10; tickets for express buses are just a few dollars more. Bus terminals don't have ticket offices; you pay the conductor, who will remember your destination whether or not he's issued you an actual ticket.

By boat

Your first experience of water transport in Belize is likely to be aboard one of the fast skiffs that ferry passengers (around 25–40 at a time) from Belize City and other mainland destinations out to the **cayes**. Many have a covered seating area, though some are still fully open-deck. They provide a quick (if sometimes bumpy), reliable and safe service.

Transport to the cayes and other popular **coastal destinations** leaves daily from the Marine Terminal, next to the Swing Bridge in Belize City, and from the San Pedro Express Water Taxi Terminal, on North Front Street. Services to Caye Caulker and San Pedro on Ambergris Caye operate approximately every ninety minutes, with most boats making both stops; see p.51 for more information. Some of the boats on the Caye Caulker/San Pedro run will also call at St George's Caye on request, although only at certain times. There are no advance bookings for these water journeys and seats are not reserved, though tickets for early-morning departures from the cayes can be purchased the night before. It's wise to show up at least fifteen minutes prior to departure; at busy times, one or two extra boats will be on hand for overflow, so it's unlikely you won't find space.

Many **tours** include boat transport in their itineraries, often to destinations, such as outlying cayes and atolls, that public routes don't serve. The only **international boat services** are skiffs from Punta Gorda to Puerto Barrios, Guatemala; Punta Gorda to Lívingston, Guatemala; and Dangriga and Placencia to Puerto Cortés, Honduras. It's

Tour operators in Belize

In addition to the overseas tour operators listed in Getting there (p.21), several Belizean agencies can expertly plan and book itineraries throughout the country. Many more specialist tour companies, often associated with hotels or resorts, are covered individually throughout this Guide.

Adventures in Belize ☏822-2800, ⓦwww.adventuresinbelize.com. Based at *Caves Branch Jungle Lodge* (see p.130) and offering everything from wilderness survival to luxury tours, all with outstanding guides.

Belize Trips ☏223-0376 or 610-1923, in the US ☏1-561/210-7015, ⓦwww .belize-trips.com. Run by the very knowledgeable Katie Valk, who is a font of information on Belize, and able to arrange and connect you with any tour in Belize.

Sun Creek Lodge & IBTM Tours ☏614-2080, ⓦwww.suncreeklodge.com. Operating from Sun Creek Lodge (p.223), and specializing in tours of southern Belize.

Maya Travel Services ☏223-1623, ⓦwww.mayatravelservices.com. Great for advice on international flights and very knowledgeable about tours and hotels in Belize.

---

best to book ahead for international departures by contacting the boat operator or their agents at least one day before.

By car

Although Belize has only four **paved highways**, driving is a popular option with visitors, and these roads offer relatively easy motoring and generally smooth surfaces. If you plan to conduct further exploration, you'll need high clearance and probably four-wheel drive. Main roads, and even most unpaved side roads, are typically well maintained and passable except in the very worst rainstorms, though mud, dust and the occasional massive pothole can be a problem at any time. Distances in Belize are generally measured in miles. When planning your journey, bear in mind that petrol stations may be scarce outside towns.

Traffic is generally light outside Belize City, but driving standards everywhere are abysmal and **fatal accidents** are high relative to traffic density. The busiest stretch of road is on the Western Highway between Belize City and Belmopan. Road signs are becoming more noticeable along the main highways, but you'll have to watch out for **speed bumps** of variable height; these are occasionally signed, but every new driver in Belize is bound to be caught unaware at least once – with potentially disastrous consequences. Look for them on entering and leaving any settlement along the highways, as well as shortly before bus stops.

Car rental

All the main rental companies offer cars, trucks and vans, including **four-wheel drive** options, for around US$70–125 per day, plus nine percent sales tax and another US$13–15 per day for insurance, depending on the class of vehicle. All companies have offices at the international airport and in Belize City.

Avis (ⓦwww.avis.com), Budget (ⓦwww .budget.com), Hertz (ⓦwww.hertz.com) and Thrifty have franchises in Belize and, along with local firm Crystal (ⓦwww.crystal-belize .com) (which offers some of the best rental prices and is the only company that allows you to take its vehicles to Tikal), accept advance bookings; there are also other local companies. **Reserving ahead** of time can save money and guarantees that a car will be waiting for you on arrival. One-way rentals typically aren't available, but your rental company can provide a pick up or drop-off at your Belize City hotel or the airport. See Listings on p.68 for details of car rental companies in Belize City.

In most cases you'll need to be 25 to rent a vehicle (if you are aged between 21 and 25 you may be required to pay a premium), and you'll probably have to leave a credit card imprint as a damage deposit when you pick up the car. Before you belt up and drive off into the sunset, check exactly what the **insurance** covers, examine the car carefully for signs of existing damage (making sure it's marked on the rental contract) and check what spares and equipment are included. A good **spare wheel** (and the tools to put it on) is essential – you'll get an average of one puncture a week from heavy driving on Belize's roads.

Hitchhiking

In the more remote parts of Belize, bus services will probably operate only once a day, if at all, so unless you have your own transport, **hitching** is the only other option. Although locals, including women and children, regularly hitch rides in rural areas, women travellers may prefer to do so with a friend; hitching in Belize is generally safer than at home or in neighbouring countries, but attacks have occurred, and the practice should never be considered entirely safe. Apart from this, the main drawback is the **lack of traffic**, but if cars or pickup trucks pass, the driver will usually offer you a lift, though occasionally you may be expected to donate some money for the ride.

Taxis

All taxis in Belize are licensed and easily identifiable by their green licence plates. Drivers operate from ranks in the centres of towns and bus stations and, particularly in Belize City, will call out to anyone they suspect is a foreigner. There are **no meters**, so you'll need to establish a rate in advance, though within the towns a fixed fare of Bz$7–8 for one or two people usually applies. You can negotiate **out-of-town fares** with the driver. Designated airport taxis from the international airport charge Bz$50 to Belize City; taxis will almost certainly be waiting for all scheduled domestic flights at Belize Municipal Airport, and at all bus stations. Some drivers (such as those

at the Marine Terminal in Belize City) are also **licensed tour guides** and have been through tourism training. It's common to share taxis in Belize, so your driver may stop to pick up another fare during your journey.

Cycling

Touring Belize by bike is fairly straightforward, particularly in the north and west where the roads are well surfaced, and also along the Hummingbird Highway – if you can manage the hills. Some locals will be surprised to see you using this form of transport, but don't assume that you're always noticed – **stay alert** to traffic. Cycling on the highways after dark is not recommended.

Cycling is a popular sport in Belize: citizens compete internationally, and several annual races, in which visitors are welcome to take part, are heavily attended. You'll find cycle **repair shops** in many towns. Mountain or beach bikes are available for rent at an increasing number of shops and resorts (sometimes free for guests). Inspect rental bikes carefully since they deteriorate quickly in coastal climes, and if you intend to cycle a lot, bring or buy your own lock, lights and a helmet, which can be difficult to find. Two of the best places to rent a bike are San Ignacio, where you can ride along the forest roads in the Mountain Pine Ridge, and Placencia, whose smooth, sandy resort road makes for an enjoyable day's riding. Renting a mountain bike in Punta Gorda will give you the freedom to explore the Maya villages and hills of Toledo.

Bikes can only rarely be carried on top of buses; few Belizean buses have the **roof racks** so common in Guatemala. If you're lucky – and if there's room – the driver may let you put your bike in the back of the bus.

Accommodation

Accommodation in Belize ranges from world-renowned resorts to cheap, clapboard hotels. In each category between, there's a wide range of prices and it's fairly easy to find somewhere both comfortable and affordable to stay.

Towns in Belize are so small that you can usually walk to the majority of hotels from the bus stop to see what's on offer. For much of the year occupancy rates are very low, and you should have little difficulty finding a room even in the high season. The few exceptions are Christmas and New Year, when you'll almost certainly need to **book ahead** in resort areas.

The cost of accommodation in Belize is notably higher than in surrounding countries, but a little investigation can often turn up good bargains. Toucan Trail, a consortium of small, affordable hotels that have met the association's standards of social and environmental sustainability, recommends places to stay on its website (@www.toucan trail.com).

Arriving early at your destination gives you time to look around for the best room in your budget. A good idea, especially in cheaper places, is to ask to see the room before you accept it; check that the light and fan work, and if you've been told there's hot water, see just what that means. In towns, it's sometimes better to get a room at the back, away from the street noise, although people-watching from the front balcony can be fascinating; an upstairs room means you're more likely to benefit from a breeze.

Budget and mid-range hotels and guesthouses

Most small hotels and guesthouses are family-run, and owners generally take pride in the **cleanliness** of the rooms. Check-in is typically informal – you'll usually have to pay on arrival and sign the register.

Budget hotels run the gamut. As a rule, a basic room will have a bed, light and fan, and all but the most rock-bottom of places will supply a towel, soap and toilet paper. You'll often have the option of a **private bathroom**, which can be worth paying a little extra for.

Resorts and lodges

With more money to spend, you could stay in a very comfortable **private cabaña** at one of the island resorts, which have spectacular beach or atoll locations. Alternatively, head inland to one of the beautiful **jungle lodges**, often in or near national parks and offering private, thatched cabañas with balconies overlooking a forest or river. These options may be expensive, but the extra dollars will soon be forgotten as you watch the sun rise over the reef or hear the rainforest's dawn chorus. Specialist diving, adventure and nature tours often use resorts and lodges as bases. Several places offer spa and

---

Accommodation price codes

Accommodation listed in this guide has been given a price code according to the following scale. The prices refer to the cost of a **double room in high season** (generally Dec to Easter) in Belize dollars, but, unless otherwise stated in the text, do not include the government hotel tax of nine percent. To get the equivalent price in US$, simply divide by two.

❶ Bz$40 and under	❹ Bz$91–120	❼ Bz$251–350
❷ Bz$41–60	❺ Bz$121–180	❽ Bz$351–500
❸ Bz$61–90	❻ Bz$181–250	❾ Bz$501 and over

The Lodge at Chaa Creek
Belize

Canoe on pristine tropical rivers,
hike in Maya Temple Cities,
horseback ride through jungle trails,
explore ancient ceremonial caves,
bike in the Maya Mountains,
relax in an exotic rainforest spa,
and enjoy candlelight dinners &
charming accommodations in our
award winning 365-acre Nature Reserve.
Caribbean Reef &Rainforest Packages.
Tours throughout Belize.

Adventure Centre and Spa
Wildly Civilized

Email: reservations@chaacreek.com Toll Free (877) 709-8708
www.chaacreek.com

PORTOFINO
A STYLISH RESORT ON THE BEACH

PO BOX 36
NORTH SAN PEDRO
AMBERGRIS CAYE, BELIZE, C.A.
BZE TEL: +501 678 5096 + 501 220 5096
US TEL: 1 212 372 7648 TOLL FREE: 1 888 240 1923
EMAIL: INFO@PORTOFINOBELIZE.COM

WWW.PORTOFINOBELIZE.COM*WWW.PORTOFINO.BZ

BASICS

28

massage services, perfect for unwinding after a day spent hiking or on horseback.

Rates may start at as low as US$80 per night for a double room, but in high season can reach over US$250.

Hostels and camping

There are very few dormitory-style cheap hostels in Belize, although you will find some in Caye Caulker and San Ignacio. Formal **camping facilities** are few and far between, and the few trailer parks that exist are small and fairly basic. Specialist camping **supplies** are scarce or unobtainable, so don't expect to find gas canisters or Coleman fuel, though kerosene is widely available; in most cases cooking will be done over a wood fire. You can only camp in forest reserves and national parks if you obtain **special permission** from the Forest Department in Belmopan.

Generally, a **tent** is useful if you plan to hike off the beaten track, usually with a guide who will lead you to places where you can set up camp. Some of the rural resorts in Cayo and villages throughout Belize (particularly Crooked Tree) have **camping areas**, but these are rare on Ambergris Caye or Caye Caulker.

Food and drink

Belizean food is a distinctive mix of Latin American and Caribbean influences, with Creole "rice and beans" cuisine dominating the scene but plenty of other dishes playing important roles. At its best, Creole food is delicious, taking fresh ingredients from the sea and mixing them with the smooth taste of coconut – a favourite ingredient – and lively spices. The range of international cuisines on offer increases every year, and you can find authentic delicacies from as far afield as Lebanon and Thailand.

You'll soon become accustomed to the **lunch hour** (noon to 1pm), observed with great devotion. This is often the main meal of the day and, though most places also serve dinner, **dining late** is not a Belizean custom; generally, planning to get to your table by 8pm will give you a good range of options, and possibly better service. Many places will be closed by nine or earlier, even in tourist areas.

Typical cuisine

A delicious Belizean breakfast treat is **fry jacks**, fluffy, fried dough usually eaten with sweet jam. The other daily meals (mostly US$7–10) are generally variations on **rice and beans**, Creole mainstays that feature heavily in most restaurants. The white rice and red beans are cooked together in coconut oil and flavoured with *recado* (a mild, ground red spice) – often with a chunk of salted pork

thrown in for extra taste – and usually served with fried fish or stewed chicken or beef. In **stewed beans and rice**, the beans are stewed, sometimes with spices, and ladled on top of boiled white rice. If you like your flavours full on, there'll always be a bottle of hot sauce on the table for extra kick; a Belizean favourite is Marie Sharp's pepper sauce.

Adventurous eaters may want to try *agouti*, a peculiarly Belizean delicacy also known as **gibnut**: in the wild, it's a large, nocturnal rodent; on the plate it looks a bit like pork, and has a gamey flavour. At the other end of the dietary spectrum, **vegetables** are scarce in Creole food, but you can opt for larger portions of side dishes, such as potato salad and fresh coleslaw along with a green salad, fried plantain and flour tortillas. As well, there are good Indian restaurants in Belize City and San Ignacio, which often have vegetarian main dishes.

Seafood is almost always excellent. Grouper and red snapper are invariably fantastic, and you might also try a barracuda steak, conch fritters or a plate of fresh shrimp. On San Pedro and Caye Caulker the food can be exceptional, with **lobster** served in an amazing range of dishes: in addition to grilled or barbecued lobster, you'll see pasta with lobster sauce, lobster and scrambled eggs and even lobster chow mein or curry.

Belize has many **Chinese restaurants**, varying enormously in quality. Chinese food will probably feature more in your trip than you anticipated, as it's often the only food available on Sundays, or late evenings in smaller places. Other Belizean ethnic minorities are now starting to break into the restaurant trade; many places serve **Garifuna dishes**, such as crispy cassava bread.

Central American-style, streetside **snack bars** are found all over the country, and provide cheap and delicious fast food. You'll find tasty *tamales* (a savoury cornmeal "pudding", usually with chicken cooked in a lightly spiced sauce inside, wrapped in a banana leaf and steamed), tacos, *empanadas* (similar to tacos but the tortilla is folded in half after filling, then deep fried) and other Latin staples, adding variety to the range of cuisine on offer.

Drinks

Belikin, the only brewery in Belize, produces almost all the **beer** consumed here. Belikin beer comes in several varieties: regular, a tasty, lager-type bottled and draught beer; bottled stout (a rich, dark beer); and Premium and Lighthouse, more expensive bottled beers and often all that upmarket hotels and restaurants offer. The **legal age for drinking alcohol** in Belize is 18.

Cashew nut and berry **wines**, rich and full-bodied, are bottled and sold in some villages, and you can also get hold of imported wine, though it's far from cheap. Local **rum**, in both dark and clear varieties, is the best deal in Belizean alcohol and there's plenty to choose from. The locally produced gin, brandy and vodka, however, are poor imitations – cheap and fairly nasty.

Despite the number of citrus plantations, fresh fruit juices are not always available, though you can generally get orange, lime and watermelon juices, and sometimes pineapple. **Tap water** in towns, though safe, is highly chlorinated, and many villages (with the exception of Caye Caulker) now have a potable water system. Filtered, bottled water and mineral water are sold almost everywhere, and pure rainwater is usually available in the countryside and on the cayes.

Health

Belize has a high standard of public health, and most visitors leave without suffering so much as a dose of diarrhoea. Tap water in all towns and many villages (though not in Caye Caulker) is safe to drink, though heavily chlorinated. Rainwater is collected in rural areas; it's usually safe, but you might want to treat it, especially for children. Restaurants are subject to stringent hygiene regulations, so ice in drinks will almost certainly be shop-bought or made from treated water. Bottled water is also widely available.

Still, it's essential to get the best **health advice** you can before you set off; always schedule a visit with your doctor or a travel clinic (see p.32). Many clinics also sell travel- related medical supplies, such as malaria tablets, mosquito nets and water filters. Regardless of how well prepared you are, **medical insurance** is essential (see p.40).

If you're **pregnant** or taking an oral contraceptive, you'll need to mention this when seeking health advice on travel medicine, as some vaccines and drugs can have harmful interactions or side effects.

Vaccinations

The only obligatory inoculation for Belize is against yellow fever, and that's only if you're arriving from a "high-risk" area (northern South America and equatorial Africa); carry your **vaccination certificate** as proof. However, there are several other inoculations that you should have anyway, particularly if you intend to spend time in remote, rural areas. At least eight weeks before you leave, check that you're up to date with diphtheria, polio and tetanus jabs, and arrange for typhoid and hepatitis A inoculations. Both typhoid and hepatitis A are transmitted through **contaminated food and water**. Although the risk of contracting hepatitis B is low unless you receive unscreened blood products or have unprotected sex, travel clinics often recommend inoculation; a joint hepatitis A and B vaccine is available from GPs and travel clinics.

Rabies exists in Belize, and vaccination is recommended for anyone travelling to Latin America for over thirty days.

Malaria and dengue fever

Malaria is endemic to many parts of Central America, especially the rural lowlands. Though it poses no great threat in Belize's tourist areas – due to an effective nationwide control programme – several thousand cases do occur each year, so you should still take precautions. Ask your travel clinic about the current, recommended malaria medicine. Avoiding bites in the first place is the best prevention: sleep in screened rooms or under nets, burn mosquito coils containing permethrin, cover up arms and legs (especially around dawn and dusk when mosquitoes are most active) and use repellent containing over 35 percent DEET (15 percent for children).

Keeping mosquitoes at bay is also important in the case of **dengue fever** – a viral infection transmitted by mosquitoes active both day and night. The first symptom is a fever, accompanied by severe joint and muscle pains, which subsides, only to recur a few days later, this time with a rash likely to spread all over the body. After this second outbreak, the fever and rash recede and recovery is usually complete.

Intestinal troubles

A bout of **diarrhoea** is the medical problem you're most likely to encounter in Belize, generally caused by the change of diet and exposure to unfamiliar bacteria. Following a few simple precautions should help keep you healthy: be sure to drink clean water (any bottled drinks, including beer and soft drinks, are already purified; for more advice on water, see box below), steer clear of raw shellfish and don't eat anywhere that's obviously dirty. If you do go down with a

Water purification

Contaminated water is a major cause of illness amongst travellers in Central America, due to the presence of pathogenic organisms: bacteria, viruses and cysts. In Belize, however, water in most hotels and resorts is treated, and bottled water is available pretty much everywhere; you will only need to consider treating water if you travel to remote areas. Bottled water is also easy to find in Flores and Tikal in Guatemala. While boiling water for ten minutes kills most micro-organisms, it's not the most convenient method. Chemical sterilization with either chlorine or **iodine tablets** or a tincture of iodine liquid is effective (except in preventing amoebic dysentery or giardiasis), but the resulting liquid doesn't taste very pleasant, though it can be masked with lemon or lime juice. Iodine is unsafe for pregnant women, babies and people with thyroid complaints. Purification, involving both sterilization and filtration, gives the most complete treatment, and travel clinics and good outdoor equipment shops stock a wide range of portable water purifiers.

dose, the best cure is also the simplest: take it easy for a day or two, eat only the blandest of foods – **papaya** is good for soothing the stomach and is also packed with vitamins – and, most importantly, ensure that you replace lost fluids and salts by drinking lots of bottled water and taking **rehydration salts**. If you can't get hold of these, half a teaspoon of salt and three of sugar in a litre of water will do the trick. If diarrhoea lasts more than three or four days or is accompanied by a fever or blood in your stools, seek immediate medical help.

Heat and dehydration

Another common cause of discomfort – and even illness – is **the sun**. The best advice is to build up exposure gradually, use a strong sunscreen and, if you're walking around during the day, wear a hat and stay in the shade. Be aware that overheating can cause **heatstroke**, which is potentially fatal. Signs are a very high body temperature without a feeling of fever, accompanied by headaches and disorientation. Lowering body temperature (with a tepid shower, cool drinks or a fan, for example) is the first step in treatment. **Avoid dehydration** by taking plenty of fluids, especially water.

Bites and stings

Aside from malaria-carrying mosquitoes, there are several other biting insects (and other animals) whose nips could leave you in varying degrees of discomfort. **Sandflies**, often present on beaches, are tiny, but their bites, usually on feet and ankles, itch like hell and last for days – antihistamine creams provide some relief.

Scorpions are common but mostly nocturnal, avoiding the daytime heat under rocks and in crevices. Species in Belize can cause a painful sting but are rarely fatal. You're unlikely to be stung, but if you camp or sleep in a rustic cabaña, shake out your shoes before putting them on and avoid wandering around barefoot.

Swimming and snorkelling might bring you into contact with some potentially dangerous or venomous sea creatures. Shark attacks are virtually unknown in Belize; **stingrays** are generally very gentle creatures, but if you step on one (they rest in the sand) it will give a very painful sting. Shuffling your feet in shallow water gives them warning that you are approaching. The Portuguese man-o'-war **jellyfish**, with its purple, bag-like sail, has very long tentacles with stinging cells that inflict raw, red welts; equally painful is a brush against **fire coral**. In both cases, clean the wound with vinegar or iodine and seek medical help if the pain persists or infection develops. For advice on mammal bites, see the information on rabies on p.31.

Getting medical help

Doctors in Belize have received training abroad, usually in the US, Mexico or Cuba; your embassy keeps a list of recommended specialists. Care is split between the public and private healthcare systems, both open to travellers. A visit to a **local public clinic** is usually by donation, and treatment at a public hospital (such as Belize City's Karl Heusner, see p.69) will usually incur a small charge and entail a long wait. **Private doctors** and clinics set their own (much higher) fees, but waits are minimal and facilities generally better – see p.69 for private clinics in Belize City. Pharmacists are knowledgeable and helpful, and sometimes provide drugs only available by prescription at home. **Herbal remedies** are also quite popular in Belize, and if you have confidence in alternative medicine, seek advice from a respected practitioner – see p.146 for details of the Ix Chel Wellness Center.

Medical resources for travellers

Whether you're a frequent traveller or this is your first trip to the tropics, check the listings below to find the latest travel health advice from the most reliable providers. By far the best source for a comprehensive assessment of health risks is the website of the **Centers for Disease Control** in the US; no matter where you live, check here first.

Australia, New Zealand and South Africa

The Travel Doctor – TMVC ☎ 1300/658 844, ⓦ www.tmvc.com.au. Lists travel clinics in Australia, New Zealand and South Africa.

UK and Ireland

Hospital for Tropical Diseases Travel Clinic ☎0845/155 5000, ☎020/7388 9600 (Travel Clinic), ⊛www.thehtd.org.
MASTA (Medical Advisory Service for Travellers Abroad) ☎0870/606 2782, ⊛www.masta.org for the nearest clinic.
Travel Medicine Clinic ☎028/9031 5220.
Tropical Medical Bureau ☎1850/487 674, ⊛www.tmb.ie. Ireland.

US and Canada

Canadian Society for International Health ☎613/241-5785, ⊛www.csih.org. Extensive list of travel health centres.
CDC ☎1-800/232-4636, ⊛www.cdc.gov/travel. Official US government travel health site.
International Society for Travel Medicine ☎1-770/736-7060, ⊛www.istm.org. Has a full list of travel health clinics.

The media

Belize, with its English-language media, can come as a welcome break in a region of Spanish-speakers. That said, many of the country's news sources can often report in a nationalistic manner, prioritizing relatively trivial local stories over important international ones.

Newspapers and magazines

There are five **national newspapers** – *The Amandala*, *The Belize Times*, *The Guardian* (no relation to the UK broadsheet), *The Reporter* and *The Independent*. *The Belize Times* is the propaganda organ of the ruling People's United Party (PUP), which *The Amandala* also generally supports, while *The Guardian* is the mouthpiece of the opposition United Democratic Party (UDP); *The Reporter* and *The Independent* try their best to be objective and impartial. For online magazines covering Belize, see the list of recommended websites on p.43.

Radio

Love FM (89.9, 95.1 and other frequencies around the country), offering easy listening, news and current affairs, has the most extensive network and also runs sister stations Estero Amor (in Spanish) and More FM (youth-oriented). Another major station is KREM (91.1 and 96.5FM), with an emphasis on talk, reggae and **punta rock**. Belize City's other stations are WAVE FM (105.9) and Positive Vibes (90.5), and each major district town has its own local station. There's also a **British forces** station, BFBS (93.1FM), and Mexican stations come through in the north, Honduran and Guatemalan ones in the south and west.

Television

There are two more-or-less national **television** stations. Channel 5 is the country's best broadcaster, producing good news and factual programmes (you can access their daily news output on the internet at ⊛www.channel5belize.com), although they don't transmit everywhere in the country. Channel 7, on the other hand, shows mostly **American programming** from various satellite channels, mixed in with some local news and rambling political discussion programmes. But it's cable TV (mostly pirated from satellite by local companies) that gets most of the nation's viewers, with its American soaps, talk shows, sports, movies and CNN.

Festivals

Festivals are popular in Belize and often involve entire communities. They range from full-on Carnival to local school fundraisers, all celebrated with flair and exuberance. The following list is just a sample of what's on when and where; check locally for exact dates and venues.

Spring

March La Ruta Maya canoe race (first week of March) from San Ignacio to Belize City.
April Regattas in Caye Caulker and Sarteneja; Easter Fair in San Ignacio and other Easter celebrations throughout the country.
May Cashew Festival in Crooked Tree village; National Agriculture Show in Belmopan.

Summer

June Día de San Pedro in San Pedro; Lobster-Fest in San Pedro, Caye Caulker and Placencia.
July Benque Viejo Fiesta in Cayo District (mid-July)
August International Costa Maya Festival in San Pedro (first week of Aug); Deer Dance Festival in San Antonio, Toledo District.

Autumn

September Independence Day celebrations nationwide (Sept 21); St George's Caye Day (Sept 10); Carnival in Belize City.
October Pan American Day: fiestas in mestizo areas.
November Garifuna Settlement Day (Nov 19) in Dangriga, Hopkins and other Garifuna communities.

Winter

December Boxing Day: parties, dances, cycle race in Belize City and horse races in Burrell Boom.
New Year's Day Horse racing in Burrell Boom village; Cycling Classic from Corozal to Belize City.
February Sidewalk Arts Festival in Placencia.

Sports and outdoor activities

The main spectator sport in Belize is football (soccer), which is avidly covered in the press. Softball, basketball and volleyball are also very popular, as is track and field, and televised American football and baseball have small followings. As elsewhere in Central America, cycling is closely followed and there are frequent races all over Belize. Finally, there are a number of horse races around Christmas and New Year.

Many of the sports that visitors to Belize can participate in are connected to the water in some way, with sailing, windsurfing, diving and snorkelling all extremely popular. **Diving courses**, for beginners or experts, are run from Belize City, San Pedro, Placencia, Caye Caulker and many other cayes. A dive with PADI certification starts at Bz$325. Sea and river kayaking, too, are becoming ever more popular, and a number of outfits organize trips. **Fly-fishing** for bonefish on a catch-and-release basis has long attracted dedicated anglers to the shallow, sandy "flats" off Belize's cayes and atolls. Several lodges, specialist operators and local guides can arrange this as well as fishing for permit, tarpon and other sportfish.

Away from the coast, **canoeing**, **rafting** and **tubing** – floating along rivers in a giant inner tube – are extremely popular, particularly in Cayo District, where plenty of people are eager to arrange this for you. Many of the same tour operators can arrange **jungle hiking**: anything from a guided walk along a medicinal plant trail to very demanding, multi-day jungle survival courses. Beneath the jungle, Belize's amazing subterranean landscape is becoming ever more accessible, with motivated, very competent **caving** guides leading tours and organizing specialist expeditions. *Caves Branch Jungle Lodge* (see p.130), owned by a founding member of the Belize Cave and Wilderness Rescue Team, makes safety a prime feature of its

caving trips; they also offer rappelling and rock climbing.

Horseriding and **mountain biking** are other possibilities in Cayo and indeed anywhere in rural Belize, with some superb routes through forested hills to Maya sites. Organizers and tour guides of these activities are listed in relevant places throughout the Guide.

Licensed guides will have a **photo ID** (often stating their main field of expertise), which must be displayed when they're conducting a tour, but it's not a bad idea to research the reputations of different companies, as quality can sometimes vary.

Culture and etiquette

On the whole, Belize is friendly and welcoming to outsiders, and, being a popular vacation destination, is relatively accustomed to visitors' sometimes peculiar habits.

Due to Belize's warm climate, clothing is mostly very casual; business people often dress smartly, but full suits are uncommon. Locals will outwardly tolerate visitors who make a habit of walking about in **skimpy swimwear**, especially in the cayes, but may think of them in less-than-generous terms.

Solo female travellers may have a hard time differentiating between a friendly greeting and a romantic overture; Belize shares Central America's **culture of machismo**, and local men can be boldly persistent, particularly in Belize City and tourist areas. Replying to them with a short greeting and moving on quickly

will usually convey your lack of interest without being insulting.

Though Belizeans rarely **tip** unless they receive exceptional service, foreigners are expected to do so in most situations. An average practice is to tip **ten percent** for food and drink, but significantly more for specialized, personal service (eg, an exceptional tour guide).

Public toilets are quite rare in Belize, though the bus station in Belize City does have them. Facilities are basic but usually very clean.

Shopping

Compared to its neighbours, Belize has less to offer in terms of traditional crafts or local markets, the latter being primarily for food. Proper craft and gift shops are found throughout the country, but you'll often get better prices from the artisans themselves, when you can find them on the street or in villages.

If time is short, the National Handicraft Market Place in Belize City (see p.58) is a great place to buy souvenirs, with a wide range of good-quality, genuine Belizean crafts, including paintings, prints and music. A good place for contemporary **Belizean art** is The Image Factory in Belize City (@www .imagefactorybelize.com; see p.57).

Wood carvings, common throughout the country, make beautiful and unusual souvenirs. Carvers often sell their wares in Belize City and at Maya sites; their exquisite renderings of dolphins, jaguars, ships and more are made from *zericote*, a two-toned wood that grows only in Belize and surrounding areas. The best wood is **kiln-dried**, though the items you see on the street may not be. **Slate carvers**, also common at Maya sites, create high-quality reproductions of gods, glyphs and stelae. In the Maya villages in southern Belize, you'll also come across beautiful **embroidery**, though the quality of both the cloth and the work is better in Guatemala. Maya, Garifuna and Creole villages produce superb drums and good basketware, including small, tightly woven "jippy jappa" baskets. Dangriga, Hopkins, Gales Point and the Toledo villages are the best places to shop for these.

One tasty souvenir is a bottle (or five) of Marie Sharp's Pepper Sauce, made from Belizean *habañero* peppers in strengths ranging from "mild" to "fiery hot". This spicy accompaniment to rice and beans graces every restaurant table in the country, and visits to the factory near Dangriga can be arranged.

Travelling with children

Belize is a very child-friendly destination, and there is plenty to keep active and inquisitive children occupied. Most Belizeans are patient and helpful, having grown up in large families themselves. Few hotels and resorts prohibit children, though it's worth asking before you book.

All community stores carry supplies of baby formula and nappies (diapers), and many restaurants have high chairs. The dearth of public toilets means **changing facilities** are rare. Larger resorts may have them, but for the most part babies are changed where necessary, in public or otherwise.

Children tend to prefer seeing Belize's **wildlife**, particularly the underwater variety (if they're old enough to snorkel), over Maya ruins. Highlights for older children include caving activities in Cayo; kayaking on the rivers; and snorkelling in the cayes. **Childcare facilities** do exist in larger resorts, and the concierge or hotel staff can usually help you find recommended, quality local babysitters.

Travel essentials

Costs

Though Belize may be the cheapest country in the Caribbean, it has the fully deserved reputation of being the **most expensive** country in Central America; if you've been travelling cheaply through the region to get here, many prices are going to come as a shock. Even on a tight budget, you'll spend at least forty percent more than you would in, say, Guatemala. Aside from some park and reserve entry fees (and occasional taxis in Belize City), however, you'll be paying the same prices as locals.

Prices in Belize are generally lower than in North America and Europe, though not by much. What you will spend depends on when, where and how you travel. **Peak tourist seasons**, such as Christmas and around Easter, tend to push hotel prices up, and certain tourist centres – notably San Pedro – are more expensive than others. A **sales tax** of ten percent increases costs, but the rate of inflation remains relatively low.

As a general rule, a **budget traveller** who is being very frugal can get by with spending about US$35 per day on basics (accommodation, food and transport); trips such as snorkelling or canoeing will add to this.

Travelling in a couple will reduce per-person costs slightly, but to enjoy a reasonable level of comfort and the best of Belize's natural attractions, you should allow at least US$45 per day per person.

Taxes

Hotel rooms in Belize are subject to a nine percent tax, sometimes included in the quoted price, and separate from the ten percent service charge that some higher-end places impose. A ten percent **general sales tax (GST)**, which applies to most goods and services (including meals in restaurants, though not to drinks), should not apply to hotel rooms; some package operators may try to slap it on anyway, so check carefully to see what you're paying for. To leave Belize by air, you'll pay a US$39.25 **exit tax** (payable in US dollars) at the international airport, although some tickets include all or part of the taxes. Land borders levy a **border tax** (payable in either Belize or US currency; around Bz$30), plus, sometimes, a small conservation fee. If you'll be returning to Belize within thirty days, hold on to your receipt to get a discount on the next exit tax.

Illegal Drugs

Belize has long been an important link in the chain of supply between producers in South and Central America and users in North America, with minor players often being paid in product, creating a deluge of illegal drugs in the country. Marijuana, cocaine and crack are all readily available in Belize, and whether you like it or not you may receive offers, particularly in San Pedro, Caye Caulker and Placencia. All such substances are **illegal**, and despite the fact that dope is sometimes smoked openly in the streets, the police do arrest people for possession of marijuana; they particularly enjoy catching tourists. If you're caught you'll probably end up spending a couple days in jail and paying a **fine** of several hundred US dollars. Practically every year foreigners are incarcerated for drug offences – the pusher may have a sideline reporting clients to the police, and catching "international drug smugglers" gives the country brownie points with the US Drug Enforcement Agency. Expect little sympathy from your embassy – they'll probably send someone to visit you, and maybe find an English-speaking lawyer, but certainly won't break you out of jail.

Crime and personal safety

While Belize has a relatively high **crime** rate, it has a great safety record for tourists, and despite the sometimes intimidating character of Belize City, you're very unlikely to experience any crime during your visit.

That said, it pays to be aware of the dangers. If you've got valuables, **insure** them properly, keep them close to you (preferably in a concealed moneybelt) and always store **photocopies** of your passport and insurance documents in a secure place. Trousers with zippered pockets are also good pickpocket-deterrents. Looking generally "respectable" without appearing affluent will go some way in avoiding unwanted attention. One fairly accurate overview of the possible dangers of visiting Belize and Central America is on the UK Foreign Office **Travel Advice Unit** website, ⓦ www.fco.gov.uk. The unit also produces a helpful leaflet for independent travellers, explaining what a consul can and cannot do for you while you're abroad. The US equivalent is the State Department's **Consular Information Service** (ⓦ www .travel.state.gov), which also publishes consular information sheets and lists the current dangers to US citizens. It can take some time for these sites to be updated, so local knowledge should also be sought out.

Break-ins at hotels are one of the most common types of petty theft – something you should bear in mind when selecting a room. Make sure the lock on your door works, from the inside as well as out. In some budget hotels, the lock will be a small padlock on the outside; for extra safety, it's a good idea to supply your own so you're the only one with keys. Many hotels will have a **safe** for valuables. It's up to you whether you use it; most of the time it will be fine, but make sure whatever you put in is securely wrapped – a lockable moneybelt does the job.

Police emergency numbers

The police emergency number in Belize is ⓣ 90 or 911; to contact the tourism police or to report a crime in Belize City, call ⓣ 227-2210 or 227-2222.

Solo women travellers, in addition to exercising the usual precautions, should be especially careful when talking to new male acquaintances in restaurants and bars, particularly in the cayes and Belize City. As in many other parts of the world, drugs intended to make women susceptible to **date rape** and other violent crimes are occasionally slipped into food or drinks. Though most victims of such acts have been local women, it's still never a good idea to accept food or drinks from anyone you don't know well.

Finally, don't let anyone without the official credentials talk you into accepting them as your "guide" – all legal tour guides in Belize are licensed and will have a **photo ID**. If you have doubts about using a certain guide, trust your instinct and report the incident to the authorities.

Tourism police and reporting a crime

In addition to its regular police force, Belize has special **tourism police**, operating from local police stations. Easily identified by their shirts and caps emblazoned with "Tourism Police", they patrol Belize City, San Pedro, Caye Caulker, Placencia and many other tourist destinations around the country. Police in Belize are poorly paid and, despite an ongoing campaign against criminals who prey on tourists, it's often difficult to convince them to do any more than simply fill out a report. Tourism police are specially trained to assist visitors and will likely prove more helpful than regular police, so it's best to track them down first if you have a problem.

If you're a victim of any crime, you should also report it to your **embassy** if you can – doing so helps the consular staff support their case for better tourist protection. This is not to say that crime against tourists is taken lightly in Belize; if criminals are caught, they're brought into court the next day, much more quickly than in other countries in the region.

Electricity

The main supply is 110 volts AC, with American-style, two- or three-pin sockets. Any electrical equipment made for the US or Canada should function properly, but anything from Britain or South Africa will need a plug adapter and possibly a transformer. The electricity supply is generally pretty dependable, but **power cuts** do occur; if you're bringing any delicate equipment, like a laptop, you'll need a good surge protector. In small villages where electricity is supplied by local generators, voltage will often be lower and less dependable.

Entry requirements

Citizens of the US, Canada, the EU, Australia, New Zealand and South Africa do not need **visas** to enter Belize as tourists. Swiss, Japanese and Israeli citizens, as well as most other nationalities, do need a visa, for which they have to apply at a **Belizean embassy** or consulate in advance, as visas are not officially obtainable at the border. There is no charge to enter Belize – just fill out the immigration form on the plane or at the border. Even if you don't require a visa, keep your **passport** or a photocopy with you at all times in Belize, as you may be asked to show it at police checkpoints.

Non-US citizens passing through the US en route to Belize will need a machine-readable passport and possibly a **US visa**. It's essential you confirm before you travel that your current passport will permit you to enter the US; allow at least two months if you need to obtain a US visa. For more on this, check the latest information on the US Department of Homeland Security website (✆www.dhs.gov/us-visit).

Citizens of countries on the visa waiver programme will need to have a machine-readable passport and to apply online for authorization to travel via the Electronic System for Travel Authorization at ✆www .cbp.gov/xp/cgov/travel/id_visa/esta (this does not apply to those arriving in the US by land).

All visitors to Belize are generally allowed a maximum stay of **thirty days**, but entry stamps can be renewed for up to a year. The vast majority of foreign **embassies and consulates** are still in Belize City, though the US embassy is in Belmopan, which is also the location of the British High Commission. All current contact numbers are under the Diplomatic Listings in the green pages of the Belize telephone directory.

Belizean embassies and consulates

These are just a few of the Belizean embassies and consulates around the world. In **New Zealand** and **South Africa**, contact the British High Commission, which represents Belize in these countries.

Australia (Honorary Consul) 81 Highfield Rd, Lindfield, NSW ✆ 02/9880 7160, ✉ belizeconsul @optusnet.com.au.
Canada (Honorary Consul) Suite 3800, South Tower, Royal Bank Plaza, Toronto M5J 2JP ✆ 416/865-7000, ✉ mpeterson@mcbinch.com; in Québec ✆ 514/288-1687; in Vancouver ✆ 604/730-1224.
Guatemala Av La Reforma 1–50, Zona 9, Edificio El Reformador Suite 803, Guatemala City ✆ 502/334-5531, ✉ embelguat@guate.net.
Mexico 215 Calle Bernado de Gálves, Col Lomas de Chapultepec, México DF 11000 ✆ 555/520-1274, ✉ embelize@prodigy.net.mx; there is also a consulate in Cancún ✆ 988-78417, ✉ nelbel @prodigy.net.mx.
UK Belize High Commission, Third Floor, 45 Crawford Place, London W1H 4LP ✆ 020/7723 3603, ✆ www.belizehighcommission.com.
US 2535 Massachusetts Ave NW, Washington DC 20008 ✆ 202/332-9636, ✆ www.embassyofbelize .org; also 5825 Sunset Blvd, Suite 206, Hollywood, CA 90028 ✆ 323/469-7343.

Gay and lesbian travellers

Belize overall is not a gay-friendly country, and local homosexuals often keep their sexuality a secret. Few people will make their disapproval obvious to foreigners, however, and many openly welcome the gay cruises that visit the country. San Pedro and Caye Caulker are probably your best bets for a hassle-free time.

Insurance

Travel insurance is important for a trip to Belize; your coverage should include emergency treatment and provision for repatriation by air ambulance. Although there is a modern, private hospital in Belize City, in emergencies you may well need treatment in a US hospital, so ensure that your policy provides you with a 24-hour emergency contact number.

Consider also taking out coverage for **loss or theft** of personal possessions, as petty

Rough Guides travel insurance

Rough Guides has teamed up with WorldNomads.com to offer great **travel insurance** deals. Policies are available to residents of over 150 countries, with cover for a wide range of **adventure sports**, 24-hour emergency assistance, high levels of medical and evacuation cover and a stream of **travel safety information**. Roughguides.com users can take advantage of their policies online 24/7, from anywhere in the world – even if you're already travelling. And since plans often change when you're on the road, you can extend your policy and even claim online. Roughguides.com users who buy travel insurance with WorldNomads.com can also leave a positive footprint and donate to a community development project. For more information go to Ⓦ**www .roughguides.com/shop**.

theft is fairly common in Belize; for more on this and how to avoid it, see p.38.

Before shopping around for a policy, check first to see what coverage you already have. Bank, credit and charge cards often have certain levels of medical or other insurance included, especially if you use them to pay for your trip. While this can be quite comprehensive, it should still be considered **supplementary** to full travel insurance.

Policies vary: some are comprehensive while others cover only certain risks, such as accidents, illnesses, delayed or lost luggage, cancelled flights, etc. In particular, ask whether the policy pays medical costs up front or reimburses you later, and whether it provides for **medical evacuation** to your home country. For any policy, make sure you know the claims procedure and the **emergency helpline number**. In all cases of loss or theft of goods, you will have to visit the local police station to have a report made out (make sure you get a copy) so that your insurer can process the claim.

Internet

You'll find **internet** cafés throughout Belize, though the speed and reliability of the service varies enormously. A growing number of hotels and other accommodation also offer wireless internet (some for a fee; others for free). In the cayes and other tourist centres, you can expect good connections and prices around Bz$8–10 for a half hour.

Living in Belize

Living in Belize is very different from visiting it. Poor infrastructure, hefty import taxes and the high cost of living in reasonable comfort

are challenges that dissuade some, though others persevere and find Belize a very rewarding place to call home.

Because any company hiring a foreigner must first prove that no Belizean could do the job, most work opportunities for foreigners are in the **voluntary sector**. Work permits, available only on a yearly basis, are required for any job, paid or not. Anyone planning to stay must also apply for **permanent residency**, a lengthy and costly process that prohibits you from leaving the country for more than fourteen days in your first year. After five years of residency (or a year of marriage to a Belizean) you can apply for **citizenship**.

Voluntary work and study

There are plenty of opportunities for **volunteer work** – mainly as a fee-paying member of a conservation expedition – or study at a field study centre or archeological field school. These options generally mean raising a considerable sum for the privilege and committing yourself to weeks (or months) of hard but rewarding work, often in difficult conditions. Many of the expeditions are aimed at students taking time off between school and university, and arrange work on **rural infrastructure projects** such as schools, health centres and the like, or on trails and visitor centres in nature reserves.

Academic **archeological groups** undertake research in Belize each year, and many of them invite paying volunteers; for details, see the box on p.264 in Contexts. There is also a growing number of **field study centres** in Belize, aimed primarily at college students on a degree course, though there are opportunities for non-students to learn about the ecology and environment of Belize; for more information, look under "field study centres" in the index. If you want to learn **Spanish** relatively cheaply, you could extend a trip to Tikal by studying at one of the language schools in and around Flores, Guatemala.

If the cost of joining a volunteer expedition deters you, there are a handful of organizations that don't collect fees, as well as opportunities to volunteer independently; the **conservation organizations** in Contexts (see box, p.264) all have volunteer programmes.

A helpful website is ⊛www.gapyear.com (UK-based, free membership), which holds a vast amount of general information on volunteering, and a huge, invaluable database on travel and living abroad.

Voluntary organizations

Barzakh Falah Children's Home Georgeville, Cayo District ☎674-4498, ⓔBarzakhfalah @gmail.com. One-week to one-year projects available in anything from childcare, teaching and counselling to gardening and arts workshops, depending on experience.
Cornerstone Foundation Belize ☎824-2373, ⊛www.cornerstonefoundationbelize.org. A Belize-based grassroots organization.
Earthwatch US ☎1-800/776-0188, UK ☎01865/318 838; ⊛www.earthwatch.org. Earthwatch matches volunteers from around the world with scientists dedicated to working on environmental and sustainable initiatives.
Ecologic Development Fund US ☎617/441-6300, ⊛www.ecologic.org. Ecologic has a great deal of experience in Central America, and aims to conserve endangered habitats by using community-based development and resource management in partnership with local organizations.
The Peace Corps US ☎1-800/424-8580, ⊛www.peacecorps.gov. Since 1962, the Peace Corps has been sending American volunteers to Belize to teach in rural areas, work in agricultural and environmental education and computer and business-training centres, and assist with women's groups, youth and community outreach and health awareness programmes.
Trekforce Worldwide UK ☎0845/241 3085, ⊛www.trekforceworldwide.com. Trekforce runs projects ranging from surveys of remote Maya sites to infrastructure development in national parks.
World Challenge Expeditions UK ☎020/8728 7200, ⊛www.world-challenge.co.uk. A youth development organization that leads an adventurous Maya route through Belize and Mexico.

Mail

Belize has a reliable internal postal system, but its **international service** can be patchy; standard cost for postcards starts at Bz$0.40, and letters at Bz$0.75. Many packages sent overseas, particularly between Belize and Europe, can spend months in transit, or may disappear altogether. An "express" service, considerably pricier than the cheap standard rates, has a better track record and is worthwhile when it comes to important parcels. Fedex and Global Express services are available in main towns and tourist centres.

Post offices are generally open from Monday through to Friday 8am to 4pm; post offices in small villages – sometimes operated by a local out of their home – are often short on stamps and packing materials, so do any major mailing from a large town.

Money

Prices and exchange rates are fairly stable, with the national currency, the **Belize dollar**, very conveniently fixed at the rate of two to the US dollar (**Bz$2=US$1**). US dollars (cash and travellers' cheques) are also accepted everywhere – and in some places even preferred – as currency. This apparently simple dual currency system can be problematic, however, as you'll constantly need to ask which dollar is being referred to; it's all too easy to assume the price of your hotel room or trip is in Belize dollars, only to discover on payment that the price referred to was in US dollars – a common cause of misunderstanding. In San Pedro and other high-end destinations around the country, many businesses quote prices in US dollars. Prices in the Guide are usually quoted in Belize dollars – always preceded by the symbol Bz$.

The Belize dollar is divided into 100 cents. Banknotes come in denominations of 2, 5, 10, 20, 50 and 100 dollars; coins come in denominations of 1, 5, 10, 25, 50 cents and 1 dollar, although 10 and 50 cent pieces are less commonly seen. All notes and coins carry the British imperial legacy in the form of a portrait of Queen Elizabeth – and quarters are sometimes called "shillings".

The Guatemalan unit of currency is the quetzal; note that costs in Guatemala are generally considerably cheaper than in Belize.

Currency exchange

For **currency exchange** on arrival, there's a branch of the Belize Bank at the international airport with an ATM that accepts foreign cards. You'll find there's at least one bank, sometimes two or three (generally Mon–Fri 8am–2 or 3pm, some also Sat 8am–12pm) in every town. It's a good idea to keep some US cash, as it's in high demand. Also, it's smart to carry smaller bills of US currency ($20 instead of $100, for example), especially towards the end of your trip, because change is always given in Belize dollars and you don't want to be stuck with too much Belize money before you go, since it's useless outside the country. Smaller banks may not be able to change your Belize dollars to US.

You can use most credit and debit cards at **ATMs** of the Belize Bank, Atlantic Bank, Alliance Bank and First Caribbean Bank (formerly Barclays) to get cash in Belize dollars at decent rates. Other banks will process cash advances on cards at the counter, though usually at less favourable rates than an ATM. Always check what the

charge will be for using your credit or debit card – many establishments add the extra five percent that the bank charges them. Visa is the most useful card in Belize (and throughout Central America), but MasterCard is also accepted fairly widely.

Opening hours and public holidays

It's difficult to be specific about **opening hours** in Belize, but in general most shops are open from 8am to noon and from 1 or 2pm to 7pm. Banks, though, do stay open during the lunch hour. Some shops and businesses work a half-day on Saturday, and everything is liable to close early on Friday. **Archeological sites**, though, are generally 8am to 4pm daily. **Public holidays**, when virtually everything will be closed – though some public transport operates normally – are listed in the box, below. Note that if the actual date of a particular holiday falls mid-week, the holiday will sometimes be observed the following Monday.

Phones

Belize's modern phone system is almost always easy to use, and payphones are plentiful. **Belize Telecommunications Limited (BTL)**, formerly a monopoly but still the country's dominant telephone service, has its main office (for international calls, fax, email and internet access) at 1 Church St, Belize City (Mon–Fri 8am–5pm).

There are no area codes in Belize, so wherever you're calling within the country you'll need to dial just the seven-digit number. **Cell phones** cover most of the country and visitors can easily rent one for about Bz$10–15 per day, plus an activation fee.

Time

Belize is on Central Standard Time, six hours behind GMT and the same as Guatemala and Honduras. Belize does not observe Daylight Savings Time, though Mexico does. This means that when DST is in operation (during the summer) the time in Belize is an hour earlier than in Mexico – something to bear in mind when you're crossing the border.

Public holidays

January 1	New Year's Day
March 9	Baron Bliss Day
Good Friday	varies
Holy Saturday	varies
Easter Monday	varies
May 1	Labour Day
May 24	Commonwealth Day
September 10	National Day (St George's Caye Day)
September 21	Independence Day
October 12	Columbus Day (Pan America Day)
November 19	Garifuna Settlement Day
December 25	Christmas Day
December 26	Boxing Day

Useful phone numbers

Calling Belize from abroad

The international direct dialling (IDD) code (also known as the country code) for Belize is ☎501. To call a number in Belize from abroad, simply dial the international access code (listed in your phone book), followed by the country code (501) and the full seven-digit number within Belize.

Useful numbers within Belize

Directory assistance ☎113   Operator assistance ☎115
International operator ☎114

Calling home from Belize

Note that the initial zero is omitted from the area code when dialling the UK, Ireland, Australia and New Zealand from abroad.

Australia international access code + 61
New Zealand international access code + 64
UK international access code + 44
US and Canada international access code + 1
Ireland international access code + 353
South Africa international access code + 27

Tourist information

The Belize Tourism Board (see below) has a main office in Belize City, and an informative website. Beyond that, you'll find a wide variety of **information about Belize**, much of it online. Several excellent websites are dedicated to Belize, and these are the best places to start and refine your search for facts and practical details. See opposite for a list of recommended sites.

An informative overview of the society, economy and environment of Belize and other Central American countries is provided by the Latin America Bureau (⊛www.latinamericabureau.org) in the UK. Also in the UK are two very useful resources, open to the public: Canning House Library (London; ☎020/7235 2303, ⊛www.canninghouse.com), which has a collection of books and periodicals on Latin America, including a comprehensive section on Belize; and The Guatemalan Maya Centre, London (☎&☎020/7371 5291, ⊛www.maya.org.uk), good for anyone planning to visit the Maya areas of Guatemala and Mexico as well as Belize.

Useful websites

⊛**www.belize.gov.bz** The government's own website is worth checking – and you can sign up for news reports and press releases.
⊛**www.belize.net** A good place to search for links to Belize websites.
⊛**www.belizeaudubon.org** Website of the Belize Audubon Society (BAS), useful for the latest info on the growing number of reserves and national parks and their associated visitor centres. See Contexts, p.264 for more on the BAS.

The Belize Tourism Board and the BTIA

The **Belize Tourism Board** website, ⊛www.travelbelize.org, is one of the best in the country, and from the main office in Belize City (see p.54) you can pick up city and regional maps, a transportation schedule and a list of hotels. The number of official tourist information offices in the country is increasing; local ones are covered in their respective chapters. The **Belize Tourism Industry Association** (BTIA; ⊛www.btia.org) represents most of the tourism businesses in the country and produces the annual *Destination Belize* magazine (free from tourist offices and many hotels), which is packed with helpful information. The BTIA has local representatives in most resort areas.

Ⓦ **www.belizefirst.com** The best online magazine dedicated to Belize, featuring accurate reviews and articles about hotels, restaurants and destinations.

Ⓦ **www.belizenet.com** A decent tourism-related site, with a range of accurate listings and links; also see Ⓦ www.belize.com, run by the same company.

Ⓦ **www.channel5belize.com** Daily TV news broadcasts from Belize on an award-winning website.

Ⓦ **www.lanic.utexas.edu** The homepage of the Latin American Information Center (LANIC) leads to a series of great links.

Ⓦ **www.mesoweb.com** Fascinating articles and links, often written by archeologists, on the latest findings in Maya research.

Ⓦ **www.planeta.com** A valuable resource for information on ecotourism and travel in Latin America.

Ⓦ **www.spear.org.bz** In-depth information on social, cultural, political and economic matters concerning Belize from the Society for the Promotion of Education and Research (SPEAR).

Travellers with disabilities

Travelling with a disability in Belize is possible, but certainly not easy. The very nature of Belize's abundant natural attractions often makes much of the country inaccessible to anyone with a disability, but there is increasing awareness of the differing needs of travellers. If you **plan ahead** and stay in higher-end resorts, you can still enjoy a visit to Belize but will need to rely on a certain level of help from staff and locals.

Travelling by **public bus** is virtually impossible, as they have no accessibility features and tend to get crowded. However, minibus **taxis** are plentiful and drivers will assist you when asked. Bicycle carts, though not the most dignified of transport options, can be a good solution in remoter areas. Streets in many areas can be difficult to negotiate, as they are mostly unpaved and **sidewalks** are rare.

Most **hotels** in Belize don't have rooms on the ground floor, and even those that do often have a few steps somewhere on the floor. It's imperative to ask about a hotel's accessibility when you call to book.

Resources for travellers with disabilities

The website Ⓦ www.makoa.org/travel.htm, provides an extensive array of useful links.

RADAR (Royal Association for Disability and Rehabilitation) UK ☎ 020/7250 3222, Ⓦ www .radar.org.uk. A good source of advice on disability organizations, holidays and travel abroad.

Society for Accessible Travel and Hospitality (SATH) US ☎ 212/447-7284, Ⓦ www.sath.org. Non-profit disability information service with a very organized website.

Irish Wheelchair Association Ireland ☎ 01/818 6400, Ⓦ www.iwa.ie. Useful information about travelling abroad for wheelchair-users.

NDS (National Disability Services) Australia ☎ 02/6283 3200, Ⓦ www.nds.org.au. National association that supports Australians with all disabilities.

Guide

Guide

Belize City

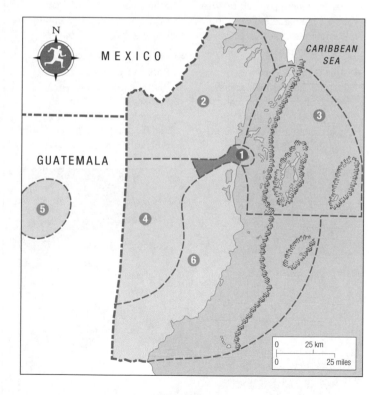

CHAPTER 1　**Highlights**

✳ **Swing Bridge** Watch the last manually operated swing bridge in the Americas open at dawn or dusk against a backdrop of brightly painted wooden fishing boats. **See p.56**

✳ **The Image Factory** Visit Belize's most provocative art gallery, where you can browse and buy unique local art and sometimes chat with artists at work. **See p.57**

✳ **Fort George** Stroll this historic area, admire some of the city's best colonial architecture and enjoy the sea breeze at the Fort George Lighthouse. **See p.58**

✳ **Museum of Belize** Marvel at the quality of Maya jades and other treasures on display in this world-class museum, housed in a beautifully restored Victorian prison. **See p.59**

✳ **The Belize Zoo** Take a day-trip from the city for close-up sightings of the animals and birds of Central America, notably Panamá the harpy eagle. **See p.63**

✳ **Monkey Bay Wildlife Sanctuary** Just a short ride from the Zoo, experience monkeys, crocodiles and plentiful bird life in their natural habitat, on an overnight trip. **See p.64**

▲ Scarlet Macaw, Belize Zoo

Belize City

The narrow, congested streets of **BELIZE CITY** can initially seem daunting and unprepossessing, even to travellers familiar with blighted urban centres. Dilapidated wooden structures stand right on road edges, offering pedestrians little refuge from cars and trucks, while almost stagnant canals are still used for some of the city's drainage. The overall impression is that the place is recovering from some great calamity – an explanation at least partly true. Belize City has suffered several devastating hurricanes, the latest in October 1961, when Hurricane Hattie tore it apart with winds of 150mph and left behind a layer of thick black mud. Such hazards, however, are often overstated by people who have never set foot within the city limits. For those who spend some time here, Belize City will reveal a distinguished history, several superb sights and fascinating cultural spectacles.

The city's astonishing energy comes from its 76,000 inhabitants, who represent every ethnic group in the country, with the **Creole** descendants of former slaves and British Baymen forming the dominant element and generating an easy-going Caribbean atmosphere. As you push your way through the throng, you'll see this relaxed attitude blending with an entrepreneurial flair, for this is the country's business capital. Banks, offices and shops line the main streets, while fruit and fast-food vendors jostle for pavement space with others selling plastic bowls or cheap jewellery. The jubilant **September Celebrations**, which pack the already full streets with music, dancing and parades, culminate in **Carnival**, with gorgeously costumed dancers who shimmer and gyrate through the city to electrifying Caribbean rhythms.

Some history

By the late sixteenth century, British **buccaneers**, attracted by Spanish treasure fleets, began to take advantage of the cayes of Belize as bases for plundering raids. Ever the opportunists, they began to cut valuable logwood (a source of textile dye) in the coastal swamps, and built a settlement at the mouth of the Belize River, constructed by consolidating the mangrove swamp with wood chips, rum bottles and coral. In the 1700s, **Belize Town** gradually became a well-established centre for **Baymen** (as the settlers called themselves), their families and their slaves, though the capital of the Bay settlement remained off the coast on St George's Caye. After floating the logwood downriver to be processed, the men would return to Belize Town to drink and brawl, with Christmas celebrations lasting for weeks. The Baymen's houses stood on the seafront while slaves lived in cabins on the south side of Haulover Creek.

Spain was still the dominant regional power, and in 1779 a Spanish raid captured many British settlers and scared off the rest. Most returned in 1783 however, when Spain agreed to recognize their rights, and Belize Town soon grew into the main centre of the logwood and mahogany trade on the Bay of Honduras. Spanish raids

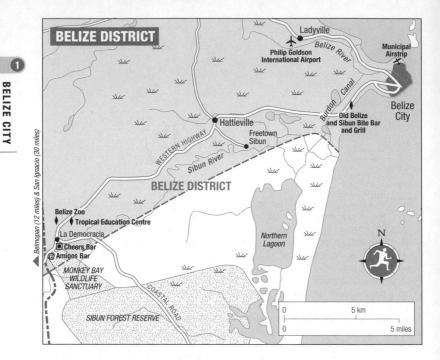

continued until the Battle of St George's Caye in 1798, when the settlers achieved victory with British naval help. In the nineteenth century, colonial-style buildings began to dominate the shoreline – the "Scottish clique" cleaned up the town's image and took control of its administration – while in 1812 Anglican mission-aries built the Anglican cathedral of St John to serve a diocese that stretched from Belize to Panama.

Fires in 1804, 1806 and 1856 destroyed large swathes of Belize Town, while epidemics of cholera, yellow fever and smallpox also wreaked havoc. Despite this, the town continued to grow with immigrants from the West Indies and refugees from the Caste Wars in Yucatán. In 1862 Belize became **British Honduras**, with Belize City (as it was now known) its administrative centre; in 1871 it was upgraded to a Crown Colony, with its own resident governor appointed by Britain.

The twentieth century was dominated by Belizean uncertainty over their relationship with the "mother country". In 1914 thousands volunteered to assist the war effort in the Middle East, but they were confronted by a wall of prejudice and racism and consigned to labour battalions. In 1919 the returned soldiers rioted in Belize City, an event that marked the onset of black conscious-ness and the **independence movement**. Compounding an already tense situation, on September 10, 1931, the city was celebrating the anniversary of the Battle of St George's Caye when it was hit by a massive **hurricane** that flooded the entire city and killed a thousand people – ten percent of the popula-tion. Many parts of the city were left in a state of squalid poverty, and together with the effects of the Depression, this added momentum to the campaign for independence, with numerous rallies in defiance of Britain. In 1961 Hurricane Hattie delivered her fury: 262 people died, and plans were made to relocate the capital inland. The instigators assumed that Belize City would become obsolete as Belmopan grew, but in fact few people chose to leave for the sterile atmosphere of the new, nominal capital, and Belize City remains by far the most populous place in the country.

Since independence in 1981, foreign investment and tourism have contributed to development, and Belize City continues in its major construction boom.

Arrival and getting around

Belize City has two airports. **International flights** land at **Philip Goldson International Airport**, 10.5 miles northwest of the city at Ladyville, just off the Northern Highway. Arriving here can be chaotic and overcrowded, but a recent expansion has alleviated some of the problems. Belize's **domestic airlines** also make stops at the international airport, so you could pick up an onward flight here, though prices to all destinations are around Bz$40 more than from the **Municipal Airport**, on the seafront north of the city centre.

From the international airport, a taxi into town costs Bz$50. If you want to cut the cost, one option is to share with other travellers. The only other way into town is by walking to the Northern Highway (25min) and flagging down one of the frequent passing buses (Bz$2 to the centre). From the Municipal Airport, a taxi to town costs around Bz$10; walking takes at least 25 minutes.

The main **bus terminal** (called Novelo's) is on the western side of the city centre (19 West Collet Canal ☎227-2255 or 227-6372), in a slightly depressed part of town known as Mesopotamia. It's only a mile from the Swing Bridge and you can easily walk – or, especially at night, take a taxi – to/from any of the hotels listed on p.54. **Boats** returning from the cayes pull in at the **Marine Terminal**, on the north side of the Swing Bridge, or at the **Brown Sugar plaza**, just along the road on North Front Street; from either it's a short taxi ride to the bus terminal or any of the hotels. For more specific information on buses from Belize City, see Travel Details, p.69; up-to-date information on buses can be found at the Marine Terminal. If you're unable to confirm departure times, your best bet is to arrive at the bus terminal in the early morning and enquire.

Although Belize City is by far the largest urban area in the country (the capital, Belmopan, is one tenth of its size), its central area is compact enough to make **walking** the easiest way to get around. The city is divided neatly into north and south halves by **Haulover Creek**, a delta branch of the Belize River. The pivotal point of the city centre is the **Swing Bridge**, always busy with traffic and opened up sometimes twice a day, to allow larger vessels up and down. **North** of the Swing Bridge, things tend to be slightly more upmarket; here you'll find the most expensive hotels, embassies and consulates and – in the King's Park area – some very luxurious homes. **South** of the Swing Bridge is the market and commercial zone, with banks, offices and supermarkets; the foreshore is the prestige area, site of the former colonial governor's residence, now a museum and arts venue. The area south and west of the main thoroughfares of Regent and Albert streets is unsafe after dark.

Taxis, identified by green licence plates, cost Bz$7–8 for one or more passengers within the city; for other journeys, agree on the fare in advance. Cars wait for passengers at the main bus station and Marine Terminal, or you can call one on ☎207-2888 or 203-4465; you should take a **taxi** to travel anywhere at night. **City buses** operate to outlying residential areas but are of little use unless you know exactly where you're going.

BELIZE CITY

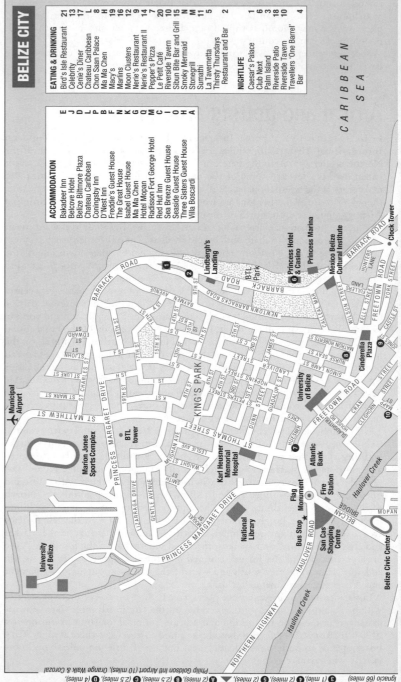

ACCOMMODATION

Bakadeer Inn	E
Belcove Hotel	J
Belize Biltmore Plaza	D
Chateau Caribbean	L
Coningsby Inn	P
D'Nest Inn	B
Freddie's Guest House	F
The Great House	N
Isabel Guest House	K
Ma Ma Chen	G
Hotel Mopan	Q
Radisson Fort George Hotel	M
Red Hut Inn	C
Sea Breeze Guest House	I
Seaside Guest House	O
Three Sisters Guest House	H
Villa Boscardi	A

EATING & DRINKING

Bird's Isle Restaurant	21
Celebrity	13
Cenie's Diner	17
Chateau Caribbean	L
Chon Saan Palace	8
Ma Ma Chen	H
Macy's	19
Marlins	16
Moon Clusters	12
Nerie's Restaurant	9
Nerie's Restaurant II	14
Pepper's Pizza	7
Le Petit Café	20
Riverside Tavern	10
Sibun Bite Bar and Grill	15
Smoky Mermaid	N
Stonegrill	M
Sumathi	11
La Tavernetta	5
Thirsty Thursdays	
Restaurant and Bar	2

NIGHTLIFE

Caesar's Palace	1
Club Next	6
Palm Island	3
Riverside Patio	18
Riverside Tavern	10
Travellers 'One Barrel'	
Bar	4

CARIBBEAN SEA

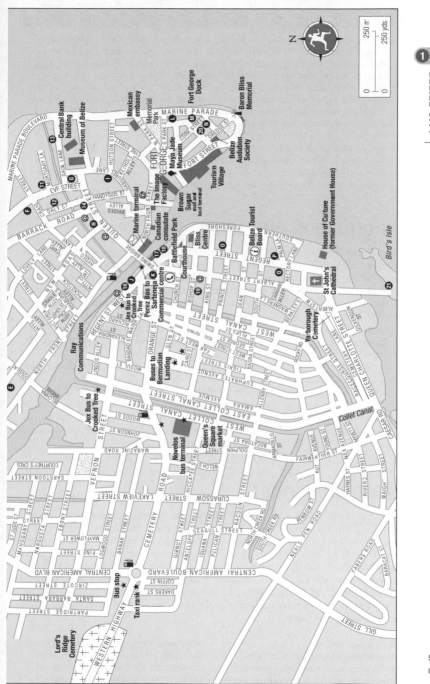

Hassle

Walking in Belize City **during the day** is perfectly safe if you observe common sense rules. The introduction of **tourism police** in 1995 made an immediate impact on the level of hassle and this, coupled with the legal requirement for all tour guides to be licensed, has reduced street crime. The tourism police are available on ☎227-6082 for advice or directions; they sport green "Tourist Unit" badges on their sleeves, and will even walk you back to your hotel if it's near their patrol route. That said, it's still sensible to proceed with caution: most people are friendly, but quite a few may want to sell you drugs or bum a dollar or two. The best advice is to stay cool and be civil; don't provoke trouble by arguing too forcefully and never bring out large wads of cash. Women wearing short shorts or skirts will attract verbal abuse from local studs. The chances of being mugged increase **after dark**. Aside from along the seafront area near the *Princess Hotel* – which gets busy in the evenings – it's advisable to take a **taxi** anywhere else in town. For more on security and avoiding trouble, see p.38.

Information and tours

The Belize Tourism Board (BTB) office is at 64 Regent Street (Mon–Thurs 8am–5pm, Fri 8am–4pm; ☎223-1913, ⓦwww.travelbelize.org). Though not an essential stop, you can pick up free bus timetables, a hotel guide and city map, nature reserve brochures and copies of **tourist newspapers**.

Should you want to escape the city, you can take a **day tour** inland. Most visit at least two of the following: the Belize Zoo, Bermudian Landing Baboon Sanctuary, Crooked Tree Wildlife Sanctuary and Maya ruins at Altun Ha or Lamanai. All but the last two are easy to visit independently – though with the exception of the zoo, you'll need to stay overnight if you don't have your own vehicle. Still, even with accommodation, it's likely to be less expensive than a tour. Ask at the following agents for local and national information, city tours and travel bookings throughout Central America: Belize Travel Adventures, 168 N Front St (☎223-3064, ⓦwww.belize-travel.net); Maya Travel Services, 42 Cleghorn St (☎223-1623, ⓦwww.mayatravelservices.com), excellent for tours and hotels within Belize; and S & L Travel, 91 N Front St (☎227-5145, ⓦwww.sltravel belize.com), which offers great birding and natural history tours.

Accommodation

There are numerous **hotels** in Belize City, many of them budget and charging Bz$30–75 for a double room, and most have good rates for singles. There's usually no need to book ahead as you'll almost always find something in the price range you're looking for – though a phone call saves time and effort. The ones listed here have good records on security; anything cheaper could well be unsafe. More **luxurious hotels** are generally located in and around the historic **Fort George area** north of the Swing Bridge. If you want a comfortable hotel in a quiet location near the international airport and within easy reach of the city, take a look at the *Black Orchid* (see p.74).

Inexpensive

Belcove Hotel 9 Regent St W ☎227-3054, ⓦwww.belcove.com. Great, secure option with attentive staff, right next to the creek with a view

of the Swing Bridge; arrive by taxi after dark as it's in a slightly less salubrious part of town. Rooms are simple and tidy, some with a/c, private bath and TV; coffee is included. Tours are arranged, including to the hotel's private island at Gallows Point, on the reef nine miles away. ❷

Freddie's Guest House 86 Eve St ☏ 223-3851, ⓔ freddies@btl.net. This long-established spot near the waterfront is excellent value. The three well-maintained, secure and peaceful fan-cooled rooms have comfortable beds and bedside lamps; two rooms share a gleaming bathroom, and one has private bath. ❷

Ma Ma Chen 7 Eve St ☏ 223-4568. A Taiwanese family runs these simple rooms and adjoining vegetarian restaurant (the only fully vegetarian option in town, see p.66). Some rooms have private bath and a/c, others have fans, and are sparsely furnished with slightly hard beds, but it's relatively central. ❶

Sea Breeze Guest House 18 Gabourel Lane ☏ 203-0043, ⓔ info@seabreeze-belize.com. Clean, airy and good-value rooms, some with a/c, private bathroom and balcony, on a quiet street in a good central location near the Museum of Belize. ❷

Seaside Guest House 3 Prince St ☏ 227-8339, ⓔ seasidebelize@gmail.com. A clean and well-run option, popular with budget travellers, in a rambling old wooden colonial house yards from the southern foreshore. Rooms are either small dorms or private, some with bath. There's internet access (Bz$10/day), a bookswap, lounge, flower-filled garden and sea-facing veranda. Breakfast available. ❶–❸

Three Sisters Guest House 36 Queen St ☏ 203-5729. Three large rooms (one triple) in an airy, wooden building run by an amiable, mainly Spanish-speaking family; each has fan and fridge. You can see the Swing Bridge from the sunny balcony overlooking Queen St. ❷

Mid-range

Bakadeer Inn 74 Cleghorn St ☏ 223-0659, ⓦ www.toucantrail.com. Twelve clean, secure, traditional rooms with a/c, ceiling fan, TV and private bath with tub, though there's little natural light. Take usual precautions when walking this area after dark. Great Belizean breakfast. Rates are excellent for three or four sharing. ❹

Coningsby Inn 76 Regent St ☏ 227-1566. Decent rooms with tiled floors, a/c, TV, private bath in a quiet part of the city centre. There's a balcony over the street and the upstairs restaurant/bar serves a Belizean breakfast, lunch and dinner. Luggage storage and laundry available; internet Bz$5/hr. ❺

Chateau Caribbean 6 Marine Parade ☏ 223-3888, ⓦ www.chateaucaribbean.com. Colonial-style hotel overlooking the seafront and Memorial Park. Well-appointed, spacious rooms all have private bath, a/c and cable TV; some with sea views, especially those with glass-fronted balconies

on the top floor. Good restaurant (see p.66), where you can start off the day with the Maya spread breakfast (Bz$14) of corn tortillas, fried beans and poached eggs. A former hospital, the property has featured in several movies. ❺

D'Nest Inn 475 Cedar St, Belama, 5km north of Belize City ☏ 223-5416, ⓦ www.dnestinn .com. A cheery, two-storey B&B in a quiet residential district. Some rooms have plush, four-poster beds; all have a/c, sparkling bathrooms, antique furniture and wi-fi. The garden flourishes with hibiscus, orchids, white lilies and a splashing bird bath, and there's a mangrove-lined canal nearby. A tasty breakfast is included. Best if you have your own transport, though a taxi is only Bz$10 into town. The airport is just six miles away. ❺

Hotel Mopan 55 Regent St ☏ 227-7351, ⓦ www.hotelmopan.com. Wood-fronted building at the quiet end of Regent St near the colonial House of Culture. Welcoming and safe, it's run by the son and daughter of the late Jean Shaw, an avid conservationist. The original building is over two hundred years old, but all rooms have private bath and cable TV, some have a/c and there's wi-fi and a bar. Relax on the comfortable verandas with a great view and evening beer. ❹

Isabel Guest House 3 Albert St, above and behind the Central Drug Store ☏ 207-3139. Small, welcoming, primarily Spanish-speaking guesthouse with four large rooms with private showers and small refrigerators. The room with four beds (❺) is a good deal for groups. ❹

Red Hut Inn 90 Bella Vista, near Mile 3, Northern Hwy ☏ 663-8986, ⓦ red-hut-inn-belize.50megs .com. Well-maintained option on the city's northern outskirts. Rooms feature firm beds along with wooden closets, a small sitting area, clean en-suite bathrooms, a/c, cable TV and wi-fi, plus there's kitchen access. Airport pickup (and rides into town) offered for Bz$10, though the distance from town can be inconvenient without your own vehicle. ❹

Villa Boscardi 6043 Manatee Drive ☏&ⓕ 223-1691 or ☏ 602-8954, ⓦ www.villaboscardi.com. Spacious, luxurious B&B with garden, two miles from downtown off the Northern Hwy. Each unique room features a/c, private bath, TV and telephone. Gracious owner Françoise can help plan tour itineraries and activities for every budget. A filling breakfast with home-brewed coffee is included and there's internet access. Nonsmoking. ❺

Expensive

Belize Biltmore Plaza Mile 3, Northern Hwy ☏ 223-2302, ⓦ www.belizebiltmore.com. Now a *Best Western*, this tranquil hotel located just off the highway has a sun-flooded lobby and spacious

1

a/c rooms around a palm-filled courtyard. The *Victoria Room* restaurant serves seafood, steaks and a varied lunch menu; there's a lively happy hour (5–7pm) with steel band at the poolside *Palm Court Bar* on Fri; and a fine selection of Caribbean rums at the *Biltmore Bar*. Facilities also include a business centre, fitness and massage rooms. Wheelchair-accessible. ❼

The Great House 13 Cork St, Fort George ☎ 223-3400, ⓦ www.greathousebelize.com. A gorgeous, modernized, four-storey wooden building, dating from 1927. The sixteen spacious a/c rooms all have private bath, TV, wi-fi, plus lots of extras, and lustrous hardwood floors; some have a balcony. The *Smoky Mermaid* restaurant (see p.67),

with a Fri evening happy hour, is in the courtyard with a wine/cigar shop and café. ❼

Radisson Fort George Hotel 2 Marine Parade, Fort George ☎ 223-3333, ⓦ www.radisson.com /belizecitybz. The city's flagship hotel is well-managed and enviably located on the seafront. All rooms have a huge TV, fridge and minibar, and most have sea views; the Colonial Wing is carpeted, the Club Wing (reached by the only glass elevator in Belize) features marble floors, and across the road, the Villa Wing has tiled balconies and wheelchair access. There's a business centre, two good restaurants, a cosy café (see p.66) and two pools and a marina, used by live-aboard dive boats. ❽

The City

Richard Davies, a British traveller in the mid-nineteenth century, wrote of the city: "There is much to be said for Belize, for in its way it was one of the prettiest ports at which we touched, and its cleanliness and order ... were in great contrast to the ports we visited later as to make them most remarkable." Many of the features that elicited this praise have now gone, though some of the distinctive **wooden colonial buildings** have been preserved as heritage showpieces, or converted into hotels, restaurants and museums. Yet even in cases where the decay is too advanced for the paintwork, carved railings and fretwork to be restored, the old wooden structures remain more pleasing than the concrete blocks that are replacing them. Fires, too, have altered city architecture; the worst in recent years claimed the historic Paslow Building, which stood in the now empty lot opposite the Marine Terminal. That said, two of the very best colonial structures have been carefully restored and are open to visitors; the former city jail, built in Victorian times, is now the **Museum of Belize**, and the even earlier **Government House** is a museum and cultural centre.

Belize City's most recognizable landmark has also changed through the years. The first wooden bridge was built in the early 1800s, replacing a system in which cattle and other commodities were winched over the waterway that divides the city – hence the name **Haulover Creek**. Its next incarnation, the Liverpool-made **Swing Bridge**, opened in 1923 and is the only manually operated swing bridge left in the Americas. Up to twice a day (around 5.30am and 5.30pm), but usually several times a week, the endless parade of vehicles and people is halted by policemen and the process of turning begins. Using long poles inserted into a capstan, four men lever the bridge until it's facing the harbour mouth. During the few minutes that the bridge is open, the creek traffic is busier than that on the roads, with the whole city jammed up.

The north side

Immediately on the **north side** of the Swing Bridge is the **Marine Terminal**, where you can catch boats for the northern cayes (see p.97). The Mundo Maya Deli (☎ 223-2923) is the last Belizean-owned stall in the terminal, and its a good place to find **information** on transport; helpful owner Ramon Cervantes keeps up-to-date bus schedules for Belize and sells tickets to Chetumal, Cancun, Flores/Tikal, San Salvador and for the boat to Honduras. There's no restaurant inside the terminal, but the toilets are clean and there are also some rather expensive **luggage lockers**.

Any sailor shipwrecked on a foreign shore would doubtless be grateful to the land that saved him, but only one who'd been unfathomably moved by the experience would want to spend the rest of his life there. That's exactly what happened to **Emory King**, American-born wit, raconteur, realtor, historian, broadcaster, writer, businessman and film extra, when his schooner *Vagabond* crashed onto the coral off English Caye, British Honduras in 1953. Realizing that the colony presented unrivalled opportunities to a young man of limited means but boundless entrepreneurial spirit, he stayed on, intrigued by this colonial backwater.

Finding the **Belize City** of the early 1950s much like a nineteenth-century village, with only a handful of cars (which, to his astonishment, drove on the left), a sickly electric power system and a few telephones to represent the modern age, he set about trying to change it. Working first as Secretary of the Chamber of Commerce, then Secretary of the Tourist Committee (when tourists were counted in dozens), Emory advised foreign investors and found land for American farmers in search of the next frontier. His most enduring gift to his adopted country, however, was persuading the **Mennonites** (see box, p.81) to settle here in 1958; their back-breaking pioneer work is Belize's greatest agricultural success story.

Emory King's involvement in Belize led to cameo roles in all the Hollywood movies filmed here. In *The Mosquito Coast* (1985), based on the novel by Paul Theroux, he played a down-at-heel, drunken landowner offering to sell Harrison Ford a piece of land – a part he claimed was not typecasting. In 1998 the government appointed him **film commissioner**, and he soon secured the production of *After the Storm*, based on the Hemingway short story and filmed in Placencia and Ambergris Caye, followed by the "reality television" series *Temptation Island*, and the establishment of the **Belize Film Festival** (Ⓦ www.belizefilmfestival.com).

King sadly died in 2007, but his **books** about Belize live on, and are sold all over the country; a good one to start with is *Hey Dad, This is Belize*, a whimsical account of family life, followed by *I Spent it All in Belize* (which includes the highly astute line 'if you want to be a millionaire in Belize, you'd better come with two million'). See p.272 for further titles. His **website**, Ⓦ www.emoryking.com, provides everything you need to know about the man – or at least everything that he was prepared to tell.

Just east of the Marine Terminal, at 91 N Front St, **The Image Factory** (Mon–Fri 9am–5pm; free but donations welcome; Ⓣ 610-5072, Ⓦ www.imagefactory.bz) is home to Belize's leading contemporary artists. The gallery holds outstanding, sometimes provocative exhibitions and you often get a chance to discuss the works with the artists themselves. If you're looking for unique gifts, browse The Image Factory Shop, in front of the gallery, which also sells a wide range of Belizean books, music and videos, along with selected souvenirs.

Continue east along North Front Street and you'll come to pedestrianized **Brown Sugar**, a striking name for a new and thoroughly unremarkable dockside shopping plaza with more options for boats to the Northern Cayes. Amongst numerous Belizean food outlets here is *Riverside Delight*, a café, internet centre and souvenir shop run by Petty Cervantes, a reliable mine of information on transport to other destinations in Central America; bus tickets are also on sale. North Front Street continues into Fort Street, where you'll immediately see the **Maya Jade Museum**, a gift shop-cum-mini-museum (Mon–Fri 8am–5pm; Ⓣ 203-1222) with a varied selection of jade jewellery – pendants, earrings, rings – for sale at decent prices, and fine replicas of jade artefacts culled from sites around Belize. In this area, you'll encounter the advance guard of trinket sellers, street musicians, hustlers and hair-braiders, announcing you're near the **Tourism Village**, Belize's **cruise ship terminal**, dominating the north side of the creek mouth. This place often handles thousands of visitors in a single day and there will almost always be a cruise ship (or five) in view as you look out to sea. Security is tight if you want to go in and are not on a ship – Belizean residents in general don't bother – and inside, too, locals are thin on the ground, with staff generally brought in from across Central America. Instead, Belizean vendors lured by US cash set up improvised stalls outside. Inside, there is a long dock with numerous outdoor restaurants and bars serving burgers, tacos and the like, and a plethora of jewellery, T-shirt and souvenir shops; most are overpriced, so buy in town. The Village has also expanded across the road to the Fort Street Plaza, with over two-dozen gift and souvenir shops along an attractive boardwalk. Note that all shops at the Tourism Village are only open when ships are in, usually Tuesday through Thursday. Cruise ships are still a relatively new and often controversial phenomenon in Belize, with those working in "traditional", low-impact tourism asserting that tours from ships are leading to irreversible environmental damage.

Fort George

Beyond the Tourism Village, the road follows the north shore of the creek mouth – an area that was once Fort George Island until the narrow strait was filled in 1924 – eventually reaching the **Fort George Lighthouse**, which sits atop the tomb of and memorial to **Baron Bliss**, Belize's greatest benefactor (see p.61). Natural history enthusiasts will benefit from a visit to two of Belize's foremost conservation organizations in the area: the **Belize Audubon Society**, 12 Fort St (℡223-5004, ⓦwww.belizeaudubon.org) is very prominent in conservation education and manages many of Belize's reserves; it has information plus a great giftshop with books, maps and posters relating to the country's wildlife reserves. Nearby, at 1 Eyre St (℡227-5616, ⓦwww.pfbelize.org), the **Programme for Belize** manages the Rio Bravo Conservation and Management Area (see p.85); staff will answer questions about Area access and progress. For more on conservation see p.264.

Rounding the point and walking along the shoreline, you pass the *Radisson Fort George Hotel*, and just north, the seafront **Memorial Park**, which honours the Belizean dead of World War I. In the streets around the park you'll find several colonial mansions: the *Chateau Caribbean* and the Mexican embassy are two fine architectural examples. On the south side of the park, the **Belizean Handicraft Market Place** (Mon–Sat 8am–4pm; ℡223-3637) sells high-quality Belizean crafts and art at fair prices. A little beyond here, at the corner of Hutson Street and Gabourel Lane, sits a superb "colonial" building – formerly the home of the US embassy, which moved to Belmopan in 2006 – actually constructed in nineteenth-century New England before being dismantled and shipped to Belize.

Marine Parade, the seaward edge of Memorial Park, marks the beginning of a massive civil engineering project; a **seawall** stretching hundreds of metres along the shore towards the *Princess Hotel* has reclaimed over fourteen acres of shallow sea, and is now used as a boulevard and pedestrian promenade. Part of the reason for this seaward expansion is to accommodate fleets of tour buses for the cruise ship industry, though it also creates lots of valuable real estate. Just beyond the *Princess*, the attractive seafront **BTL Park** was built on land reclaimed much earlier; it was here that Charles Lindbergh landed the *Spirit of St Louis*, the first aeroplane to touch down in Belize, in 1927. The park, with a children's playground, is popular with families and often hosts open-air concerts. The biggest party takes place during the Independence Day celebrations in September.

The Museum of Belize

Near the giant Central Bank building at the north end of Queen Street, the former colonial prison has undergone a beautiful transformation to become the **Museum of Belize** (Mon–Fri 8.30am–5pm, closed at weekends) Bz$10; ℡ 223-4524, Ⓦ www .nichbelize.org). Built in 1857 and housing prisoners until 1993, it was reopened as a museum in 2002, the 21st anniversary of Belize's independence. Today, the elegantly proportioned, two-storey structure of sand-coloured brickwork, set in lawns and gardens, looks more like a country mansion than its former incarnation.

The lower floor, with plenty of exposed, original brick and bars on the windows, displays photographs and artefacts celebrating the history and the people of the city as it grew over the last 370 years. Here you can also peruse a

▲ Maya pottery, Museum of Belize

complete collection of the country's stamps; the earliest one, depicting Queen Victoria, dates to 1837. The building's original role is not glossed over, either; there's an old jail door and small exhibit of before-and-after photos chronicling the structure's evolution.

The star attractions are upstairs, however, in the **Maya Masterpieces** gallery; a permanent, world-class collection of some of the best artefacts recovered from Belize's Maya sites. Well-lit glass cases display fine painted ceramics, including the striking Buenavista Vase, which depicts the mythical Hero Twins dancing in the costume of the young Maize Gods after having defeated the Lords of Death – the central theme of the Maya creation story, the Popol Vuh (see p.273). If you want to visit the site of Buenavista del Cayo, where the vase was found, see p.159. Other treasures include painstakingly formed **eccentric flints**, carved from a single piece of stone, and an exceptionally well-preserved wooden figurine, probably of a ruler, from a cave in Toledo District. Upstairs are the splendid **Jades of Belize**, the country's trove of jade discoveries including a replica of the famous jade head from Altun Ha, stunning mosaic masks, pendants, ear flares and necklaces. The museum also features one of the best-displayed collections of insects in Belize; bug-lovers won't want to miss it.

The south side

The **south side** is generally the older section of Belize City; in the early days, the elite lived in the seafront houses while the backstreets were home to their slaves and labourers. These days it's the city's commercial centre, with shops, banks and travel agencies. Right by the Swing Bridge is the three-storey **commercial centre** (also called the new market), which opened in 1993 on the site of a rather decrepit old market from 1820. Though the new one is much cleaner, it's not very popular with either traders or shoppers, most preferring the goods on display on the streets outside or the bustling Queen's Square market, next to the bus terminal.

Albert Street, running south from the Swing Bridge, is the main commercial thoroughfare, with banks, supermarkets and T-shirt and souvenir shops. On the parallel **Regent Street**, a block closer to the sea, are the former colonial administration and court buildings, known together as the **Courthouse**. These well-preserved examples of colonial architecture, with their columns and finely wrought iron, were completed in 1926 after an earlier building was destroyed by fire. The Courthouse overlooks a tree-lined square with an ornamental fountain in the centre, known as Central Park until it was renamed **Battlefield Park** in the early 1990s, commemorating the heated pre-independence political meetings that took place here; nowadays most of the noise is the raucous chatter of grackles, which roost here in their thousands.

Bliss Centre for the Performing Arts

On the waterfront a block south of the Courthouse is the extensively refurbished **Bliss Centre for the Performing Arts** (Mon–Fri 8am–5pm; ☏227-2110; ⓦwww.nichbelize.org). A sleek, marble-lined entrance hall opens onto a six hundred-seat theatre, with space for drama workshops and the studios of the **Belize National Dance Company** (BNDC) upstairs. Benefiting from a generous grant from the Mexican government, this is the centre of Belizean cultural life, hosting concerts, plays and exhibitions as well as accommodating the country's **National Art Collection**. It's certainly worth a visit to see what's on – here and elsewhere – or to enjoy a drink at the café/bar. Concerts and events usually take place from 6 to 9pm. If there's a BNDC performance on, don't miss it: aimed at preserving Belizean traditional dance, they amalgamate Afro-folkloric styles including Garifuna and Creole brukdown and bram dance, alongside Cuban, creative and contemporary techniques.

The cultural programme is spearheaded by the **Institute of Creative Arts** (ICA), also housed here, with a remit to keep traditional culture alive and promote new talent. The organization was originally known as the Bliss Institute, funded by the legacy of Baron Henry Ernest Edward Victor Bliss, an eccentric Englishman with a Portuguese title and considerable wealth, the origins of which remain a mystery. Bliss arrived off the coast of Belize in his yacht *Sea King* in 1926 after hearing about the tremendous amount of game fish in local waters. Unfortunately, he became ill soon after and died without ever having been ashore, but he must have been impressed by whatever fish he did catch, as he left most of his estate to the colony – meticulously stipulating how the money was to be spent. This became the Bliss Trust, which has been used to help build markets and libraries, improve roads and water supplies and create the Bliss School of Nursing. In gratitude, March 9 (the date of his death) was declared an official public holiday – **Baron Bliss Day** – commemorated by boat races and the La Ruta Maya canoe race (see p.148) from San Ignacio to Belize City. See p.58 for his tomb and memorial.

St John's Cathedral and Yarborough Cemetery

At the southern end of Albert Street is **St John's Cathedral** (daily 6am–6pm; free), the oldest Anglican cathedral in Central America and one of the oldest buildings in Belize. Its construction lasted from 1812 to 1820 and used red bricks brought over as ballast in British ships. With its square, battlemented tower, it looks like a large, English parish church. The main structure has survived almost two hundred years of tropical heat and hurricanes, though a fire in 2002 destroyed most of the roof, now fully restored. In the first half of the nineteenth century, several indigenous kings of the Mosquito Coast held their coronation ceremonies here.

Just west of the cathedral, **Yarborough Cemetery** was named after the magistrate who owned the land and permitted the burial of prominent people here from 1781; commoners were admitted only after 1870. Although the graves have fallen into disrepair, a browse among the stones will turn up fascinating snippets of history. Nearby, connected to the mainland by a wooden causeway, **Bird's Isle** is a popular venue for parties and concerts, and there's a pleasant outdoor restaurant (see p.66).

The House of Culture

East of the cathedral, in a beautiful, breezy, seafront setting, shaded by royal palms and complete with an immaculate lawn, is the colonial Government House, now restored and renamed the **House of Culture** (daily 9am–4pm; Bz$10; ☏227-3050, Ⓦ www.nichbelize.org). Built in 1814, it was the governor's residence when Belize was a British colony; at midnight on September 20, 1981, the Belize flag was hoisted here for the first time as the country celebrated independence.

The house has always been used for official receptions, particularly on Independence Day. But the present governor-general, Sir Colville Young, wanted to make this superb example of Belize's colonial heritage open to everyone, so in 1996 it was designated a **museum**, later becoming the House of Culture. A flight of steps under a columned portico leads to the front door; inside, a plush, red carpet stretches down the hall to a great mahogany staircase, and beyond here doors open onto the back porch, overlooking the sea. On the grounds, the carefully restored *Sea King*, the tender of Baron Bliss's yacht of the same name, stands as testimony

▲ House of Culture

to the skill of Belizean boatbuilders. The plant-filled gardens are a haven for birds and it's worth bringing a pair of binoculars.

A wide range of Belizean arts are presented here, among them painting, dance, **Garifuna** drumming, musical performances and, in a room off the front porch, contemporary visual arts. It's also a popular venue for weddings and banquets. In the main room, a panoramic painting of Belize City in the early 1900s overlooks the collection of colonial silverware, glass and furniture, while a different room displays the **Eric King collection**, a fascinating compilation of vintage photographs and postcards of Belize.

Around Belize City

A number of sights outside Belize City along the Western Highway make memorable day-trips: among them, the superb Belize Zoo, and beyond, Monkey Bay Wildlife Sanctuary. As you leave the city, however, you first pass through the Lord's Ridge cemetery, then skirt the coastline, running behind a tangle of mangrove swamps and past **Old Belize** – a fine museum showcasing the history and cultures of the country. A few miles further, the highway crosses the **Sir John Burden Canal**, an inland waterway that serves as a nature reserve and valuable wildlife corridor connecting the Belize and Sibun rivers; some small boat tours take this canal to the **Northern and Southern lagoons** and Gales Point (see p.187). After fourteen miles the highway passes through **HATTIEVILLE**, named after the 1961 hurricane that gave the village its first inhabitants in the form of refugees. From here, a paved road leads north to **Burrell Boom** (see p.74), while slightly west, on the south side of the highway near the Sibun River, **Gracie Rock** is the highest of several curious limestone outcrops quarried for road-building, and used as the fictional settlement of Geronimo in the film *The Mosquito Coast*.

Old Belize Cultural and Historical Center

The informative, well-run **Old Belize Cultural and Historical Center** (Mon–Sat 10am–9pm, Sun 10am–6pm; Bz$10; ☏222-4129, ⓦwww.oldbelize .com), on Mile 5 of the Western Highway, was created as a colourful, inter-active overview of the country all under one roof, targeted towards time-pressed visitors such as cruise ship passengers with nine hours or less to spend in port. The centre successfully draws the cruise crowd, but thanks to its adjoining open-air **restaurant** (see p.67) and man-made beach with water slide and zip line, it's also a hit with the locals. You enter the experiential museum through a mahogany tree, wander past videos on the country's varied ethnic groups and natural riches, and then explore a series of rooms, each highlighting a different era in the country's history. The humid rainforest room contains a waterfall and a cage of fluttering Blue Morpho butterflies, then there's a dimly lit Maya village, with life-sized stone carvings and a replica wood-and-thatch home. Early industry also features, with a steam-powered sugar mill, and chicle (the base ingredient of chewing gum) trade and logging. A Garifuna dwelling has piped-in beats of traditional drumming, and you can also walk along a re-created, early-twentieth-century Belize City street lined with wooden homes. Old Belize is also a great place for one-stop **souvenir shopping**, with reasonably priced wooden products, local hot sauces and books on Belize.

From Tuesday to Thursday, when the cruise passengers are scheduled to visit, you might catch Belizean dancing and singing, usually during the late morning and at lunch. The **beach** (daily 10am–4.30pm; included in museum entrance fee), fashioned out of reclaimed land, is fairly small but well groomed, with plenty of water activities for youngsters. There is also the **Cucumber Beach Marina** here, attracting both recreational and commercial boats.

The Belize Zoo

Twenty-six miles outside Belize City, at Mile 29 of the Western Highway, the **Belize Zoo** (daily 8.30am–5pm; Bz$20 adult, $10 child, volunteers and military personnel; ☏220-8004, ⓦwww.belizezoo.org) is easily visited on a half-day trip or as a stop on the way to or from the west. And, unless you're a seasoned wildlife photographer, this is likely to be the best place to get excellent **photographs** of the animals of Belize. By **bus**, take any service between Belize City and Belmopan (except James Bus) and ask the driver to drop you off; there's a sign on the highway and zoo staff know the times of onward buses. A 100yd walk brings you to the entrance and the Gerald Durrell Visitor Centre, with displays of children's art and exhibits on Belize's ecosystems.

Probably the finest zoo in the Americas south of the US, and long recog-nized as a phenomenal conservation achievement, the zoo opened in 1983 after an ambitious wildlife film (*Path of the Rain God*) left Sharon Matola, the film's production assistant, with a collection of semi-tame animals no longer able to fend for themselves in the wild. This now means the chance to see the native animals of Belize at close quarters, housed in spacious enclosures that resemble their natural habitats. The zoo's menagerie has never been supplemented by animals taken from the wild – all are either donated or confiscated pets, injured wild animals, sent from other zoos (for its internationally-recognized **captive breeding programmes**) or residents since birth. All schoolchildren in Belize benefit from a free, educational trip here.

The zoo's trail is arranged as "a walk through Belize", taking you to the pine ridge, the forest edge, the rainforest, lagoons and the river forest; hand-painted signs identify what you're seeing. Along the river forest trail you'll find April, a venerable **Baird's tapir** (known locally as a "mountain cow") well known to the schoolchildren of Belize, who visit in their hundreds on her birthday (in April) to feed her a huge, vegetable birthday cake. All the Belizean cats are represented and some, including the **jaguars**, have bred successfully; you can enter an enclosure with a young, tame jaguar (with the keeper) for Bz$100, while there's even a rarer melanistic (black) jaguar. Numerous aviaries house vividly coloured **scarlet macaws**, toucans, parrots, jabiru storks, a spectacled owl and several vultures and hawks, though Panamá, a magnificent **harpy eagle** (named for his home country) is most well-known for his role in an ambitious breeding programme crucial to the reintroduction of the eagle to Belize. Other inhabitants include deer, spider and howler monkeys, peccaries, agoutis, numerous snakes and the two species of **crocodile** found in Belize.

Visit the **gift shop** for interesting souvenirs: Sharon, the zoo's founder, has written several extremely popular children's books with a strong conservation message. If you're really keen on supporting the zoo, you can become a Friend and receive a regular newsletter; the zoo's website is a good information source for current conservation issues in Belize.

The Tropical Education Center

Across the highway from the zoo, the **Tropical Education Center** (☎220-8003, ⓔtec@belizezoo.org; free) focuses on school and tour guide training groups, though it's open to all and has research opportunities for overseas students. There is **internet access** and a well-equipped library, alongside self-guided **nature trails** and observation decks around two small lagoons.

Anyone can stay in the wonderful **accommodation** here (ask at the zoo office for pick up), seated in the pine savannah and equipped with bug screens, electric lights, hot showers, flush toilets and a communal kitchen. Wooden **dorms** with tiled floors (Bz$60 per person) have either double or single beds, though for a fraction more, a couple can stay in the comfortable "Forest Cabana" (❺) on stilts (shared showers). A third option is the secluded Guest House (❹; long-term rates available) with private bath, stove, fridge and peaceful views. Guests can take a special nocturnal tour of the zoo for Bz$25.

Monkey Bay Wildlife Sanctuary

A little over a mile beyond the Belize Zoo, the unpaved **Coastal Road** (or Manatee Road; marked by a sign, a petrol station and a bar) heads south to isolated yet beautiful **Gales Point** (see p.187), and eventually to **Dangriga**. The route is only served by two buses per week, with no onward service to Dangriga, though hitching is feasible. Just past the junction, the much-maligned and barely-occupied new residential area of **Mahogany Heights** is on the right, built amidst a political firestorm of corruption, while a mile further on is *Cheers* (☎822-8014), a friendly, Canadian-run **restaurant/bar** and **gift shop** set back one hundred yards from the roadside, where you can find good food and even **accommodation** in cabañas (❹). Just beyond, next to Monkey Bay, *Amigos Bar* (☎802-8000) has great **meals** and desserts, a daily happy hour and **internet**.

Marking the boundary between Belize and Cayo districts, and located four hundred yards south of the road here (signposted at Mile 31.5; most buses stop), the **Monkey Bay Wildlife Sanctuary and National Park** (☎820-3032 or 600-3191, ⓦwww.monkeybaybelize.org) is a 28-square-mile protected area extending to the **Sibun River** and beyond, offering birding and nature trails through a variety of habitats. The "bay" part of the name comes from a beautiful swimming spot by a sandy beach on the river, overhung with trees once inhabited by howler and spider monkeys; the monkeys are now returning after a long absence following hurricane disturbance, while the river watershed also supports abundant birdlife, jaguars, tapirs and Morelet's crocodiles. From Monkey Bay you can arrange one- or multi-day guided **canoe**, **camping and birding trips** on the Sibun River and explore little-visited **caves** in the Sibun Hills to the south, all showing evidence of use by the ancient Maya. You'll need a guide for the three-day trek along the **Indian Creek Trail** to Five Blues Lake (Marcos Cucul is also an excellent guide for the trail, see p.128). All trips should be arranged in advance.

The sanctuary headquarters comprises a handsome, wooden **field research station**, serving as library, museum and classroom, as well as a screened, dining room and bunkhouses. Although it specializes in hosting academic programmes in natural history and watershed ecology for students and teachers (it's also the Belize base for Conservation Corridors), it is a wonderfully relaxing **place to stay** for anyone, either in rooms, cabins, the bunkhouse, or else camping on raised platforms under thatched roofs (❶–❸) – all have mosquito-nets and use shared rainwater showers. You could also stay in the "Savanna Cabaña", a private home with bath, veranda and kitchen (❻). To make a **booking**, contact directors Matt and Marga Miller on the number above, or just turn up and ask if there's space available. The field station attempts to be a viable exponent of **sustainable living**, utilizing solar and wind power, rainwater catchment and biogas fuel for cooking; the food, some of it grown in the station's organic gardens, is delicious, plentiful and inexpensive. An **internet** café and free wi-fi access is also available to guests.

Monkey Bay is also the contact point for visits to **Cox Lagoon Crocodile Sanctuary**, a 70-square-mile private wetland reserve north of the highway in the Mussel Creek watershed. Home to over one hundred Morelet's crocodiles, it also hosts numerous other reptiles, jabiru storks, howler monkeys and jaguars. Visitors can camp, canoe, hike and fish, though all trips should be arranged well in advance.

Eating

There are a good variety of **restaurants** in Belize City, though the tasty but humble **Creole** fare of rice and beans still predominates the lower to mid range. There's plenty of seafood and steak, and a preponderance of **Chinese** restaurants – some good for **vegetarians** – as well as the odd **Lebanese** and **Indian** establishment. Fine dining tends to be found in larger **hotels**. Note that some restaurants close fairly early in the evening (by 8.30 or 9pm, and sometimes earlier), and many smaller places are closed on Sunday.

Amazingly, the only US-based chain to make inroads into Belize is *Subway*, with a single branch; *HL's Burger* (the self-proclaimed "Burger King of Belize") serves as the principal purveyor of fast food until others inevitably arrive. A more grassroots fast food is fried chicken – known as "dollar chicken" whatever the price – available from small stands, while Brodie's supermarket (below) has a deli counter with sandwiches and fajitas.

If you're shopping for food, the main **supermarkets** are Brodie's on Albert Street (which has a pharmacy, and good selection), and the cheaper, larger Bottom Dollar on North Front Street opposite Holy Redeemer Cathedral. Naturally enough, local **fruit** is cheap and plentiful.

Cafés, snacks and fast food

Moon Clusters 25 Daly St (above Chinese store). Open 9am–6pm Tues–Sat. Quirky and popular coffee bar selling espressos, smoothies and snacks including quesadillas and sandwiches. Try their Cholie's frozen coffee or iced chocolate and whipped cream.

Pepper's Pizza 4 St Thomas St ☏ 223-5000. Popular pizza restaurant with reliable deliveries. Mon–Thurs 10am–10pm, Fri & Sat 10am–11pm, Sun 10am–9pm. There's also a small branch (until 5pm; closed Sun) on Albert St where you can buy by the slice.

Le Petit Café Cork St, in the Villa Wing of the *Radisson*. Enjoy good coffee, baked treats including (very un-French) croissants, and a pleasant café atmosphere at the outdoor tables. Ideal for a continental breakfast.

Local restaurants and Chinese

Bird's Isle Restaurant South end of Albert St ☏ 207-6500. Relax under a thatched roof by the sea and enjoy nicely priced Belizean fare (Bz$15–20, like grilled conch, stewed chicken, plantains and, on Sat, a boil-up – the one-pot stew of root vegetables and chicken or beef. A friendly, community-oriented place, with kids encouraged to use the adjoining basketball court. Karaoke Thurs and happy hour Fri (6–8pm).

Cenie's Diner Upstairs in the commercial centre, just south of the Swing Bridge. Great breakfasts – eggs, fry jacks, *longanissa* sausage – and numerous kinds of chicken (and other options) for lunch, served cafeteria-style. Great fresh juices. Enjoy the best harbour and bridge views in the city. Mon–Sat 7am–4pm.

Chon Saan Palace 1 Kelly St (by Cinderella Plaza) ☏ 223-3008. Indisputably Belize City's best Chinese, in a smart dining room, and featuring a large and varied menu (Bz$20–30), plus dim sum and, surprisingly, a sushi bar.

🏃 **Macy's** 18 Bishop St ☏ 207-3419. Long-established Creole restaurant with plaid tablecloths, popular with locals and very busy at lunchtime. The menu (Bz$12–20) includes whole snapper – pan-fried, steamed or broiled – and deep-fried chicken with tomato sauce, and also traditional game: armadillo, deer and gibnut (a type of large rodent).

Ma Ma Chen 7 Eve St ☏ 223-4568. The only vegetarian restaurant in town, with a tasty Taiwanese menu of spring rolls stuffed with carrots, cabbage, mushrooms and tofu, vegetarian lunchboxes and sushi (on Fri). It's a no-frills but comfortable family spot. Mon–Sat 10am–6pm.

Marlins 11 Regent St W, next to the *Belcove* ☏ 227-6995. Tasty, large portions of inexpensive Belizean and Mexican-influenced dishes – *escabeche*, stewed chicken, grilled catch of the day – served indoors or on the veranda overlooking the creek. Filling breakfasts.

Nerie's Restaurant 12 Douglas Jones St ☏ 223-4028. Excellent Belizean fare served in clean, well-run and brightly lit surroundings. Choose from the chalkboard menu featuring local specialities, including a flavourful conch soup made with potatoes, okra and cocoa. Great fresh juices. Very busy at lunchtimes, with a daily special. Mon–Sat 7am–5.30pm. *Nerie's II* at Queen St and Daly St (daily 7.30am–10pm) is also good, with occasional live music at the *Bodega Lounge* upstairs.

Thirsty Thursdays Restaurant & Bar 164 Newtown Barracks ☏ 223-1677. The newest option on the strip is the sister restaurant to the long-established Jambel's Jerk Pit in San Pedro, with Chef Garnet Brown cooking up delicious, Jamaican dishes at reasonable prices; jerk chicken, spicy fish, shrimp and lobster, and soups, salads and burgers – indoors or on the patio. Closed Sun.

International and fine dining

Celebrity Marine Parade, behind the Central Bank ☏ 223-7272. Good international cuisine (Bz$25–40) – thick T-Bone steaks, grilled snapper, shrimp kebabs, *köfte* meatballs, chicken fajitas – at this bright, airy (yet strangely carpeted) restaurant. You can catch glimpses of the Caribbean Sea in the near-distance. Good take-out Belizean lunches (Bz$12) also.

Chateau Caribbean 6 Marine Parade ☏ 223-3888, ⊛ www.chateaucaribbean.com. For undisturbed views of blue sea, head up to this cool, first-floor hotel restaurant, where prices for Chinese (try noodles with lobster) and international dishes are more reasonable than you might guess from the gleaming white linen (Bz$25–35). The restaurant is often quite empty, but the outdoor bars at the *Radisson* and *Great House* are nearby for a post-meal drink.

Riverside Tavern 2 Mapp St ☏ 223-5640. A gleaming, four-sided bar, with bottles lining back-lit shelves, stands in the centre of this high-end tavern on the riverbank. Fill up on "Coco Loco" shrimp (Bz$35), pan-seared grouper, seafood ceviche and excellent juicy burgers (Bz$20), at wooden tables or on the breezy outdoor deck. See nightlife listings, p.158.

Sibun Bite Bar and Grill Old Belize, Mile 5 Western Highway ☎ 222-4129. Featuring high ceilings made of native hardwoods, this large and popular place serves well-presented and nicely priced Belizean and international dishes (Bz$18 upwards) - pineapple curry shrimp, seafood burritos and stewed chicken – on its outdoor terrace. Great bar, too. Daily 11am–9pm.

Smoky Mermaid 13 Cork St ☎ 223-4759. Superb option for seafood al fresco (Bz$40 upwards), including ceviche, the catch of the day crusted with shredded yucca, and "Naked Lobster", steamed and served with garlic and butter. Sit amid the gnarled roots and heavy branches of native trees – and a mermaid fountain, with the colonial *Great House* (see p.56) looming behind. Excellent cocktails are served either at the bar or in the upstairs *Budda Bar*, reclining on low couches.

Stonegrill Cork St, in the Colonial Wing of the *Radisson* ☎ 223-3333. Poolside restaurant where you select your dish – seafood, chicken or beef,

kebab-style (Bz$40 upwards)– and cook it yourself on a slab of volcanic rock heated to 350°C. Mild or spicy sauces accompany your creation. Sizzling fun and surprisingly healthy, as there are no added fats or oils.

Sumathi 31 Eve St ☎ 223-1172. Good north Indian and tandoori food (Bz$20–40) in a quiet, smart environment. Vegetarian dishes include chickpea curry and *aloo gobi* (cauliflower, potatoes, sweet pepper and ginger). Tues–Sun 10am–11.30pm.

La Tavernetta 2 Dolphin Drive, Buttonwood Bay, off the Northern Hwy ☎ 223-7998. The city's only Italian restaurant serves up great food from a brick oven, in a sedate dining room with rose walls and white tablecloths. The Italian owner imports most ingredients, with choices (Bz$25 upwards) including shrimp pasta, risotto in a creamy mushroom sauce and good tiramisu and home-made ice cream. Bz$15 taxi ride to town. Convenient if staying along the highway. Closed Mon & Tues.

Nightlife and entertainment

Belize City's more sophisticated **bars** are to be found in the higher-end hotels; try the poolside bar of the *Biltmore* (with occasional steel band music), or the *Radisson*, where you can sip frothy cocktails on an outdoor patio while tapping your toes to Caribbean tunes. The *Smoky Mermaid* (see above), in the patio beneath *The Great House*, is another pleasant spot for an outdoor drink amid tropical foliage. Most of the above tempt the after-work crowd with Friday evening **happy hours** (usually 5–7pm).

At the other end of the scale are low-lit rum-drinking dives, which you won't need any help to find. Though you might be offered drugs or feel uneasy in these places, you're more likely to spend a casual evening in the company of easy-going, hard-drinking guys. *Nu Fenders Bar*, just opposite *Nerie's* (see opposite), does a brisk trade at the weekends with a local crowd knocking back local drinks.

Between these two extremes is a smattering of amiable, local spots – many with comfortable outdoor decks – perfect for enjoying a Belikin beer or two. Many of these places have **karaoke** sessions, belting out hits weekdays or weekends. *Bird's Isle* (see opposite) is currently one of the best for both karaoke, DJs and live music, while the *Bodega Lounge*, upstairs at *Nerie's Restaurant II*, also features karaoke on some weekend nights. The liveliest strip in the city is the relatively safe stretch of Barracks Road around BTL Park. At weekends, the sidewalks fill with a youngish, local crowd traipsing from one nightspot to the next, kicking back on various **outdoor decks**.

The *Princess Hotel* looms over this part of town, with a popular club and a flashy **casino**, where you don't have to be a high roller to try your luck at blackjack, Caribbean poker and roulette, though you will need a passport or photo ID; the dress code is no shorts or sandals. There's a Bz$50 minimum play charge (any tokens you don't use are changed back into currency), and local (as opposed to imported) drinks are free. For the viceless or underage, there's an eight-lane bowling alley and Belize City's only **cinema**, showing the latest releases in air-conditioned comfort.

Caesar's Palace Newtown Barracks Rd, across from BTL Park. The nights get going here after 10pm on Fri and Sat, when a lively, packed house grooves to techno, Latin, soca and reggae on the small dancefloor. *MJs Bar* is a near-identical place next door.

Club Next In the *Princess Hotel*. Hip DJs spin blaring tunes in the city's most popular club, from reggaetón to contemporary rock, for a dance-savvy crowd fuelled on potent cocktails. Fri & Sat 10pm–4am. Bz$20 cover.

Palm Island 1 1/2 miles, Northern Hwy. New, smartish club with a large dancefloor and two lounge areas. Dress code no sneakers, sleeveless or caps. Music is reggae dancehall, soca, punta, electronic and reggaetón. Bz$15 upwards.

Riverside Patio On the creekside behind the commercial centre. Depending on the crowd – usually lots of hard-drinking, local fishermen – this place can get loud and rowdy. If that's your scene, grab a beer with the guys and watch the bridge swing.

Riverside Tavern 2 Mapp St ☎223-5640. The classiest nightspot in this part of town swells with a lively crowd of Belizeans and foreigners. Dark-wood-and-brass interior and a spacious outdoor deck are matched by an extensive cocktail menu, including the "Rainwater", watermelon and cranberry juice spiked with vodka. Secure parking.

Travellers 'One Barrel' Bar 2 1/2 miles, Northern Hwy. Raised wooden bar next to the Travellers brewery with a friendly atmosphere and Caribbean sounds. Ideal for a late beer or rum – people in groups buy a bottle for the table and keep going till it's gone.

Shopping

Albert and Regent streets, south of the Swing Bridge, hum with commerce, from discount shoe stores to the city's largest supermarket and department store, **Brodie's**. **Sing's** at 35 Albert St, stocks a wide range of souvenirs, from mahogany carvings to Maya crafts and jewellery; there's also a Sing's in the Tourism Village.

On the north side of town lies the well-stocked department store **Mirab**, on Fort Street, with everything from postcards and batteries to appliances and furniture. For souvenirs, stop in at the **Belizean Handicraft Market Place** (see p.58), with Belizean hardwood crafts, including bowls, picture frames and cutting boards, Maya basketry and hot sauces and spices. **The Image Factory** (see p.57) also carries quality souvenirs, books and local art, and **Old Belize** (see p.63) has its own excellent array, as does the Audubon Society (see p.58).

Listings

Airlines American, New Rd at Queen St ☎223-2522; Continental, 80 Regent St ☎227-8309; Maya Island Air, Municipal Airport ☎223-1140 or 226-2435; Taca, in Belize Global Travel, 41 Albert St ☎227-7363; Tropic Air, Municipal Airport ☎224-5671 or 226-2012; US Airways toll-free to US office ☎0800/872-4700.

Banks and exchange Most banks are on Albert St (usually Mon–Thurs 8am–2pm, Fri 8am–4.30pm); The Belize, First Caribbean and Scotia banks have ATMs that accept foreign-issued cards; others will process cash advances over the counter. Cash in US$ is usually only available if you can show a ticket to leave the country. *Casas de cambio* in shops, hotels and restaurants change travellers' cheques and accept US$. Guatemalan and Mexican currency is often difficult to obtain except at the borders, but some shops in the Marine Terminal generally have quetzales and pesos. Western Union is located at Belize Chamber of Commerce, 63 Regent St ☎227-0014.

Books Angelus Press, 10 Queen St (Mon–Fri 7.30am–5.30pm, Sat 8am–noon; ☎223-5777), has a wide range of books on Belize, maps and guides, including *Rough Guides*. Many larger hotels also sell books, magazines and newspapers.

Car rental Highly reputable Crystal, Mile 5, Northern Hwy ☎223-1600 or toll-free in Belize ☎0800/777-7777, ⓦwww.crystal-belize.com, has the largest rental fleet in the country, and is the only outfit that allows you to take vehicles over the Guatemalan border. Other companies which also arrange vehicle pick up and drop-off anywhere in the city, or at the airports, at no extra charge, are: Avis ☎ 225-2385 or 225-2629 (24hr), ⓦ www .avis.com.bz; Budget, Mile 2, Northern Hwy ☎ 223-2435, ⓦ www.budget-belize.com; and Hertz, 11A Cork St ☎ 223-5935. For more information on driving in Belize, see p.23.

Embassies and consulates Several EU countries have honorary consulates in Belize City, open mornings Mon–Fri; contact details are in the green pages of the Belize telephone directory. The US and Irish embassies and UK consulate are in Belmopan (see p.127). Canada (cannot issue passports), 83 N Front St ☎ 223-1060; Guatemala, 8 A St, Kings Park ☎ 223-3150; Mexico, 18 North Park St ☎ 223-0194. For passport photos, try Spooner's, 89 N Front St, or Tito's Photo Studio, 7 Barrack Rd.

Immigration The Belize Immigration Office is in the Government Complex on Mahogany St, near the junction of Central American Blvd and the Western Hwy (Mon–Thurs 8.30am–4pm, Fri 8.30am–3.30pm; ☎ 222-4620; this is a bad area so take a taxi). Thirty-day extensions of stay cost Bz$35.

Internet Several internet centres are dotted about the city: Angelus Press (see books, above) is reliable (just over Bz$4/hr); Hi-Tech Arena Internet Cafe nearby at 44 Queen St (corner with Barrack Rd) Mon–Sat 8am–8pm, Sun 1.30–7pm, Bz$4/hr; and TT internet café in the Downtown Shopping Plaza, 27 Albert St (opposite Brodies), Mon–Sat 9am–6pm, BZ$5/hr, coffee available.

Laundry Central America Coin Laundry, 114 Barrack Rd (Mon–Sat 8.30am–9pm; reduced hours Sun), and in many hotels.

Massage Oltsil Day Spa, 148A Barrack Rd ☎ 223-7722, ⓔ oltsil@yahoo.com. Holistic massage, body scrubs, herbal wraps, facials, waxing, pedicures and spa treatments using local natural products and ingredients, including mud – properly sterilized – from cave systems in northern Belize. Closed Sun.

Medical care The Karl Heusner Memorial Hospital (Princess Margaret Drive, near Northern Hwy ☎ 223-1548 & 223-5686, ⓦ www.khmh.bz), is the principal hospital of the Belizean health service. It has most medical specialities and a 24hr accident and emergency department. For quick but expensive medical care there are two private hospitals: Belize Medical Associates, 5791 St Thomas St ☎ 223-0302, ⓦ www.belizemedical .com, and Belize Healthcare Partners Ltd, Chancellor Ave and Blue Marlin Ave ☎ 223-7870, ⓦ www.belizehealthcare.com. Both have all the main specialities and 24hr emergency rooms.

Pharmacy In Brodie's, 2 Albert St ☎ 227-7070. Open Mon–Thurs 8:30am–7pm, Fri 8:30am–8pm, Sat 8:30am–5pm, Sun 8:30am–1pm.

Police The main police station is on Queen St, a block north of the Swing Bridge (☎ 227-2210). For emergencies, dial ☎ 90 or 911 nationwide. Alternatively, contact the tourism police; see the box on p.54.

Post office The main post office (including parcel office) is on N Front St, northeast of the Swing Bridge (Mon–Fri 8am–4.30pm).

Telephones There are payphones (which need a phonecard) dotted around the city and a/c phone booths at the main BTL office, 1 Church St (Mon–Fri 8am–6pm), which also has fax facilities.

Travel Details

Moving on from Belize City is easy, with domestic **flights** to all main towns from the Municipal Airport, and **boats** to the northern cayes from the Marine Terminal or Brown Sugar plaza. There are regular departures by **bus** to all parts of the country, across the border to Chetumal in Mexico and to Benque Viejo in Cayo, for the Guatemalan border.

Buses

Most buses depart from the Novelo's terminal, west of the city centre, in a fairly rundown section of town; it's safest to take a taxi. Transport peters out at dusk and there are no overnight buses. Tickets are always bought on the bus; schedules are available at ⓦ www .nationaltransportbelize.com and ⓦ www .guidetobelize.info.

Belize City Novelo's Bus Terminal (NTSL, James Bus, Gilharry, BBOC and others) to: Belmopan (every 15min; 1hr 15min; 5am–9pm); Benque Viejo, for the Guatemalan border (at least hourly; up to 3hr; 5am–9pm); Chetumal, Mexico (10 daily; up to 3hr 30min; 5.30am–7pm); Corozal (hourly; 2hr 30min; 5.30am–7pm); Dangriga via Belmopan (at least hourly; 3hr 30min; 6am–5pm); Gales Point (1hr 40min; 5pm Mon & Fri only; confirm in advance); Hopkins via Dangriga (6 daily;

4hr; 7am–2pm); Maskall, for Altun Ha (1hr 30min; Mon–Sat 3.30, 5.30 & 7pm); Orange Walk (hourly; 1hr 30min; 5am–7pm); Placencia via Dangriga (4 daily; 4–6hr; 7am–2pm; far quicker to go via the ferry from Mango Creek); Punta Gorda via Dangriga and Mango Creek (8 daily; 5–7hr; 5.30am–3.30pm); San Ignacio via Belmopan (at least hourly; up to 2hr 30min; 5am–9pm);

Belize City, Regent St West/Albert St (Perez Bus) to: Sarteneja via Orange Walk (Mon–Sat 10.30am; 3hr 30min; noon & 4pm).

Belize City, Cairo Street/Euphrates Ave (Russell's and McFadzean's bus) to: Bermudian Landing (3 daily; 1hr 15min; Mon–Sat).

Belize City, Regent St W and Collet Canal (Jex and Sons bus) to: Crooked Tree (2 daily; 1hr 30min; Mon–Fri, 1 Sat).

Boats

Marine Terminal, N Front St by the Swing Bridge and Brown Sugar Plaza, N Front Street to: Caye Caulker (every 90min; 45min; 8am–5.30pm) Bz$30 one-way, Bz$40 same-day return; T 223-5752. Most services also continue to San Pedro, Ambergris Caye and will call at St George's Caye on request. For more detail on boat schedules, see the boxes, p.102 & p.113. For boats to Honduras, see p.191, and to Guatemala, p.210; check with Ramon or Petty Cervantes at the Mundo Maya Deli/Riverside Cafe at the Marine Terminal or Brown Sugar respectively (see p.51), for schedules and connecting buses.

Flights

Belize City Municipal Airport to: Punta Gorda (8–10 flights daily; 1hr), stopping on request at Dangriga (25min) and Placencia (45min); and San Pedro (hourly; 25min; 7.30am–5pm daily), stopping on request at Caye Caulker. All flights are with Maya Island Air and Tropic Air (see p.68).

Belize International Airport to: Flores, for Guatemala City (2–4 daily; 45min); Roatán (1 daily; 1hr 45min); San Pedro Sula (1 daily; 1hr); and San Salvador (1 daily; 1hr 30min). See Basics for further destinations, and for details of international and domestic airlines.

The north

CHAPTER 2 **Highlights**

✱ **Bermudian Landing** Get up close to the black howler monkey – the largest primate in the New World – in this small village on the banks of the Belize River. **See p.76**

✱ **Birding in Crooked Tree Wildlife Sanctuary** Stroll this leafy sanctuary to spot a fabulous array of birds. **See p.78**

✱ **Lamanai** Journey by boat along the tranquil New River to reach this astonishing Maya city, with some wonderfully restored temples. **See p.83**

✱ **Rio Bravo Conservation and Management Area** A massive swath of the best-protected forest in Belize, and one of the most likely places to catch a glimpse of a wild jaguar. **See p.85**

✱ **Sarteneja** Relax and enjoy small-town Belizean life at this quiet, lobster-fishing village. **See p.88**

✱ **Corozal** Relax in this quiet village, and enjoy a stroll along its palm-shaded shoreline. **See p.90**

▲ Lamanai

The north

Swamps, savannahs and lagoons mix with rainforest and farmland in **Northern Belize**. For many years this part of the country was largely inaccessible and had closer ties with Mexico than Belize City; most of the original settlers were refugees from the Caste Wars in Yucatán, who brought with them the sugar cane that formed the basis of the Belizean economy for much of the twentieth century. Indian and mestizo farming communities were connected by a skeletal network of dirt tracks, while boats plied the route between Belize City and Corozal. In 1930, however, the Northern Highway brought the region into contact with the rest of the country, opening up the area to further waves of settlers.

The largest town in the north is **Orange Walk**, the main centre for sugar production. Further north, **Corozal** is a small and peaceful Caribbean settlement with a strong Mexican element – not surprising, as it lies just nine miles from the border. Throughout the north, Spanish is as common as Creole, and there's a distinctive Latin flavour to life.

Most visitors to northern Belize come to see the **Maya ruins** and wildlife reserves. The largest archeological site, **Lamanai**, features some of the most impressive pyramids in the country; it's served by regular boat tours along the New River. East of Lamanai, **Altun Ha**, reached by the Old Northern Highway, is usually visited as part of a day-trip from Belize City or San Pedro. Other sites in the region include Cuello and Nohmul, respectively southwest and north of Orange Walk, and Santa Rita and Cerros, both near Corozal.

The north is also a haven for wildlife, and each of the four main **reserves** in the region offers insight into a specific habitat or conservation strategy. At the **Community Baboon Sanctuary** in the Belize River valley, a group of farmers has combined agriculture with conservation, much to the benefit of the black howler monkey, while at **Crooked Tree Wildlife Sanctuary**, a network of lagoons and creeks gives protection to a range of migratory birds, including the endangered jabiru stork. By far the largest and most ambitious conservation project is the **Rio Bravo Conservation and Management Area**, comprising 378 square miles of tropical forest and river systems in the west of Orange Walk District. This vast, practically untouched area, containing several Maya sites, adjoins the borders of Guatemala and Mexico. The most northerly protected area is **Shipstern Nature Reserve**, where a large tract of tropical hardwood forest, mangroves and wetland is preserved with the help of several conservation organizations.

Getting around the north

Travelling around the north is fairly straightforward if you stick to the main roads. National Transport has **bus services** (around five daily, 5am–7pm) along the Northern Highway between Belize City and Chetumal, Mexico, calling at Orange

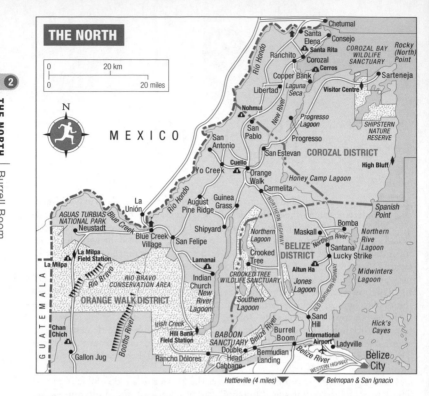

Hattieville (4 miles) ▼   ▼ Belmopan & San Ignacio

Walk, Corozal and the border town of Santa Elena along the way. Smaller roads and centres are served by a fairly regular flow of buses and trucks. Several companies also operate **tours** to the Maya sites and nature reserves.

Burrell Boom

BURRELL BOOM, on the Belize River, is about twenty miles from Belize City, and is reached down the Northern Highway turn-off to Bermudian Landing. In logging days, a huge, heavy, metal chain called a "boom" was stretched across the river to catch the logs floating down. Burrell Boom is a pleasant base for exploring the area; if you plan on spending the night, try the restful *Black Orchid Resort* (T 225-9028, W www.blackorchidresort.com; ❽). Perched on the banks of the river, the **hotel** offers freshly scrubbed rooms surrounded by leafy grounds. The cosy **restaurant** features home-made Belizean specialities.

In Burrell Boom, the river is never far from view, and to fully understand its role in the surrounding area, head on a boat journey. **Old River Adventures** (T 225-9008) offers informative riverboat tours (from 1–2hr) where you can spot crocs, iguanas and howler monkeys. Tours start at Bz$75.

The Community Baboon Sanctuary

The **Community Baboon Sanctuary** (ⓦ www.howlermonkeys.org), established in 1985 by primate biologist Rob Horwich and a group of local farmers (with help from the Worldwide Fund for Nature), is one of the most interesting conservation projects in Belize. A mixture of farmland and broadleaf forest, the sanctuary stretches along nineteen miles of the Belize River valley – from Flowers Bank to Big Falls – and comprises a total of eight villages and over 250 landowners. Farmers here voluntarily harmonize their own needs with those of the wildlife in a project combining conservation, education and tourism; visitors are welcome and you'll find plenty of places to rent canoes or horses.

▲ Black howler monkey

The main focus of attention here is the **black howler monkey** (locally known as a "baboon"), the largest monkey in the New World and an endangered subspecies of howler that exists only in Belize, Guatemala and southern Mexico. They generally live in troops of between four and eight, and spend the day clambering through the leafy canopy, feasting on leaves, flowers and fruits. You're pretty much guaranteed to see them up close, feeding and resting in the trees along the riverbank, and they're often as interested in you as you are in them. At dawn and dusk they let rip with their famous howl, a deep and rasping roar that carries for miles.

The sanctuary is also home to around two hundred **bird** species, plus anteaters, deer, peccaries, coatis, iguanas and the endangered Central American river turtle. Special trails are cut through the forest so that visitors can see it at its best; you can wander these alone or with a guide, and canoe or horseback tours in the sanctuary are also possibilities.

At the heart of the sanctuary, twenty-seven miles northwest of Belize City, lies the Creole village of **BERMUDIAN LANDING**, a former logging centre dating to the seventeenth century. On arrival at Bermudian Landing, you'll need to register at the sanctuary's **visitor centre** (daily 8am–5pm; Bz$10; ☎220-2181) at the western end of the village. The fee includes a short, guided trail walk and entry to Belize's first natural history museum, inside the centre, with exhibits and information on the riverside habitats and animals, and a library.

Altun Ha

Thirty-four miles north of Belize City, and just six miles from the sea, is the impressive Maya site of **Altun Ha** (daily 8am–5pm; Bz$10). With a peak population of about ten thousand, it was occupied for around twelve hundred years until the Classic Maya collapse between 900 and 950 AD. The site was also inhabited at various times during the Postclassic period, though no new monumental building took place during this period. Its position close to the Caribbean coast suggests that it was sustained by trade as much as by agriculture – a theory upheld by the discovery of trade objects such as jade and obsidian, neither of which occurs naturally in Belize; both are very important in Maya ceremony. The jade would have come from the Motagua valley in Guatemala, and would probably have been shipped onwards to the north.

Around five hundred buildings have been recorded at Altun Ha, but the core of the site is clustered around two Classic-period plazas, with the main structures extensively restored, exposing fine stonework with rounded corners. Entering from the road, you come first to **Plaza A**. Large temples enclose it on all four sides, and a magnificent tomb has been discovered beneath Temple A-1, **The Temple of the Green Tomb**. Dating from

550 AD, this yielded a total of three hundred artefacts, including jade, jewellery, stingray spines, jaguar skins, flints and the remains of a Maya book.

The adjacent **Plaza B** is dominated by the site's largest temple, B-4, **The Temple of the Masonry Altars**, the last in a sequence of buildings occupying this spot over the centuries. If its exterior seems familiar, it's because you might already have seen it on the Belikin beer label. Several priestly tombs have been uncovered within the main structure, but most of them had already been desecrated, possibly during the political turmoil that preceded the abandonment of the site. Only two of the tombs were found intact; in 1968 archeologists discovered a carved jade head of **Kinich Ahau**, the Maya sun god, in one of them. Standing just under 15cm high, it is the largest carved jade found anywhere in the Maya world. At the moment it's hidden away in the vaults of the Belize Bank, though there is a splendid replica in the Museum of Belize in Belize City (see p.59).

Practicalities

Altun Ha is fairly difficult to reach independently, as the track to the site is located along the Old Northern Highway and is not well served by buses. Any travel agent in Belize City will arrange a tour (see p.54), and increasing numbers of visitors come on day-trips from San Pedro. In theory there are buses from the terminal in Belize City to the village of **MASKALL**, passing the 1.8 mile side road to the site from **Lucky Strike**, but the service is erratic and unreliable.

For a real splurge, try the hedonistic (and undoubtedly therapeutic) pleasures at the primitive-meets-posh *Maruba Resort and Jungle Spa*, at Mile 40 near Maskall (☎225-5555, ⓦwww.maruba-spa.com; ❾). Each room and suite is luxurious: think gleaming mahogany ceilings, billowing silks, feather beds and wafting incense, along with mosaic-tiled bathrooms. What sets the *Maruba* apart from the usual high-end resort are the quirky, jungle-chic touches: a carved penis for a toilet paper holder in the lobby bathroom; rough-hewn walls studded with glass bottles of Belikin beer and Fanta; and palm fronds as placemats. The message is clear: little goes to waste at this largely self-sustaining resort, where the lush, natural surroundings are incorporated whenever possible. Fabulous **spa treatments** include the honey-bee scrub and mood mud body wrap. The thatched **restaurant** is surrounded by palms and bougainvillea and serves excellent Belizean and international fare. The resort offers a shuttle service to and from Belize City for around US$75 round-trip.

Crooked Tree Wildlife Sanctuary

Back on the Northern Highway, roughly midway between Belize City and Orange Walk, you pass the well-signposted branch road heading three miles west to **Crooked Tree Wildlife Sanctuary**, a five-square-mile reserve encompassing inland waterways, logwood swamps and four separate lagoons. It's an ideal nesting and resting place for the sanctuary's greatest treasure: tens of thousands of migrating and resident **birds**, including snail kites, tiger herons, snowy egrets, ospreys and black-collared hawks. Representatives of over three hundred bird species (two-thirds of Belize's total) have been recorded here.

The reserve's most famous visitor is the **jabiru stork**, the largest flying bird in the New World, with a wingspan of 2.5m. Belize has the biggest nesting population of jabiru storks at one site; they arrive in November, the young hatch in April or May, and they leave just before the summer rainy season gets under way. The **best time to visit** is from late February to early June, when the lagoons shrink to a string of pools, forcing wildlife to congregate for food and water.

Crooked Tree village

In the middle of the reserve, connected to the mainland by a causeway, the village of **CROOKED TREE** straggles over a low island in the wetlands. Over three hundred years old, it's the oldest inland community in Belize, with an economy based on fishing, farming and, more recently, tourism. The Bz$8 visitor fee is payable in the **Sanctuary Visitor Centre** (Mon–Sat 8am–5pm, usually closes at noon on Sun), at the far end of the causeway. Inside, a diorama displays fantastically lifelike models of the birds, mammals and insects found at Crooked Tree; there's also a good wildlife reference library with some books for sale.

The main attraction at Crooked Tree is taking guided **boat trips** on the lagoons and along sluggish, forest-lined creeks. Trips start at around Bz$150 per person; check at the visitor centre or the hotels in town. You can also explore on your own; stroll down the sandy, tree-lined lanes and along the lakeshore trails, and you'll spot plenty of birds and turtles, and hear frogs croaking languidly from the shallows. Some of the mango and cashew trees around the village are over one hundred years old, and in January and February the air is heavy with the scent of cashew blossoms. The village celebrates a yearly **Cashew Festival** during the first week of May with music, dance, storytelling and crafts that offer a glimpse of village traditions and culture.

Practicalities

There are a couple of daily **buses to Crooked Tree** from Belize City; note that buses returning to Belize City (Mon–Sat) usually leave in the early morning. If you plan on spending the night, try the lakeshore *Bird's Eye View Lodge* (T 225-7027, W www.birdseyeviewbelize.com; 6). The amiable restaurant serves tasty Belizean food. Also a good bet is *Sam Tillett's Hotel* (T 220-7026, W www.crookedtree belize.com; 6), near the village centre. Rooms are in a large, thatched cabaña, and have private bath, and the restaurant offers good local food. They also run boat tours, including through Crooked Tree, and further afield, to Lamanai, Altun Ha and the Belize Zoo.

Around Crooked Tree: Chau Hiix

A 760-yard **boardwalk**, 1.8 miles north of the village, is supported above the swamp on strong logwood posts. You'll need to get here by boat most of the year, but in the dry season it's possible to drive. Built in 1997, the walkway allows access through the otherwise impenetrable low forest at the edge of a lagoon, and an observation tower affords panoramic **views** – a great place to enjoy the sunset. **Chau Hiix** ("small cat") is a Maya site on the western shore of the lagoon. Climbing the nearby **observation tower** (also with a boardwalk) will give you a clearer idea of the site, though admittedly much of what you'll see are just forested mounds.

Orange Walk

ORANGE WALK is the largest town in the north of Belize and the centre of a busy agricultural region. The tranquil, slow-moving **New River**, a few blocks east of the centre, was a heavily used commercial waterway during the logging days, and today provides a lovely starting point for a visit to the ruins of Lamanai, to which several local operators offer tours (see p.85).

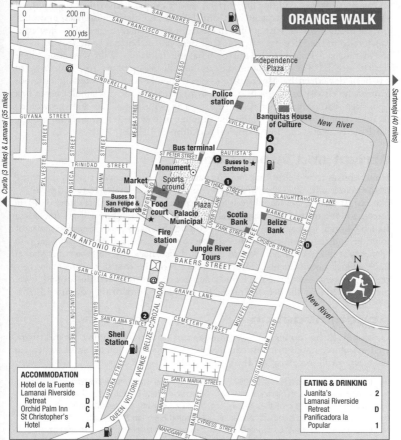

ORANGE WALK

0   200 m
0   200 yds

SAN ANDRES STREET

SAN FRANCISCO STREET

Independence Plaza

CINDERELLA STREET

PROGRESSO

Police station

Banquitas House of Culture   New River

GUYANA STREET

MEJIBA STREET

AVILEZ LANE

A

SYL VESTER STREET

FONSECA STREET

TRINIDAD STREET

DUNN STREET

Bus terminal

ST PETER STREET   BAUTISTA'S

Buses to ★ Sarteneja

B

C

Monument   Sports ground

Market

BETHIAC STREET

SLAUGHTERHOUSE LANE

Buses to San Felipe & Indian Church   Food court

Plaza

Scotia Bank

MARKET LANE

Belize Bank

RIVERSIDE STREET

SAN ANTONIO ROAD

Palacio Municipal

Fire station

LOVER'S LANE

PARK STREET

CHURCH STREET

MAIN STREET

SAN LUCIA STREET

ASUNCION STREET

GUADALUPE STREET

Jungle River Tours

BAKERS STREET

GRAVEL LANE

MUFFEL STREET

New River

N

SANTA ANA STREET

Shell Station

CEMETERY STREET

LOUISIANA FARM ROAD

QUEEN VICTORIA AVENUE (BELIZE-COROZAL ROAD)

AURORA STREET

SANTA MARIA STREET

BANAK STREET

MAIN STREET

SANTA CYPRESS STREET

MAHOGANY ST

ACCOMMODATION
Hotel de la Fuente   B
Lamanai Riverside Retreat   D
Orchid Palm Inn   C
St Christopher's Hotel   A

EATING & DRINKING
Juanita's   2
Lamanai Riverside Retreat   D
Panificadora la Popular   1

Cuello (3 miles) & Lamanai (35 miles)

Sarteneja (40 miles)

Like Corozal to the north, Orange Walk was founded by mestizo refugees fleeing from the Caste Wars in Yucatán in 1849, who chose as their site an area that had long been used for logging camps and was already occupied by the local Icaiché (Chichanha) Maya. From the 1850s to the 1870s, the Icaiché Maya were in conflict with both the Cruzob Maya, who were themselves rebelling against mestizo rule in Yucatán (and supplied with arms by British traders in Belize), and with the British settlers and colonial authorities in Belize. The leader of the Icaiché, **Marcos Canul**, organized successful raids against British mahogany camps, forcing the logging firms to pay "rent" for lands they used, and Canul even briefly occupied Corozal in 1870. In 1872 Canul launched an attack on the barracks in Orange Walk. The West India Regiment, which had earlier retreated in disarray after a skirmish with Canul's troops, this time forced the Icaiché to flee across the Río Hondo, taking the fatally wounded Canul with them. This defeat didn't end the raids, but the Maya ceased to be a threat to British rule in northern Belize; a small monument opposite the park in Orange Walk commemorates the last (officially the only) battle fought on Belizean soil.

Orange Walk has traditionally thrived on its **crops**, first with the growth of the sugar (and the consequent rum distillation) and citrus industries, and after the fall in sugar prices, with profits made from marijuana. In the 1990s, however, pressure from the US government forced Belizean authorities to destroy many of the marijuana fields, and today the town has much less of a Wild West atmosphere than it once did. The land around the satellite villages of Blue Creek and Shipyard has been developed by **Mennonite** settlers, members of a Protestant religious group who choose to farm without the assistance of modern technology (see box opposite). You'll often spot them, the men in wide-brim hats and the women in ankle-length dresses, shopping for supplies in town – it's an arresting image, particularly against the dusty, tropical backdrop of Belize.

Arrival and information

Hourly **buses** from Belize City and Corozal pull up on the main road in the centre of town, officially called Queen Victoria Avenue but always referred to as the Belize–Corozal Road. Services to and from Sarteneja (see p.88) stop at Zeta's store on Main Street, a block to the east, while local buses to the surrounding villages (including Indian Church, for Lamanai) leave from around the market area, near the centre of town behind the town hall and fire station. You can **change money** and get cash advances at the Belize Bank (with ATM) on the corner of Main Street and Market Lane, a block east of the plaza. The **post office** is on the west side of the main road, right in the centre of town. You'll find a number of **internet facilities** around town, including K&N, on the Belize–Corozal Road a block south of the post office.

Accommodation

Orange Walk has a range of accommodation options, including several smart, well-appointed hotels that cost considerably less than you might pay elsewhere, as the town is still somewhat off the visitor trail.

Hotel de la Fuente 14 Main St ☎322-2290, ⓦwww.hoteldelafuente.com. This bright, inviting hotel has tidy rooms with a/c, cable TV, fridge and private hot-water bath, along with thoughtful extras like a coffeemaker with complimentary coffee. You'll find a range of rooms, from basic doubles (❸) to larger suites (❺). The friendly owners can offer lots of tips on exploring the area, including tours to Lamanai. Internet access available for guests. ❹

Lamanai Riverside Retreat Lamanai Alley ☎302-3955, ⓔlamanairiverside@hotmail.com. This relaxing retreat takes full advantage of Orange Walk's prime perch on the New River. Wooden cabañas, with a/c and hot-water bath, are simple, but the surroundings make the place: wake up to birds chirping and the gentle rush of the river, followed by a tasty breakfast served on the open-air deck of the restaurant. The owner,

a long-time wildlife enthusiast, can arrange trips down the New River to Lamanai with Jungle River Tours (see p.85). Internet available for guests. ❹

Orchid Palm Inn Belize-Corozal Rd ☎322-0719, ⓦwww.orchidpalminn.com. This hotel pays homage to its elegant namesake throughout, from the garden to the colour photos that hang in the well-kept rooms, many of which come with a/c, cable TV, coffeemaker and refrigerator. ❺

St Christopher's Hotel 10 Main St ☎322-2420, ⓦwww.stchristophershotelbze.com. Plain but clean rooms with wooden furnishings, all with private bath and most with access to a balcony; some have a/c and fridge. The colourfully painted hotel, set on grounds that sweep down to the river, is run by a friendly family, who can arrange for tours to Lamanai departing from the hotel dock. Plenty of secure parking for guests with vehicles. Internet access. ❹

The Town

Orange Walk centres around a distinctly Mexican-style, formal plaza, shaded by large trees, and the town hall across the main road is called the Palacio Municipal, reinforcing the strong historic links to Mexico. The town isn't heavy on sights, but, on the riverbank just north of the centre, it does feature the **Banquitas House of Culture** (Mon–Fri 8.30am–5.30pm; free), a small museum and cultural centre. The *banquitas* in the name refer to the little benches in a riverbank park, used for generations by courting couples and for simply relaxing on warm evenings. There's still a leafy park here, now with an amphitheatre for outdoor performances, but the highlights are in the main building, a renovated former market. The

Mennonites in Belize

The **Mennonites** arose from the radical Anabaptist movement of the sixteenth century and are named after the Dutch priest Menno Simons, leader of the community in its formative years. Recurring government restrictions on their lifestyle, especially regarding their pacifist objection to military service, forced them to move repeatedly. Having removed to Switzerland, they travelled on to Prussia, then in 1663 to Russia, until the government revoked their exemption from military service, whereupon some groups emigrated to North America, settling in the prairies of Saskatchewan. World War I brought more government restrictions, this time on the teaching of German (the Mennonites' language). This, together with the prospect of conscription and more widespread anti-German sentiments in the Dominion of Canada, drove them from Canada to Mexico, where they settled in the arid, northern state of Chihuahua. When the Mexican government required them to be included in its social security programme, it was time to move on again. An investigation into the possibility of settling on their own land in British Honduras brought them to the British colony of **Belize** in 1958.

They were welcomed enthusiastically by the colonial authorities, who were eager to have willing workers to clear the jungle for agriculture. Perseverance and hard work made them successful farmers, and in recent years prosperity has caused drastic changes in their lives. The Mennonite Church in Belize is increasingly split between the *Kleine Gemeinde* – a modernist section that uses electricity and power tools, and drives trucks, tractors and even cars – and the *Altkolonier* – traditionalists who prefer a stricter expression of their beliefs. Members of the community, easily recognizable in their denim dungarees and straw hats, can be seen trading their produce and buying supplies every day in Orange Walk and Belize City.

▲ Mennonites travelling by horse and cart

one-room permanent exhibition charts the history of Orange Walk District from Maya times to the present. Glass cases contain artefacts from local Maya sites, along with maps and drawings of the sites themselves. Other panels display archival materials documenting the stories of logwood, mahogany and chicle, which tell of the boom-and-bust cycles of extracting natural resources.

Eating and drinking

Many of the **restaurants** in and around Orange Walk serve Mexican-influenced Creole fare. *Juanita's*, on Santa Ana Street by the Shell station towards the south end of town, serves up tasty Mexican dishes. Try *pan dulces* (sweet bread and pastries) and fresh bread at *Panificadora la Popular*, on Bethias Street, off the northeast side of the plaza. Behind the town hall, near the market, is the bustling **food court** (usually open daily until mid-afternoon), where you can graze cheaply on Mexican treats, from tacos to enchiladas. For outdoor dining, stroll over to the *Lamanai Riverside Retreat* (see p.80), where you can sip Belikin beer and savour local dishes – pork *salpicón*, lobster salad – on an airy wooden deck overlooking the New River.

Maya sites around Orange Walk

Although the Maya sites in northern Belize (with the notable exception of Lamanai) are not as monumentally spectacular as those in the Yucatán, they have been the source of very important archeological finds. The area around Orange Walk has some of the most productive farmland in Belize, and this was also the case in Maya times; aerial surveys in the late 1970s revealed evidence of raised fields and a network of **irrigation canals**, showing that the Maya practised skilful, intensive agriculture. In the Postclassic era, this region became part of the powerful Maya state of Chactemal (or Chetumal), controlling the trade in cacao beans, which were used as currency and grown in the valleys of the Hondo and New rivers. For a while the Maya here were even able to resist the conquistadores, and long after nominal Spanish rule had been established in 1544, there were frequent Maya rebellions: in 1638, for example, they drove the Spanish out and burned the church at Lamanai.

Cuello and Nohmul

Cuello is a small Maya site three miles west of Orange Walk. It was excavated in 1973 by Norman Hammond, who found structures dating back to 1000 BC, making it one of the earliest sites from the Middle Preclassic Maya lowlands. That said, the site is more interesting to archeologists than the casual visitor; there's not much to look at except for a single small, stepped pyramid (Structure 350), rising in nine tiers – a common feature of Maya temples – and several earth-covered mounds.

The ruins are behind a factory where **Cuello rum** is made, and the site is on the Cuello family's land, so you should ask permission to visit by phoning ☏322-2141. Tours of the distillery are given on request. You can reach Cuello from Orange Walk by simply walking west from the town plaza for a little under an hour; a taxi to the site costs around Bz$15 each way.

A rather more arresting Maya site is **Nohmul** ("great mound"), situated on the boundary with Corozal District, eleven miles north of Orange Walk. It was a major ceremonial centre with origins in the Middle Preclassic period, but was abandoned before the end of the Classic and subsequently reoccupied by newcomers from

Yucatán during the Early Postclassic (known here as the Tecep phase, around 800–1000 AD). The ruins cover a large area, comprising the East and West groups connected by a *sacbe* (causeway), with several plazas around them. The main feature is an acropolis platform (Structure 2) surmounted by a later pyramid, which, owing to the site's position on a limestone ridge, is the highest point for miles around.

Nohmul lies amid sugar cane fields 1.2 miles west of **San Pablo**, on the Northern Highway. Any bus between Corozal and Orange Walk passes through the village. To visit the site, ask around the village for a local guide.

Lamanai

Extensive restoration of the ancient structures and a spacious museum make **Lamanai** (Mon–Fri 8am–5pm, Sat, Sun & holidays 8am–4pm; Bz$10) undoubtedly the most impressive Maya site in northern Belize. It's one of only a few sites whose original Maya name – *Lama'an ayin* – is known; it translates to "submerged crocodile", which explains the numerous representations of crocodiles among the ruins. "Lamanai", however, is a seventeenth-century mistransliteration that actually means "drowned insect". The site was continuously occupied from around 1500 BC until the sixteenth century, when Spanish missionaries built a church next door to lure the Indians from their "heathen" ways.

More than seven hundred structures have been mapped by members of the Lamanai Archeological Project, the majority of them still buried beneath mounds of earth, and the site extends far north and south of the restored area.

The site

Lamanai's setting on the shore of the New River Lagoon, in an isolated swathe of jungle protected as an archeological reserve, gives it a special serenity long gone from sites served by the torrent of tourist buses – though increasing numbers of speedboats now carry cruise ship visitors here. Over a dozen troops of black howler monkeys make Lamanai their home, and you'll certainly see them peering down through the branches as you wander the trails; mosquitoes too, are ever-present, so you'll need to be armed with a good **repellent**. Many trees and other plants bear name labels in English, Creole and Maya, and your guide will explain what the ancient Maya used them for.

The most impressive feature at Lamanai, prosaically named N10-43 (informally called the "High Temple", or "El Castillo", the castle), is a massive, Late Preclassic **temple**, towering 115ft above the forest floor. When it was first built around 100 BC, it was the largest structure in the entire Maya world, though one which was extensively modified later. The view over the surrounding forest and along the lagoon from the top of the temple is magnificent and well worth the daunting climb. On the way to the High Temple you pass N10-27, a much smaller pyramid, at the base of which stands a fibreglass replica of **Stela 9**, which bears some of the best-preserved carvings at Lamanai. Dated to 625 AD, it shows the magnificently attired Lord Smoking Shell participating in a ceremony – probably his accession. This glyph has become emblematic of Lamanai and features on many of the T-shirts on sale here. North of the High Temple, structure N9-56 is a sixth-century pyramid with two stucco masks of a glorified ruler, represented as a deity (probably Kinich Ahau, the sun god), carved on different levels. The lower mask, 13ft high, has survived especially well, and shows a clearly humanized face wearing a crocodile headdress and bordered by decorative columns. The temple overlies several smaller buildings, the oldest of which is a superbly preserved temple from around 100 BC, and there are a number of other clearly defined glyphs throughout.

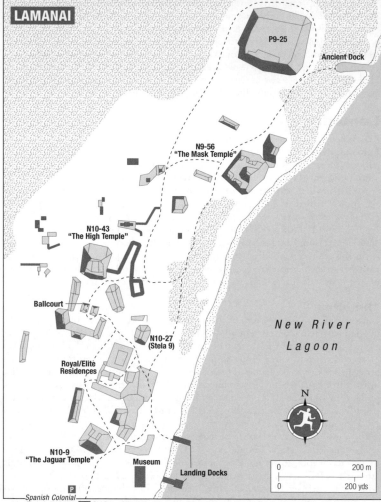

The **archeological museum** at the site houses an excellent collection of artefacts, arranged in chronological order; the majority of these are figurines depicting gods and animals, particularly crocodiles. The most beautiful exhibits are the delicate eccentric flints – star- and sceptre-shaped symbols of office – skilfully chipped from a single piece of stone. More unusual items include a drum the size and shape of a pair of binoculars and a phallus carved from a manatee bone. Traces of later settlers can also be seen near the museum: immediately to the south are the ruins of two churches built by Spanish missionaries, while a short trail behind the building leads west to the remains of a nineteenth-century sugar mill, built by Confederate refugees from the American Civil War. These refugees settled in several places in Belize, in an attempt to recreate the antebellum South using indentured labourers in place of slaves – but their effort failed, and within a decade most had returned to the States.

Practicalities

Buses for **INDIAN CHURCH**, 2km from the site (schedule varies, so confirm with locals; buses usually run Mon & Fri afternoons; Bz$5), leave from the street next to the market, behind the town hall, in Orange Walk. The bus usually departs for Orange Walk at 5.30am on the same days, so, unless you have your own transportation, you'll have to stay a few nights.

By far the most memorable way to journey to Lamanai is along the New River, and a number of Orange Walk operators organize **day-trips** for about US$50 per person, departing around 9am; the price will usually include a picnic lunch at the site. The most informative are run by the Novelo brothers of ✈ **Jungle River Tours**, in the centre of town at 20 Lover's Lane (☎ 302-2293, ✉ lamanaimaya tour@btl.net). Their round-trip Lamanai tour, with lunch included, costs from Bz$90 per person and lasts from half a day. Besides being extensively knowledgeable about Maya sites, the Novelos are also wildlife experts, and will point out the lurking crocodiles, iguanas, bats and dozens of species of birds that you might otherwise miss. The boat also floats past the only operating sugar mill in the country. The guides will advise what to bring; especially important are mosquito repellent and a pair of sturdy shoes, as the trails are muddy and the temple steps slippery when it rains.

To get to Lamanai in your own vehicle, head to the south end of Orange Walk and turn right (west) by Dave's Store, where a signpost gives the distance to Lamanai as 35 miles. Continue along the Yo Creek road as far as San Felipe, where you should bear left for the village of Indian Church, 1.2 miles from the ruins. Visitors can also inquire at one of the Orange Walk operators about trips to Indian Church

Staying in Indian Church on a budget is not especially convenient, but it enables you to visit Lamanai in the quieter times, as soon as it opens and after the crowds have left. If you're travelling here by bus, you won't have a choice anyway. A couple of places offer **rooms** (❸); try asking in the Artisan Center, where you can see villagers making jewellery and other craft items, if someone can rent you a room or let you **camp**. In either case you'll be invited to eat with the family.

Excellent **accommodation** is available nearby in the well-run and very comfortable thatched cabañas at *Lamanai Outpost Lodge* (☎ 220-9444 or 670-3578, ⓦ www .lamanai.com; ❾), set in extensive gardens sweeping down to the lagoon just south of the site. Each cabaña has 24-hour electricity, hot water and a private deck; guests enjoy free **internet** access and there's also a small library. The restaurant serves great Belizean and international food and has a wooden deck overlooking the lagoon. Guests can head on a sunrise canoe expedition; follow a Maya medicinal trail; and join a night nature trek under the light of the moon.

The Río Bravo Conservation and Management Area

In the far northwest of Orange Walk District is the **Río Bravo Conservation and Management Area**, an enormous tract of land designated for tropical forest conservation, research and sustainable-yield forest harvests. This conservation success story actually began with a disastrous plan in the mid-1980s to clear the forest, initially to fuel a wood-fired power station and later to provide Coca-Cola with frost-free land to grow citrus crops. Environmentalists were alarmed, and their strenuous objections forced Coca-Cola to drop the plan, though the forest remained threatened by agriculture.

Following this, a project to save the forest by purchasing it – known as the **Programme for Belize (PFB)** – was initiated by the Massachusetts Audubon Society and launched in 1988. Funds were raised from corporate donors and conservation organizations, but the most widespread support was generated through an ambitious "adopt-an-acre" scheme, enthusiastically taken up by schools and individuals in the UK and North America. Coca-Cola itself, anxious to distance the company from charges of rainforest destruction, donated more than 137 square miles of land it owned on the perimeter of the conservation area.

Today, rangers with powers of arrest patrol the area to prevent illegal logging and to stop farmers from encroaching onto the reserve with their *milpas* (slash-and-burn maize fields). The guarded boundaries also protect dozens of Maya sites, most of them unexcavated and unrestored, though many have been looted.

The **landscape** ranges from forest-covered, limestone escarpments in the northwest, near the Guatemalan border, to palmetto savannah, pine ridge and swamp in the southeast, around the New River Lagoon. Crossing through the middle of the region are several river valleys. The Río Bravo area has over 240 endemic tree species, and the forest teems with **wildlife**, including tapirs, monkeys and all five of Belize's large cats, as well as four hundred bird species – almost ninety percent of the country's total. The strict ban on hunting, enforced for nearly twenty years now, makes this the best place in Belize to see these beasts; even pumas and jaguars, extremely reclusive creatures, are spotted fairly frequently. Wildlife-viewing is also excellent in the protected territory around **Gallon Jug**, a private estate to the south of the Río Bravo area that's home to the fabulous *Chan Chich Lodge* (see p.88), regarded as one of the finest eco-lodges in the Americas and an incredibly beautiful place to stay.

Getting there

There's no public transport to the Río Bravo Conservation and Management Area, but if you want to visit or stay at either of the **field stations** (see below), see the PFB entry in Contexts (see p.264) for more information. Getting here from Orange Walk means you have to pass through the modern Mennonite settlement of **Blue Creek**, high up on the Río Bravo escarpment, where you'll find one of the more surprising artefacts in Belize: the fuselage (and more) of a **Super Constellation**, the world's first real airliner. On the Constellation's last flight from Mexico to Guatemala City, in the mid-1970s, it first lost a propeller before its two other engines cut out. The pilot attempted an emergency landing in Belize City, but on the final approach the port undercarriage failed to operate and the aircraft skidded off the runway. Luckily, no passengers were on board, and all three crew members survived.

In the valley below Blue Creek, the Río Hondo forms the boundary with Mexico. The border crossing here is usually only for use by Belizeans, who pole canoes over to the Mexican village of **La Unión**, where a brisk trade in cigarettes and beer fuels the local economy.

La Milpa and Hill Bank field stations

One of the aims of the PFB is environmental education; as such, **field stations** have been built at **La Milpa** and **Hill Bank** to accommodate both visitors and students. Both are quite difficult to get to, but you could visit either on a day-trip with your own vehicle, or you might be able to get a ride in with a ranger or other staff; see p.264 for contact details.

Each field station has comfortable **dorms** (❹), facilities that utilize the latest green technology, including solar power and composting toilets, and a natural history library. Both sites also have lovely, thatched **cabañas** with private bath and a loft bedroom (**❺**). The field stations also offer a range of activities, from early morning birding to rainforest treks. To visit or stay at either station, contact the appropriate station manager through the PFB office, 1 Eyre St, Belize City (**T** 227-5616, **W** www .pfbelize.org), who will arrange transport.

La Milpa: the field station and Maya site

Set in a former *milpa* clearing in the higher, northwestern forest, **La Milpa Field Station** has a tranquil, studious atmosphere; deer and ocellated turkeys feed contentedly around the cabins, grey foxes slip silently through the long grass and vultures circle lazily overhead. There are binoculars and telescopes for spotting birds and you'll see turtles from the boardwalk bridge over the pond. Guests are mainly students on tropical ecology courses, though anyone is welcome to stay. A day-visit to the field station includes a guided tour of La Milpa ruins or one of the trails. Getting here on public transport is not easy: you'll have to catch a bus from Orange Walk to San Felipe, 23 miles away, and arrange to be picked up there – the PFB office will give details. To get here in your own vehicle, take the road west from Orange Walk via San Felipe to the Mennonite village of Blue Creek. Beyond there the road is paved and in good condition, climbing steeply up the Río Bravo escarpment, then turning south to the field station and Gallon Jug. Charter flights use the airstrips at Blue Creek and Gallon Jug.

Three miles west of the field station is the huge, Classic-period **Maya city of La Milpa**, the third largest archeological site in Belize. After centuries of expansion, La Milpa was abandoned in the ninth century, though Postclassic groups subsequently occupied the site and the Maya here resisted both the Spanish conquest in the sixteenth century and British mahogany cutters in the nineteenth. Recent finds include major elite burials with many jade grave goods. The **ceremonial centre**, built on top of a limestone ridge, is one of the most impressive anywhere, with at least 24 courtyards and two ball-courts. The site also contains one of the largest public spaces in the Maya world: the **Great Plaza**, flanked by four temple-pyramids. The tallest structure in the group, the **Great Temple**, rises 77ft above the plaza floor, and you can climb its steep, rocky face using roots for handholds and a rope for support. Beyond here are some of the site's *chultunes* – cave-like, underground chambers carved out of stone. For a unique perspective on a *chultun*, you can enter one through a collapsed side, view the tightly fitting capstone (similar to a manhole cover) from beneath and ponder what the ancient Maya used these spaces for.

Hill Bank Field Station

At the southern end of the New River Lagoon and 43 miles west of Belize City, **Hill Bank Field Station** is a former logging camp that has been adapted to undertake scientific forestry research and development. The emphasis here is more on extractive forest use, with the aim of revenue generation on a sustainable basis. Selective logging is allowed on carefully monitored plots, chicle is harvested from sapodilla trees and there's a tree nursery. These and other projects are at the cutting edge of tropical forest management, and there are often students and scientists working here. There's plenty of wildlife too, particularly birds and crocodiles, and butterflies abound. The **dorms** here (identical to those at La Milpa, see above) have a screened veranda with table and chairs overlooking the lagoon, and there are also **cabañas**. For an even better view, climb the 40ft fire tower nearby.

There's **no public transport** to Hill Bank, but with your own vehicle you can get here by following the road west and north from the village of Bermudian Landing (see p.76). It's also possible to approach Hill Bank from Lamanai, by boat along the New River Lagoon.

Gallon Jug and Chan Chich Lodge

Twenty-five miles south of La Milpa Field Station, the former logging town of **GALLON JUG**, set in neat, fenced pastures, is today the private property of Barry Bowen, reportedly the richest Belizean. In the 1980s, his speculative land deals led to international outcry against threatened rainforest clearance. The experience apparently had a powerful effect upon Bowen, who is now an ardent conservationist, and most of the 190 square miles on his estate are strictly protected. Around eight square miles of Gallon Jug are still under cultivation and produce the excellent coffee served at the luxurious, world-class **Chan Chich Lodge** (T223-4419, in US T1-800/343-8009, W www.chanchich.com; 9), the focal point of the estate. The lodge, which regularly wins awards in the travel press, consists of twelve large, thatched cabañas and suites, each with lovely verandas and hammocks, set in the grassy plaza of the Classic Maya site of Chan Chich ("little bird"). It's surrounded by superb forest and there's a refreshing, fully screened pool, complete with waterfall. Activities abound, from horseriding through the jungle, canoeing on Laguna Verde and some of the best birdwatching in Belize.

The construction of the lodge on this spot was controversial at the time (all Maya sites are technically under government control), but it received Archeology Department approval once its intent to cause minimal disturbance became clear. Certainly the year-round presence of visitors and staff does prevent looting, which has been a real problem in the past. It is a truly awe-inspiring setting: grass-covered temple walls, crowned with jungle, tower up from the lodge and the forest explodes with a cacophony of birdcalls at dawn. The nine miles of **guided trails** are incomparable and the guides excellent; day and night wildlife sightings are consistently high, with around seventy jaguar sightings per year, half of them during daylight. You can drive here from Orange Walk (through Blue Creek and La Milpa), but most guests fly in to the airstrip at Gallon Jug; the lodge can help arrange flights.

Sarteneja and Shipstern Nature Reserve

The **Sarteneja peninsula**, jutting out towards the Yucatán in the northeast of Belize, is covered with dense forests, swamps and lagoons that support an amazing array of wildlife. Though the area is largely unpopulated and could once be reached only by boat, the lobster-fishing village of **Sarteneja**, the peninsula's main settlement, is beginning to attract tourism. Sarteneja and the shoreline are pretty enough, but the region's main attraction is **Shipstern Nature Reserve**, on the road three miles before the village.

Sarteneja

SARTENEJA, from Tzaten-a-ha (meaning "water among the rocks"), was largely settled in 1854 by refugees from the Caste Wars of Yucatán. Due to its historic isolation from the rest of Belize, it still retains close ties to **Mexico** – its inhabitants are primarily Spanish-speaking mestizos – which locals can easily reach by boat, though such services are currently not offered to tourists.

It's relatively easy to get here by **bus from Belize City** (see p.69). Buses pass through Orange Walk ninety minutes after departure, stopping on Main Street, where the bus crew takes a break, and it's a further ninety minutes to Sarteneja. Buses returning to Belize City leave Sarteneja in the early morning, as does a

Underwater Belize

A complex, living wall stretching nearly two hundred miles from just south of Cancún, Mexico down the entire coastline of Belize, the Barrier Reef is the longest in the Americas – and one of the most amazing and colourful ecosystems on earth. The ocean here provides a firm floor; warm, shallow water; and strong sunlight, all essential ingredients for coral growth, which happens gradually over thousands of years. Small sections of the reef are protected as World Heritage Sites, and many local reserves help to nurture this fragile and important environment, which in turn supports an array of land and sea habitats. Belize's cayes (pronounced "keys"), integral parts of the reef system, provide dry land for human settlements and bases for water-based recreation.

Starfish ▲

Fan coral ▼

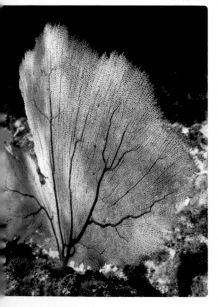

Stingray ▼

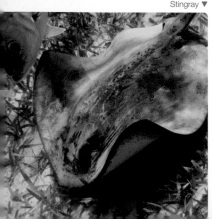

Sea creatures

The reef is an underwater wilderness populated by creatures ranging in size from the practically microscopic to the plain enormous. Some of the tiniest organisms are the individual units of the reef itself: billions of **coral polyps**, most in the family of "hard" or "stony" corals, that come in an array of electric colours. "Soft" corals, such as gracefully wafting **sea fans** and stinging **fire corals**, are also integrated into the reef's structure.

Swarming around the coral are over four hundred species of **fish**, several playing important roles in the ecosystem. **Cleaner wrasse** feed on the parasites of larger species, and **butterfly fish** regulate algae build-up on the reef. Most reef fish also spend time among the mangrove roots on the edges of the cayes, where they lay their eggs and seek shelter from storms and predators.

Sometimes spotted within the reef, but more often in calm lagoons or just offshore, the compelling **West Indian manatee** is distantly related to the elephant. Manatees are **endangered**, but activists are working hard to save them and Belize's manatee population is the largest in the region.

The Blue Hole

The magnificent **Blue Hole** (see p.122), formed over a million years ago and now protected as a Natural Monument, is a massive shaft that opens out into a network of caves and crevices. Its immense depth gives it a vibrant blue colour, and while it's a magnet for divers, offering spectacular drop-offs, seeing it from the air is the best way to truly appreciate it. Local travel agents can book flights and helicopter tours over this splendid landmark.

Get wet

The best way to appreciate the amazing variety of marine life in Belize is in a bathing suit. **Diving** and **snorkelling trips** abound in the coastal communities, although the best tours can be found on the cayes, notably Ambergris Caye and Caye Caulker. Some of the southern cayes are so close to the reef that you can swim right out to it, though to do this you'll often have to stay at an exclusive — and expensive — **resort**.

▲ Kayaking, Ambergris Caye

Many outfits offer night dives, enabling you to explore the mysteries of life below the sea during darkness, often with just a flashlight for guidance. Creatures you might spy by night include octopuses and colorful parrotfish. Belize's shallow seas and pleasant climate also make for excellent **sailing** in the shelter of the reef or the deeper water beyond. Skippered sailing tours leave from several cayes and coastal towns, and many offer sunset sails or overnight camping.

▲ Snorkelling

▼ Sailing boats, Caye Caulker

Windsurfers will have no problem finding rentals and lessons in either San Pedro or Caye Caulker. **Sea kayaking** is popular wherever there's water in Belize — in fact, the fishermen who ply the country's coastal and inland waterways have always used agile, kayak-like boats. All coastal resorts offer kayak rental, and many have organized tours.

For visitors who want something to show for their efforts (in a photo or on a plate), saltwater **fishing** trips are possible. Dedicated fishing lodges on the cayes attract anglers with all-inclusive packages, and local day-trips can be arranged virtually anywhere. Sand flats are the perfect, year-round locale for catch-and-release fly-fishing, and there's excellent deep-water fishing further offshore.

▼ Catching a barracuda

Nurse sharks ▲

Gray angelfish ▼

Caye carnivores

Belize is home to two dolphin species: the **spotted dolphin**, which lives beyond the reef and often frolics alongside boats to the outer atolls, and the more restrained **bottlenose**, larger in size but usually seen in smaller pods between the reef and land. Several species of large **shark** – including tiger, bull, lemon and hammerhead – patrol the outer Belizean waters, although the harmless **nurse shark** is usually the only one found within the reef. On full-moon nights between April and June, majestic and docile **whale sharks** congregate to feast on snapper eggs at Gladden Spit, offshore from Placencia; trips here can be arranged (see p.214).

Whale shark ▼

Glover's Reef ▼

Exploring the atolls

An **atoll** is a ring of coral reef enclosing a sheltered lagoon and often providing the foundation for a cluster of islands. There are four such formations in the Caribbean Sea, and Belizean waters contain **three** of them:

▶▶ **Lighthouse Reef:** Belize's eastern-most atoll, it surrounds the famous Blue Hole, best appreciated from the air but also a popular dive site. On the atoll's southeast edge is Half Moon Caye Natural Monument, the country's first marine conservation area and a protected colony of red-footed boobies. See p.122

▶▶ **Turneffe Islands:** Considered by some to be the most biologically diverse region in the Caribbean, these largely unsettled isles support many fish and crocodile nurseries as well as opportunities for snorkelling, diving and some of Belize's best fly-fishing. See p.121

▶▶ **Glover's Reef:** South of Lighthouse and Turneffe, the smallest and least accessible of Belize's atolls is a World Heritage Site with incredible diving and snorkelling. See p.195

service from Chetumal. The *Thunderbolt*, a **skiff** running between Corozal and San Pedro on Ambergris Caye, stops at Sarteneja if there's sufficient demand (call ℡226-2904 to check); the dock is near the village centre. There's also a small airstrip, where Tropic Air **flights** between Corozal and San Pedro will stop on request (℡226-2012, Ⓦwww.tropicair.com). If arriving by plane, arrange a pickup by your guesthouse in advance, as there are no taxis from the airstrip and the road into the village is long and rough.

Despite its remote location, there are several guesthouses, and a number of **restaurants** provide decent sustenance, among them *Richie's*, in the village centre (℡423-2031; 7am–9pm or later), offering fast food and home-made ice cream. Near *Richie's* is *Tiny's Internet Café*, with several computers and simple meals, snacks and shakes. Sarteneja has a small but adequate choice of accommodation, given its size, and most places will serve meals if asked in advance. *Fernando's Guesthouse* (℡423-2085, Ⓔsartenejabelize@hotmail.com; ❹), toward the western end of North Front Street, is Sarteneja's original guesthouse and offers comfortable rooms with private bath. *Candelie's Sunset Cabañas* (℡423-2005, Ⓔcandeliescabanas @yahoo.com; ❻), at the western end of the village, has two large cabañas, each with two double beds, cable TV and air conditioning. The dinette serves Belizean meals on advance request, and the owners can arrange fishing and birding trips. They also run *Krisami's Lodge* next door, which is undergoing renovations.

Shipstern Nature Reserve

Established in 1981, the unique **Shipstern Nature Reserve** (daily 8am–4pm; Bz$15; ℡223-3271, Ⓦwww.shipstern.org) – named for an unexcavated Maya centre in its forested depths – crosses two bio-geographical regions and is home to numerous species, some found only in Belize. Its approximately 27,000 acres, dotted with small mangrove islands, saline swamps and wetlands, contain much of Shipstern Lagoon. Roughly a third of the reserve is tropical moist forest, which includes over a hundred plant species, though the effects of Hurricane Janet, which whipped through in 1955, still show in the absence of mature growth. Elsewhere are wide belts of savannah, covered in coarse grasses, palms and broadleaf trees. Several guided trails invite exploration, occasionally in one of the reserve's safari-type vehicles, and it's possible to arrange after-dark tours, as well as overnights in the guesthouse or further afield. Simply by spending an hour on the superb botanical trail from the **visitor centre** (off the main road, served by all Sarteneja buses), you'll encounter more recorded plant species than on any other trail in Belize.

Shipstern is a nature-lover's paradise. The lagoon system supports blue-winged teal, American coot, thirteen species of egret and huge flocks of American wood stork, while the forest is home to flycatchers, warblers, keel-billed toucans, collared aracari and at least five species of parrot. In addition to birds, there are crocodiles, manatees, coatis, jaguars, peccaries, deer, raccoons, pumas (though the tracks of larger animals are more commonly seen than the animals themselves) and an abundance of insects, particularly butterflies, which you can view at the **butterfly farm**. Camouflaged **treehouses** throughout the reserve enable you to get good views of wildlife without disturbing the animals, though you'll need a guide to find them, and the **Xo-Pol Ponds** offer an unparalleled chance to see Morelet's crocodiles and waterfowl throughout much of the year. Before trekking into the bush, make sure to cover exposed skin with clothing and a slathering of repellent – the bugs can be nasty.

The Shipstern management also runs the **Mahogany Tree Park and Museum**, with an informative visitor's centre (opened on request; included in reserve fee) detailing the life cycle of Belize's national tree and historic export.

Corozal and around

COROZAL, thirty miles north of Orange Walk along the Northern Highway, is Belize's most northerly town, just twenty minutes from the Mexican border. Its location near the mouth of the New River enabled the ancient Maya to prosper here by controlling river and sea trade, and two archeological sites – Santa Rita and Cerros – are within easy reach. The town was founded in 1849 by refugees hounded south by the Caste Wars of Yucatán, and underwent substantial reconstruction after Hurricane Janet in 1955; today it's an interesting mix of Mexican and Caribbean culture, with mestizos in the majority. This is a fertile area – the town's name derives from the cohune palm, which the Maya recognized as an indicator of fecundity – and much of the surrounding land is planted with sugar cane.

Corozal is a relaxed town to spend a few days in and perhaps use as a base for day-trips throughout northern Belize, though the atmosphere is much more lively on Pan American Day (October 12; also known as Columbus Day), an occasion that merges the Mexican fiesta with Caribbean carnival. Palm trees shade Corozal's breezy, shoreline park, and the **town hall** is worth a look inside to see the interior

Ruins of Santa Rita (0.5 miles) & Mexican Border (9 miles)

COROZAL

Consejo (7 miles)

EATING & DRINKING
Al's Café	5
Cactus Plaza	7
Chon Kong	6
Marcelo's Pizza	3
Patty's Bistro	4
RD's Diner	2
Scotty's	1

SANTA RITA ROAD
3RD STREET NORTH
2ND STREET NORTH
11TH AVENUE
10TH AVENUE
1ST STREET NORTH
Bus terminal
Police station
Atlantic Bank
Market
Bank
COTTAGE ROAD
2ND STREET SOUTH
Taxis
Town Hall
Central Park
Library
Bank
3RD STREET SOUTH
4TH STREET SOUTH
5TH STREET SOUTH
Thunderbolt Dock

Corozal Bay

G STREET SOUTH
9TH AVENUE
7TH AVENUE
6TH STREET SOUTH
7TH ST SOUTH
8TH ST SOUTH
1ST AVENUE
4TH AVENUE
9TH STREET SOUTH
D ST SOUTH
C STREET SOUTH
B ST SOUTH
A STREET SOUTH
10TH STREET SOUTH
8TH AVENUE
SOUTH STREET

N

ACCOMMODATION
Corozal Bay Resort	F
Hok'ol Kin Guest House	D
Mark Anthony Hotel	A
Hotel Maya	E
Mirador Hotel	B
Las Palmas Hotel	C
Tony's Inn and Beach Resort	G

0	200 m
0	200 yds

F, **G**, Airstrip (1.5 miles), Copper Bank (5 miles), Cerros (10 miles), Sarteneja (25 miles), Orange Walk (30 miles) & Belize City (84 miles)

mural's vivid depiction of local history. The block northwest of Central Park, with the post office and police station, was previously the site of **Fort Barlee**, built in the 1870s to ward off Indian attacks.

Arrival and information

In addition to **buses** from Belize City to Corozal, those to Chetumal, Mexico pass through town roughly hourly from 7am to 9pm, and from 3.30am to 6.30pm in the opposite direction. A couple of local companies also operate shuttles to the border, which can be caught at the terminal on 7th Avenue near the market. The *Thunderbolt* skiff provides a **fast boat service** to San Pedro, Ambergris Caye, leaving from the dock daily at 7am and 3pm (1hr 30min; around Bz$50 one way; ⊤226-2904); it's important to call ahead, because in low season the schedule is sometimes limited. Both Tropic Air and Maya Island Air operate daily **flights** between Corozal and San Pedro; the airstrip is a few miles south of town, and taxis meet all flights. If you'd like to travel directly to Tikal in Guatemala, check at *Hotel Maya* (see below) for information on the Linea Dorada **express bus from Chetumal to Flores**, which will stop at the hotel if you book ahead.

For general information, check out Corozal's well-designed **website** (ⓦwww .corozal.com). The **post office** is northwest of Central Park (Mon–Fri 8.30am–4.30pm), and a number of banks, most near the park, have ATMs. You'll also find several **internet cafés** in the area. George and Esther Moralez run a good tour service (⊤422-2485, ⓦwww.gettransfers.com) to the surrounding region, including to Altun Ha. You can also inquire at your hotel for organized tours.

Accommodation

Corozal has plenty of hotels in all price ranges, and you'll always be able to find something suitable.

Corozal Bay Resort 1.8 miles south of the centre ⊤422-2691, ⓦwww.corozalbayinn.com. Large, thatched cabañas on a private beach, each with two double beds, a/c, TV with cable and nice bathroom. There's wireless internet and a beachfront pool, and the *Rainforest Restaurant & Bar* serves tasty meals and plenty of tropical cocktails. ❽

Hok'ol K'in Guest House At the sea end of 4th St South ⊤442-3329, ⓔcorozal@btl.net. Decent hotel near the seafront with private baths, balconies (with hammocks) and cable TV in most rooms. The ground floor is wheelchair-accessible. The restaurant serves Mexican-Belizean fare. Prices vary according to room size and a/c or fan. ❹–❺

Hotel Maya South of the centre ⊤422-2082, ⓦwww.hotelmaya.net. Clean, well-priced rooms with private bath, some with a/c and cable TV. The upstairs balcony gives refreshing sea views, and tasty breakfasts are served at the downstairs restaurant. The owner has extensive local knowledge on the surrounding region, and there are also several long-stay apartments. ❻

Las Palmas 123 5th Ave South, between 4th & 5th ⊤422-0196, ⓦwww.laspalmashotelbelize.com.

Spacious, white hotel with a variety of room styles, all with a/c, wi-fi and cable TV. The hotel is very secure, and they can arrange meals for groups. ❺

Mark Anthony Hotel On 3rd St North, close to the seafront ⊤422-3141, ⓔmark@localgringos .com. Clean rooms with a/c, cable TV and private bathrooms, above a local bar and restaurant serving Belizean food. Locals also know it as "Butch's Place". ❹

Mirador Hotel 4th Ave at 2nd St South, near the seafront ⊤422-0189, ⓦwww.mirador.bz. Large, well-maintained hotel with rooftop views both across the bay and over Corozal, best enjoyed from the hammocks or chairs. Rooms (of varying sizes) come equipped with wi-fi and cable TV, and some have a/c and bay views. ❻

Tony's Inn and Beach Resort 1.8 miles south of the centre ⊤422-2055 or 422-3555, ⓦwww.tonysinn.com. A touch of well-run luxury in a superb location. The large rooms with a/c and king-sized (or two double) beds overlook landscaped gardens and an inviting beach bar, and the hotel's *Vista del Sol* and *Y-Not Grill* restaurants are excellent. There's internet access for guests. Tours, many with an ecological focus, can be arranged. ❽

Eating and drinking

In addition to several small restaurants around town, some hotels serve good food. On Sundays, when many small businesses are closed, these may be your best bet. *Tony's Inn* has good fine dining, and *Corozal Bay Resort* offers a decent menu.

Al's Café 5th Ave. Homey, no-frills, petite restaurant with inexpensive Mexican and Belizean fare.

Cactus Plaza 6 6th St South ☏ 422-0394. This great cactus-shaped restaurant and bar serves reasonably priced Mexican-style meals. At the weekend, it hosts the town's liveliest weekend club night (Fri–Sat from around 9pm–2am). Restaurant open Wed–Sun from 6pm.

Chon Kong 42 5th Ave ☏ 422-0169. The best Chinese joint in town, with fresh, flavourful, decently priced favourites – including takeaway options. Daily 10.30am–11pm.

Marcelo's Pizza 4th Ave, two blocks from Central Park ☏ 422-3275 or 422-2310. A reliable choice

for late nights and Sun, also delivering cheap fast food all over town. Daily 8am–12am.

Patty's Bistro 4th Ave, one block from Central Park ☏ 402-0174. Excellent, well-priced Belizean, Mexican and American dishes. Closed Sun.

RD's Diner 4th Ave, four blocks northwest of Central Park ☏ 422-3796. Spacious, inviting restaurant with diverse offerings at mid-range prices, from Belizean dishes (cooked on a traditional "fire hearth") to Mexican fajitas and quesadillas to burgers. They also serve hearty breakfasts – with good brewed coffee. Mon–Sat 7am–11pm, Sun 7am–3pm.

Scotty's North of town. Tasty, reasonably priced burgers and pizzas, along with decent cocktails. Wed–Sun for lunch and dinner.

Santa Rita

Of the two small Maya sites within reach of Corozal, the closer is **Santa Rita** (no set opening hours, no charge), about a fifteen-minute walk northwest of town. Follow the main road toward the Mexican border and bear left at the fork, bringing you to the raised archeological site.

Founded as a small settlement around 1800 BC, Santa Rita appears to have been continuously occupied until the arrival of the Spanish, by which time it was in all probability the powerful Maya city known as Chactemal (Chetumal), which dominated regional trade. It was certainly still thriving in 1531 AD, when the conquistador **Alonso Dávila** entered the town, which had been tactically abandoned by its inhabitants; he was driven out almost immediately by Na Chan Kan, the Maya chief, and his Spanish adviser Gonzalo Guerrero (see Contexts).

Being so close to modern-day Mexico, it's not surprising that the site shares many attributes with ruins found to the north. **Pottery** found here connects the site with others in Yucatán, and, before it was bulldozed in the late 1970s, Structure 1 contained superb, Mixtec-style Postclassic murals similar to those found at Tulum in Quintana Roo. Due to this destruction, and the strong possibility that much of the ancient city lies beneath present-day Corozal, the only visible remains of Santa Rita are a few mounds and Structure 7, a fairly small but attractive **pyramid**. Burials excavated here include that of an elaborately jewelled elderly woman, dated to the Early Classic period, and the tomb of a Classic-period warlord, interred with the symbols of his elite status. Unfortunately the site is no longer maintained and bears some marks of abuse, namely litter and graffiti.

Cerros

On another peninsula jutting from the southern shore of Corozal Bay, the Preclassic Maya centre of **Cerros** (daily 8am–4.30pm; Bz$10) benefited from its position at the mouth of the New River, which enabled it to dominate regional water-borne trade. Beginning around 50 BC, it grew in only two generations from a small fishing village to a major city, one of the first to be ruled by a king. A canal bordered the central area, providing drainage for the town and the raised field system that sustained it. Despite initial success, however, Cerros was abandoned by the Classic period, made obsolete by shifting trade routes. The site today contains three large acropolis structures, ball-courts and plazas flanked by pyramids. The largest structure is a 22-metre-high temple with superb views of Corozal from its summit. Keep an eye out for the temple's intricate **stucco masks**, representing the rising and setting sun and Venus as morning star and evening star; note that they are periodically covered to prevent erosion.

Practicalities

The easiest way to arrange a trip to Cerros is by asking at a Corozal hotel, which can arrange transportation. Daily buses also connect Corozal to the village of **Copper Bank**, whose accommodation is good for staying near the ruins, but departure points and times vary. Once you're in Copper Bank, it's easy enough to rent a bike for the twenty-minute ride to the site.

Copper Bank has a few worthwhile **places to stay**, though you should call ahead to make sure they're operating. *Copper Bank Inn* (☎608-0838, ⓦwww .copperbankinn.com), has large rooms (❹) with air conditioning. Just off the road to Cerros, the eco-friendly *Cerros Beach Resort* (☎623-9766, ⓦwww.cerros beachresort.com) is solar-powered, with several thatched cabañas offering single and double accommodation (❹–❻).

The Mexican border crossing

Corozal is only nine miles from the Mexican border and one of the two land border crossings in Belize open to tourists. Many northbound buses heading into Mexico will take you to either the **bus terminal** in Chetumal (with plenty of onward express services up the coast to Cancún, or inland to Mexico City) or the nearby market. The whole journey from Corozal takes under an hour, including the **Santa Elena border crossing** on the south side of the Río Hondo. After you've cleared Belizean immigration, the bus carries you to the Mexican immigration and customs posts on the northern bank.

Border formalities for entering Mexico are straightforward, and few Western nationalities need a visa; simply pick up and fill out a **Mexican tourist card**. If you want visa advice, check with the Mexican embassy in Belize City (see Listings, p.69). There's no fee for entering Mexico, though you can convert your US or Belize dollars to pesos with the help of **moneychangers** on the Belize side of the border. **Entering Belize** from Mexico is also simple: there's no fee, and you'll get a maximum of thirty days by filling out the Belize immigration form.

In between the two border posts you'll pass through the **Corozal Free Zone**, a fairly chaotic area of shopping malls and petrol stations designed to encourage customers returning to Mexico to part with their US dollars. Once you've left Belize, you can enter this low-brow collection of duty-free shops, which all sell pretty much the same range of cut-rate electronic and household goods, clothes, shoes and canned food.

Travel details

Buses

Bus company information and details of services from Belize City to destinations in the north are given on p.69.

Bermudian Landing to: Belize City (2–3 daily Mon–Sat; 1hr 15min), via Burrell Boom.

Chetumal to: Belize City (hourly; 3hr 30min, express services 3hr), via Corozal and Orange Walk; Sarteneja (1 daily Mon–Sat at 6am; 3hr 30min).

Corozal to: Belize City (hourly; 2hr 30min), via Orange Walk (1hr); Chetumal (hourly; under 1hr).

Crooked Tree to: Belize City (several daily Mon–Sat; 1hr 30min).

Orange Walk to: Belize City (at least hourly from 5am–7pm; 1hr 30min); Corozal (hourly; 1hr); Indian Church, for Lamanai (3 weekly Mon, Wed & Fri in the afternoon; 2hr).

Sarteneja to: Belize City (3 daily Mon–Sat; 3hr 30min); Chetumal (1 daily Mon–Sat; 3hr 30min).

Flights

Corozal to: San Pedro (25min), calling at Sarteneja on request, are run daily by Tropic Air (☎ 226-2012, ⓦ www.tropicair.com) and Maya Island Air (☎ 223-1140, ⓦ www.mayaregional.com).

The northern cayes and atolls

CHAPTER 3   # Highlights

✳ **San Pedro** Enjoy Caribbean breezes – and rum cocktails – at this laidback resort village, made famous by Madonna in her song La Isla Bonita. **See p.100**

✳ **Caye Caulker** Go barefoot on the sandy streets and snorkel the Barrier Reef just offshore from this relaxed little island. **See p.112**

✳ **Sail the Caribbean** Watch the glorious sunset from a handsome wooden sailing boat on an excursion from Caye Caulker. **See p.119**

✳ **Turneffe Islands** Spend the day diving at Belize's largest atoll and marvel at the colourful marine life in this biologically diverse environment. **See p.121**

✳ **The Blue Hole** View the unique splendour of the famous Blue Hole from the air – or underwater – and then discover booby birds on Half Moon Caye. **See p.122**

▲ Caye Caulker

The northern cayes and atolls

B elize's spectacular **Barrier Reef**, which begins just south of Cancún and runs the entire length of the Belize coastline, is the longest in the western hemisphere. Its dazzling variety of underwater life and string of exquisite islands – known as cayes (pronounced "keys") – is the main attraction for most first-time visitors to the country. One of the planet's richest marine ecosystems, it's a paradise for scuba divers and snorkellers, who come for the incredible coral formations teeming with hundreds of species of brilliantly coloured fish. Such is the importance of this astonishing marine life that virtually the entire reef, including the portions surrounding the outlying atolls, and all of Belize's marine reserves – known jointly as the **Belize Barrier Reef Reserve System** – were declared a **World Heritage Site** in December 1996.

Most of the cayes lie in shallow water behind the shelter of the reef, with a limestone ridge forming larger, low-lying islands to the north and smaller, less frequently visited outcrops – often merely a stand of palms and a strip of sand – clustered toward the southern end of the chain. Though the four hundred cayes themselves form only a tiny portion of the country's total land area, and only around ten percent have any kind of tourism development, Belize has more territorial water than land, and the islands' lobster-fishing and tourism earnings account for a substantial proportion of the country's income.

More than anywhere in the cayes, the town of **San Pedro**, on **Ambergris Caye**, has experienced a major transition from a predominantly fishing-based economy to one dominated by tourism. There are still some peaceful spots on Ambergris, however, notably the protected areas of the island, including **Bacalar Chico National Park** in the north and **Hol Chan Marine Reserve** in the south. **Caye Caulker**, south of Ambergris Caye and home to another marine reserve, is smaller and more Belizean in feel. The budget-friendly caye has long been dubbed the "backpacker isle", but it has also expanded into a more high-end market. Further south still, the original Belizean capital of **St George's Caye** holds a celebrated place in the nation's history and has some fine colonial houses along with an exclusive diving resort. **Swallow Caye**, near the tip of Belize City, is protected as a manatee sanctuary. Many of the other cayes are inhabited only by tiny fishing communities whose populations fluctuate with the season; a few have just a single luxury lodge offering diving and sport-fishing to big-spending visitors.

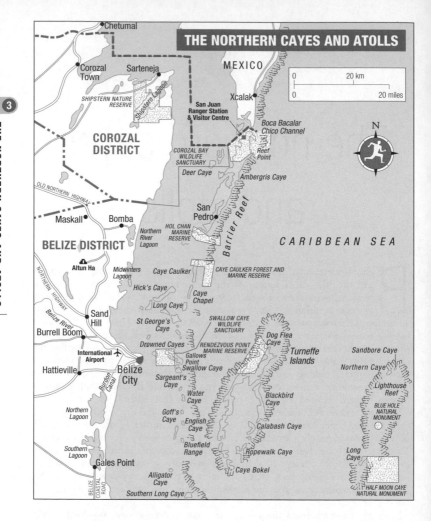

Beyond the chain of islands and the coral reef are two of Belize's three **atolls**: the **Turneffe Islands** and **Lighthouse Reef**. In these breathtakingly beautiful formations, a ring of coral just below the surface encloses a shallow lagoon, often with a caye sitting right on its edge; here you'll find some of the most spectacular diving and snorkelling sites in the country, if not the world. To the east, Lighthouse Reef is the site of beautiful **Half Moon Caye**, where you can view nesting red-footed boobies, and the unique **Blue Hole Natural Monument** – an enormous, collapsed cave that attracts divers from all over the world. All of these destinations are regularly visited by day-trips or live-aboard dive boats from San Pedro and Caye Caulker.

A brief history of the cayes

The earliest inhabitants of the cayes were **Maya** peoples or their ancestors. By the Classic period (300–900 AD), the Maya had developed an extensive trade network stretching from the Yucatán to Honduras, with settlements and shipment centres on several of the islands. At least some cities in Belize survived the Maya "collapse", and the trade network lasted throughout the Postclassic era until the arrival of the conquistadors. **Christopher Columbus** may have sighted the coast of Belize on his last voyage to the "Indies" in 1502; his journal mentions an encounter with a Maya trading party in an immense dugout canoe off Guanaja, one of the Bay Islands of Honduras. Traces of Maya civilization remain on some of the cayes today, especially Ambergris Caye, which has the site of **Marco Gonzalez** near its southern tip.

Probably the most infamous residents of the cayes were the **buccaneers**, usually British, who lived here in the sixteenth and seventeenth centuries, taking refuge in the shallow waters after plundering Spanish treasure ships. In time the pirates settled more or less permanently on some of the northern and central cayes. But life under the Jolly Roger grew too risky for them in the late 1600s, after Britain agreed to stamp out privateering under the terms of the Madrid Treaties, and a number of pirates turned instead to logwood cutting. The woodcutters, known as **Baymen**, kept their dwellings on the cayes – specifically **St George's Caye** – whose cool breezes and fresh water offered a welcome break from the steaming swamps where the logwood grew. The population of the cayes stayed low during the seventeenth and eighteenth centuries, but the St George's Caye settlement remained the Baymen's capital until 1779, when a Spanish force destroyed it and imprisoned 140 Baymen and 250 of their slaves. The Baymen returned to their capital in 1783, but waited until 1798 to take revenge on the Spanish fleet in the celebrated **Battle of St George's Caye** (see p.243). After, although the elite of the Baymen still kept homes on St George's Caye, the population of the islands began to decline as Belize Town (later Belize City) grew.

During this period, fishermen and turtle hunters continued to use the cayes as a base for their operations, and refugees fleeing the Caste Wars in Yucatán towards the end of the nineteenth century also settled on the islands in small numbers. Descendants of these groups have steadily increased the islands' population since the mid-twentieth century, assisted by the establishment of **fishing cooperatives** in the 1960s, which brought improved traps, ice manufacturing (for shipping seafood) and access to the export market.

At around the same time the cayes of Belize, particularly Caye Caulker, became a hangout on the **hippie trail**, and then began to attract more lucrative trade. The islanders generally welcomed these new visitors: rooms were rented and hotels built, and a burgeoning prosperity began to transform island life. Luxuries not usually associated with small fishing communities in the developing world – colour televisions, skiffs with large outboard motors – are all evidence of the effects of tourism over the years. So profound are these changes that fishing has now become a secondary activity; many of the inhabitants of the two largest northern cayes, Ambergris Caye and Caye Caulker, now depend almost solely on tourism.

Visiting the cayes

Life on the cayes is supremely relaxing, tempting you to take it easy in a hammock, feast on seafood and sip rum punch as the sun sets. If you adopt the "no shirt, no shoes, no problem" philosophy of locals and expats alike, you'll fit right in. **Snorkelling** or **diving** trips to the reef are easily arranged from Caye Caulker and Ambergris Caye; dive instruction is also readily available. You can visit areas of almost unbelievable beauty and isolation by joining a group day-trip, visiting three or four different reef sites in a day, or by staying at a lodge on one of the atolls. For a spectacular aerial view of the **Blue Hole Natural Monument**, ask a local travel agent to book you onto a flight over this amazing landmark and other sections of the reef; you can also choose from a variety of helicopter tours with Belize City-based Astrum Helicopters (☎222-9462, ⓦwww.astrumhelicopters.com).

Safeguarding the coral reef

Coral reefs are among the most complex and **fragile** ecosystems in the world. Once damaged, coral is far more susceptible to bacterial infection, which can quickly lead to large-scale, irreversible decline. Unfortunately, a great deal of damage has already been caused on the Barrier Reef by snorkellers and divers standing on the coral or holding onto outcrops for a better look. All tour guides in Belize are trained in reef ecology before earning a licence (which must be displayed as they guide), and if you go on an organized trip, as most people do, the guide should brief you on the following **precautions** to avoid damage to the reef.

Never anchor boats on the reef – use the permanently secured buoys.

Never touch or stand on coral – protective cells are easily stripped away from the living polyps on their surface, destroying them and thereby allowing algae to enter. Coral also stings and can cause **burns**, and even brushing against it causes cuts that are slow to heal.

Don't remove shells, sponges or other creatures from the reef or buy reef products from souvenir shops.

Avoid disturbing the seabed around coral – aside from spoiling visibility, clouds of sand settle over corals and smother them.

Don't use suntan lotion in reef areas – the oils remain on the water's surface. Wear a T-shirt instead to protect your skin from **sunburn**.

Don't feed or interfere with fish or marine life; this can harm not only sea creatures and the food chain, but snorkellers too – large fish may attack, trying to get their share.

Birdwatching in the cayes is fascinating, as it is almost everywhere in Belize. Over 250 species live in or visit the region, from ospreys and sandpipers to flamingos and finches. Catch-and-release **fly-fishing** for bonefish is popular, particularly on the Turneffe Island flats, where a couple of luxury fishing lodges can fulfil any angler's dream. Fishing trips for species such as snapper, barracuda and grouper are easily arranged from Caye Caulker or San Pedro, and a local guide can take you to the best spots.

Finally, some words of **warning**: occasionally the northern cayes (and other coastal areas of Belize) suffer direct hits by devastating hurricanes. The official **hurricane season** lasts from June to the end of November, though the worst storms usually occur during September and October – tourist low season. There are excellent warning systems in place, and if you are on the cayes during the hurricane season you can keep yourself informed about developing storms by checking Ⓦ www.belizenet .com/weatherix.shtml. If there is a hurricane developing *anywhere* in the Caribbean, prepare to leave as quickly as possible or postpone plans for a visit to the cayes.

Ambergris Caye and San Pedro

Ambergris Caye is separated from Mexico by the narrow **Boca Bacalar Chico channel**, created partly by the ancient Maya. It's the most northerly and, at 25 miles long, by far the largest of the cayes, though the vast majority of its population is concentrated near the southern end. The island's main attraction and point of arrival is the former fishing village of **SAN PEDRO**, facing the reef about a mile from the caye's southern end. Development continues to spread north from the town, with plenty of beach resorts and plans for ever-larger hotels constantly in the making.

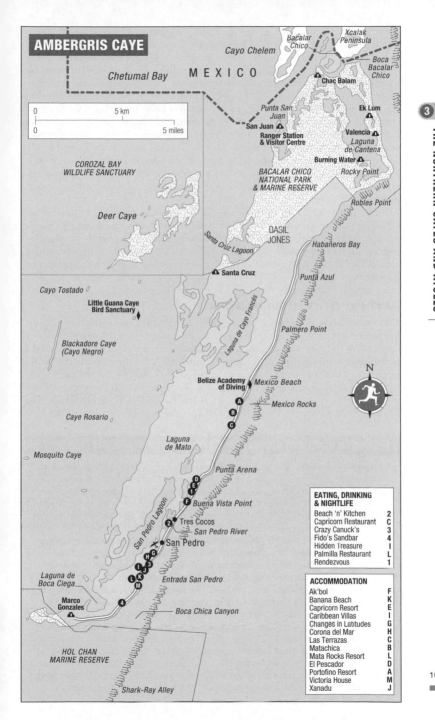

AMBERGRIS CAYE

Xcalak Peninsula

Cayo Chelem

Bacalar Chico

Chetumal Bay

MEXICO

Boca Bacalar Chico

Chac Balam ⌂

0 ——————— 5 km
0 ——————— 5 miles

Punta San Juan

San Juan ⌂
Ranger Station & Visitor Centre

Ek Lum ⌂

Valencia ⌂
Laguna de Cantena

COROZAL BAY WILDLIFE SANCTUARY

Burning Water ⌂

Rocky Point

BACALAR CHICO NATIONAL PARK & MARINE RESERVE

Deer Caye

Robles Point

BASIL JONES

Santa Cruz Lagoon

Habañeros Bay

⌂ **Santa Cruz**

Punta Azul

Cayo Tostado

Little Guana Caye Bird Sanctuary ▼

Palmero Point

Blackadore Caye (Cayo Negro)

Laguna de Cayo Francés

Caye Rosario

Belize Academy of Diving

Mexico Beach

Ⓐ

N

Mosquito Caye

Mexico Rocks

Ⓑ

Ⓒ

Laguna de Mato

Punta Arena

Ⓓ
Ⓔ
①

Ⓕ *Buena Vista Point*

② *Tres Cocos*

San Pedro River

San Pedro Lagoon

San Pedro

Ⓗ
Ⓖ
①
③
Ⓚ
Ⓛ
Ⓜ

Laguna de Boca Ciega

Entrada San Pedro

Marco Gonzales

④

Boca Chica Canyon

HOL CHAN MARINE RESERVE

Shark-Ray Alley

EATING, DRINKING & NIGHTLIFE

Beach 'n' Kitchen	**2**
Capricorn Restaurant	**C**
Crazy Canuck's	**3**
Fido's Sandbar	**4**
Hidden Treasure	**I**
Palmilla Restaurant	**L**
Rendezvous	**1**

ACCOMMODATION

Ak'bol	**F**
Banana Beach	**K**
Capricorn Resort	**E**
Caribbean Villas	**I**
Changes in Latitudes	**G**
Corona del Mar	**H**
Las Terrazas	**C**
Matachica	**B**
Mata Rocks Resort	**L**
El Pescador	**D**
Portofino Resort	**A**
Victoria House	**M**
Xanadu	**J**

If you fly into San Pedro, as most visitors do, the views are breathtaking: the water appears so clear and shallow as to barely cover the sandy seabed, and the mainland and other islands stand out clearly. The most memorable sight is the white line of the reef crest, dramatically separating the vivid blue of the open sea from the turquoise water on its leeward side. After your first glimpse of the sun-speckled island, it's easy to see why Madonna crooned "Last night I dreamt of San Pedro" in her famous song "La Isla Bonita". Though not a large town – you're never more than a shell's throw from the sea – its population of over five thousand is the highest in all the cayes. San Pedro is the main destination for over half of all visitors to Belize, catering mainly to North American package tourists. Almost all prices in town are quoted in US dollars, which are accepted island-wide. Some of the country's most exclusive **hotels** and **restaurants** are here; a few budget places sit in the "original" (pre-tourism expansion) village of San Pedro, which is also where most of the action takes place, particularly in the evenings.

During the daytime, for those not shopping, relaxing or enjoying some other land-based activity, the **water** is the focus of entertainment on Ambergris Caye, from sunbathing on the docks to **windsurfing**, **sailing**, **kayaking**, **diving** and **snorkelling**, **fishing** and even peering through the floor of a glass-bottomed boat. All of the trips described on p.107 can be booked from local companies or through your hotel.

Arrival and information

Arriving at San Pedro's **airport**, you're at the north end of Coconut Drive and about five hundred yards south of the centre. It's within easy walking distance of any of the hotels in town, though golf buggies and **taxis** will be waiting too. A ride to the centre (or anywhere else in town) starts at around Bz$7, but always verify this before agreeing to a ride, and never let a driver take you to a hotel of his choosing.

Boats usually pull in at the water taxi dock, on the front (reef) side of the island at the east end of Black Coral Street, or at the east end of Caribeña Street. The *Thunderbolt*, however, pulls in at Back Dock, at the back of the island at the west

---

Getting to and from Ambergris Caye

Flying to San Pedro is the easiest and most popular approach. **Maya Island Air** (☏226-2435, ⊛www.mayaregional.com) and **Tropic Air** (☏226-2012, ⊛www.tropic air.com) both operate flights from Belize International Airport (from Bz$120 return; see p.51) and Belize Municipal Airport (from Bz$67 return; see p.51) to San Pedro (25min; at least hourly, 7.30am–5pm), calling at Caye Caulker on request (same price). Tropic Air also operates daily flights from **San Pedro to Corozal**.

From Belize City, boats to Ambergris Caye are operated by the **Caye Caulker Water Taxi Association** (1hr 20min; Bz$20 one way, $40 return; ☏226-0992, ⊛www .cayecaulkerwatertaxi.com) and leave from the Marine Terminal around nine times daily, most calling at Caye Caulker on the way. The **San Pedro Express Water Taxi** (1hr 20 min; BZ$25 one way, BZ$45 return; ☏226-2194, ⊛www.sanpedrowatertaxi.com) also runs around seven daily trips to San Pedro and Caye Caulker; it departs from the San Pedro Water Taxi Terminal, on North Front Street near the Tourism Village. Note that both water taxis often offer special seasonal deals; inquire when booking. The **Thunderbolt** runs between San Pedro and Corozal, stopping at Sarteneja on request (1hr 30min; daily 7am & 3pm; starting at Bz$45 one way, $90 return). The Thunderbolt sometimes offers limited service in the off season, so call ahead. From San Pedro to other cayes, any of the boats above also stop at Caye Caulker, and will also call at St George's Caye or Caye Chapel on request, though you should check with them first for availability.

end of Black Coral Street. All docks are within a few blocks of the centre, marked by the tiny Central Park, on the seafront along Barrier Reef Drive.

The official tourist **information** centre (Mon–Sat 10am–1pm, and occasionally in the afternoon; T 226-2198) is in a small building next to the town hall. You can also get general island and country information at the BTB (Belize Tourist Board) office (Mon–Thurs 8am–5pm, Fri 8am–4pm), near the library. Beware other "information booths" dotted around town, as they are all fronts for timeshares or resorts. Ambergris Caye's official website (W www.ambergriscaye.com), one of the best in the country, is a reliable source of information, with good maps and links to most of the island's businesses. It's also worth picking up a copy of *The San Pedro Sun* or *Ambergris Today*, the island's **tourist newspapers** (both Bz$1), or the *Hot Guide to Ambergris Caye*, a free listings magazine; all three are available from the tourist information centre and most hotels and restaurants. San Pedro's **radio station**, Reef Radio (92.3FM), is worth listening to for both the music and events announcements.

You needn't worry about **changing money** here, as US dollars are accepted everywhere – even preferred – in both cash and travellers' cheques.

Several **internet cafés** offer high-speed access and cheap **international phone calls** including Caribbean Connection (T 226-4664), on Barrier Reef Drive at Black Coral Street; and Coconet, a few blocks north. The **post office** is in the Alijua Building near the middle of Barrier Reef Drive, and the police and fire stations and the **BTL** office are all at the northern end of Pescador Drive.

Getting around

The town centre is small enough to **get around** on foot; pleasant at any time, it's particularly enjoyable on weekend evenings, when the street nearest the shore, Barrier Reef Drive, is closed to vehicles. The town, however, has expanded rapidly to the north and south, and some outlying hotels have **courtesy bikes** for guests – something you might want to consider when choosing a place to stay. You can also **rent bikes** from Joe's Bike Rental, on Pescador Drive at Caribeña Street (Bz$14/ half day, $20/full day; T 226-4371).

You'll see many people using **golf carts** to zip around, and if you'd like your own, there are several places to rent them. At the southern end of Barrier Reef Drive, Castle Cars (T 226-2421, W castlecarsbelize.com) charges US$12 for an hour, $60 for a full day. Further south, at Island Supermarket on Coconut Drive, is Island Tour Rental, which charges similar prices for its well-maintained vehicles (T 226-2351, W www.ambergrisgolfcart.com). Carts Belize (T 226-4084, W cartsbelize.com), one block north of the airstrip, also offers a good fleet of carts for similar prices.

To head north, to visit the more remote resorts and restaurants, you might need to hire a **water taxi**. *Island Ferry* (starting at Bz$20; T 226-3231, W islandferry .net) is a regular **fast ferry** running the length of the caye, with departures from Fido's Dock from 7am to 10pm, later on weekends. *Coastal Xpress* (T 226-2007, W coastalxpress.com), charging similar prices, also travels throughout Ambergris Caye. They also offer charter trips – and ask about their weekly passes if you plan on taking boats regularly.

Accommodation

Ambergris Caye has the highest concentration of **hotels** in the country. Many of these, including all the **inexpensive** options, are in San Pedro itself, just a short walk or taxi ride from the airport. Resorts, some very luxurious, stretch for many miles along the beaches north and south of town. **Prices** here are much higher than in the rest of Belize, but **discounts** on quoted rates are often available, especially in the low season, so it's worth asking. During Christmas, New Year and Easter

▲ Northern Resorts & Bacalar Chico Reserve

SAN PEDRO

N

Boca del Rio

BOCA DEL RIO AND BRIDGE

Park and
Basketball Court

LAGUNA STREET

Tanisha Eco
Tour

Ⓐ

Patajo's Dive Shop

BOCA DEL RIO DRIVE (BEACH ROAD)

High
School

SANDPIPER STREET

JEWFISH STREET

Polo's Golf
Carts

Fire station

Police station

Ⓑ

Laguna de San Pedro

Hol Chan Marine
Reserve Office

Amigos Dive
Shop

Texaco Dock

CARIBENA STREET

CORAL STREET

Joe's
Bikes

Ⓒ
Ⓓ
Ⓔ

PESCADOR DRIVE

@

San Carlos
Medical

Ⓕ

Belizean Arts

❶

Fido's Dock (Island Ferry)

PELICAN STREET

❷

AMBERGRIS STREET

ANGEL STREET

❸

Ⓖ

❹

BARRIER REEF DRIVE

Central
Park

BUCCANEER STREET

❺

❼

Ⓗ

Ambergris Jade Museum

Back Dock

❾

BLACK CORAL STREET

❽

Ambergris Divers

Town Hall

Front Dock (Water Taxis to
Caye Caulker & Belize City)

Nellie's
Laundry

@

Castle
Cars

❶❶

Sailsports Belize

Ⓙ

TARPON STREET

❿

Ⓚ

Primary
school

ESMERALDA STREET

Ⓘ

ⓘ

Lion's Medical
Centre

Maya
Island

Tropic Air

Hyperbaric Chambers

Ⓛ

Airship

COCONUT DRIVE

Ⓜ

Orange Gift Shop
& Gallery

EATING & DRINKING

Blue Lotus	5
Blue Water Grill	L
Caliente	6
Elvi's Kitchen	3
Estel's Restaurant	7
El Fogón	10
Red Ginger	B
The Reef	2
Sunset Grill	9
Wild Mango's	11

NIGHTLIFE

Fido's	1
Jaguar Temple	4
Palapa Bar and Grill	3
Pier Lounge	G
Playa Lounge	8

ACCOMMODATION

Holiday Hotel	I
Martha's	G
Mayan Princess Resort	F
The Phoenix	B
Ramon's Village	M
Ruby's	J & K
San Pedrano	C
Spindrift Hotel	H
Sunbreeze Hotel	L
Thomas Hotel	D
The Tides	A
Tio Pil's Place	E

0   100 m
0   100 yds

▼ Island Supermarket & Wine de Vine

you should definitely **book ahead**. All hotels have air-conditioning and private bath (unless otherwise stated). It also has more **apartments**, condominiums and timeshares than anywhere else in Belize, and you can often get good package or long-term deals if you book ahead; check with Caye Management (☎226-3077, ⓦwww.cayemanagement.com).

Hotels in San Pedro

Holiday Hotel Barrier Reef Drive, just south of the centre ☎226-2014, ⓦwww.sanpedroholiday .com. San Pedro's central, first hotel, with all modern facilities, including fridges, TV and a/c. Rooms face the sea and come in a variety of sizes. There's a restaurant and a weekly beach barbecue with live music. **❸**

Martha's Pescador Drive, across from *Elvi's Kitchen* ☎206-2053, ⓔmarthashotel@yahoo.com. A bargain in the town centre, offering clean, comfortable, fan-cooled rooms with private bath and bedside lamps. **❸**

Mayan Princess Resort Barrier Reef Drive ☎226-2778, ⓦwww.mayanprincesshotel.com. Central beachfront suites with kitchenette and a large balcony – some with hammocks – overlooking the sea. Daily maid service, complimentary internet and free taxi from airport. **❸**

The Phoenix Barrier Reef Drive near Caribeña St ☎226-2083, ⓦwww.thephoenixbelize.com. Sleek, stylish, and wonderfully perched on the beach, this condominium-hotel features spacious, light-flooded suites with full dining room and kitchen. Choose from a dip in the pool, a visit to the Sol Spa or cocktails at the outdoor bar overlooking the Caribbean. The *Phoenix* is ideal for longer stays; check the website for ongoing deals. **❸**

Ramon's Village Coconut Drive, near the airstrip ☎226-2071, ⓦwww.ramons.com. This friendly resort enjoys a prime position: It's within strolling distance of town, but also right on the beach. Roomy thatched-roof cabañas have plenty of amenities, and the leafy grounds feature a pool, presided over by "Rey Ramon," a huge replica of a Maya mask, and a dock for sunning, swimming and napping. **❾**

Ruby's Barrier Reef Drive, south of the centre ☎226-2063, ⓔrubys@btl.net. Decent, family-run budget hotel on the seafront. The clean rooms (some with a/c) get better views (and increased rates) the higher up you go; all are good value, those with shared bath especially so. **❸**

San Pedrano Barrier Reef Drive at Caribeña St ☎226-2054, ⓔsanpedrano@btl.net. Popular hotel in a wooden building with nice rooms, some with a/c. Set back slightly from the beach, but with fine views and breezy verandas. **❹**

Spindrift Hotel On Barrier Reef Drive at Buccaneer St ☎226-2174, ⓦambergriscaye.com /spindrift. Centrally located (near plenty of nightlife)

and on the beach, this concrete hotel offers some rooms with great views across the sea and others around a patio. Four levels of rooms are available, the top three with a/c. **❻–❽**

Sunbreeze Hotel South end of Barrier Reef Drive ☎226-2191, ⓦwww.sunbreezehotel.com. Curving around a sandy courtyard and a pool, this well-run beachfront hotel has comfortable rooms with large bathrooms; some have a jacuzzi. Excellent restaurant and good gift shop. **❸**

Thomas Hotel North end of Barrier Reef Drive ☎226-2061. A good budget option with clean and simple rooms. **❹**

The Tides On the beach, about a half mile from the centre ☎226-2283, ⓦwww.ambergriscaye .com/tides. Family-run hotel, with comfy rooms, with a/c, refrigerator and two double beds. Rooms face the pool and bar with the ocean beyond. Dive packages with Patojo's Dive shop are available. **❾**

Tio Pil's Place On the beach near Caribeña St ☎206-2059, ⓦwww.ambergriscaye.com/lilys. Formerly *Lily's*, this family-owned beachfront wooden-and-concrete structure has rooms with fridge and a/c and TV; some have sea views. **❼**

Hotels south of San Pedro

Banana Beach Resort On Mar de Tumbo Beach, one mile south of town ☎226-3890, ⓦwww .bananabeach.com. Variety of suites, with cable TV, rattan furniture and Mexican weavings; some with kitchens, and balconies overlooking the grounds or facing the ocean. Good weekly rates and off-season discounts. The excellent *El Divino* restaurant serves up tasty seafood and cocktails. Tours can be arranged by the friendly and efficient in-house Monkey Business Travel Shop (ⓦwww.ambergris tours.com). **❸**

Caribbean Villas Coconut Drive, about one mile south of town ☎226-2715, ⓦwww.caribbeanvillashotel.com. Ample grounds, with a wildlife-viewing platform and excellent birdwatching. A great spot for nature lovers that's also close to town. A variety of large rooms and well-equipped suites, all with ocean views, on the beachfront. Plenty of peace and quiet and opportunities to relax; snooze in a hammock or immerse yourself in the hot tub. **❸**

Changes in Latitudes Coconut Drive, about a half mile south of town, near the Belize Yacht Club

⏱&ℱ 226-2986, ⓦ www.ambergriscaye.com /latitudes. Friendly B&B set in relaxing gardens half a block from the sea – guests can use the yacht club facilities, including the pool, next door. Smallish but clean rooms, with use of common area, including full kitchen. Rates include a cooked breakfast, different every day. ❻

Corona del Mar On the beach, just over a half mile south of town ⏱ 226-2025, ⓦ www .ambergriscaye.com/coronadelmar. Lots of local flavour and spacious rooms and suites with kitchens and TV. Rates include a full breakfast and use of the *Coconuts* pool next door. Has the only elevator in San Pedro and good disabled access, including wide steps to a swimming area from the pier. ❼–❽

Mata Rocks Resort Around two miles south of town ⏱ 226-2336, ⓦ www.matarocks.com. Small family resort with rooms around the pool and bar, complimentary breakfast and free bikes for exploring. ❼–❾

Victoria House On the beach, around two miles south of town ⏱ 226-2067, ⓦ www.victoria -house.com. Gorgeous, award-winning resort with a range of fabulous accommodation in a splendid location. Luxurious, colonial-style hotel rooms, thatched cabañas, suites and villas are set in spacious grounds – not surprisingly, it's one of the most popular wedding hotels on the island. Excellent service and very relaxing; you can sun yourself near the beachfront pool and enjoy cocktails in your bathing suit or enjoy fine dining at the restaurant *Palmilla* (see p.111). Prices start at US$200 for a double room in high season, and go up to over US$1000 for a full villa. ❾

🏃 **Xanadu** On the beach, about 1.5 miles south of town ⏱ 226-2814, ⓦ www .xanaduresort-belize.com. *Xanadu* more than lives up to its name – defined as a "beautiful, idyllic place" – with nineteen lovely condominium suites, all built in environmentally-friendly monolithic domes that are grouped around a palm-shaded pool, with the beach just a few lazy paces away. All suites have a full kitchen, internet access, and wooden decks, and the staff is delightful. They also run Carts Belize (see p.103), with a top fleet of carts to rent. ❾

Hotels north of San Pedro

If you're looking for remote and swanky, head north of town. This part of the caye is best accessed via boat or taxi (if they're willing to go the distance). You can also visit on golf cart (in dry season), but ask ahead: many companies don't allow use of their carts in the north. As for accommodation – it's largely populated with high-end resorts, such as luxury getaways like *Matachica* (ⓦ www.matachica.com; ❾). Especially popular in recent years are condo-hotels, including the sleek *Las Terrazas* (ⓦ www.lasterrazasresort.com; ❾).

Ak'bol On the beach, 2.5 miles north of town ⏱ 226-2073, ⓦ www.akbol.com. Belize's first yoga resort invites you to "renew your spirit" with yoga and wellness classes and retreats. You can stay in breezy thatched cabañas (❽–❾) amid a meditation garden, or go for the budget option, and bed down in the yoga "barracks" (❺), which has comfy single rooms and shared bathrooms with carved mahogany sinks. Even if you don't stay, pay a visit to the on-site *Shade Beach Bar*, where you can enjoy "create-your-own" fruit smoothies.

Capricorn Resort On the beach, just north of *El Pescador* ⏱ 226-2809, ⓔ capricorn@btl.net. Most people come here for the incredibly good food (see p.111), but there are also some delightful, secluded wooden cabins with porches overlooking a pristine beach; all make perfect hideaways. Breakfast is included, as is a water taxi from town on arrival and departure. ❾

El Pescador On the beach, about 2.5 miles north of town ⏱ 226-2398, ⓦ www.elpescador.com. With a choice of several rooms in a colonial-style house rich with hardwood furnishings, or one-, two- or three-bed villas (up to US$725), there's plenty of choice at this family-run establishment, where fishing and diving are the most popular activities. Complimentary bikes, kayaks and wi-fi are available. ❾

Portofino Resort On the beach, 5.5 miles north of town ⏱ 220-5096, ⓦ www.portofinobelize.com. A mix of beautiful wooden and concrete cabañas arranged to one side of a large pool and all with ocean views, colourful, Mexican-tiled bathrooms and hardwood floors. All amenities, including free boat transfer to town. Service is friendly and the restaurant is excellent (see p.111). ❽

The Town

San Pedro's main streets are only half a dozen blocks long, and the town does not boast any standout sights, but in a place so devoted to tourist pleasure you're never far from a bar, restaurant, gift shop – or the Caribbean Sea. Despite all the development, the town manages to retain some elements of its **Caribbean charm** with a few two-storey, clapboard buildings in the centre. However, lofty, concrete structures are an increasingly common feature, and traffic has increased considerably in recent years.

One of the most interesting (and hectic) times to visit San Pedro is during August's **Costa Maya Festival** (Ⓦwww.costamayafestival.com), a week-long celebration featuring cultural and musical presentations from the five Mundo Maya countries (Belize, Mexico, Guatemala, Honduras and El Salvador). Another event that draws crowds is the **Annual Eco-challenge Lagoon Kayak Race and Reef Festival**, held at the end of April to raise awareness of the coral reef. Kayakers race 42 miles over two days, then celebrate at a blow-out beach party. And, lobster lovers won't want to miss the mid-June **San Pedro Lobster-Fest**, with a host of events celebrating the island's most famous crustacean.

Shops and galleries

San Pedro's **gift shops** and **art galleries** offer an array of Belizean handicrafts and souvenirs. Belizean Arts on Barrier Reef Drive (Ⓣ226-3019, Ⓦwww.belizeanarts .com) features an excellent range of **arts**, **crafts** and **jewellery**. Orange Gift Shop & Gallery, south of the centre along Coconut Drive, displays interesting works, from wooden sculptures to colourful tropical paintings by Belizean artists.

In the middle of Barrier Reef Drive, Ambergris Jade has **carved jade** replicas of Maya artefacts.

Exploring the caye and reef

North of the town centre, the **Boca del Rio** (usually referred to simply as "the river" or "the cut") is a narrow but widening erosion channel now crossed by a substantial bridge (free on foot and after 10pm, Bz$2 for bikes and Bz$10 for golf carts during the day). The largest vehicle permitted across is a golf cart, although most rental companies don't allow clients to head much further north; check with your company, or call a taxi at Ⓣ602-1073. On the northern side of the river, a rudimentary road (navigable for some distance in the dry season, much less during wet weather, though bikes can usually pass) leads to the village of **Tres Cocos** and the northern resorts along miles of gorgeous, mostly deserted beaches. The northernmost region of the caye, now accessible on organized day-trips or overnights, features the spectacular **Bacalar Chico National Park and Marine Reserve**, as well as several **Maya sites** (see p.110).

Following Coconut Drive **south** from the city, San Pedro becomes **San Pablo**, the semi-official name for this area of beach resorts and houses for the often Spanish-speaking workforce. Set back from the sea, the road runs for a couple miles to the Maya site of **Marco Gonzalez**. The site is hard to find and there's not much to see, but studies have shown that it was once an important trade centre with close links to Lamanai (see p.83); archeological teams still conduct excavations here. The southernmost tip of the caye is the terrestrial section of **Hol Chan Marine Reserve**.

Before **snorkelling** or **diving** here, whet your appetite for the wonders of the reef with a visit to the Hol Chan Marine Reserve office and **visitor centre**, on Caribeña Street in San Pedro (Mon–Fri 8am–noon & 1–5pm; Ⓣ226-2247), which has photographs and informative maps and models. For additional information on Hol Chan, contact Green Reef (Ⓣ226-2833, Ⓦwww.greenreefbelize.org), a non-profit organization.

Diving

The reef in front of San Pedro is a heavily used area that's been subject to intensive fishing and souvenir hunting. You'll find it in much better condition to the north, toward **Mexico Rocks**, or south, toward **Hol Chan**, both locations exhibiting fascinating "spur and groove" formations. Large marine life found here can include

sharks (hammerhead, bull and tiger, as well as the common and harmless nurse shark), turtles, spotted eagle rays and, if you're really lucky, manta rays and whale sharks. For the best diving in Belize and high-voltage excitement in a relatively pristine environment, you really need to take a trip to one of the **atolls** (see box below). **Night diving** and **snorkelling** are also available.

PADI diving certification starts at around US$325. A more basic, single-dive **resort course** (which doesn't lead to PADI certification) starts at around US$150. All options should include equipment. For diving trips to the Blue Hole, expect to pay around US$250; for the Turneffe Islands, around US$200.

Snorkelling

Almost every dive shop in San Pedro also offers **snorkelling** trips, although specialized snorkelling outfits will provide more personal attention; going with a dive

---

Snorkel, dive and watersports operators

In addition to the dive and snorkel shops at several hotels and resorts, there are many independent **operators**. The best are not necessarily the most well known, as these often cater to large groups and leave some divers unsatisfied. Smaller, locally owned outfits usually take smaller groups and provide more personal service. Beware of any guides that encourage clients to touch the reef or animals or feed the fish. Equipment sales and repairs and underwater camera rentals are available at **Island Diver Supplies** on Black Coral Street, near the Front Dock (☏226-4023). San Pedro also has the only **hyperbaric chamber** in Belize, located behind the airstrip; your dive operator should have all the details in case of emergency.

Adventure Belize On the Front Dock ☏226-2636. Offers a variety of snorkel tours, including Bacalar Chico.

Amigos del Mar Dive Shop ☏226-2648, ⓦwww.amigosdive.com. Well-run diving outfit that offers several dives a day, as well as snorkelling and fishing trips, and night dives on request.

Belize Diving Adventures ☏226-3082, ⓦwww.belizedivingadventures.net. Family-run business organizing dive trips to the Turneffe Islands, Blue Hole and other local dive sites, as well as fishing and inland tours.

Ecologic Divers North of the centre ☏226-4118, ⓦwww.ecologicdivers.com. Offers a variety of dive trips.

Island Roots ☏226-3773, ⓔislandroots@btl.net. A small operation specializing in snorkel tours to Bacalar Chico.

Patojo's Next to *The Tides* ☏226-2283, ⓦwww.ambergriscaye.com/tides. A wide variety of local dives, and qualified to teach to Divemaster level. Offers good packages for keen divers.

Red Mangrove Eco Adventures Near Anchorage Resort ☏226-0069, ⓦwww.mangrovebelize.com. Offers educational and eco-aware small-group tours, specializing in local sites and Turneffe.

Reef Runner ☏226-2180, ⓦwww.ambergriscaye.com/reefrunner. Good snorkelling trips, and a glass-bottomed boat that allows even non-snorkellers to enjoy the reef.

Seaduced by Belize In the town centre ☏226-3221, ⓦwww.seaducedbybelize.com. Their sailing boats visit all the local snorkelling areas, and they also run sunset, sunrise and inland tours. Owner Elito is a great guide.

Searious Adventures In the town centre ☏226-4202, ⓦwww.seariousadventures.com. Snorkel tours by sailing boat; sunset and inland tours as well.

Tanisha Ecological Tours ☏226-2314, ⓦwww.tanishatours.com. Both snorkel and inland tours. Guide Daniel Nuñez is a fantastic naturalist.

boat may mean you're left on your own while the staff concentrates on the divers. Several trips are offered from San Pedro, the most popular being to Hol Chan Marine Reserve, focusing on a decent section of reef that is sometimes overcrowded. Local tours cost US$30–50 for two to four hours, depending on where you go and whether a beach barbecue is included.

Snorkelling **guides** (who must also be licensed tour guides) have a great deal of experience with visitors, and they'll show you how to use your equipment before setting off. Generally, trips either head north to the spectacular **Mexico Rocks** or **Rocky Point** or, more commonly, south to **Hol Chan Marine Reserve** and **Shark-Ray Alley** (see below). Trips to Caye Caulker are also popular, but travelling there on your own by water taxi and taking a local tour is cheaper. There are also several independent sailing boat owners who will charter their craft for the day; ask at your hotel or at the information centre next to the town hall.

Windsurfing, sailing and swimming

Great **windsurfing** and **sailing** rental and instruction is offered by Sailsports Belize (☎ 226-4488, ⓦ www.sailsportsbelize.com), on the beach in front of the *Holiday Hotel*. A beginner sailing course is US$265 for a five-hour session. Boat rental is US$22–50 per hour; windsurfers are also available for rent at US$22–27 per hour. Rates for both grow cheaper as rental hours increase.

Very comfortably equipped **charter catamarans** are an increasingly popular, if expensive, activity. You can book a catamaran with TMM Bareboat Vacations, on Coconut Drive just past the Tropic Air Office (☎ 226-3026, in the US ☎ 1-800/633-0155, ⓦ www.sailtmm.com). All catamarans have dinghy, lifejackets, first-aid kit, cruising guide and snorkel equipment; a skipper and cook are also available for an extra daily fee.

If you plan on **swimming**, you should know that **beaches** on Ambergris Caye are narrow and the sea immediately offshore is shallow, with a lot of seagrass – meaning you'll usually need to jump off the end of a dock or take a boat trip to the reef if you want a proper paddle. A word of **warning**: There have been a number of swimming accidents in San Pedro caused by boats speeding past the piers. A line of buoys, not always clearly visible, indicates the "**safe area**", but speedboat drivers are sometimes recklessly macho; be careful when choosing where to swim.

The south: Hol Chan Marine Reserve and Shark-Ray Alley

Hol Chan Marine Reserve, five miles south of San Pedro at the southern tip of the caye, takes its name from the Maya word for "little channel", and it is indeed a break in the reef that forms the focus of the reserve. Established in 1987 and the first of Belize's marine reserves, its three zones preserve a comprehensive cross-section of the marine environment, including **coral reef**, **seagrass beds** and **mangroves**. Approaching with a boat tour, you'll be met by a warden who explains the rules and collects the entry fee (Bz$20), which is sometimes included in the cost of your tour. If arriving in your own boat, purchase tickets beforehand at the Hol Chan office in town (see p.107). You'll see plenty of **marine life**, including some very large snappers, groupers and barracuda.

Included in most of the tours is another part of the reserve, **Shark-Ray Alley**, where you can swim in shallow water with three-metre **nurse sharks** and enormous **stingrays**. Watching these creatures glide effortlessly beneath you is an exhilarating experience and swimming here poses almost no danger to snorkellers, as humans are not part of the fishes' normal diet. However, note that the area can get quite crowded and there's also the possibility that a shark could accidentally bite a hand – as has occasionally happened.

The north: Bacalar Chico National Park and the Maya sites

A visit to the remote and virtually pristine northern section of Ambergris Caye is a highlight, both for the obvious attractions of the **Bacalar Chico National Park and Marine Reserve** (☎226-2833 for park manager) and for the chance to see a number of **Maya sites** along the coast. Several companies offer trips up here (see box, p.108). On a day-trip from San Pedro you can visit several areas of the reserve and take in a few Maya sites.

On standard trips with local companies, you'll travel by boat through the Boca del Rio and up the west coast, stopping briefly to observe colonies of wading birds roosting on small, uninhabited cayes, such as the bird sanctuary of **Little Guana Caye**. Several species of heron and egret live in the area, and you might even spot the beautiful and much rarer **roseate spoonbill**, though landing on the islands or disturbing the birds is prohibited. To return to town you'll pass through **Bacalar Chico**, the channel partly dug by the Maya about 1500 years ago to create a shorter trading route between their cities in Chetumal Bay and the coast of Yucatán.

The **Maya sites** in the north are sometimes undergoing archeological investigation, and therefore may not be accessible. About two thirds of the way up the west coast of the caye, **Santa Cruz** is a large site with stone mounds, and was once used for the shipment of trade goods in the Postclassic era. Further on is **Chac Balam**, which was an ancient ceremonial and administrative centre, and has burial chamber remains.

The national park and marine reserve

Covering the entire northern tip of Ambergris Caye, **Bacalar Chico National Park and Marine Reserve** is the largest protected area in the northern cayes. Its 42 square miles extend from the reef, across the seagrass beds to the coastal mangroves and the endangered **caye littoral forest**, and over to the salt marsh and lagoon behind. The park and reserve are patrolled by rangers based at the headquarters and **visitor centre** at **San Juan**, on the island's northwest coast, where you register and pay the park fee. Near the ranger station, a 23-foot-high **observation tower** allows views over undisturbed lagoon and forest. Despite all the development to the south, there's a surprising amount of **wildlife** here, including crocodiles, deer and, prowling around the thick forests, several of the wild cats of Belize, including **jaguars**.

Trips inland

Increasingly popular inland **day-trips** are the Maya sites of **Altun Ha** (around US$95; see p.76) and **Lamanai** (starting at US$125; see p.83), as well as river **cave tubing** (starting at US$120) and jungle zip-lining (starting at US$175). A number of the local tour companies, including Tanisha Ecological Tours and Seaduced by Belize (see p.108), run these trips. Prices usually include lunch, soft drinks and beer and entrance fee.

Eating and drinking

San Pedro features some of the best **restaurants** in the country, and an island highlight is, naturally, **seafood**, including excellent lobster. **Prices** are generally higher than elsewhere in Belize, but you can also find plenty of local places offering excellent value. Many hotels also have their own dining room, and in some cases hold **beach barbecues**.

There are a number of supermarkets around the island, including Island Supermarket, on Coconut Drive at the southern end of town. If you're staying further south, try the small but bustling Marina's Market, near Xanadu Resort, which has some of the better prices on the island for basic groceries (including the popular Marie Sharp's sauces which are cheaper here than at a souvenir shop). The island's best wine shop is Wine de Vine, on Coconut Drive near the Island Supermarket.

Restaurants in San Pedro

Blue Lotus. At the *Brahma Blue* resort, a five-minute water taxi ride from the west side of the caye, at Buccaneer St ☎610-2583. If you're up for a splurge – and a short water taxi ride – try this fine Indian-Belizean restaurant, which sits on stilts, surrounded by the lagoon. The cuisine may not quite deserve the price tag – but it's plenty romantic, particularly when lit up at night.

Blue Water Grill At the *Sunbreeze Hotel* ☎226-3347. On a deck overlooking the beach, this is one of the best restaurants in town, serving imaginative seafood – like grilled tilapia with a pineapple sauce – and fresh pasta and pizza, along with fine wines.

Caliente On the beach at *Spindrift Hotel* ☎226-2170. A popular place for locals and tourists alike, with tasty Mexican-Belizean fare, from *ceviche* and conch fritters to fat burritos.

Elvi's Kitchen Pescador Drive, across the street from *Martha's* ☎226-2176. A San Pedro institution, *Elvi's* started out as a "humble burger stand", and now has an expanded menu that includes top-notch seafood, chicken and steaks. Fri is Maya Buffet night. Gentle live music in the evenings. Closed Sun.

Estel's Restaurant On the beach, at the end of Buccaneer St ☎226-2019. A great spot for breakfast, with fresh juices, Johnny cakes, *huevos rancheros*, and the like – all at fair prices.

El Fogón Off Tarpon St, just north of the airstrip. This casual, thatched-roof restaurant is one of the few on the island where traditional Belizean cuisine is cooked over an actual "fire hearth" (in Creole, "faiya haat"). Try any number of local delicacies, including *gibnut* (a type of nocturnal rodent – much better than it sounds) and cow foot soup. Mon–Sat 11.30am–3pm.

Red Ginger In *The Phoenix* ☎226-4623. Well-groomed restaurant with fresh, flavourful tropical cuisine, like *ceviche* soaked in mango juice and braised grouper with black beans. Closed Tues.

The Reef Pescador Drive, between Pelican and Ambergris streets ☎226-4145. Good Belizean food, including fresh seafood, in an atmospheric local restaurant cooled by fans.

Sunset Grill Lagoon-side of the island, just south of the soccer field ☎226-2600. This breezy restaurant overlooks the lagoon, and serves up fresh seafood, including coconut shrimp and almond snapper, as well as meatier offerings, from steak to pork chops. The restaurant is also known for this fun twist: feeding the tarpon at the restaurant pier.

Guests are given sardines (first bucket is free) to hold over the water, as the tarpon leap powerfully to nab their meal.

Wild Mango's On the beach between Tarpon and Esmeralda streets ☎226-2859. Owned by locally renowned chef Amy Knox (who has twice been voted Belize's best chef) and featuring an innovative menu of Caribbean-Latin cuisine – from mid-range to pricey – and good desserts.

Restaurants south of San Pedro

Hidden Treasure South of *Banana Beach Resort*. Enjoy fine Belizean fare, from snapper seasoned with Maya spices and wrapped in a banana leaf to marinated ribs. The breezy, open-sided restaurant appeals with its rustic elegance, featuring mahogany tables and wood-beamed ceilings.

Palmilla Restaurant At *Victoria House* ☎226-2067, ⦿www.victoria-house.com. Excellent fine-dining menu in a romantic, candlelit setting overlooking the hotel's pool. Also serves breakfast and lunch.

Restaurants north of San Pedro

Note that to reach this part of the island, you'll need to travel via water taxi or, when the road is passable, by land taxi.

Beach n' Kitchen About a half mile north of the bridge ☎226-4456. Open for full breakfast and lunch, serving salads, sandwiches, Belizean food and daily specials at reasonable prices.

Capricorn Restaurant At *Capricorn Resort* ☎226-2809. Excellent gourmet food in a beautiful location, with such dishes as French crêpes, crab claws and *filet mignon* with Portobello mushrooms. Great breakfasts, too. Best to book in advance in high season. Closed Wed in low season.

Portofino At *Portofino Resort* ☎220-5096. Excellent restaurant with great views, wines and cocktails and a wide range of seafood, poultry and meats. Call ahead for dinner reservations, which include free pickup from town. Open 7am–4pm & 6–9pm.

Rendezvous On the beach, 3.5 miles north of town ☎226-3426. A delicious and unique fusion of Thai and French cuisines, accompanied by wines from the restaurant's own winery. Try the seafood sour curry, with shrimp, snapper and mussels. Around Bz$10–15 for an entree, but well worth it. Heavenly desserts, too.

▲ Fido's, San Pedro

Bars and nightlife

San Pedro is the tourist capital of Belize and, correspondingly, it also has the liveliest nightlife in the country. You'll find the buzziest bars and nightlife in town, along the beach, including *Fido's* (see below), which is a great place to start out the night. Locals often gather in Central Park in the evening, which fills with food vendors, making this a good spot to grab a cheap snack after a boozy night out.

Crazy Canuck's South of town, at *Exotic Caye Beach Resort*. Fun beach bar with live music on Mon, and plenty of good-natured drinking.
Fido's On the beach, just north of the park. This *palapa*-style beach club draws a healthy mix of locals and visitors to the ample bar and outdoor seating. Live music most nights of the week, and a great spot to meet other travellers. For those on the south side, try *Fido's Sandbar*, 2.5 miles south of town, which has chilled beers and outdoor bowling.
Jaguar Temple Near Central Park. A hopping dance club, where locals and visitors come to groove under pulsating lights.

Palapa Bar and Grill Around a mile north of the bridge, on the north side of the island. Ease into the Caribbean evening over a rum cocktail at this lovely *palapa* bar on the water.
Pier Lounge At the *Spindrift Hotel*. Relaxed bar that gets packed every Wed evening for the caye's famous "chicken drop". They also host karaoke nights.
Playa Lounge On the beach, just south of Buccaneer St. Just as the name says, this is a lounge on the beach, with low couches, throw pillows and a chill-out vibe, along with the usual assortment of tropical cocktails and chilled beer.

Caye Caulker

The beautiful, palm-clad island **CAYE CAULKER** derives its name from a local wild fruit, the *hicaco*, or coco plum. The island lies south of Ambergris Caye and 22 miles northeast of Belize City, and has long had a reputation as a sleepy, laidback fishing village. While it's always a popular spot on the backpacker trail through Belize, it now also attracts families as well as upmarket travellers. The sunny little island offers a relaxing, traffic-free escape, but with plenty of opportunities for comfort and entertainment, and its wide spectrum of hotels runs from basic backpacker dormitories to luxury, poolside lodging.

Until about twenty years ago, tourism existed almost as a sideline to the island's main source of income, **lobster fishing**. Although the lobster catch increased for many years after fishing cooperatives were set up in the 1960s, the deployment of more traps over an ever-wider area led to the rapid depletion of the **spiny lobster**, once so common that it could be scooped onto the beaches with palm fronds. Their numbers remain low today, and in some years the creatures are so scarce that the fishermen call it quits by mid-January, a month before the end of the legal season. Despite this, there are always plenty of lobsters around for the annual **Lobster-Fest**, held in June to celebrate the opening of the season.

Caye Caulker's five-mile length is split into two unequal sections by the "Split", originally a small passage cut by local fishermen that's since grown into a swiftly-moving boat channel, widened by successive tropical storms. The main village, and most hotels, are on the northern end of the south island. The north island has long been mostly uninhabited and remains without electricity, but the caye as a whole is experiencing a build-up on both sides of the Split. Still, most visitors have little reason to venture to the north island, except perhaps for an occasional trip to the land section of the **Caye Caulker Forest and Marine Reserve** (see p.116), whose littoral forest takes up roughly half a square kilometre on the northern tip of the caye. The smaller **Caye Caulker Mini Reserve**, on Back Street just north of the airstrip, makes for an easier trip (see p.117) and has an informative visitor's centre.

Arrival and information

Arriving **by boat**, you'll be dropped off at one of two piers on the eastern edge of the caye, both in the main village. By plane, you'll fly in to the airstrip, about 1.5km south of the centre. From here, you can catch a golf cart taxi into the centre. Getting around the island is a breeze: You'll find three sandy main streets running roughly parallel to the eastern shore: "Front", "Middle" and "Back" streets (officially, these are called Avenida Hicaco, Avenida Langosta and Avenida Mangle, respectively, but the original names are the ones always used). Outside the village, the main streets end and only a single road leads north and south, turning into a winding path beyond the airstrip.

There's no official tourist office in Caye Caulker, but the village council (Ⓦ www .cayecaulkerbelize.net) and the Belize Tourism Industry Association (BTIA; Ⓦ www.gocayecaulker.com) both have excellent **websites**. The **post office** is just south of the centre on Front Street, and good **internet** access is available at Caye Caulker Cyber Café on Front Street. The Atlantic Bank, on Middle Street, has an ATM that takes foreign and local cards, and most businesses accept credit cards and US travellers' cheques; all take US dollars.

Getting to and from Caye Caulker

Most visitors to Caye Caulker arrive by **boat**: the Caye Caulker Water Taxi Association (☏ 226-0992, Ⓦ www.cayecaulkerwatertaxi.com) has departures around nine times daily from the Marine Terminal in Belize City (45min; Bz$15–20 one way). The San Pedro Express Water Taxi (see p.102) also runs daily trips to Caye Caulker. As well, boats travel regularly between Caye Caulker and San Pedro.

You can buy your ticket in advance but they usually don't take reservations. Standby boats are available at busy times. **Flights** (starting at Bz$65–70) to San Pedro stop on request at the Caye Caulker airstrip, one mile south of the village centre. The offices of Maya Island Air and Tropic Air are at the airstrip, and there are agents around the village.

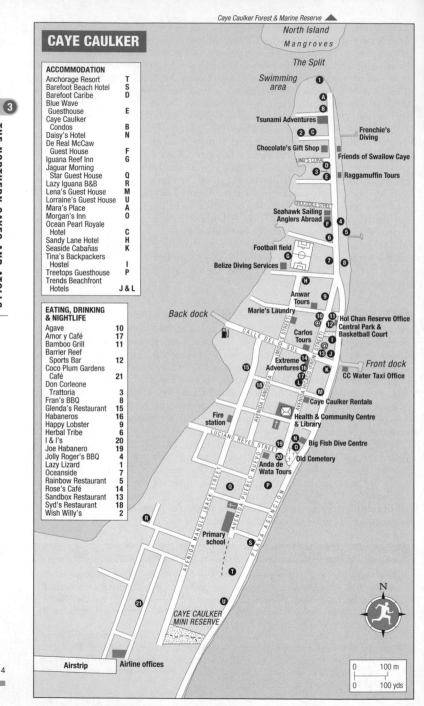

Caye Caulker Forest & Marine Reserve

North Island

Mangroves

The Split

CAYE CAULKER

Swimming area

ACCOMMODATION
Anchorage Resort	T
Barefoot Beach Hotel	S
Barefoot Caribe	D
Blue Wave Guesthouse	E
Caye Caulker Condos	B
Daisy's Hotel	N
De Real McCaw Guest House	F
Iguana Reef Inn	G
Jaguar Morning Star Guest House	Q
Lazy Iguana B&B	R
Lena's Guest House	M
Lorraine's Guest House	U
Mara's Place	A
Morgan's Inn	O
Ocean Pearl Royale Hotel	C
Sandy Lane Hotel	H
Seaside Cabañas	K
Tina's Backpackers Hostel	I
Treetops Guesthouse	P
Trends Beachfront Hotels	J & L

EATING, DRINKING & NIGHTLIFE
Agave	10
Amor y Café	17
Bamboo Grill	11
Barrier Reef Sports Bar	12
Coco Plum Gardens Café	21
Don Corleone Trattoria	3
Fran's BBQ	8
Glenda's Restaurant	15
Habaneros	16
Happy Lobster	9
Herbal Tribe	6
I & I's	20
Joe Habanero	19
Jolly Roger's BBQ	4
Lazy Lizard	1
Oceanside	7
Rainbow Restaurant	5
Rose's Café	14
Sandbox Restaurant	13
Syd's Restaurant	18
Wish Willy's	2

Tsunami Adventures

Frenchie's Diving

Chocolate's Gift Shop

Friends of Swallow Caye

LIND'S CORAL

Raggamuffin Tours

CROCODILE STREET

Seahawk Sailing
Anglers Abroad

Football field

Belize Diving Services

Anwar Tours

Back dock

Marie's Laundry

Hol Chan Reserve Office

Central Park & Basketball Court

Carlos Tours

CALLE DEL SOL

Extreme Adventures

Front dock

CC Water Taxi Office

Caye Caulker Rentals

Fire station

LUCIANO REYES STREET

Health & Community Centre & Library

Big Fish Dive Centre

Anda de Wata Tours

Old Cemetery

AVENIDA MANGLE (BACK STREET)

AVENIDA PUEBLO NUEVO

AVENIDA LANGOSTA

AVENIDA HICACO (FRONT STREET)

PLAYA ASUNCION

Primary school

CAYE CAULKER MINI RESERVE

N

Airstrip | Airline offices

| 0 | 100 m |
| 0 | 100 yds |

One thing to be aware of in Caye Caulker is the **tap water**, which smells sulphurous at times. This may be the result of natural chemicals in the groundwater, but since most businesses and residences use septic tanks for waste disposal, it could be the result of effluent seeping into the water table. A clean water system has been in the planning stages for quite some time, but until it actually materializes, tap water on the caye should be regarded as **unfit to drink**. Some hotels provide drinking water, or you can buy bottled water.

Though there is a near-constant sea breeze, when this drops the air gets very sticky, and **sandflies and mosquitoes** can be unbearably irritating, making a good insect repellent essential.

Accommodation

Caye Caulker has an abundance of simply furnished, inexpensive shared-bath rooms in attractive **clapboard hotels**, plus plenty of more comfortable options with private bathrooms (and many with a/c) – but to arrive at Christmas or New Year without a **reservation** could leave you stranded. Even the furthest **hotels** are no more than fifteen to twenty minutes' walk from the Front Dock. Almost everywhere has hot water and many accept credit cards. For excellent **house rentals**, check at Caye Caulker Rentals, south of the Front Dock (☎226-0029, ⓦwww .cayecaulkerrentals.com). You can also rent houses and cabañas from their owners; ask around town or look for signs.

North of the Front Dock

Barefoot Caribe Just past *Blue Wave* ☎226-0161. Run by a friendly family, this amiable spot offers a wide range of comfortable rooms with a/c and private bath. They also run *Sobre las Olas* across the street, where you can fill up on decent breakfasts and seafood. ❻

Blue Wave Guesthouse Toward the north end of Front St ☎206-0114, ⓔbluewave @btl.net. Pleasant family-run place, just paces from the shoreline, with well-maintained comfortable a/c rooms with showers and cable TV, with both shared and private bath. ❹

Caye Caulker Condos One block from the Split ☎226-0072. Excellent-quality apartments with full kitchens, wi-fi, a safe for valuables, a/c and large showers decorated with river stones. Take a dip in the swimming pool, borrow one of the complimentary bicycles or drink in the lovely sea views from the large rooftop *palapa*. ❽

De Real Macaw Guest House Front St, south of the Split ☎226-0459, ⓦwww.derealmacaw.biz. Comfortable, good-value rooms and thatched cabañas facing the sea. Variety of accommodation, including beachfront rooms with a/c, cabañas with ceiling fan and condo with hardwood floors, kitchen and TV. Doubles ❹, condo ❾

Iguana Reef Inn At the back (west side) of the caye, across the football field ☎226-0213, ⓦwww.iguanareefinn.com. One of the more luxurious hotels on the island, with well-furnished suites with tiled floors, local artwork, a/c and

ceiling fans, queen-sized beds – and great sunset views. They rent kayaks, and also have a pool and complimentary continental breakfasts. ❽

Mara's Place Near the Split ☎206-0056. Simple, family-run, good-value wooden cabins facing the sea, with private bath, TV and porch – and it's one of the closest spots to the Split, good for splashing around in the water (and getting cocktails at the *Lazy Lizard*). ❹

Ocean Pearl Royale Hotel Toward the back of the island, two blocks from the Split ☎226-0074, ⓔoceanpearl@btl.net. Simple but comfy, well-tended rooms, some with a/c. The owners can offer plenty of local information and there's complimentary coffee in the lobby. ❺

Sandy Lane Hotel On Middle St, one block north of Atlantic Bank ☎226-0117. Small, quiet and clean, with both shared-bath rooms and cabañas with private bath. ❸

Tina's Backpacker's Hostel Eighty yards along the beach from the Front Dock ☎206-0019, ⓔtinasbackpackershostel@yahoo.com. A range of accommodation, including a relaxing beach house with dorm beds (Bz$22 per person; shared bathroom), private rooms and suite apartments with cable TV and a/c. You can cook in the communal kitchen, and outside is a pretty garden with hammocks and a dock for sunbathing. ❸

Trends Beachfront Hotel On the beach, north of the Front Dock ☎226-0094, ⓦwww.trendsbze.com. Large rooms in a pastel-painted wooden building with comfortable beds, private baths and tiled floors.

There's a deck with hammocks outside, and they also offer fully furnished apartments with decent weekly and monthly rates. ❸

South of the Front Dock

Note that some of the accommodation on the southern part of the caye can be up to a twenty-minute walk from town, which can be a drag at night (as there are minimal street lights). Consult the map (see p.114) to confirm, and if you are staying at one of the further places, inquire about the availability of bicycles, which are helpful for zipping to town.

Anchorage Resort South of the centre, past the school, near the airstrip ☎ 226-0304. Clean, tiled rooms with comfortable beds, private bath, fridge, cable TV and balconies overlooking the sea in a three-storey concrete building in palm-shaded grounds. Rates for top-floor rooms are higher, but include great views. ❼

Barefoot Beach Hotel On the beach, just south of the school ☎ 226-0205, ⓦ www.barefootbeach belize.com. Comfortable, colourful rooms with private bath, a/c and small fridge in a concrete house on the beach. There are also two roomy, wooden cottages. ❼

Daisy's Hotel On Front St ☎ 206-0150. Set just back from the sea, these simple but well-tended budget rooms with shared showers, are run by a friendly family. ❸

Jaguar Morning Star Guest House Across from the school ☎ 226-0347, ⓦ jaguarmorningstar.com. Two rooms on the third floor feature a deck and great view. Also, there's an a/c cabin with a shady porch and hammock in a leafy garden setting; all rooms have private shower, fridge and coffeemaker. A quiet, secure, relaxing place to stay. ❹

Lazy Iguana Bed & Breakfast At the back of the island, just north of the airstrip ☎ 226-0350, ⓦ www.lazyiguana.net. Lovely B&B, with four comfortable, well-maintained a/c rooms, each with

a private bathroom. The top floor has a thatched deck with hammocks to enjoy 360-degree views over the sea and the lagoon. Wake up to a breakfast of fresh fruit, baked goods and brewed coffee. Friendly owners Mo and Irene Miller are great sources of island information. ❼

Lena's Guest House On the beachfront ☎ 226-0106, ⓔ lenas@btl.net. Budget rooms in a wooden building by the water, some with private bath. Good sea views from the shady porch at the front. ❹

Lorraine's Guest House On the beach beyond *Anchorage Resort* ☎ 206-0162. A good bargain on the beach. Simple but comfortable wooden cabins with private hot-water showers run by an amiable family. ❹

Morgan's Inn Opposite Galería Hicaco, where you enquire ☎ 226-0178, ⓔ siwaban@gmail.com. Quiet, roomy cabins, set just back from the beach. Perfect for long stays and fine for just a night or two. The Galería features Belizean artwork, and the owner can take you on birdwatching and reef tours. Kayaks and windsurfers for rent. ❹

Seaside Cabañas Just steps south of the Front Dock ☎ 226-0498, ⓦ www.seasidecabanas.com. Well-designed and furnished rooms and thatched cabañas, all with a/c, fridge, cable TV, and veranda with hammocks. Beautifully decorated both inside and out in rich colours, and arranged around a pool. There's also a thatched rooftop bar. No children under 11. ❽

Treetops Guesthouse On the beachfront, past the cemetery ☎ 226-0240, ⓦ www.treetopsbelize .com. One of the better hotels on the island, right near the water. Bright, clean and comfort-able ground-floor rooms with fridge, cable TV and ceiling fans, and lovely rooftop a/c suites with fantastic views, all set in a small, peaceful garden. Deservedly popular, so booking ahead is advised. Rooms ❺, suites ❼

Exploring the caye and reef

The **Barrier Reef** lies only about a mile from the shore, and the white foam of the reef crest is always visible to the east. The entire length of the reef off Caye Caulker was declared a **marine reserve** in 1998, and visiting it (Bz$10) is an experience not to be missed. You'll swim along **coral canyons**, surrounded by an astonishing range of fish, with perhaps a harmless nurse shark or two.

At the island's northern tip is the **Caye Caulker Forest and Marine Reserve**, home to such trees as red, white and black mangroves, gumbo limbo and poison-wood. This area was a coconut plantation before Hurricane Hattie hit in 1961, but has not been in active use since, so the native littoral forest has had nearly fifty years to regenerate. The mangrove shallows support fish nurseries and small species called "sardines" by fishermen, who use them as bait to catch snapper. Sponges, anemones and other colourful sea creatures grow on the mangrove roots. **American saltwater**

▲ Wooden boat, Caye Caulker

crocodiles are sometimes seen here, but you're more likely to find them in the wild on the Turneffe Islands (see p.121) or in the more remote coastal areas. Other native inhabitants of the littoral forest include **boa constrictors**, scaly-tailed iguanas (locally called "wish willies"), geckos and five species of land crab.

A small section of the original littoral forest has been preserved closer to town in the **Caye Caulker Mini Reserve**, just north of the airstrip and approached from the beach or Back Street (always open; free, but donations appreciated). The visitor's centre (usually 8am–noon) provides good information about the species you can see here. Walking the cleared paths will give you some idea of the variety and density of jungle that can grow on bare sand and coral rubble.

Swimming, snorkelling and diving

Caye Caulker has only a small beach, as the proximity of the reef stops sand building up on the foreshore, and the water's too shallow for true **swimming**, which is done from the end of piers or at the Split at the north end of the village. Swimming out to the reef is discouraged, since it requires crossing a busy boat lane where fatal accidents have occurred in the past, as captains do not expect swimmers.

Your most rewarding **snorkelling** experiences are likely to be on an organized tour, which can educate you on what you're seeing. Tours are easily arranged and cost around Bz$60–150 per person, depending on duration and location – generally a half or full day and stopping at a number of sites. Some trips visit Hol Chan Marine Reserve and Shark-Ray Alley (see p.109), but these tend to be busier and more expensive, and you'll be just as happy in either Caye Caulker's own marine reserve or the outer atolls, Turneffe in particular (p.121) – keep an eye out for the **dolphins** that often accompany boats on the way. Rental of decent equipment is usually included in the cost of your tour.

Snorkel, dive and watersports operators

You'll find many snorkel and dive shops on Caye Caulker, including those listed below. When looking around, note that some of the cheaper tours may limit your time in the water, use inexperienced guides or overload boats.

Anda De Wata Tours On Luciano Reyes St ☏601-6757, ⒲aguallos.com/andade wata. Offers a variety of snorkelling and inland tours – their fun slogan is "Cos it's Hot Anda de Wata".

Anwar Snorkel Tours Two blocks north of the Front Dock ☏226-0327, ⒲www.anwar tours.page.tl. One of the oldest tour companies, offering snorkelling tours and inland trips to Altun Ha, Lamanai and river cave tubing.

Belize Diving Services At the far side of the football field ☏226-0143, ⒲www.belize divingservices.net. Offers a variety of well-run diving services.

Big Fish Dive Center Front St, south of the Front Dock ☏226-0450, ⒲www.bigfish divecenter.com. Features a range of guided dives.

Carlos Tours Near the *Sandbox Restaurant* ☏600-1654, ⒠carlosayala@gmail.com. Tours, led by the knowledgeable, conscientious guide Carlos Ayala, place an emphasis on conservation and education.

Chocolate's Tours At Chocolate's Gift Shop ☏226-0151, ⒠chocolateseashore@gmail .com. Lionel "Chocolate" Heredia is Caye Caulker's longest-serving tour guide, and was instrumental in securing Sanctuary status for Swallow Caye.

Frenchie's Towards the northern end of the village ☏226-0234, ⒲www.frenchies divingbelize.com. This very popular company runs a wide range of dive tours, including overnight trips to the Blue Hole (book at least a few weeks in advance).

Ras Creek Between the Front Dock and the Split. Ras runs laidback trips in his little boat *Heritage* (Bz$25), taking you to the reef right in front of the caye. Plenty of rum punch is provided, and guests help prepare lunch, arriving back as the sun is setting.

Tsunami Adventures Near the Split ☏226-0462, ⒲www.tsunamiadventures.com. A wide variety of snorkelling and diving trips, they can also book flights and tours throughout Belize.

Xtreme Adventures Front St, just north of the Front Dock ☏206 0065 or 206 0225, ⒠xadventures@hotmail.com. Dive trips to Hol Chan and Blue Hole. This is also where you can buy tickets for the San Pedro Express Water Taxi.

Other popular snorkelling destinations include Goff's Caye, English Caye and Sergeant's Caye, tiny specks of sand and coral with a few palm trees. A trip to any of these may be combined with a stop at Swallow Caye Wildlife Sanctuary (see p.121), a mangrove caye with seagrass beds near Belize City, where you can view (but not swim with) **manatees**.

All dive shops (see box opposite) on the caye offer great reef diving and visits to coral gardens (two tanks starting at US$65, usually including equipment), as well as **night dives**. A day-trip to **Lighthouse Reef** and the **Blue Hole** is an unforgettable experience, although some people are disappointed by the lack of marine life in the depths. After the unique, slightly spooky splendour of diving over 115ft into the hole, many groups visit the fantastic 87yd wall off Half Moon Caye. A brief stop on the island itself lets you observe red-footed boobies and huge hermit crabs before climbing back in the boat for the Long Caye wall. The **Turneffe Islands** have world-class dive sites, too – some believe the best diving in Belize. North Turneffe and Turneffe Elbow are the most popular trips from Caye Caulker. Several dive shops offer PADI **instruction** (around US$325) for an Open Water or Advanced Open Water course.

Sailing, fishing and other day-trips

A relaxing way to enjoy the sea and the reef is to spend the better part of a day on one of the caye's **sailing trips**, costing around Bz$65–90 and usually including a couple of snorkelling stops and lunch before returning in the evening. **Sunset cruises** are also on offer. Raggamuffin Tours, near the north end of Front Street (☎226-0348, ⓦwww.sailingadventuresbelize.com) operates many trips, including **camping trips** (Bz$600) starting in Caye Caulker and ending in Placencia (see p.206). Experienced paddlers can **rent a kayak** for around Bz$23–40, or ask at Galería Hicaco (☎226-0178), which also offers windsurfers. A **fishing trip** is a common outing from the caye, and Anglers Abroad, near the Split (☎226-0303, ⓦwww.anglersabroad.com) features fishing trips (including overnight) and has fly-fishing equipment for rent. You can also simply ask around the village and you'll be pointed in the direction of a guide. Informative **birdwatching tours**, led by local naturalists, can be arranged at Galería Hicaco (☎226-0178, Ⓔsiwaban@gmail.com).

Eating, drinking and entertainment

Reasonable prices and local cuisine characterize many of the island's **restaurants**, a lot of which are sprinkled along Front Street. Aim to eat in the early-to-mid-evening, as many places close by 9–10pm. **Lobster** (in season) is served in every dish imaginable, from curry to quesadillas; other **seafood** is also generally well priced. You can buy groceries at several **shops and supermarkets** around the village.

Restaurants north of the Front Dock

Agave Just north of the dock ☎226-0403. The draw here is the spacious, raised dining deck, offering a breezy perch to enjoy the Caribbean-Mexican fusion fare, from fresh lobster to grilled snapper. Also on the menu are tasty – and potent – cocktails, thanks to the owner, who is an accomplished bartender.
Bamboo Grill Beachfront place serving fresh, grilled seafood for lunch and dinners. Late bar.
Don Corleone Trattoria ☎226-0025. High-end, comfortable Italian restaurant with pastas, gnocchi and salads.

Fran's BBQ. North of the Front Dock, on the beach. Look for this green-painted beach grill for excellent lobster and other fresh seafood, which you can enjoy at picnic tables.
Happy Lobster North of the centre. Inexpensive restaurant ladling out rice and beans, seafood and local dishes, as well as hearty breakfasts. One of the better values on the caye. Also has lodging in clean and pleasant rooms upstairs.
Jolly Roger's Barbecue On the beach, opposite *DeReal Macaw*. The jolly Roger Martinez grills up lobster and fish at great prices. The generous portions are served on picnic tables.

Rainbow Restaurant ☎226-0281. Bask in sea breezes at this popular restaurant over the water. Try lobster in coconut sauce – or the nicely priced lobster quesadilla – washed down with a fresh watermelon juice or a chilled Belikin beer.

Sandbox Restaurant Immediately north of the dock ☎226-0200. Offering a variety of good meals, including fresh seafood, and excellent breakfasts. A favourite evening hangout among expats, especially for its tropical cocktails.

Wish Willy's At the north end of the island ☎660-7194. A true Caye Caulker experience: Friendly, relaxed restaurant in a ramshackle building at the back of the island, where Belizean chef Maurice Moore creates some of the most delicious seafood dishes in the country.

Restaurants south of the Front Dock

Amor y Café Just south of the centre. Greet the morning on the breezy deck of this cosy spot, which serves tasty breakfasts – fresh baked goods, sandwiches, fruit smoothies and *café*, of course.

Coco Plum Gardens Café South of the centre, just north of the airstrip ☎226-0226. "Wholefood" café serving great breakfasts –

think multigrain pancakes, crêpes with melted gouda cheese and home-made granola – as well as salads and desserts. The lush garden setting also features an art gallery and spa, with a variety of luxurious massages; it's well worth the walk. Also has delicious Belizean fruit jams and sells books, artwork and herbal remedies. Open 9am–4pm; closed Sun.

Glenda's Restaurant At the back of the island, south of the Back Dock ☎226-0148. Justly famous for its delicious cinnamon rolls and fresh orange juice. Closed Sun.

Habaneros Just south of the Front Dock ☎226-0487. The island's top restaurant, serving creative gourmet international meals, with fine wine and slick bar service; it's often busy, so call for reservations. Sometimes closed Thurs. They also run *Joe Habaneros*, further south on Front St, an open-air casual bar and eatery with pizza, nachos and other finger foods, as well as rum cocktails.

Rose's Café On Calle del Sol ☎206-0085. Good for breakfasts, Belizean food and takeout pizza.

Syd's Restaurant On Middle St, just south of the bank ☎206-0294. Popular for its well-priced local food, including chicken and rice and beans. Closed Sun.

Bars and nightlife

Caye Caulker's social scene revolves around its various bars and restaurants, particularly along Front Street. The best place to ease into the evening is *Lazy Lizard*, which has an outdoor bar at the Split. The three-storey *I & I's*, with reggae tunes, chilled beers and swing chairs, offers a good taste of island nightlife. Other popular bars are the *Oceanside*, sometimes featuring live music, and the relaxed *Herbal Tribe*, both on Front Street. *Barrier Reef Sports Bar* has plenty of TVs to keep the sports fans happy.

Other northern cayes and atolls

Although Caye Caulker and San Pedro are the only villages anywhere on the reef, there are several **other islands** that you can visit and even stay on. Some of these are within day-trip distance of the main northern cayes or Belize City, and often contain a few superbly isolated, package-deal hotels.

Caye Chapel

Immediately south of Caye Caulker, **Caye Chapel** (Ⓦ www.cayechapel.com) is a privately-owned corporate retreat with an airstrip, luxury hotel, marina and eighteen-hole **golf course**. The island is open to visitors who want to visit for the day to play golf (Bz$300), which includes golf club rental and use of golf carts. On a historical note, it was on Caye Chapel that the defeated Spanish fleet paused for a few days after the **Battle of St George's Caye** in 1798. According to legend, some of their dead are buried here.

Swallow Caye Wildlife Sanctuary

Just a ten-minute boat ride from Belize City (forty from Caye Caulker), the Drowned Cayes (which include Swallow Caye) form the **Swallow Caye Wildlife Sanctuary** (Bz$10 entry fee), a secure refuge for the area's healthy population of **West Indian manatees**. Belize has one of the largest surviving populations of these gentle giants, which congregate here to feed on the abundant turtle-grass beds, their primary food source, and use the deeper areas near Swallow Caye as resting places. The sanctuary, covering fourteen square miles sustains an array of other marine life including bottlenose dolphins, American crocodiles and the upside-down jellyfish. It's co-managed by the Friends of Swallow Caye (℡226-0151, ⓦwww .swallowcayemanatees.org) and the Ministry of Natural Resources, and **day-trips** are available, mainly departing from Caye Caulker. On one of these ventures, the skipper will turn off the motor as you near, quietly pushing the boat towards the manatees in order not to disturb them.

St George's Caye

Tiny **St George's Caye**, around nine miles from Belize City, was the capital of the Baymen in the seventeenth and eighteenth centuries, and still manages to exude an air of colonial grandeur; its beautifully restored houses face east to catch the breeze and their lush, green lawns are enclosed by white picket fences. Eighteenth-century cannons are still mounted in front of some of the finer houses, and for another glimpse into the past you could head to the small graveyard of the early settlers on the southern tip of the island.

Though there's not much for the casual visitor, some fishing and snorkelling trips from other islands call here for lunch. Should you choose to stay, a lovely option is *St George's Lodge* (℡220-4444, ⓦwww.gooddiving.com; ➒), an all-inclusive **dive resort** comprised of a main lodge and six luxury, wood-and-thatch cottages with private verandas and a beautiful dining room. The superb lodge was Belize's first dedicated diving resort.

The Turneffe Islands

Though shown on some maps as one large island, the virtually uninhabited and numerous **Turneffe Islands** are part of Belize's largest atoll, an oval archipelago rising from the seabed and enclosed by a beautiful coral reef. Situated 25 miles from Belize City, they are primarily low-lying mangrove islands – some quite large – and sandbanks around a shallow lagoon. Thanks to relatively minimal human development, the islands make up one of the most biologically diverse areas of the Caribbean. **Fishing** the shallow flats here, typically for bonefish and permit, is world-class, with most of the sport-fishing on a catch-and-release basis. The **diving** and **snorkelling** is also sublime.

The resorts here are generally very pricey, and all-inclusive, including transport from Belize City (and usually from the international airport), all meals and whatever diving and/or fishing package is arranged; all the resorts have electricity and most have air-conditioning. Most guests will be fishing or diving much of the time, but there are always hammocks to relax in and the snorkelling right offshore is superb. Although staying out here has a heavenly, even dreamlike quality, **sandflies** and **mosquitoes** can bring you back to earth with a vengeance – so pack repellent.

The most northerly of the Turneffe resorts is *Turneffe Flats* (in US ℡1-888/512-8812, ⓦwww.tflats.com), offering diving packages at around US$2300 for a week, and fishing packages for US$3600 a week. On **Blackbird Caye**, halfway down the eastern side of the archipelago, *Blackbird Caye Resort* (in US ℡1-800/326-1724, ⓦwww.blackbirdresort.com) has luxury wood-and-thatch cabañas and a beautiful thatched dining room. A week's high-season package, including transfers, all meals, and diving/snorkelling starts at US$2050; three- to four-night packages are also available.

At the southern tip of the archipelago, **Caye Bokel** boasts *Turneffe Island Resort* (in the US ☎1-800/874-0118, ⊛www.turnefferesort.com), with luxurious, air-conditioned cabins on a twelve-acre private island. Catering to upmarket fishing and diving groups, packages cost US$1590–3000 per person for a week, depending on the activity. Half-weeks are also available.

If you'd prefer to visit the Turneffe Islands on a **day-trip**, you can do so easily from San Pedro or Caye Caulker; see the boxes on p.108 & p.118, respectively.

Lighthouse Reef, the Blue Hole and Half Moon Caye

About fifty miles east of Belize City is Belize's outermost atoll, **Lighthouse Reef**, made famous by Jacques Cousteau, who visited in the 1970s. The two main attractions here are the Blue Hole, which drew Cousteau's attention (he cleared the passage through the reef), and Half Moon Caye Natural Monument (Bz$80 entrance for both). The **Blue Hole**, now also protected as a Natural Monument, is technically a "karst-eroded sinkhole", a shaft about 984ft in diameter and 442ft deep that drops through the bottom of the lagoon and opens out into a complex network of **caves and crevices**, complete with stalactites and stalagmites. It was formed over a million years ago when Lighthouse Reef was a sizeable island – or even part of the mainland. Investigations have shown that caves underlie the entire reef, and that the sea has simply punctured the cavern roof at the site of the Blue Hole. Its great depth gives it a peculiar deep-blue colour, and even swimming across it is disorienting as there's no sense of anything beneath you. Unsurprisingly, the Blue Hole and Lighthouse Reef are major magnets for **divers**, offering incredible walls and drop-offs, bright corals and tropical fish, although seeing it from the air is arguably the best way to appreciate it.

The **Half Moon Caye Natural Monument**, the first marine conservation area in Belize, was declared a national park in 1982. Its lighthouse was built in 1820 and has not always been effective: several wrecks, including the *Ermlund*, which ran aground in 1971, testify to the dangers of the reef. The medium-sized caye is divided into two distinct ecosystems: in the west, guano from thousands of seabirds fertilizes the soil, allowing the growth of dense vegetation, while the eastern half has mostly coconut palms growing in the sand. A total of 98 bird species have been recorded here, including frigate birds, ospreys, mangrove warblers, white-crowned pigeons and – most important of all – a resident population of four thousand **red-footed boobies**, one of only two nesting colonies in the Caribbean.

There's no accommodation on the caye, but **camping** is sometimes allowed with the permission of the Belize Audubon Society (☎223-5004, ⊛www.belizeaudubon .org), which manages the reserve; many of the overnight diving or snorkelling expeditions camp here, and are often your best bet, since independent campers are discouraged. Visitors must register with the rangers prior to arrival and pay the Bz$20 **entrance fee**; the **visitor centre** will help you understand the caye's ecology.

Travel details

For details of **flights** and **boats** to the cayes from Belize City and between the cayes themselves, see the boxes on p.102 & p.113.

Cayo and the west

CHAPTER 4

Highlights

✳ **Actun Tunichil Muknal** Hike across rivers and through jungle before descending into an astonishing cave that was, for the Maya, the underworld and abode of the Lords of Death. See p.127

✳ **River tubing and mountain adventures at Caves Branch** Experience one of a kind river adventures at this wonderful jungle lodge. See p.130

✳ **Green Hills Butterfly Ranch and Botanical Collections** Relax surrounded by clouds of colourful butterflies in this fascinating and informative botanical garden. See p.136

✳ **Mountain Pine Ridge Forest Reserve** Escape the jungle's humidity to the cooler air of the pine forest and its many clear streams and waterfalls. See p.138

✳ **Caracol** The greatest Maya city in Belize, where you can ascend Caana, a 1200-year-old palace and temple complex that's still one of the tallest buildings in the country. See p.142

✳ **San Ignacio** Stay in a comfortable, affordable hotel and choose from dozens of adventure trips in this charming town, still full of colonial buildings. See p.145

✳ **The Macal River** Observe iguanas in the trees and watch the scenery slide by as you take a tranquil float along this gentle, jungle river. See p.155

▲ Caracol

Cayo and the west

eading along the fast **Western Highway** from Belize City to the Guatemalan border, eighty miles away, you trade the heat and humidity of
the low-lying city for a range of varied landscapes, from sometimes
swampy savannah, scattered with palmetto scrub and low pines, to river
valleys, rich pastures and citrus groves, and finally to the rolling hills with dense
tropical forest beyond. Belmopan, established in 1970, is still the smallest national
capital city in the world, and though not holding particular interest in itself, is
surrounded by phenomenal natural sights and adventure options; among them
Guanacaste National Park, and the Blue Hole National Park, with its numerous
caves and hiking possibilities.

West of Belmopan, following the Belize River valley, the road skirts the lush
foothills of the Maya Mountains, a beautiful area with clear air and astonish-
ingly fertile land. You're now nearing the heart of **Cayo District**, the largest
of Belize's six districts and arguably the most beautiful. It's certainly one of the
greenest: most of southern and western Cayo, including the entire mountain
range, is under official protection as part of a vast network of national parks,
wildlife sanctuaries and forest and archeological reserves stretching from
the Caribbean coast to the Guatemalan border. The **Mountain Pine Ridge
Forest Reserve**, to the south of the highway, is a pleasantly cool region of hills,
pine woods and waterfalls, boasting some of the finest lodge accommodation
in the country.

The ideal base for exploring the forests, rivers and ruins of western Belize is the
busy main town of **San Ignacio**, on the Macal River just nine miles from the
Guatemalan border. A canoe or kayak trip through the **Macal River valley**, as
the river tumbles from the Maya Mountains into the calmer waters of the tree-
lined Macal gorge, is a highlight of any visit to Cayo, and cabins to suit all budgets
line the riverbanks. South of San Ignacio, deep in the jungle of the Vaca Plateau,
lies **Caracol**, the largest Maya site in Belize and a current focus of archeological
research and restoration; many of its **caves** hold more astonishing Maya treasures
for adventurous visitors.

Between San Ignacio and the Guatemalan border, the road climbs past the
hilltop ruin of **Cahal Pech**, then descends along the valley of the **Mopan
River**, passing several delightful riverside lodges. Belize's westernmost Maya
site, **El Pilar**, eleven miles northwest of San Ignacio, actually extends into
Guatemala, and is the first international archeological reserve anywhere in
the Maya region. A couple of miles before the border itself, at the village of
San José Succotz, an ancient ferry crosses the Mopan River to bring visitors
to **Xunantunich**, a hilltop Maya site whose highest structures offer stunning
views into Guatemala's department of Petén.

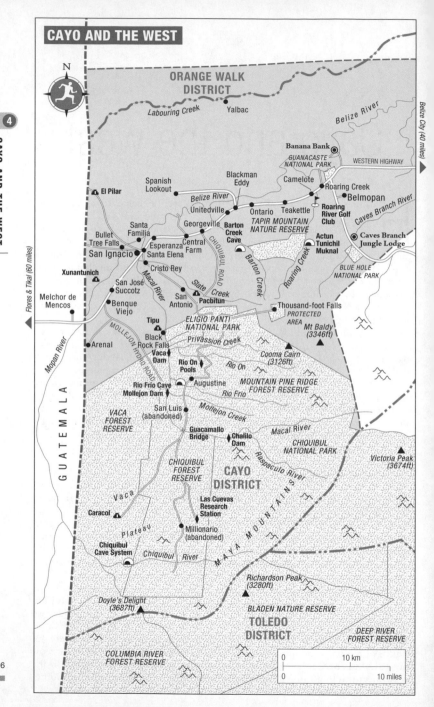

Belmopan and the Mountain Pine Ridge

Served by frequent buses between Belize City and San Ignacio, the Western Highway provides easy access to nearby sights, including tiny **Guanacaste National Park**, which offers a fascinating introduction to the country's vast network of national parks and reserves, and the **Roaring River Golf Club**, where you can swing clubs in an extraordinary eco-friendly setting. The **Hummingbird Highway** leads south to Belize's diminutive capital **Belmopan** and on to the **Blue Hole National Park**, while nearby **Caves Branch Jungle Lodge** is home to Belize's original cave-tubing outfit. West of Belmopan the scenery becomes more rugged, with thickly forested ridges always in view to the south. Although the strictly protected **Tapir Mountain Nature Reserve** here is not open to casual visitors, you can get a taste of what it holds by visiting **Actun Tunichil Muknal**, one of the most extraordinary **caves** in the country. The Western Highway stays close to the valley of the Belize River, crossing numerous tributary creeks and passing through a series of villages: Roaring Creek, Camelote, Teakettle, Ontario, Unitedville and Esperanza. There's been something of an accommodation boom along this route, with a couple of long-established, cottage-style **lodges** now joined by several newer enterprises. With your own vehicle, you might choose to abandon this route by turning south at Georgeville, sixteen miles from the Belmopan junction, and taking the **Chiquibul Road** to the **Mountain Pine Ridge Forest Reserve** and the ruins of **Caracol**. Along this unpaved road are several places to stay, as well as Belize's best **butterfly exhibit** and **horseback riding**.

Belmopan and around

Heading along the Western Highway from Belize City, you know you're arriving in Belmopan when you pass **Art Box** (W www.artboxbz.com; Mon–Sat 8am–6pm), a giant arts and crafts shop standing alone on the southern side of the road. Alongside a collection of wonderful Belizean paintings, jewellery, pottery, music, books, T-shirts and the like, there is also a marvellous **café** here, serving espresso coffees and tropical fruit ice cream.

Just beyond, a paved branch road leads a mile south to Belize's tiny capital, **BELMOPAN**, before becoming the Hummingbird Highway to the coast at Dangriga. For most people, the town is no more than a pause in the bus ride to or from San Ignacio or the south – though it's also the location of most foreign embassies and government departments. Belmopan was founded in 1970 in a Brasília-style bid to focus development on the interior, nearly a decade after Hurricane Hattie swept much of Belize City into the sea. The name combines the words "Belize" and "Mopan", the language spoken by the Maya of Cayo. The layout of government buildings is modelled on a Maya city; the National Assembly even incorporates a version of the traditional roof comb, a decorative stonework and stucco crest. Though these grey and ageing concrete buildings won their British architect an award, they now present a dismal facade, out of line with their importance. Belmopan originally symbolized the dawn of the new era of independence: the population was planned at five thousand with an expected increase to thirty thousand, but few Belizeans other than government

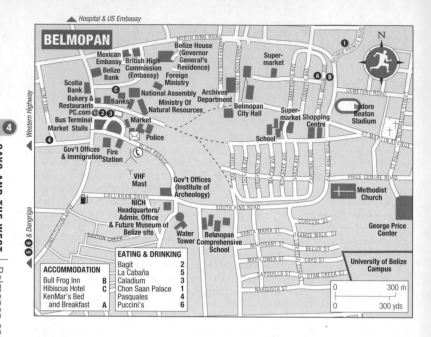

BELMOPAN

Mexican Embassy
British High Commission (Embassy)
Belize House (Governor General's Residence)
Foreign Ministry
Belize Bank
Scotia Bank
Bakery & Restaurants
PC.com @
Bus Terminal
Market Stalls
Gov't Offices & immigration
Fire Station
Banks
National Assembly
Ministry Of Natural Resources
Market
Police
VHF Mast
Gov't Offices (Institute of Archeology)
NICH Headquarters/ Admin. Office & Future Museum of Belize site
Water Tower
Belmopan Comprehensive School
Archives Department
Belmopan City Hall
Super-market
Super-market Shopping Centre
School
Supermarket
Isidoro Beaton Stadium
Methodist Church
George Price Center
University of Belize Campus

ACCOMMODATION
Bull Frog Inn — B
Hibiscus Hotel — C
KenMar's Bed and Breakfast — A

EATING & DRINKING
Bagit — 2
La Cabaña — 5
Caladium — 3
Chon Saan Palace — 1
Pasquales — 4
Puccini's — 6

0 — 300 m
0 — 300 yds

officials (who had no option) have moved here. With a present population of sixteen thousand, Belmopan is still the smallest capital city in the world.

Though there's no particular reason to stay, if you have some time here visit the **George Price Centre** (Mon–Fri 9am–6pm; free; ☎822-1054, ⓦwww.gpcbelize .com), on the east side of the city. Here you will find the first Belizean flag, photos of damage caused by Hurricane Hattie, and an excellent display in tribute to the first Prime Minister and the architect of Belize's independence. Exhibits by local artists and concerts are scheduled regularly, and well-informed Curator Elsie Alpuche is a great source of information. On the south side of town, next to the water tower, is the National Institute of Culture and History (NICH) with the Institute of Archeology (☎822-3302) on the second floor. The **Archives Department**, 26–28 Unity Blvd (Mon–Fri 8am–5pm; free; ☎822-2248, ⓦwww.belizearchives.gov.bz), welcomes visitors to its air-conditioned reading room, where photographs, documents, newspapers and sound archives provide fascinating glimpses of old Belize.

Practicalities

Buses from Belize City to San Ignacio, Benque Viejo, Dangriga and Punta Gorda all pass through the main bus terminal in Belmopan, and there's at least one service every thirty minutes east and west – the last bus from Belmopan to Belize City leaves at 7pm, to San Ignacio at 10pm. Heading south, the first bus is at 6.30am, leaving roughly hourly until 7pm. Not all buses heading east or south stop at every town along the way, so be sure to check if your destination is on the itinerary.

The best **tour guide** in the area is Marcos Cucul of ☈**Maya Guide Adventures** (☎670-3116, ⓦwww.mayaguide.bz, ⒺMarcos@mayaguide.bz); one-of-a-kind tours include single- or multiple-day jungle treks, Maya ruins, trips to Chiquibul Caves – which contain the largest cave in the Americas – and kayaking expeditions. Overnight camping is usually undertaken in Hennessy hammocks with Belizean food cooked at camp, while a porter carries all equipment.

Hotels in Belmopan cater to the needs and expense accounts of diplomats; though nearby lodges and San Ignacio – just an hour away – have much more interesting and affordable accommodation. If you do have to stay here, best in town is the *Bull Frog Inn*, 25 Half Moon Ave (☏822-2111, ✉bullfrog@btl .net; ❻), which has a good restaurant and **bar** frequented by politicians. Just behind, *KenMar's Bed and Breakfast*, 22–24 Half Moon Ave (☏822-0118, ⓦwww .kenmar.bz; ❹–❺), offers homely air-conditioned rooms and a tropical breakfast, and *Hibiscus Hotel* off Constitution Drive (☏822-1418, ✉hibiscus@btl.net; ❹) is also reliable, with a gift shop and restaurant on site.

For **eating**, the **market** near the bus terminal has numerous food and fruit stalls: Dora at *DMD's Fast Food* (☏660-7330), is a mine of local **information** – she's in the northwest corner near the terminal. As for **restaurants**, the nearest to the terminal is *Caladium*, with air conditioning, clean toilets and tasty, inexpensive Belizean dishes. A few doors down, tiny *Bagit* is a good spot for coffee, sandwiches and salads (10am–2pm Mon–Fri only). If you're willing to go a few blocks, the large *Chon Saan Palace* at 7069 George Price Blvd is the town's best Chinese, also serving sushi (open until 10pm); *Pasquales* serves decent pizza, just a little way down Forest Drive, while *Puccini's* is a new, popular, Italian restaurant next to the roundabout on the southwest edge of the city, serving great pasta dishes. Nearby is *La Cabaña* bar, Belmopan's most lively evening **entertainment** spot.

Blue Hole National Park

Heading southeast from Belmopan through hills and lush forest, the scenic **Hummingbird Highway** is lined with the green, eastern slopes of the **Maya Mountains** rising to the right. The road leads all the way south to Dangriga (see p.188), but twelve miles out of Belmopan crosses the **Caves Branch River**, a tributary of the Sibun whose valley holds some of Belize's finest **caves**. Just beyond, the wildlife-rich **Blue Hole National Park**, established in 1986 and managed by the Belize Audubon Society, is named for its most famous feature: the **Blue Hole** (or "Inland Blue Hole", to distinguish it from the one on Lighthouse Reef), a short, ten-yard-wide stretch of underground river revealed by a collapsed karst cavern, or *cenote* in Maya. The river continues to flow on the surface for about fifty yards beyond the "hole" before disappearing beneath another rock face. Its cool, fresh, turquoise waters, surrounded by dense forest and overhung with vines, mosses and ferns, are perfect for a refreshing dip. Three of the five species of **cats** found in Belize – the jaguar, ocelot and jaguarundi – have also been sighted within park boundaries; black howler monkeys are occasionally heard; and other mammals seen here include tapir, collared and white-lipped peccaries, tamandua (anteaters), gibnut, coatimundi, opossum, deer, kinkajou and many species of bats. It's also home to more than 175 species of birds, including the slaty-breasted tinamou, black hawk-eagle, crested guan, lovely cotinga, nightingale wren and red-legged honeycreeper. The **Hummingbird Loop**, a mile-long, self-guided trail undulating through the forest, provides a worthwhile glimpse of the park – but to enjoy it comfortably you'll need insect repellent.

St Herman's Cave and Crystal Cave

Just beyond the Caves Branch River, by the roadside on the right, is **St Herman's Cave** (daily 8am–4.30pm; Bz$8, includes the Blue Hole), the most accessible cave in Belize. Any bus between Belmopan and Dangriga will drop you at the cave or the Blue Hole, making this an easy day-trip (rangers know the times of onward buses), but to really experience the excitement of caving in Belize you need to stay nearby, at *Caves Branch Jungle Lodge* (see p.130).

The National Park **visitor centre** (call the Audubon Society on ☎223-5004) is located at the entrance, and has good displays on the plant, bird and animal life found here – particularly bats. There's a marked trail for ten minutes to the cave entrance, beneath a dripping rock face; you'll need a torch to descend the steps, originally cut by the Maya. Inside, you scramble over rocks and splash through the shallow river for about twenty minutes, admiring the strange rock formations, before the cave appears to end. To continue beyond, and emerge from another opening, you need to go on a **tour**; the best is organized by Marcos Cucul of Maya Guide Adventures (see p.128) – also great for any sort of caving, climbing or jungle survival trip, including a tour of the impressive **Crystal Cave**, also in the park (US$80 includes entrance fee, all equipment and lunch). Behind the cave – which sports some crystal formations and intriguing Maya artefacts – a **trail** leads past unusually shaped rocks, yet more caves and a spectacular observation platform, arriving after a little over two miles at a **campsite**.

Caves Branch Jungle Lodge

One of the best places to stay in the whole region is ⚶ **Caves Branch Jungle Lodge**, at Mile 41.5 (☎822-2800, ⒲www.cavesbranch.com), a mile beyond St Herman's Cave and just before the Blue Hole. It's under a mile from the highway, easily accessible and signposted; all passing buses will stop at the entrance. The lodge is set in a 58,000-acre estate of high canopy forest surrounding the banks of the beautiful **Caves Branch River**, and though maintaining some of the communal atmosphere of its early days, it's been transformed into a mid to higher-end jungle retreat. **Accommodation** suits all budgets: from luxurious treehouse suites, elevated twenty feet off the ground with a spectacular view of the river (❽–❾) to spacious jungle suites with wicker furniture (marginally cheaper, ❽), and bungalows with tiled roofs, painted murals and wraparound verandas (❼); all have spacious hot showers, though only treehouses have electricity. Screened cabañas on stilts (❺) are less expensive, and the screened **bunkhouse** is a bargain (❷, Bz$30 per person). Most people book a three- or five-night **package** including tours, taxes and delicious buffet-style meals served above the river. A bar, massage cabañas, tiered swimming pools and an orchid garden assist with relaxation. Plan at least two nights here; one day just isn't long enough, and the birding is superb.

Caves Branch is run by Canadian Ian Anderson, and with some of the most experienced guides in the country, they lead excellent wildlife treks, ruin tours, overnights and survival courses through seven spectacular on-site cave systems and along sparkling rivers (starting at US$95 per person, including lunch and equipment). All the caves contain Classic-period **Maya artefacts**; some are dry (don't touch the glittering – but brittle – crystal formations as you clamber over rocks), and others have extensive subterranean rivers – *Caves Branch* was the first to pioneer **river tubing** in Belize, and offers a phenomenal seven-mile trip with headlamps piercing the darkness. Stupendous waterfall climbing, **rappelling** through a sinkhole into the enormous Actun Loch Tunich cave entrance, **rock-climbing**, and three-night **kayaking** and **camping** trips on both the white-water of the upper Sibun and the calmer lower section, are all available. If you haven't brought hiking boots, the lodge has a good selection to borrow.

For group travel, the nearby thatched *Sibun Education and Adventure Lodge* (see ⒲www.adventuresinbelize.com; US$130 per person per night including transfers, all meals, drinks and a tour) overlooking the Sibun River, offers comfortable dorms and private bungalows, with hot showers and classrooms with fantastic views; an ideal place to study tropical ecology.

Guanacaste National Park

Back on the Western Highway at the junction for Belmopan, **Guanacaste National Park** (daily 8am–4.30pm; Bz$5, includes a short, ranger-led tour) is Belize's smallest protected area at 52 acres, but it's also the easiest to visit (**buses** stop right outside the entrance); sign in at the **visitor centre** – which has a superb exhibit on the life cycle of leaf-cutter ants – admire the courtyard orchid display, and follow three short **trails** through lush rainforest at the confluence of Roaring Creek and the Belize River, with the chance to plunge into a lovely swimming hole at the end of your visit. There's a large wooden deck for picnicking and sunbathing. Bring mosquito repellent.

The main attraction here are the many **guanacaste** (or tubroos) trees, tall spreading hardwoods that support some 35 other species of plants: hanging from their limbs are bromeliads, orchids, ferns, cacti and strangler figs, which blossom spectacularly at the end of the rainy season. The partially water-resistant wood is traditionally favoured for feeding troughs and dugout canoes. In season, the tree produces ear-shaped fruit, used as cattle feed. A mature guanacaste can be found along the River Path.

Other botanical attractions include young mahogany trees, cohune palms, a ceiba (the sacred tree of the Maya, also known as a silk-cotton tree) and quamwood, while the forest floor is a mass of ferns and mosses. Your chances of seeing any four-footed **wildlife** here are fairly slim so close to the road, though agoutis, jaguarundis and the like have been spotted, and howler and spider monkeys use the park as a feeding ground. Around one hundred species of **birds** are present, among them blue-crowned motmots, black-faced ant-thrushes, black-headed trogons, red-lored parrots and squirrel cuckoos.

Banana Bank Lodge

Located on the north bank of the Belize River, and accessed by road from Mile 49, signposted at the turn-off northwards just west of **Roaring Creek** village, **Banana Bank Lodge** (T 820-2020, W www.bananabank.com; ⑤–⑦, includes breakfast) is a four thousand-acre working cattle ranch – half of which is still primary forest – with great **horseback riding**, canoeing and swimming, and there are also dozens of Maya mounds to explore. A pickup can be arranged from Belmopan, or you can even hike here via an alternative route: alight the bus opposite the airstrip at Mile 46, a mile east of the Belmopan turn-off, and head north; the signed road ends after two miles at the south bank of the river and you cross in a small boat.

Accommodation comprises five impressive high-roofed cabañas with two bedrooms, each with two beds, fan and private bath, and nine air-conditioned rooms and suites in the original lodge, some with private balconies and internet; all rooms are decorated with artistic touches and colour schemes, testament to the work of top Belizean-American artist and owner Carolyn Carr, whose work is exhibited all over the country (visit her studio on-site). Tasty, home-cooked meals are served family-style.

Banana Bank was renowned for its racetrack, popular with the Belize elite from the 1920s until the 1970s – and the lodge now has sixty well-trained horses and a training arena. With both beginner and expert trails, guides are very friendly, knowledgeable and ready to help (non-guests also welcome). If there's a full moon, a moonlit ride is an especially memorable experience. More sedentary visitors can delight in the *Lodge's* natural history: two hundred recorded bird species from an observation tower, a beautiful **lagoon** with resident Morelet's crocodiles, and a resident collection of animals including spider monkeys, a jaguar, and an aviary. There is a **swimming pool** modelled on the Inland Blue Hole (see p.129), and a fourteen-inch **mini observatory** (Meade telescope), with fantastic views of the galaxies.

Belize Jungle Dome

Immediately adjacent to *Banana Bank* on the banks of the Belize River, the intriguing *Belize Jungle Dome* (℡ 822-2124, Ⓦ www.belizejungledome.com; ❻) is another great accommodation option, specializing in adventure travel and owned by ex-Premier League footballer Andy Hunt. All five rooms back onto a superb swimming pool, while a bar, romantically set in the treetops, serves coffees and smoothies alongside cocktails and beers. With a reputation for personalized service, the intimate family feel is also evident in the on-site restaurant, with Maya chefs cooking delicious Belizean and international meals with the property's own organic fruit and veg. All rooms have air conditioning, TV and there's also a bookstore, wi-fi and computer access. Good value packages are available including tours to Maya ruins, cave, river and jungle treks, as far away as the barrier reef.

Roaring River Golf Club

CAMELOTE village, a couple of miles west of Roaring Creek and five miles west of Belmopan, is home to the remarkable **Roaring River Golf Club**, located at Mile 50.25 of the Western Highway (℡ 614-6525). The Belizean mainland's only public course, it's the pride of South African owner Paul Martin, with immaculately maintained fairways and greens, screened by mature and newly planted trees on the bank of the crystal-clear Roaring River. Paul designed and built the nine-hole course himself, and it has gained a fine reputation, with none of the snobbery that can permeate other golf clubs. Prices are generous: weekend fees are only Bz$35, and it's Bz$15 to rent a set of clubs. On weekdays, you can golf all day for Bz$20. The course is regularly patronized by Belmopan diplomats and other members of the expatriate community, but you'll just as often encounter off-duty clerks or Mennonite families swinging their clubs. Paul's policy of minimal pesticide use encourages an abundance of wildlife; it's now an official location on Audubon's annual Christmas Bird Count, and the water hazard on the eighth hole is home to thousands of fish and two crocodiles.

If you're arriving by bus, get off at *One Barrel Bar* at the junction of the two mile track to the course; call from the bar and Paul will pick you up.

Tapir Mountain Nature Reserve

Six miles south of the highway, between Roaring and Barton creeks, **Tapir Mountain Nature Reserve** protects seventeen square miles of the foothills of the Maya Mountains. The reserve, managed by the Belize Audubon Society, is a rich, well-watered habitat covered in high canopy and moist tropical forest, and home to all of Belize's **national symbols**: Baird's tapir, the keel-billed toucan, the black orchid and the mahogany tree. Nature reserves are Belize's highest category of protected land and, as the designation aims to "maintain natural processes in an undisturbed state", Tapir Mountain can only be visited by accredited researchers. Unfortunately, the category does not guarantee the reserve protection from hunters, or even from farmer's encroachment.

Pook's Hill Jungle Lodge

Although you aren't allowed to enter the reserve, you can enjoy spectacular scenery from a distance at **Pook's Hill Jungle Lodge** (℡ 820-2017, Ⓦ www.pookshilllodge .com; ❼). The turn-off from the highway is signposted at Mile 52, at the village of **Teakettle**; the five-mile track is bumpy but in good condition. If travelling by bus, call ahead and someone will pick you up from the junction, where there's a payphone.

The lodge is set in a clearing on a terraced hillside within a three hundred-acre private holding. Thirteen comfortable, thatched cabañas overlook the thickly forested Roaring River valley, with breathtaking views of the Mountain Pine Ridge; two are reached by a bridge over a creek and offer more seclusion; all have electricity and hot water. This spectacular location clearly held attractions for the ancient Maya: the lodge sits atop a platform with cabañas arranged around the remains of an ancient habitation, plans of which can be viewed. The site was recently excavated with the remarkable discovery that it held the only purpose-built "sweatbath" found so far in Belize. Excellent **meals** (not included) are served in a dining room at the edge of the forest; above, a thatched, deck with easy chairs and hammocks serves as a bar in the evenings. There's also a small **library** with a focus on archeology and natural history.

To see **wildlife**, you don't have to stray far: superb birding almost always reveals a raptor, perhaps a **bat falcon**, hunting or feeding in view of the lodge, and every year a pair of spectacled owls raises a brood near the cabañas; it's also a centre for the green iguana breeding. There are self-guided **nature trails** and superb **horseback riding**, and you can hike or ride to more substantial ruins, including **Actun Tunichil Muknal**, further up the valley. To cool off you can swim or go **tubing** in the river.

Actun Tunichil Muknal

A few miles up Roaring Creek valley, south of *Pook's Hill*, lies **Actun Tunichil Muknal** ("cave of the stone sepulchre"), one of the most spectacular caves in the country. Known as "ATM", it was discovered in 1986 by archeologist Thomas Miller, who named it for the well-preserved skeletons of Maya human sacrifices found within: fifteen individual skeletons including six infants under 3 years old and a child of about 7; the adults range from their 20s to 40s. None was actually buried: they were simply laid in shallow pools in natural travertine terraces. Alongside the skeletons are over four hundred ceramic vessels, probably originally containing food - most have been ceremonially "killed" by piercing the base to release the powerful energy of the vessel.

Although looting occurred in one chamber, the main chamber, much higher up the cave wall, has not been touched and its **megalithic artefacts** are spellbinding: carved slate representations lean upright, models of bloodletting implements that are an indisputable indication of the ceremonies performed here over 1200 years ago. Perhaps the most dramatic sight is the skeleton of a young woman lying below a rock wall, with the stone axe that may have killed her nearby. To the ancient Maya, caves were entrances to Xibalba – "the place of fright" and the abode of the Lords of Death – yet the worshippers made the difficult descent over nearly a mile with only pine torches to light their way. Such rituals must indeed have been terrifying journeys to an utterly frightful place.

As the cave is a registered archeological site (entry fee Bz$30), only specially trained guides are allowed to lead groups. A number of experienced guides based in San Ignacio (see p.146) run excellent, adventurous trips (around US$80 with transportation, entrance fee and lunch included). You'll need to be pretty fit and able to swim: it's unsuitable for small children as you'll be wading waist- or even chest-deep in water some of the time. Good **hiking boots** or closed-toe footwear are mandatory for navigating rocks, and don't wear anything you don't want to get muddy. While ATM is certainly worth exploring, its massive popularity places great stress on its carrying capacity and this has begun to compromise both visitor experience and **safety**. The best tack is to find a reputable guide to take you when fewer people are visiting, and to go with the smallest group possible.

Spanish Lookout and the Chiquibul Road

Heading west from Teakettle, you'll pass the roadside eatery *McWolf's*, a great spot for burgers and fries (Mon–Sat 11am–7pm, Sun 11am–5pm). Whichever direction you're headed, you can get off the bus here and catch the next one in half an hour. Once you've filled up and arrived at the village of **Blackman Eddy** (Mile 57), a well-signposted road north from the highway leads to **Spanish Lookout**, Belize's wealthiest **Mennonite** settlement. Its neat farmhouses, white-fenced fields, paved roads, car and tractor showrooms and the *Golden Coral* diner (closed Sun) successfully evoke the American Midwest. The Mennonites here have enthusiastically embraced modern technology, and have the best auto parts shops in the country. **Crude oil** was discovered here recently, bringing a burgeoning settlement further into the spotlight. While the oil strike suggests a windfall for debt-strapped Belize, questions still remain over how a modest infrastructure can keep up with the available fifty thousand barrels per day. The oil is currently trucked all the way south to Big Creek near Placencia, where a 45,000-barrel barge transports it to Texas – with associated transportation risks. On the positive side, oil industry cash has been released to fund social projects across the country.

Further along, on the north side of the highway at Mile 60, **Caesar's Café and Guest House** (☎824-2341, ✉cayo@orangegifts.com; ④–⑤) sits on the bank of pretty Barton Creek, run by Julian Sherrard since the retirement of his pioneering father Caesar. Guests stay in attractive rooms with private bath and air conditioning, while there are trailer hook-ups and camping spots (Bz$9 per person), and a smart house for longer rentals. The family **bar/restaurant** is a great place for breakfast, lunch and dinner (6am–8pm), serving delicious, pan-American **home cooking** including superb burgers and delicious "pibil pork" baked in banana leaves – and there's always a vegetarian option. A short trail leads down to a beautiful **swimming** hole on the creek, and Julian can organize canoe or caving trips. The ♣ **Orange Gift Shop** is one of the best in Belize, featuring superb wooden furniture, sculpture, games boards and bowls, carved mostly on site (tours of the woodshop on request) and properly dried in a solar kiln, plus slate reproductions of Maya artwork and a wide selection of Central American contemporary art, textiles and silver jewellery. The book section is a good place to pick up information about the Maya and maps and guides to Guatemala and Mexico.

West of *Caesar's*, just over the Barton Creek bridge, two prominent grass-covered **pyramids** mark the unexcavated Maya site of **Floral Park**; simply looking out as you pass by gives a good sense of what's there. Three and a half miles further lies **Georgeville**, a linear community from where (with your own transport) you can head south along the **Chiquibul Road** (see below), while westwards the highway continues, passing Central Farm after a few miles, the University of Belize's Agricultural Research station. To the north, another road leads to **Spanish Lookout** via a ferry crossing, and four miles further west lies Santa Elena and San Ignacio (see p.145).

The Chiquibul Road

Reaching deep into the Mountain Pine Ridge Forest Reserve and onward to Caracol (see p.142), the unpaved **Chiquibul Road** (known also as the Georgeville Rd) offers some entertaining diversions. Though there are no buses, you could hitch to the reserve headquarters at **Augustine/Douglas Silva**, and a mountain bike or four-wheel-drive vehicle is ideal for exploring this fascinating area of hills, waterfalls, caves and jungle. A great **accommodation** option for exploring the region lies just two miles from Georgeville. **Gumbo Limbo Village Resort** (☎665-3112,

@ www.gumbolimboresort.com; **❼**, including continental breakfast) is a supremely attractive collection of spacious family-style stone cabañas set around a pool, with a view south across forested valleys to the Mountain Pine Ridge. Each room offers tasteful decor, large showers and wide French windows opening onto private terraces; with plentiful breeze there's no need for air conditioning, while solar and wind power provide most of the power. Owned by a friendly British family, **lunch** here is also available to non-guests, served in a large bar/dining *palapa*, with a good range of burgers, burritos and salads (around Bz$10). A four-course **evening meal** (Bz$40) is available by arrangement.

Barton Creek Cave

Of the many **cave trips** in Cayo, one of the most fascinating is to **Barton Creek Cave**, accessible only by river (around 4hr; Bz$55 plus $20 entry fee). Barton Creek is a registered archeological site and nothing must be touched or removed; although many outfits now offers trips here, the original and one of the **best guides** is David Simpson, a multilingual Belizean who runs David's Adventure Tours in San Ignacio (see p.147). He'll carefully show you the astonishing Maya artefacts in the cave, and will usually include a visit to Green Hills Butterfly Ranch (see p.136).

The official, signposted turnoff to the cave is four miles along the Chiquibul Road from Georgeville, but this route has become largely impassable; instead, tour groups use a private track which turns east off the road after two miles, kindly granted access by the traditional Mennonite settlement of **Upper Barton Creek**. The road fords the creek and eventually reaches a jade-green pool. On the far side, the water disappears into the jungle-framed cave entrance, and you follow the river underground in a canoe, crouching down in places where the cave roof dips low. After 1600yd you emerge into a gallery blocked by a huge rockfall. If it's been raining, a subterranean waterfall cascades over the rocks – an unforgettable sight. Beyond lie many more miles of passageways, accessible only on a fully equipped expedition. The clear, slow-moving river fills most of the cave's width, though the roof soars 100yd above your head in places; powerful lamps are a must. Several **Maya burial sites** surrounded by pottery vessels line the banks, the most awe-inspiring indicated by a skull set in a natural rock bridge used by the Maya to reach the sacred site.

After a tour of Barton Creek Cave, you can stop by **Barton Creek Outpost** (☎ 662-4797, @ www.bartoncreekoutpost.com), complete with restaurant and bar, showers, rope swings and canoe rental (Bz$20). If you're inclined to stay overnight, camping is free – mattress and sleeping bag rental is Bz$10 and you can catch a ride back to San Ignacio with a tour the next day.

Mountain Equestrian Trails

Seven miles from Georgeville, **✤ Mountain Equestrian Trails** (☎ 820-4884, in the US ☎ 1-800/838-3918, @ www.metbelize.com; **❼**) is unquestionably Belize's premier **horseback riding** centre, with sixty miles of superb forest trails. It offers very comfortable **accommodation** – ten rooms in thatched, oil lamp-lit cabañas, set in tropical forest on the edge of the Pine Ridge – and the *Cantina* restaurant dishes out tasty Belizean and Mexican **meals** in large portions. The managers can also arrange hiking, birding, kayaking and caving trips into the rarely visited interior, and the centre is a base for low-impact wildlife safaris deep into the Chiquibul Forest. Owner Jim Bevis and his wife, Marguerite, are founding members of the Slate Creek Preserve, a privately owned, ten-square-mile tract of limestone karst forest. Landowners, recognizing the importance of conservation and sustainable development, helped to establish the preserve in 1992 by following the guidelines in UNESCO's Man and the Biosphere Programme – turning environmental concerns into practical projects to benefit local people.

Green Hills Butterfly Ranch and Botanical Collections

On the opposite side of the road from *Mountain Equestrian Trails*, the ☩ **Green Hills Butterfly Ranch and Botanical Collections** (daily 8am–4pm; Bz$12.50 with guided tour, last tour at 3.30pm; ☎820-4017, ⓦwww.green-hills.net) is Belize's biggest butterfly exhibit. It's run by Dutch biologists Jan Meerman and Tineke Boomsma, both of whom have published extensively – including a *Checklist of the Butterflies of Belize* – on insects, reptiles, amphibians and flowers (see the excellent website for free downloads of their numerous articles). They've also discovered several new species in Belize, including a **tarantula** – *Citharacanthus meermani* – at Green Hills itself.

▲ Green Hills Butterfly Ranch

The main attraction is the enclosed, beautifully landscaped **flight area**, where flocks of gorgeous tropical butterflies flutter around, settling occasionally on flowers to sip nectar. Over eighty different species have been bred here, though you'll usually see around twenty-five to thirty at any one time, depending on the time of year and the breeding cycle. In the early morning you can watch one of nature's wonders as butterflies emerge from jewelled chrysalises; many of the chrysalises are shipped for exhibit in the US. Also worth seeing is the flight of large owl butterflies which happens at dusk; this can be arranged by appointment. Fascinating as this is, there is also a lot more – with enthusiastic, well-trained local guides giving excellent briefings. To raise butterflies you also need to know about their food plants; the botanical garden here is home to **Belize's National Passion-flower Collection**, as well as countless **epiphytes** (air plants), cycads, heliconias and orchids, and a tropical fruit orchard.

Pacbitún

As the Chiquibul Road meets the Cristo Rey Road from San Ignacio just over a mile on, a short diversion west lies the **ruins of Pacbitún** (meaning "stones set in the earth"), a major Maya ceremonial centre. One of the oldest Preclassic sites in Belize (dated to 1000 BC), it continued to flourish throughout the Classic period, and farming terraces and mounds are still evident in the surrounding hills. Only the area around high Plaza A has been cleared (out of 24 temple pyramids and a ball-court), and here you can find the tombs of two elite women, which yielded a massive haul of Maya drums, flutes, ocarinas and maracas. Though the site is not always open, José Tzul, who lives just to the right of the entrance, runs Blue Ridge Mountain Rider and arranges a wonderful **horseback tour** (US$60/day), here and along little-known trails to the lodges in the Mountain Pine Ridge. If he's not home, Maria at the Tanah Museum in San Antonio (below) can help you find him.

San Antonio

Two miles west of Pacbitún heading towards the Macal River valley along the Cristo Rey Road, is **SAN ANTONIO**, a village surrounded by scattered *milpa* farms with the forested Maya Mountains in the background. Its inhabitants are descendants of Yucatec Maya (or *Masawal*) refugees who fled the Caste Wars in Yucatán in 1847. Most people here, whose oral history is transcribed in Alfonso Antonio Tzul's fascinating *After 100 Years*, still speak Yucatec and Spanish as well as English. San Antonio was the home of the famous Maya *Curandero* (healer) **Don Eligio Panti**, and his house has become a small, informal **museum** (opening by request) dedicated to his life and the simple tools he used. His name has been further honoured by a national park.

The village is a fine place to learn about traditional **Maya healing** methods. Go see one of Don Eligio's nieces, **Maria Garcia**, who grew up here and runs the *Chichan Ka Guest House* (☏ 820-4023; ❶–❷) here; the **Mesh bus** from San Ignacio (2 daily Mon–Sat; 1hr) stops right outside. **Meals** are catered upon request, prepared in traditional ways using organic produce from the garden. Maria is president of the Itzamna Society, a local organization which protects local environment and culture, and she offers courses in the use of medicinal plants. The community is renowned for its **slate carvings**, and two **gift shops** here have become favourite tour-group stops. Next door is the small **Tanah Museum** (Bz$8), with displays of village life and history and slate carvings.

Maria Garcia played a prominent role in the establishment of the **Eligio Panti National Park**, a project to allow local Maya to manage a protected area covering 31 square miles of rugged forest, hugging the perimeter of the Mountain Pine Ridge.

Wardens and guides are well trained to take you on horseback to see caves and water-falls, and there's a visitor centre, trails among medicinal plants and campsites (Bz$10). Few visitors come here, but the landscape is breathtaking.

The Mountain Pine Ridge and Caracol

Southeast of San Ignacio, the **Mountain Pine Ridge Forest Reserve** is a spectacular range of rolling hills, peaks and gorges. Its heights are formed from some of the oldest rocks in Central America, granite intrusions that have thrust upwards from the bedrock that underlies the entire isthmus. Amongst this are also some sections of limestone, riddled with superb caves, the most accessible of which is **Rio Frio** in the village of Augustine/Douglas Silva. The landscape here is a mixture of grassland and pine forest growing in the nutrient-poor, sandy soil, though in the warmth of the river valleys the vegetation is denser. The pines give way to rainforest south of the Guacamallo Bridge, which crosses the upper Macal River on the road to **Caracol**.

The smooth roads in the Pine Ridge are difficult to use in the rainy season, though the water feeds a number of small streams, running off into the Macal and Belize rivers. One of the most scenic is the **Río On**, rushing over cataracts and forming a gorge – a sight of tremendous natural beauty within view of a picnic shelter. On the northern side of the ridge is **Thousand-foot Falls**, actually over 1600ft and the highest in Central America.

The Pine Ridge is virtually uninhabited but for a handful of **tourist lodges** and the small forest reserve headquarters at **Augustine/Douglas Silva**. The whole area is perfect for **hiking**, but **camping** is allowed only at Augustine/Douglas Silva and at Bol's Nature Tours, by the Mai Gate at the entrance to the reserve (see p.140). Officially you need permission from the Forest Department in Belmopan to camp, but in practice you'll almost certainly be allowed if you ask politely when you arrive. It's fairly hard – though rewarding – to explore this part of the country on your own, and unless you have a car or a mountain bike or come on an organized tour, you may have to rely on hitching, making sure you're near somewhere to stay

The Pine Ridge lives on

Belizeans regard their pine forest as a national treasure, so news of a very severe infestation of the **southern pine bark beetle** in the Mountain Pine Ridge in early 2000 caused anguish throughout the country. As they feed, the beetle larvae kill the trees, and a new generation of larvae appears every four or five weeks. Sweeping through the forest, their progress was helped by the government's policy of fire suppression, which allowed trees to grow more densely than they would naturally. Initially, it was thought that the entire forest might be destroyed, but a rapidly implemented **reforestation programme** has made sure that the forest will eventually recover. As you drive around the sandy roads in the Pine Ridge, you will see large areas of bare, lifeless pines, stretching to the horizon in places, but already saplings are up to 2.5 yards tall and growing vigorously. Even dead trees make an important contribution, providing hunting grounds for woodpeckers and other insect-eaters and thinning the forest as they fall, which makes recurrences of the infestation less likely and reveals new vistas for visitors to enjoy. Though the forest's appearance has been altered, it's still a beautiful place, and, by good fortune, the trees around Thousand-foot Falls were untouched – you can still see this magnificent sight in all its glory.

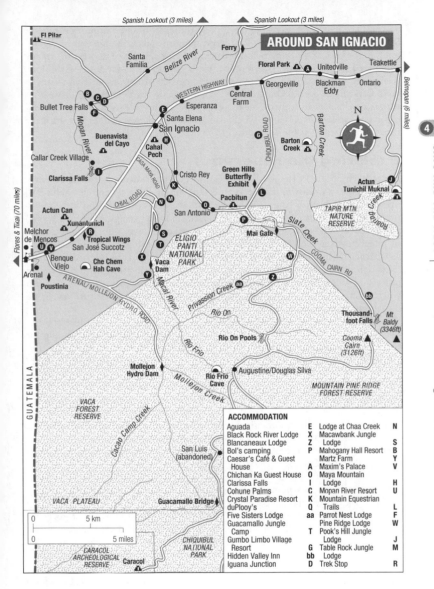

ACCOMMODATION

Aguada		Lodge at Chaa Creek	N
Black Rock River Lodge	X	Macawbank Jungle	
Blancaneaux Lodge	Z	Lodge	S
Bol's camping	P	Mahogany Hall Resort	B
Caesar's Café & Guest		Martz Farm	Y
House	A	Maxim's Palace	V
Chichan Ka Guest House	O	Maya Mountain	
Clarissa Falls	I	Lodge	H
Cohune Palms	C	Mopan River Resort	U
Crystal Paradise Resort	K	Mountain Equestrian	
duPlooy's	Q	Trails	L
Five Sisters Lodge	aa	Parrot Nest Lodge	F
Guacamallo Jungle		Pine Ridge Lodge	W
Camp	T	Pook's Hill Jungle	
Gumbo Limbo Village		Lodge	J
Resort	G	Table Rock Jungle	M
Hidden Valley Inn	bb	Lodge	
Iguana Junction	D	Trek Stop	R

when it gets dark. To explore the many forestry roads branching off the Chiquibul Road, you really need to study one of the 1:50,000 topographic maps of the area, on display at many area resorts and attractions but, unfortunately, available for purchase only at the Forest Department in Belmopan.

There are **two entrance roads** to the reserve: the **Chiquibul Road**, from Georgeville on the Western Highway, and the **Cristo Rey Road**, from Santa Elena, served by the Mesh bus from San Ignacio and passing through the village of **San Antonio** (see p.137); they converge before ascending to the park entrance. If you're up to it, a good way to explore these routes is to rent a **mountain bike** in San Ignacio; buses on the Cristo Rey Road transport bikes, though you could also put it in the back of a passing pick-up truck. All tour agents and resorts can arrange **organized tours**: if you're staying at a Cayo resort, a full-day tour of the Pine Ridge costs around US$45–70 per person for a group of four, more if you want to go to Caracol (see p.142). Ongoing road improvements, particularly the all-weather surface on the road to Caracol, make a trip perfectly feasible most of the year, but reports of incidents involving Guatemalan *bandidos* in the past couple of years make trips to the latter advisable only in tour convoy.

Exploring the reserve

A steady climb marks the journey toward the official **entrance to the reserve**. On the way is a **campsite** (Bz$15 per person) run by Fidencio and Petronila Bol, owners of Bol's Nature Tours. On a ridge with views over to Pacbitún and Xunantunich, it's a good base for exploring the park. Fidencio can guide you to several nearby **caves**, including the aptly named **Museum Cave**, which holds dozens of intact bowls and other ceramics. Across from the campsite is *Misty Mountain* restaurant and bar, serving tasty burgers, pizzas and Belizean fare. About three miles uphill is the **Mai Gate**, a forestry checkpoint offering information as well as toilets and water. Though there are plans to levy an **entrance fee**, for the moment you just have to leave your name, or that of the tour group, to ensure there's no illegal camping.

Once you've entered the reserve, pine trees quickly replace leafy forest. After two miles, the often-rough Cooma Cairn Road heads off to the left, running for ten miles (through dead pines) to a point overlooking **Thousand-foot Falls**. The setting is spectacular, with thickly forested slopes visible across the gorge. The long, slender plume of water disappears into the valley below, giving rise to the falls' other, more poetic name: Hidden Valley Falls. The waterfall itself is half a mile from the viewpoint, but try to resist climbing around for a closer look: the slope is a lot steeper than it appears, and even if you manage to make the descent, the scramble back up is more difficult. Dawn and dusk are the best times to view the falls as you'll very likely be the only visitors; you'd almost certainly need your own vehicle, however, or a room at the *Hidden Valley Inn*. You can't see the river below, but this is the headwater of Roaring Creek, whose confluence with the Belize River you can appreciate in Guanacaste National Park (see p.131). There's a shelter with toilets at the viewpoint, and since the site is also a **National Monument**, you'll be asked by caretaker Pedro Mai for the entrance fee (Bz$3).

One of the reserve's main attractions has to be the **Rio On Pools**, a gorgeous spot for a swim seven miles further on the Chiquibul Road. Here the river forms pools between huge, granite boulders before plunging into a gorge right beside the main road. Another five miles from here you reach the reserve headquarters at **Augustine/Douglas Silva**. Now housing only a few forestry workers, this small settlement was known as Augustine until it was renamed **Douglas Silva** after a local politician; however, only some of the signs were changed and a complete transition never occurred. If you're heading to **Caracol**, Forest Department staff here will give advice on road conditions and **safety**. You can also **camp** here, and be sure to make the short hike to Big Rock Falls, one of the area's waterfall treasures.

A twenty-minute walk from Augustine/Douglas Silva, along the signposted track, is **Rio Frio Cave**. It burrows under a small hill, the Río Frio flowing right through it. If you enter the foliage-framed cave mouth, you can clamber over limestone terraces the entire way until you're back out in the open. Sandy beaches and rocky cliffs line the river on both sides.

Accommodation

The **resorts** in the Mountain Pine Ridge Forest Reserve include some of the most exclusive accommodation in Belize. These lodges, mostly cabins set amongst pines, are surrounded by undisturbed natural beauty and have quiet paths to secluded waterfalls; they're also ideal if you're visiting **Caracol** (see p.142). Bugs can be a problem so bring insect repellent. Listings here are in order of their location (see map, p.139).

🏃 **Blancaneaux Lodge** 0.5 mile beyond *Pine Ridge Lodge*, then 1.2 miles down a signposted track, by the airstrip ☎824-3878, ⓦwww.blancaneauxlodge.com. Owned by Francis Ford Coppola, this is a sumptuous lodge. Comfortable and spacious hardwood and thatch cabañas and villas overlooking Privassion Creek, while the grounds are beautifully landscaped, from the palm-lined driveway to the croquet lawn and organic garden. Villas (sleep 4) have two enormous rooms with hardwood floors, Guatemalan textiles and screened porches with gorgeous views. There's a wood-fired pizza oven and Italian specialities served with home-grown organic vegetables and Coppola's wines. A heated pool and Indonesian massage house ensure relaxation, while service is exceptional. Prices are considerably lower off-season; packages available with Placencia's *Turtle Inn* (see p.211) and *La Lancha*, Guatemala (see p.170). ❾

Five Sisters Lodge 2.5 miles past *Blancaneaux*, at the end of the main reserve road ☎820-4005, ⓦwww.fivesisterslodge.com. Set on a hillside among granite and pines, this superbly-located lodge is the only local Belizean-owned property; the pride and joy of Carlos Popper. Nineteen comfortable palmetto-and-thatch cabañas have hot showers and a deck with hammocks. Electricity is via an unobtrusive hydro, and oil lamps are wonderfully romantic. Popular with honeymooners, there are gorgeous flowered gardens and a nature trail through broadleaf forest to waterfalls. The Five Sisters Falls, viewed from the dining-room deck, can also be explored via a tiny funicular. A rocky island in nearby Privassion Creek offers a thatched bar and small beach. Good value meals also availale to non-guests. ❻–❼

🏃 **Hidden Valley Inn** Five miles along the Cooma Cairn Rd to Thousand-foot Falls ☎822-3320, ⓦwww.hiddenvalleyinn.com. Twelve spacious cottages at a high elevation, within a twenty square mile reserve. You'll forget you're in the tropics here with pines, tree ferns and fireplaces stacked with logs to ward off the chill. Hiking, mountain bike and 4WD trails take you to secret waterfalls; there are so many that guests can arrange to have one entirely to themselves – popular with honeymooners. Guides, maps, radios and bikes included. Great meals (not included), on-site pool, and if you get chilly you can jump in the hot tub. Excellent birding, with frequent sightings of the rare orange-breasted falcon. Private airstrip. ❽

Pine Ridge Lodge Chiquibul Rd, just past the Cooma Cairn junction ☎606-4557, in the US ☎1-800/316-0706, ⓦwww.pineridgelodge.com. A small resort on the banks of Little Vaqueros Creek, with a choice of simple, Maya-style thatched cabins or more modern ones with red-tiled roofs. The grounds and trees are full of orchids, and trails lead to pristine waterfalls. The restaurant is a favourite refreshment stop on tours of the Pine Ridge. Continental breakfast included. ❺–❻

Caracol

The main ridges of the Maya Mountains rise up to the south of Augustine/ Douglas Silva. Ten miles past the reserve headquarters, the Chiquibul Road crosses the Macal River (and a fault line) over the low **Guacamallo Bridge**. South of here, the vegetation changes from riverbank pine to the broadleaf jungle of the **Chiquibul Forest**. The turn-off for **Caracol** (daily 8am–4pm; Bz$20) is 1.5 miles past the bridge; eleven miles along this road brings you to the **visitor centre**, where you sign in. Many tour operators in San Ignacio run trips to Caracol: Everald Tut has a daily **shuttle** (US$50 per person; ☎820-4014). All groups leave by 9am and, due to robberies in the area, travel with a military escort. For a directory of guides, see the box on p.146.

If you've driven here on your own (inadvisable due to robberies by Guatemalan *bandidos*), you'll be accompanied by a knowledgeable site ranger or by an archeology student – not so much to inform you as to ensure you won't damage recently exposed surfaces or artefacts; many new monuments and stucco carvings have been left under simple, thatched shelters until they can be removed to storage or laboratories. A **stela house** is planned to display some of these findings. Despite the presence of rangers, Caracol's isolated, remote location just three hours on foot from Guatemala makes it vulnerable to looting; the British Army and Belize Defence Force frequently patrol the area.

The **visitor centre**, the best at any Maya site in Belize, is an essential first stop, with a scale model of the ruins, some excellent displays (follow them from right to left) and several artefacts. There's also a large, thatched picnic shelter and clean toilets. Only the city's core, covering 24 square miles and containing 32 large structures and twelve smaller ones around five main plazas is currently open to visitors – though this is far more than most will see. It's an incredible experience to be virtually alone in this great, abandoned city, the horizon bounded by jungle-covered hills.

The site
Towering above the forest, Caracol's largest architectural complex – **Caana**, or "sky place" – is, at 141ft, the tallest Maya building in Belize (and still one of the tallest buildings in the country), the central structure of the **B Group**. At the top of this immense, restored edifice is a plaza, with yet three more sizeable pyramids above. When you finally (and breathlessly) climb B-19, the tallest of the three, you'll be rewarded with views of seemingly endless ridges and mountains – a perfect environment to contemplate the Maya concept of time's enormity. Beneath Caana, a series of looted tombs still show traces of original, painted glyphs on their walls; some have lintels of iron-hard sapodilla wood supporting their entrances and are decorated with painted text. Excavation on **Temple B5**, facing Caana across Plaza B, has uncovered fantastically detailed, stucco **monumental masks** on either side of the central staircase. They portray jaguars and the Witz ("sacred mountain") monster, wearing a headdress of water-lily pads being nibbled by small fish. In Maya cosmology, this design symbolizes the evening sun transforming into the jaguar god of the underworld and descending into the watery underworld of Xibalba to fight the Lords of Death. Legend dictates that if he's successful, he will rise again as the sun god. To the side of Plaza B lies **Altar 23** – the largest altar here – depicting two bound, captive lords from Ucanal and Bital, once-subdued cities located in present-day Petén; glyphs date the structure to 810 AD. Other glyphs and altars tell of war between Caracol and **Tikal** (see p.170), with regional control alternating between the two great cities. One altar dates a victory over Tikal to 562 AD – setting the seal on the city's rise to power.

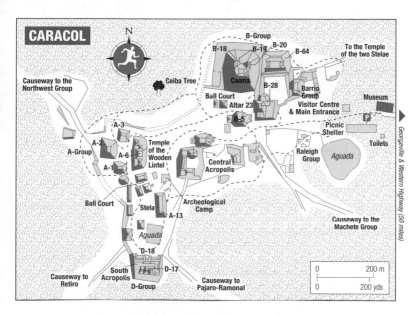

Caracol: facts and mysteries

The most extensive and magnificent Maya site in Belize (and one of the largest in the Maya world), **Caracol** was lost in the rainforest for over a thousand years until its rediscovery by *chiclero* (see p.148) Rosa Mai in 1937. Research has revealed that the name the ancient Maya gave to the city was **Oxwitzá**, or "three hill water", making this one of the few sites whose true name is known. The locale was first systematically explored by archeologist A.H. Anderson in 1938; he renamed the site Caracol – Spanish for "snail" – because of the large number of snail shells he found. Anderson was accompanied by Linton Satterthwaite of the University of Pennsylvania in the 1950s, but many of their records were destroyed by Hurricane Hattie in 1961, and several altars and stelae were deliberately broken by logging tractors in the 1930s.

In 1985 the first detailed, full-scale excavation of the site, the "Caracol Project", began under the auspices of Drs Arlen and Diane Chase of the University of Central Florida, with research unearthing a tremendous amount of artefacts relating to all levels of Maya society. Over a hundred **tombs** have been found, one of the best-preserved being B-19, under the largest temple on the summit of Caana (see p.143). This is almost certainly the tomb of **Lady Batz Ek**, or "black monkey", who married into the ruling K'an dynasty in 584 AD and who may even have been a ruler. Other ceremonially buried caches contain items as diverse as mercury and amputated human fingers. There are also hieroglyphic inscriptions, enabling epigraphers to piece together a virtually complete dynastic record of Caracol's Classic-period rulers from 599 to 859 AD.

Apparently there was a large and wealthy middle class among the Maya of Caracol, and dates on stelae and tombs suggest an extremely long occupation, beginning around 600 BC. The last recorded date, carved on Stela 10, is 859 AD; evidence points to a great fire around 895 AD. At the height of its dominion, roughly 700 AD, Caracol covered 55 square miles and had a population estimated at around 150,000, with over thirty thousand structures – a far greater density than at Tikal (see p.170). So far, only around ten percent of Caracol's full extent has been mapped, and research continues each field season. What continues to puzzle archeologists is why the Maya built such a large city on a plateau with no permanent water source – and how they managed to maintain it for so long.

Caracol is also a **Natural Monument Reserve** and home to abundant wildlife. Bird sightings include the **orange-breasted falcon** and the very rare **harpy eagle**. You may catch sight of ocellated turkeys feeding in the plazas, and tapirs dine at night on succulent fresh shoots in the clearings. Another awe-inspiring sight is an immense, centuries-old **ceiba tree** – sacred to the Maya – with enormous buttress roots twice as tall as a human being.

The Chiquibul Cave System

Nine miles beyond the Caracol turn-off, the Chiquibul Road arrives at the vast **Chiquibul Cave System**, still the longest system discovered in Central America, with the largest chamber in the western hemisphere. The entire area is dotted with caves and sinkholes, certainly used for ceremonies by the ancient Maya; as yet a cave has never been found in Belize without artefacts. The area is impossible to reach on your own, but contact expert guide Marcos Cucul (see p.128) if you're interested in an organized expedition; he will also arrange the relevant permissions from the Forest Department in Belmopan. Just northeast of the cave system are the wooden cabins of the **Las Cuevas Research Station**, where visitors in organized groups sometimes stay – though it's generally closed to the public. South of the cave system, **Puente Natural** is an enormous, natural limestone arch.

San Ignacio and around

On the west bank of the Macal River, 22 miles from Belmopan, **SAN IGNACIO** is a friendly, relaxed town that draws together much of the best of inland Belize. The heart of Cayo District and the focus of tourism in western Belize, it offers good food, inexpensive hotels and restaurants and frequent bus connections. The evenings are relatively cool here, and the days fresh – a welcome break from the heat of the coast – and there are far fewer biting insects and mosquitoes. The **population** is varied,

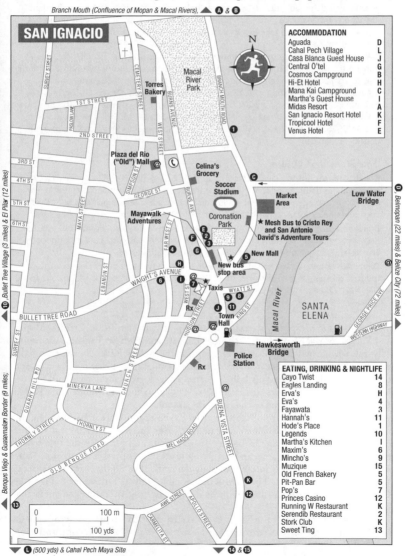

Branch Mouth (Confluence of Mopan & Macal Rivers), ▲ Ⓐ & Ⓑ

SAN IGNACIO

Macal River Park

Torres Bakery

Plaza del Rio ("Old") Mall

Celina's Grocery

Soccer Stadium

Mayawalk Adventures

Coronation Park

Market Area

Low Water Bridge

★ Mesh Bus to Cristo Rey and San Antonio
David's Adventure Tours

New Mall

New bus stop area

Taxis

Rx

Town Hall

Hawkesworth Bridge

SANTA ELENA

Police Station

Rx

Bullet Tree Village (3 miles) & El Pilar (12 miles)

Belmopan (22 miles) & Belize City (72 miles)

Bullet Tree Road

Benque Viejo & Guatemalan Border (9 miles)

Ⓛ (500 yds) & Cahal Pech Maya Site

⑭ & ⑮

ACCOMMODATION	
Aguada	D
Cahal Pech Village	L
Casa Blanca Guest House	J
Central O'tel	G
Cosmos Campground	B
Hi-Et Hotel	H
Mana Kai Campground	C
Martha's Guest House	I
Midas Resort	A
San Ignacio Resort Hotel	K
Tropicool Hotel	F
Venus Hotel	E

EATING, DRINKING & NIGHTLIFE	
Cayo Twist	14
Eagles Landing	8
Erva's	H
Eva's	4
Fayawata	3
Hannah's	11
Hode's Place	1
Legends	10
Martha's Kitchen	I
Maxim's	6
Mincho's	9
Muzique	15
Old French Bakery	5
Pit-Pan Bar	5
Pop's	7
Princes Casino	12
Running W Restaurant	K
Serendib Restaurant	2
Stork Club	K
Sweet Ting	13

Tours and tour operators from San Ignacio

Numerous **companies and guides** in San Ignacio offer a wide assortment of tours – sometimes travelling as far as the Barrier Reef – though most operators specialize in one type of tour or destination. The best way to sort through the options is to identify what kind of tour you prefer and how much you want to spend. It's generally cheaper to book directly with a local operator than through a hotel, but make sure anyone you choose to go with is a **licensed tour guide**. Some locations are difficult or impossible to visit on your own; particularly **caving**, for which a licensed guide qualified in cave rescue is mandatory, though also for the Maya ruins of Caracol. That said, several destinations are just as easy to visit on your own: if you have a vehicle, you can reach local Maya archeological sites, the Belize Botanic Gardens, the Rainforest Medicine Trail and butterfly farms, some of which have guides on location. Be aware that for cave trips, you should go in a small group; six or eight people is typical.

Average rates for trips from San Ignacio are listed as follows, usually inclusive of transportation, lunch (on full-day trips) and admission fees, but exclusive of border fees to Tikal, admission to some archeological sites (around US$5) and gratuities.

Actun Tunichil Muknal: US$75/full day **Barton Creek Cave**: US$55/half day **Birding**: US$10–15/morning walk, $50/half day, $75/full day **Caracol**: US$80/full day **Cave tubing**: US$30–40/half day **Horse riding**: US$50–70/full day **Mountain Pine Ridge**: US$55/full day **Tikal**: US$100–120/full day (cheaper for groups) **Xunantunich**: US$20–40/half day

Operators and guides

Belize Culture Tours *Casa Blanca* hotel (see p.150) ☏824 2080 or ☏610 6474, ⓦwww.belizeculturetours.com, ⓔtikaldaytrip@yahoo.com. A specialist in Mayan archeology and specifically Tikal, Elias Cambranes is a licensed guide in both Belize and Guatemala, enabling him to take tourists for the whole trip.

Belizean Sun ☏823-2781 or 601-2360, ⓦwww.belizeansun.com. Former US forester Ken Dart organizes customized trips to Cayo's interior, including caves that nobody else visits. Family trips and adventure tours to most attractions.

Cayo Adventure Tours ☏824-3246, ⓦwww.cayoadventure.com. Bespoke group tours, in reliable off-road vehicles, to all Cayo attractions. Run by Elbert Flowers and Ces Neal – based in Santa Elena.

---

mostly made up of Spanish-speaking mestizos but with significant Creoles, Mopan and Yucatec Maya, Mennonites, Lebanese, Chinese and even Sri Lankans. Undoubtedly the town's best feature is its location on the Macal River, however, amidst beautiful countryside and near several reserves. It's an excellent base for day-trips and overnights to the surrounding hills, streams, archeological sites, caves and forests. Several local tour operators run excursions south into the **Mountain Pine Ridge Forest Reserve** and beyond to the ruins of **Caracol**.

San Ignacio is divided from its sister town to the east, **SANTA ELENA**, by the mighty **Hawkesworth Bridge**, built in 1949 over the Macal River and still the only road suspension bridge in Belize. To all intents and purposes the two towns make up the same urban area, and yet, lying just on the opposite riverbank, Santa Elena is of distinctly less interest to tourists, with few of the attractions of its slightly larger neighbour. The town's one notable sight is Dr Rosita Arvigo's **Ix Chel Wellness Center**, using traditional Maya healing methods and medicinal plants (for more, see p.157).

Although you can easily use San Ignacio as a base for day-trips, numerous guesthouses and lodges in the surrounding countryside also offer **accommodation**

David's Adventure Tours In a blue booth across from the market ☎804-3674, 🌐www.davidsadventuretours.com. Multilingual Belizean David Simpson is the original (and best) guide to Barton Creek Cave, his African and Maya heritage lending added perspective. He also offers overnight jungle trips to Caracol and most regional tours. See *Guacamallo Jungle Camp*, p.157.

Easy Rider Burns Ave under Central O'tel ☎824-3734, ✉easyrider@btl.net. Charlie Collins organizes excellent horseback riding, carefully matching riders to the right mount (US$30 half day, US$50 full day).

Everald's Caracol Shuttle *Crystal Paradise Resort* (see p.156); evenings ☎820-4014 or 804-0050. Everald Tut runs affordable van tours to Caracol almost daily (US$60); he also operates King Tut Tours for other excursions around Cayo and to Tikal.

Hun Chi'ik Tours Ask at *Martha's*, or call ☎670-0746, ✉hunchiik@belizemail.net. Six guides from nearby village San José Succotz organize archeological and naturalist tours in the Cayo district, drawing on their Maya heritage and family knowledge.

Maya Guide Adventures ☎670-3116, 🌐www.mayaguide.bz. Though based in Belmopan, guide Marcos Cucul is one of the country's best, especially for overnight jungle treks and caves, including Victoria Peak and Chiquibul Caves.

Mayawalk Adventures 19 Burns Ave ☎610-1129, 🌐www.mayawalk.com. Aaron Juan leads small groups on both day and a unique overnight trip to Actun Tunichil Muknal (around US$80), as well as caving, rapelling, rock climbing, horseriding and birdwatching expeditions.

Pacz Tours 30 Burns Ave ☎824-0536, 🌐www.pacztours.net. Specialist archeology guide Jamal Crawford arranges expert trips to Actun Tunichil Muknal and other Maya sites, including new caves, and Tikal, while Toni Santiago runs the oldest and best guided canoe trip on the Macal River.

Paradise Expeditions *Crystal Paradise Resort* ☎824-4014 or 610-5993, 🌐www .birdinginbelize.com. Jeronie Tut runs superb, personalized bird and nature tours throughout Belize, with multi-day trips, spotting scopes and up-to-date equipment.

River Rat ☎625-4636, 🌐www.riverratbelize.com. Gonzo Pleitez, who lives up the Macal River, arranges customized cave and jungle trips, as well as archeological tours. For river tours, Gonzo can put you in touch with Henry Link of Phoenix Tours.

and organized trips; standards are very high, with most of these lodgings catering to upmarket, package tourists who come after a spell on the cayes – a "surf and turf" vacation. However, there are admirable places in every price bracket: a wide selection is covered on p.156.

The people of San Ignacio are justifiably proud of their beautiful surrounding countryside, and there are several specific attractions to visit in or near town, including the Green Iguana Exhibit at the *San Ignacio Resort Hotel* and the Maya site of **Cahal Pech**. Slightly further afield, the **Rainforest Medicine Trail** and the **Belize Botanic Gardens** can be seen on relaxing **canoe trips** along the mostly gentle **Macal River**; resorts along the faster **Mopan River** offer tubing or **kayaking**. The nearby farmland and forest are ideal for exploring on **horseback** or **mountain bike** – you can even take a bike on the Mesh bus to San Antonio and the Mountain Pine Ridge; see p.137.

One of the prettiest walks around San Ignacio is the twenty-minute stroll north of town to **Branch Mouth**, where the Macal and Mopan rivers merge to form the Belize River; the forested hills that begin at this confluence roll all the way south to Toledo and west across Guatemala. Follow the track from the football field past rich farmland and thick vegetation. At the confluence is a huge tree, with branches arching over the jade water, swallows skimming the surface, parrots flying overhead and scores of tiny fish. Local boys leap off the pedestrian **suspension bridge** at the final stretch of the Mopan. Raw earth on the opposite bank is evidence of the severe floods of recent years, which have risen within feet of the Hawkesworth Bridge and inundated San Ignacio.

Cahal Pech

A twenty-minute, uphill walk out of town to the southwest, clearly signposted from the highway to Benque Viejo, the hilltop Maya site of **Cahal Pech** (daily 6am–6pm; Bz\$12) has undergone extensive restoration and is well worth a visit – particularly pleasant and peaceful at sunset. The **visitor centre and museum** has a model of the site, excellent display panels showing paintings of Cahal Pech in its heyday, plus lots of artefacts, such as ocarinas, chocolate pots, arrows and carved flints, including one that looks remarkably like a modern wrench; watch the 47-minute **video** (also for sale on DVD) for a deeper understanding of the site and its treasures.

Cahal Pech means "place of ticks" in Mopan and Yucatec Maya, but that's certainly not how the elite who lived here would have known it; this was the royal acropolis-palace of a Maya ruling family during the Classic period. There's evidence of construction from the Early Preclassic, around 1200 BC, after which the city

---

Cayo: from missionaries to the Ruta Maya race

Named **El Cayo** by the Spanish, San Ignacio is still usually referred to as **Cayo** by locals (and is the name often indicated on buses). Meaning "island", it's an apt description of the location, on a peninsula between two converging rivers, and a measure of how isolated the European settlers felt, with indigenous jungle inhabitants that valued their independence. **Tipú**, a Maya city at Negroman on the Macal River (five miles south), was the capital of Dzuluinicob, where the Maya resisted attempts to Christianize them. The early wave of European conquest, in 1544, made little impact, and the area remained a centre of rebellion for decades. Two **Spanish friars** arrived in 1618, but a year later the entire population was still practising "idolatry". Outraged, the friars smashed the idols and ordered the native priests flogged, but by the end of the year the Maya once again drove out the Spaniards. In 1641 the friars returned to Tipú – but expressing their defiance the Maya priests conducted a mock Mass using tortillas as communion wafers. From then on Tipú remained an outpost of Maya culture, providing refuge to other Maya fleeing Spanish rule. It retained a good measure of independence until 1707, when the population was forcibly removed to Flores.

Like many places in Belize, San Ignacio probably started its present life as a logging camp. A map drawn up in 1787 states that the Indians of this area were "in friendship with the Baymen" – an intriguing situation, considering the strained relations of less than a century earlier. Later it was a centre for self-reliant *chicleros*, as the collectors of chicle gum were called, who knew the forest and Maya ruins intimately. When the black market price of Maya artefacts skyrocketed, many *chicleros* turned to looting. Until the Western Highway was built in the 1930s (though the section beyond San Ignacio wasn't paved until the 1980s), local transport was by mule or water. It could take ten days of paddling to reach San Ignacio from Belize City, though later small steamers shortened the trip. Nowadays river traffic, which had at one point almost died out, is enjoying a revival. Perhaps the best time to visit San Ignacio is for Belize's premier **canoe race**, La Ruta Maya, held in early March to celebrate Baron Bliss Day, when teams of paddlers race to Belize City over two days. Anyone can enter, but local guides always win.

probably dominated the central Belize River valley. Studies of the buildings and ceramics show that the site was continuously occupied until around 800 AD; most of what you see dates from the eighth century AD.

Entering the site through the forest, you arrive at **Plaza B**, surrounded by temple platforms and the remains of dwellings, and your gaze is drawn to Structure 1, the **Audiencia**, the site's largest building. If you're used to finely executed, exposed stonework at Maya sites, then the thick overcoat of lime-mortar here may come as a shock. The Classic Maya viewed bare, stone facings as ugly and unfinished, and covered all surfaces with a layer of plaster or stucco, which was then brightly painted. You can climb the steps at the front of the structure, but the best way to enjoy the site is to walk around the side and through **Plaza D** and its maze of ancient corridors and stairways, which gradually reveal an enchanting view of **Plaza A** – a sacred space entirely enclosed by walls and tall buildings. You're now across the plaza from Structure 1; make your way to the front, and you can then descend to your starting point. After your visit, you can poke around the **gift shop** for local crafts.

Arrival and information

Several **buses** run regular services from Belize City to San Ignacio, stopping at the south end of Coronation Park before continuing to Benque Viejo for the Guatemalan border; a shared **taxi** to the border from San Ignacio costs Bz$7 per person. While looking for a room, you can **leave luggage** at David's Adventure Tours, just around the corner from the bus stop and across from the market. There's no official tourist office in San Ignacio, but you'll be bombarded with **information** nonetheless: the long-established *Eva's Bar* on Waights Avenue is a good first starting point, the walls festooned with framed brochures listing what the town has to offer, while close by on West Street, Aguallos travel agency (℡669 7585, Ⓦwww.aguallos.com) offers excellent free advice and publishes *The Belize Review* magazine. Air conditioning and **internet access** is to be found at Tradewinds, at Waight's Avenue/West Street (daily 7am–10pm; also offers free coffee for patrons) or the cheaper Computer Excell at Plaza del Rio ("old mall"), 38 West St (Mon–Sat 9am–1pm, 2–8pm).

San Ignacio's main street is **Burns Avenue**; nearby, you'll find almost everything you need, including the best produce market in Belize. This is also where you'll find the **banks**; Belize, Scotia and Atlantic banks all have ATMs. If you need Guatemalan quetzales, you can sometimes avoid extra time at the border (but get slightly less favourable rates) by using the services of **moneychangers** who will approach you. The **post office** is next to Courts furniture store in the centre of town, and the **BTL office** is on the north end of Burns Avenue near Macal River Park. **Car rental** is available at Western Auto Rental (℡824-3328 or 668-2819), next to the *Venus Hotel*. For **bike rental**, check at *Eva's* or the *Crystal Paradise Resort* office on Branch Mouth Road (℡824-2823); for canoe rental, enquire at *Cosmos Campground* (see p.150), or at David's Adventure Tours.

For domestic and international **air tickets**, try Exodus Travel, 2 Burns Ave (℡824-4400). **Laundry** can be dropped off at *Martha's Guest House* on West Street (see Accommodation, below). If you're looking for a great **massage** after a tiring expedition, visit Eva Buhler at 46 Pond Ave (℡824 3423), a Swiss woman who's lived in San Ignacio for many years.

Accommodation

Hotels in San Ignacio offer some of the best budget accommodation in the country; you'll almost always find space once you arrive, but you should book ahead during busy periods – if pickings are slim, try nearby Bullet Tree Falls (see p.152). For more upmarket options, consider the lodges on the Mopan River (see p.153). All but the really inexpensive places take credit cards. For **camping**, try: *Cosmos Campground* (T824-2116; Bz$10 per person) on Branch Mouth Road by the river (just past *Midas Resort*), a ten-minute walk north of town, which has flush toilets and shared, hot-water showers; or *Mana Kai Campground*, at the start of Branch Mouth Road (T824-2317), where you can also rent tents for Bz$7 per person.

Aguada Santa Helena T804-3609, Wwww
.aguadahotel.com. Signposted on the north of the highway as you approach town, this hotel is run by a very welcoming family, with clean, comfortable a/c rooms with private bath. An inexpensive restaurant, pool and patio are in the landscaped grounds, and internet access is available. Only a short drive/taxi ride from the centre. **3**

Cahal Pech Village Cahal Pech Hill, just across from the Maya site (see p.148), 1.2 miles from town T824-3740, Wwww.cahalpech.com. With a spectacular view of San Ignacio, this well-designed hotel has spacious, private rooms and comfortable, thatched cabañas, each named after a Maya site, and with private bath, TV and Guatemalan textiles; cabañas have wooden decks with hammocks. There's a decent restaurant and internet access. **6**

Casa Blanca Guest House 10 Burns Ave
T824-2080, Wwww.casablancaguest
house.com. Great value, with immaculate a/c rooms – all have private bath, and cable TV, plus there's a comfortable sitting area with microwave, fridge, coffee and tea. It's a bright, friendly place, and owner Betty Guerra is quietly proud that it won Belize's "Best Small Hotel" award soon after opening. Laundry available, and booking is advised. The *Mallorca Hotel* next door is run by the same family and is almost identical. **2–4**

Central O'tel 24 Burns Ave T824-3734,
Eeasyrider@btl.net. Very cheap yet clean rooms, sharing a couple of small bathrooms in an old wooden building. The front balcony with hammocks is a great place to watch the street below. **1**

Hi-Et Hotel Waight's Ave T824-2828 or
665-1488, Wwww.aguallos.com/hietguesthouse. A rightly popular budget hotel in an attractive, wooden colonial building with a wraparound balcony and bench-swing. Original rooms each have their own tiny balcony and share a hot-water bathroom, while larger rooms in an adjacent concrete building have private bathrooms. Fridge and internet available. **1–2**

Martha's Guest House West St and
Waight's Ave T804-3647, Wwww.marthas
belize.com. Recent renovations and an additional building have made this popular hotel even better; owners Martha and John August manage to retain the original homey atmosphere. Rooms are very comfortable and well furnished; most have beautiful, tiled bathrooms, cable TV and either private or shared balcony, and there are also two guest lounges. Luxurious top-floor suites have grand views. There's a range of good books on Belize, a gift shop, drop-off laundry, wi-fi, shuttle to Belize City and restaurant (see opposite). Booking is advised. **3–5**

Midas Resort Branch Mouth Rd, a ten-minute walk from the bus terminal T824-2322, Emidas@btl.net. Set in trees and pasture above the riverbank, *Midas* is the only resort actually in town – and it's one of the best cabaña places in Cayo, within walking distance of the town centre but with the peace and quiet of the countryside. Accommodation is in comfortable wooden or concrete cabañas, all with a porch and private bath. There's also a restaurant, wireless internet and laundry service. Camping (Bz$8 per person) and trailer hook-ups are available. **3–5**

San Ignacio Resort Hotel 18 Buena Vista St
T824-2034, from the US T1-800/822-3274, Wwww.sanignaciobelize.com. Ten minutes' walk uphill from the town centre with views over the Macal River, the town's premier hotel hosted Queen Elizabeth on her 1994 visit. All a/c rooms are spacious, some with balconies; one economy room offers good value, while the honeymoon suite has a jacuzzi on the balcony. The *Running W* restaurant (see opposite) overlooks the pool, and the *Stork Club* nightclub (see p.152) is on-site. Tennis court, internet /wi-fi access. The Medicinal Jungle Trail down to the river is ideal for birding, and there's a display on the threatened green iguana (they're raised here for one year before being released). **6–9**

Tropicool Hotel 30 Burns Ave T804-3052,
Etropicool@btl.net. Bright, well-priced and clean rooms with shared, hot-water bathrooms, and wooden cabins in the attractive garden, with private hot showers, fridge, cable TV and verandas. Laundry area. Ground-floor rooms are wheelchair-accessible from the street. **1–4**

Venus Hotel 29 Burns Ave T824-3203, Wwww
.venushotelbelize.com. A two-storey hotel, one of the biggest in town, with good rates and a 24hr front desk. Good deals are available when booking several days. Modern rooms have clean, tiled bathrooms, a/c and TV, and the rear balcony has views over the market to the river. **3**

Eating

Like its budget hotels, San Ignacio's **restaurants** are plentiful and of high quality. If you have somewhere to cook, then the Saturday **market** is worth a visit: it's one of the best in Belize, with farmers bringing in fresh produce, and it's also a good place to stock up on provisions for trips; see Chris Lowe for his Fruit-A-Plenty trail mix, granola bars and home-made peanut butter. For general **groceries**, Celina's Store, two blocks down from the *Venus Hotel* on Burns Avenue, has the widest selection, while there are plenty of **fruit stands** around town, and you can pick up fresh **bread** and other baked goods from Torres Bakery, at the end of Far West Street. The Old French Bakery on the main square, sells croissants, baguettes, plus delicious cinnamon rolls and other pastries (open 7am–6pm). There are several reliable **fast-food stalls** in town, including a very popular taco stand (in front of the post office), which does spicy business until 2 or 3am. On most afternoons, small boys sell tasty, freshly cooked *empanadas* and *tamales* on the street. *Cayo Twist* (Thurs–Sun 4–10pm), uphill at the intersection of Old Benque Road and Buena Vista Street, is the best place in town for **ice cream** and related treats, just around the corner from *Sweet Ting* (below).

Erva's 4 Far West St. A huge and very reasonably priced menu of Belizean staples, plus steaks, seafood, burritos and burgers, all served up from a proud open kitchen – expect a little wait for your food. Especially good for breakfast.

Eva's Cnr Waight's Ave and Far West St. This Cayo institution has moved around the corner from where it stood for twenty years (the old location is now *Flava's* bar), but the vibes, drinks, characters and food (fast food, Mexican and Belizean) are much the same. Meet fellow travellers and tour guides here 7am–10pm.

Hannah's 5 Burns Ave. A small restaurant with some of the most delicious food in the country at great prices (Bz$12–20), much of it is grown on the owner's farm. Serves everything from Belizean specialities to Burmese curry, all accompanied by freshly prepared salads; get here early or you'll have to wait. Open 6am–9pm.

Martha's Kitchen West St. Located below the guesthouse of the same name and just as well run. Great breakfasts with strong, locally grown coffee, and main dishes of traditional Creole food and pizza (Bz$20–35). There's always a vegetarian choice and delicious cakes for dessert, and good service, too. The patio tables, romantically candlelit in the evenings, are a popular place to plan an excursion. Open from 7am–10pm.

Maxim's Far West St, behind *Martha's*. The best of San Ignacio's many Chinese restaurants, rapidly serving large portions of the standards. Chow mein or a great fish chop suey are both Bz$6–8. Open 10am–3pm & 5–10.30pm.

Mincho's Burns St, next to *Hannah's*. Identified by a blue awning, this takeaway food stand serves incredible *salbutes* and burritos at even more incredible prices (Bz$2–4). Arguably the best bargain if you're on a tight budget. There are great breakfast burritos here as well.

Pop's West St, across from *Martha's*. A tiny and popular local restaurant, serving very tasty Belizean dishes, including a daily lunch special and all-day breakfast (Bz$6). Open 6.30am–2pm.

The Running W Restaurant At the *San Ignacio Resort Hotel*, 18 Buena Vista St. Excellent food in tranquil surroundings, and not too expensive. Good steaks and seafood (including fish and chips) with a distinctive Lebanese influence, accompanied by Mediterranean olives. Breakfasts are especially good value.

Serendib Restaurant 27 Burns Ave. Excellent Sri Lankan curries and seafood at very reasonable prices (Bz$12–18) and with good service. Open 10am–3pm & 6–10.30pm, closed Sun.

Sweet Ting Old Benque Rd ☎610-4174. A tiny but brilliant little café serving espresso coffees, a wide variety of teas and delicious pastries – supplied to restaurants around the country; if you can't make up your mind, try the cheesecake. Daily noon–9pm.

Drinking and entertainment

Nightlife in San Ignacio is surprisingly lively at weekends, with plenty of **dancing** on offer. The younger party crowd tends to congregate at *Fayawata* on Burns Avenue, which opens nightly with a full bar, football and pool tables, and DJs at weekends; or

▲ Nightlife in San Ignacio

at *Pit-Pan*, a grimy bar by the Old French Bakery with spirited reggae dancehall and punta sound system parties. After hours, you can head to *Legends* on Bullet Tree Road, which blasts more dancehall and punta rock until 5am. Other nightclubs to look out for are the new *Muzique*, near Cahal Pech, or *Benque Rock* (see p.161). If you're in need of sustenance or refreshments in the early hours, 24-hour restaurant/bar *Eagles Landing* on Wyatt Street has a massive menu of wraps, burgers, nachos and breakfasts.

For a more relaxed drink and occasional live music, *Hode's Place Bar and Grill* on Branch Mouth Road has a large, open-air patio with pool tables, TV and a children's playground, while *Pit Pan Tavern* (not to be confused with the *Pit-Pan* above) is a smarter, smaller bar with a preference for rock music, near the bus stop. The *Stork Club* at the *San Ignacio Resort Hotel* is a slightly more sophisticated nightspot, popular during its Friday evening **happy hour**, after which things liven up with a DJ or band (until 2am) – or when belting out your favourite karaoke tunes on Thursdays. Next door is the small Princes Casino. San Ignacio's **cinema** (one of only two in Belize), Movies Seven, is located at Plaza del Rio mall ("old mall") at 38 West St, with nightly films Tuesday to Sunday and matinees at weekends (times vary).

Bullet Tree Falls and El Pilar

Three miles northwest of San Ignacio, along Bullet Tree Road, is **BULLET TREE FALLS**, a predominately Spanish-speaking, mestizo farming village spread out along the forested banks of the Mopan River. A bridge crosses the river at the falls – really just a set of rapids – and there are several very pleasant and good value **places to stay** on the riverbank nearby; all make a good base for visiting El Pilar. Several restaurants and bars create quite a busy scene here on weekends; of these, the *Riverside Lodge* right by the bridge is the liveliest place for a drink.

In the middle of the village, immediately before the bridge, is the **El Pilar Cultural Centre**, or *Be Pukte*, which means "road to Bullet Tree" in Maya (opening hours vary; call Don Beto at ☎662-2079 to check). Inside there's a good model of the Maya site of El Pilar, as well as trail guides and booklets relating to the site; if you'd like a **local guide**, ask in the village for Teddy Waight, or contact **Tony Chuc** (T 667-6060, e cherica@hotmail.com), who specializes in river sports and can lead you on an excellent combo tour that includes a visit to El Pilar and then rafting five sets of rapids back to Bullet Tree Falls. His wife Erica worked on the archeological team at El Pilar (see Contexts, p.258), and often shares her perspective. Closer to town on Pasloe Falls Road just along the river, the **Three Sister Rock Medicinal Trail** has been established; guided tours are given by donation.

A shared (*colectivo*) taxi from opposite the Belize Bank in the centre of San Ignacio to Bullet Tree Falls costs Bz$2 per person (slightly more to each accommodation). Bullet Tree Road passes through Bullet Tree Falls and eventually leads to Spanish Lookout (see p.134). The route is known as the home of well-known artists George Landero (abstract cubism) and Marcos Manzanero (rainforest and interior scenes; T 600-6225); visit their studios to say hello and view their work. Before Spanish Lookout is the village of **Santa Familia**, where Beatrice Waight (T 602-2655, e marlin_waight@hotmail.com) – a **traditional Maya healer** – works next to the village community centre. Beatrice is a seventh-generation shaman and was trained by the legendary Don Eligio (see p.137). A visit to her Healer's Hut can help cure you of your spiritual illnesses; she offers treatments such as prayers, herbal massages and teas (fees by donation).

Accommodation

Most options will arrange (often free) transport from San Ignacio, and have (or can easily procure) kayaks, tubes or mountain bikes for guests. Each option has a wonderful location along the banks of the Mopan, ideal for exploring or relaxing after a tour; all are highly recommended.

Cohune Palms T 824-0166 or 664-7508, W www.cohunepalms.com. Four unique, thatched and screened deluxe cabins, each with tiled floor, rugs and bathroom. There's a good gift shop, free internet, plus restaurant serving delicious Belizean and vegetarian meals on a veranda above the Mopan. Lounge on the outdoor decks with hammocks or try the rope swing. Yoga retreats also on offer. ❹
Iguana Junction T 824-2249, W www.iguana junction.com. Four comfortable elevated wooden cabins within riverside gardens, all with private bathroom and fan. The large palapa and restaurant are attractive communal areas, while the friendly British owners serve tasty, filling meals and offer local tours. ❹

Mahogany Hall Resort Pasloe Falls Rd T 664-0084, W www.mahoganyhallbelize.com. Brand new three-storey luxury property with superb views and very comfortable rooms and king-size suites (one with a jacuzzi) and all with local hardwoods and artwork. Giant doors and winding staircases give it an unlikely (though not forbidding) medieval fortress feel. Restaurant/bar on site. ❽
Parrot Nest Lodge T 820-4058 or 669-6068, W www.parrot-nest.com. Four simple, clean (some thatched) cabins, and two guanacaste treehouses, set among beautiful riverside gardens, some with verandas and two with private bathroom (shared bathrooms have hot showers). Great home-cooked meals are served by owner Theo Stevens at a friendly communal table. ❸–❹

El Pilar

The Maya site of **El Pilar** (daily 8am–4pm; Bz$10) is a rough uphill eight-mile drive northwest of Bullet Tree Falls on the Guatemalan border (taxis charge Bz$75 per carload; drivers wait two hours while you explore the site). The Belize River Archaeological Settlement Survey (BRASS) from the University of California has been working here since 1992 (usually March–June), and they welcome volunteer participation (see Contexts, p.258) – their very informative website (W www.marc .ucsb.edu/elpilar) also offers a downloadable *Trail of El Pilar* **guide**, detailing the story of the ruins according to archeologists (available locally at the *Be Pukte* centre in

Bullet Tree). Local accommodations arrange trips here by horse or mountain bike, or else contact Tony Chuc (above). Site caretaker Marcos Garcia also offers a fascinating history. The site is considered one of the finest **birding** areas in Cayo; enthusiasts for avifauna and monkeys should definitely bring binoculars. Setting aside generations of mutual suspicion, Belize and Guatemala have created the **El Pilar Archaeological Reserve for Maya Flora and Fauna**, covering an area of over five square miles on both sides of the border.

One archeological theory is that the area was originally a cultivated "forest garden", using the tree cover to support a variety of crops. Much more than "slash and burn", this "select and grow" technique has been simulated in an educational exhibit, including the reconstruction of a traditional Maya house discovered on the Lakin trail, on the east side of the road from Bullet Tree Falls. The "Tzunu'un" (meaning "hummingbird", guardian of forest and flowers) residential area of El Pilar was fully consolidated in the late 1990s, and provides (so far) the only view into the suburban communities that surrounded all the Maya cities.

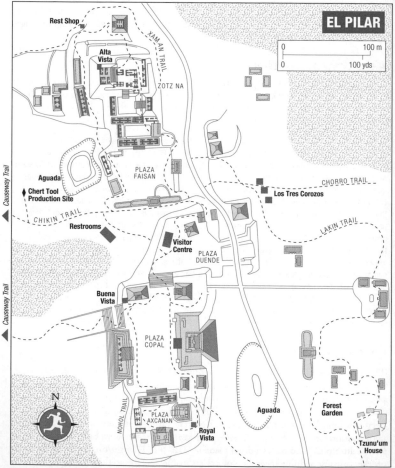

Construction on El Pilar began in the Preclassic period, around 800 BC, and continued until the Terminal Classic, around 1000 AD, when some structures were completely rebuilt. Such a long period of occupation was due to numerous springs and creeks – El Pilar is Spanish for "water basin". The city's prosperity still shows in the seventy major structures grouped around 25 plazas, appreciated along six **hiking trails** that criss-cross the five thousand-acre reserve. The four most impressive pyramids with ball court are between fifteen and twenty yards high, grouped around the **Plaza Copal**, from whose west side a flight of steps leads down to a thirty-yard-wide causeway running to **Pilar Poniente** in Guatemala. Due to the conservation policy, most structures are still largely mantled by the forest, which avoids erosion. Some portions of caved-in stonework have been uncovered and are on display; among them, an underground, corbelled tunnel, a standing temple and examples of elite architecture.

Very few of El Pilar's ruins have been altered since their discovery, offering an atmosphere similar to that experienced by the first archeologists. Scattered all around are shards of coloured pottery indicating the various periods of occupation. **Chert flakes** – by-products of the manufacture of stone implements – are visible in huge quantities along the Chikin Trail. It's easy to construe that the Maya had a concern for properly disposing of sharp stones, and therefore to walk the path without shoes. The Community Creek Trail is more strenuous, with structural remains and evidence of land use allowing you to piece together a historical narrative. For a longer hike, the 1.5-mile Chorro Trail brings you to a delicate waterfall, though the prehistoric Chorro settlement (inhabited from the Classic period) is currently inaccessible.

The Macal River and Cristo Rey Road

The mighty Macal River arises from tributaries in the Mountain Pine Ridge and the Chiquibul Forest, and in its upper reaches is sometimes fast and deep enough for **whitewater kayaking**, though you'll need an expert guide (see box, p.146). If instead the idea of a gentle day (or more) on the river appeals, then any of the resorts south of the Western Highway will rent canoes, though you'll see far more wildlife with a guide than you ever will alone. A very popular choice is to take a **guided canoe trip** up the Macal to *The Lodge at Chaa Creek* to visit the famous **Rainforest Medicine Trail** and **Chaa Creek Natural History Centre**, two of Cayo's premier attractions and both on the lodge grounds; a combined ticket costs Bz$25, though lodge guests visit for free. Even further upstream, there's the impressive and rapidly growing **Belize Botanic Gardens** at *duPlooy's*. Heading in the opposite direction, you can also make the trip downriver all the way to Belize City: up to a week of paddling, camping on the riverbank each night.

Steep limestone cliffs and forested hills edge the lower Macal valley, and there's plenty of **accommodation** in all price ranges along its banks, accessed by road via the **Chial Road**, to the west of San Ignacio, or the **Cristo Rey Road** just to the east. On any branch over the river or amidst the bank-side vegetation you can see **green iguanas**, the males resplendent in spring with their orange and brown mating colours. Higher up, you might hear the deep-throated roar of **howler monkeys**, which have been successfully reintroduced here from elsewhere in Belize. Over the past fifteen years, three **dams** have been built along the river's upper half, one – the Chalilo Dam – extremely controversially (see p.264); for most visitors, however, the only visible impact is silting of the river due to the periodic release of blockages.

On the river's eastern side, the **Cristo Rey Road** snakes its unpaved way south-wards, providing an access point to a number of river resorts before arriving at the village of San Antonio (see p.137), en route to the Mountain Pine Ridge. **CRISTO REY** itself is a pretty village of scattered wooden and cement houses and gardens on a high bank above the Macal. Near the entrance to the village, Orlando and Martha Madrid run *Sandals Restaurant* (☎614-7446), **rent canoes** at reasonable rates, and – if you're looking for budget accommodation for a night on the way to the *Mountain Pine Ridge* – rent a few simple, inexpensive **cabins** (☎614-7446; ❶).

Accommodation

Most accommodation along the Macal tends toward upmarket **cabaña resorts**, beautifully located in the forest above the riverbank. Many offer reduced low season prices, and also give discounts to *Rough Guides* readers, while there are one or two comfortable cheaper options, too. A taxi from San Ignacio to any of the lodgings costs Bz\$40–60. Most organize superb **horseback tours** to nearby Maya ruins, as well as **mountain bike** and **canoe** rental, and birding trips into the surrounding area. You can also choose to leave your accommodation via an easy **canoe float** downstream to San Ignacio; your host will take your luggage ahead while you drift along and enjoy the scenery. Each lodge offers home cooking – or at some – gourmet dining.

The following listings are in order of their appearance as you travel away from San Ignacio on the Macal River, though all can be reached by road from the Western Highway, the Cristo Rey Road or the Chial/Negroman Road (six miles from San Ignacio towards Benque Viejo) – though to get to two options you cross the Macal River in a canoe or boat. See the map on p.145 for locations.

Maya Mountain Lodge Cristo Rey Rd ☎824-2164, ⓦwww.mayamountain.com. Set in rich forest 1.5 miles south of Santa Elena, a short walk from the river. Colourfully decorated cabañas and a larger wooden "Parrot's Perch" building housing seven rooms; all have private bath and the latter a/c and a huge, shared deck with hammocks. Delicious meals are served in an open-sided room, great for birding: motmots, aracaris and trogons fly yards from your table. The lodge sometimes hosts students and has a well-stocked library and occasional after dinner presentation. Families are welcome; kids will enjoy the pool and illustrated trail guide. Tour/adventure packages available, and *Rough Guides* discount. ❺

🏃 **Crystal Paradise Resort** Cristo Rey Rd ☎824-2772 or 824-4014, ⓦwww.crystal paradise.com. Owned by the Belizean Tut family, this is a welcoming, relaxed place with wooden rooms and thatched cabañas, all with private hot water bath. The deck outside the dining room overlooks the Macal valley (you can't see the river but it's an easy walk), and attracts numerous hummingbirds. Victor built many of the thatched roofs amongst the resorts in Cayo, and sons Jeronie and Everald arrange birding and adventure tours throughout the district and to Tikal; see p.170. Free pickup in San Ignacio; internet provided; rates include Teresa's delicious and filling breakfast and dinner, plus there's a *Rough Guides* discount. ❻

Table Rock Jungle Lodge Cristo Rey Rd ☎670-4910, ⓦwww.tablerockbelize.com. Named after a well-known marker on the Macal River trail, this beautifully appointed property offers three spotless, tiled cabañas along a landscaped stone path through the rainforest. Each has poster beds with nets and an imaginative colour scheme, while surrounding them are soursop, orange and mango trees and a series of decks and trails. The stretch of riverfront here is one of the area's most attractive, and you can relax in the thatched *palapa* restaurant/bar, where the friendly staff serve excellent food and cocktails (breakfast and dinner charged at US\$29). ❼

🏃 **The Lodge at Chaa Creek** Chial Rd ☎824-2037, ⓦwww.chaacreek.com. Beautiful, whitewashed, wood-and-stucco cabañas and wooden "treetop" jacuzzi suites (sleeping four) in gorgeous grounds high above the Macal, with a deserved reputation for luxury and ambience. Very comfortable beds, tiled floors, large bathrooms, screened windows and spacious, wooden decks. Modern and stunning hilltop spa, fine restaurant and bar with large deck. A cheaper on-site option is the *Macal River Camp* – eminently comfortable wooden cabins with tarp roofs (US\$60 per person, including meals). Guided tours to the *Lodge's* attractions (see opposite & p.158), an early-morning bird walk, canoes, and internet access all included. ❼–❾

duPlooy's Chial Rd, just beyond *Chaa Creek* ☎824-3101, ⓦwww.duplooys.com. First-rate eco-friendly lodge which powers its generators mainly by vegetable oil and sources almost everything locally. Beautifully located on the Macal's west bank, it's also home to the Belize Botanic Gardens (see p.158). Guests choose between spacious, private bungalows with deck, king-sized and sofa beds, fridge and coffeemaker, or "Jungle Lodges", each with queen-sized bed and porch, or the budget seven-room Belize River House (for larger groups), with kitchen (latter US$500, sleeps up to fourteen). For followers of Maya philosophy, look out for their Dec 2012 "Apocalypto" package. **❼–❽**

Macawbank Jungle Lodge Access via Cristo Rey Rd ☎608-4825, ⓦwww.macawbankjungle lodge.com. Noticeably different from its counterparts, set within forty acres of beautiful and spacious grassland savannah and fruit trees surrounded by thick jungle, a short walk from the river. Mountain biking, kayaking, tubing and yoga are all on offer, or kick back in a hammock or walk the numerous trails spotting toucans, trogans and orange-breasted falcons. Five comfortable and artistic cabañas (three on stilts) sleep up to four and have river-rock-lined showers, varnished floors and verandas. Tasty and filling meals available: US$40 per person per day full board. **❺–❼**

Guacamallo Jungle Camp Macal River east bank (access via Chial Rd and canoe) ☎804-3674 or 628-2837. If you're looking for rustic jungle accommodation, this is it, perched high above the river on the edge of the mysterious unexcavated Maya site of Tipú. No frills (candle-light and real fire) but with a hot water shower, plus lots of tasty food, much of it organically grown here, and a wonderful sense of timeless-ness at night as you sit on a Maya mound outside your cabin, watching the stars. Explore Tipú on your own or canoe along the river. Contact David's Adventure Tours in San Ignacio; advance booking not normally necessary. Rates include transport, dinner and breakfast. **❹**

Black Rock River Lodge Via Chial Rd, at the end of "Black Rock Road" ☎820-3929, ⓦwww.black rocklodge.com. Drive here on your own, or arrange for a pickup from San Ignacio or the airport. Set high above the west bank of the Macal River with stunning views of jungle-clad limestone cliffs and the gushing rapids of the upper river. Each solidly built deluxe cabaña has private bathroom and floor made of smooth river stones; some have a spacious deck and all are powered by hydro and solar. Trails lead to waterfalls, hilltops and caves, some of which contain Maya pottery. Horses, mountain bikes and canoes available. Excellent meals taken in an exquisite open cabaña above the river. **❻–❽**

The Rainforest Medicine Trail

A canoe trip along the Macal is the best way to get to *Chaa Creek*'s **Rainforest Medicine Trail** (daily 8am–5pm; free for lodge guests, Bz$15 for non-guests, $22 combined ticket with Natural History Centre, $35 with guided tour). When first built, the trail was dedicated to Don Eligio Panti, a Maya bush doctor from San Antonio village who died in 1996 at the age of 103. At the entrance there's a thatched shelter with hammocks to rest in, and visitors enjoy a refreshing drink during the explanatory talk before the hike, which winds through the forest above the riverbank.

Maya medical knowledge was extensive, and signs along the trail identify about a hundred species of healing plants, many now used in modern medicine. It's a fascinating journey: there are vines that provide fresh water like a tap; poison-wood, with oozing black sap; its antidote, the peeling bark of the gumbo limbo tree, always growing nearby; and the bark of the negrito tree, once sold in Europe for its weight in gold as a cure for dysentery. You'll also see herbal teas and blood tonic; the **gift shop** sells all, including Traveller's Tonic, preventing diarrhoea, and Jungle Salve, for insect bites.

Before his death, Don Eligio passed on his skills to Dr Rosita Arvigo, who founded the Medicine Trail and still lives nearby. She now operates the **Ix Chel Wellness Center** in Santa Elena (1458 Eve St, just off the highway on Loma Luz Blvd; open year-round, but Rosita is there only in winter), and visitors can benefit from her natural healing methods and massage (call ☎804-0264 for an appointment, ⓦwww.arvigomassage.com; classes available in medicine and cooking, and herb walks around San Ignacio). Several plants from the Belize rainforest are being investigated as potential treatments for AIDS, and Rosita and the staff at Ix Chel, in collaboration with the New York Botanical Garden, are at the forefront. Rosita wrote about her apprenticeship to Don Eligio (see Books, p.272), and newsletters by the Belize Association of Traditional Healers are available at the Ix Chel gift shop.

Chaa Creek Natural History Centre and Butterfly Farm

A visit to the marvellous **Chaa Creek Natural History Centre** (daily 8am–4pm; Bz$15, includes guided tour, every hour), on the grounds of *The Lodge at Chaa Creek* next to the Rainforest Medicine Trail, is a great sampler of Cayo's history, geography and wildlife. If you're spending more than a couple of days in the area, try to see this first: call ☎824-2037 to check on current events. The centre has fascinating and accurate displays of the region's flora and fauna, vivid archeological and geological maps, a scale model of the Macal valley and a library with relevant books and journals – all of which make for an engaging visit.

Nearby, at the **Blue Morpho Butterfly Breeding Centre** (included in Natural History Centre entry fee), you can walk among enormous, magnificent Blue Morpho butterflies, and even watch them emerge from chrysalises most mornings. There's also a **Maya Farm**, where *Chaa Creek* staff use traditional methods to grow corn, beans, tomatoes, squash and other crops; the produce is incorporated into the meals served at the lodge (see p.156).

The Belize Botanic Gardens

South of *Chaa Creek*, and reached either by road or river, the ⚘ **Belize Botanic Gardens** at *duPlooy's* (daily 8am–5pm; Bz$10, $20 with guided tour; ☎824-3101, Ⓦ www.belizebotanic.org) is a remarkable project established in 1997 on fifty acres of former farmland and forest. The garden is the brainchild of *duPlooy's* owners and avid plant-lovers Ken and Judy duPlooy. Ken, who died in 2001, was held in such high esteem that a new species of orchid was named after him – *Pleurothallis duplooyii*, a tiny, purple variety. Daughter Heather now manages the gardens, with four hundred tree species, a nursery with a thousand seedlings and miles of interpretive **trails**. A first-class educational and study resource, they conserve many of Belize's native plant species within small reproductions of natural habitats. You approach the gardens through an avenue of fruit-bearing trees, which attract wild **birds**, and you can either explore on your own or follow **expert naturalists** Lloyd and Martin. A firetower, dedicated to Ken DuPlooy, offers breathtaking views of the surrounding hills, and bird hides on the two ponds allow you to spy on least grebes, black-bellied whistling-ducks and northern jacanas. The magnificent **orchid house**, with over one hundred species, is the best in Central America.

East to Benque and the Mopan River

Leaving San Ignacio past the entrance to the Maya ruins of Cahal Pech (see p.148), the Western Highway continues to the border town of **Benque Viejo** via the village of **Succotz** and the famous Maya ruins of **Xunantunich**. It's a fairly straight route, which parallels the Mopan River after a couple of miles, faster flowing than its neighbour, the Macal. There are some attractive and not too serious **whitewater rapids** here, and it's easy enough to arrange kayak or rafting trips; check at *Clarissa Falls* (see opposite). Take care when swimming as rapids that appear minor from the bank do present a real danger, and there are a number of hidden whirlpools; for your own safety, always wear a **lifejacket** on the Mopan.

On its east bank, two miles outside of San Ignacio, a sign points northwards to the small Maya site of **Buenavista del Cayo**, once the centre of a political region that included Cahal Pech. The ruins are on private land, and to visit you need permission from the owner, Pablo Guerra, a shopkeeper in Benque Viejo; the best way to visit is on horseback, however – Easy Rider (see box, p.147) runs excellent tours. Excavations between 1984 and 1989 by Jennifer Taschek and Joseph Ball discovered a palace, ball-courts, carved stelae, plazas and courtyards, alongside burial items including the famous Jauncy vase, now in the **Museum of Belize** (see p.59); there's evidence that the Maya established workshops here to mass-produce pottery. Most of the structures are overgrown with vegetation, but you can still visit a small but charming palace structure and arched courtyard in a glade.

Just before Succotz, *Trek Stop* (see p.160) offers well-positioned **accommodation** for visiting the ruins, though it's better known as the site of **Tropical Wings Nature Center** (daily 8am–5pm; Bz$6, including guided tour), a delicate, enchanting world full of tropical colour. Native plants arch upwards, pressing against the netting on the roof, and about two dozen species of butterfly breed here, laying their eggs on the leaves. Outside you can see caterpillars in all stages of development. Inside, there are child-friendly exhibits on biodiversity, Maya ethno-botany, as well as a *marimba* xylophone. A rather unique activity here, popular with school groups, is a round of **frisbee golf** on the only course in the country.

Both *Clarissa Falls* and *Trek Stop* serve good **food**, but there are also options in Succotz village; walk three blocks uphill from the bus stop on the highway to *Benny's Kitchen* – an open-air, very reasonable Belizean **restaurant** (try the milkshakes). *On 'D' Way*, on the highway between *Trek Stop* and Xunantunich, sells fried tacos and *salbutes* – quick, delicious snacks. For souvenirs, also in Succotz, the Magaña family's art gallery and **gift shop**, just south of Hua Young Supermarket, deals in superb wood and slate carvings.

Accommodation

Clarissa Falls signed 1.5 miles north of the Western Hwy (Mile 70) ☎824-3916, ⓦ www.clarissafalls.com. Part of a working cattle ranch, this is a very restful place right by a set of (often dangerous) rapids on the Mopan. Simple thatched cottages are all wheelchair-accessible and have private bath; suites have full kitchen. Space for camping (Bz$15 per person) and hook-ups for RVs. Owner Chena serves great home cooking, and there's a quiet bar overlooking the falls. Activities on offer include horseback riding, canoeing, rafting, tubing and guided jungle walks; birding here is stellar. Discounts for student groups. ❺

Martz Farm Eight miles along the Arenal/Mollejon Hydro Rd from Benque Viejo ☎663-3849 or 614-6462, ⓦ www.martzfarm.com. Run by the Martinez family, an ideal budget river resort if you're crossing the border to/from Guatemala; the owners will pick up from there or San Ignacio. On the Macal River two miles upriver from *Black Rock* (see p.157), with comfortable thatched cabins perched in trees above a rushing, crystal-clear creek, inexpensive rooms and home-cooking.

To reach the river you climb down a gorgeous, thirty-yard waterfall (you can also camp here) to a remote beach; across the river, the forest beckons and there's great riding on the Martz mules. ❸

Maxim's Palace 41 Church Hill St, Benque Viejo ☎823-2360, ⓔ cayobenque@yahoo.com. A clean, safe, yet simple guesthouse in the middle of town, popular with Belizeans. Twelve rooms with private hot-water bath; some have king-sized beds, others two double beds. ❷

Mopan River Resort Benque Viejo, on the west bank of the Mopan (cross by boat) ☎823-2047, ⓦ www.mopanriverresort.com. Belize's first all-inclusive inland resort, this is the place to be pampered while staying in very attractive cabañas; all have comfortable beds, mahogany floors and rattan furniture, a tub, large porch and numerous extras; some have kitchens. This is a social vacation: meals are served family-style, and each evening you're briefed on the next day's excursion. Great on-site birding. Three-nights minimum; rates include transfers, gourmet meals, all drinks, a tour each day (including Tikal and Caracol), use of kayaks and taxes. With all the extras it's very good value, quite possibly the best deal in the country. Closed in low season. **❾**

Trek Stop Five hundred yards east of Succotz ☎823-2265, ⓦwww.thetrekstop.com. Set in a quiet forest clearing near the highway, ten non-smoking cabins have comfortable beds, mosquito nets and porch. Run by a Succotz family, it uses composting toilets and solar-heated showers. As part of the Tropical Wings Nature Center (see p.159), plants here include Maya medicinal varieties. Great library on Maya and natural history. Restaurant serves large portions of good food, including vegetarian choices; also self-catering kitchen. Guided river and nature trips. **❷–❸**

San José Succotz and Xunantunich

The village of **SAN JOSÉ SUCCOTZ** lies beside the Mopan River just east of Benque Viejo. It's a traditional place, inhabited largely by Mopan Maya, who throw a fiesta here on the weekend after Holy Saturday (Easter). Under colonial administration, the Maya of Succotz cooperated with the British, a stance that angered other groups such as the Icaiché, who burnt the village to the ground in 1867. People here identify strongly with their culture, and many of the men work as caretakers at Maya sites throughout Belize. Outside fiesta times, it's a sleepy place; the main reason for coming is to see the Classic-period site of **Xunantunich**, up the hill across the river.

To **get here**, take any bus or shared taxi running between San Ignacio and Benque. Try to visit in the afternoon and on days when cruise ships aren't in town as the site can get unpleasantly crowded. You cross the Mopan River via a hand-winched **cable ferry** (daily 8am–3.30pm; free); from the opposite bank, walk or drive up a steep, 1.5-mile road to the site entrance (daily 8am–4pm; Bz$10). The marvellous **visitor centre** is one of the best in Belize, with a superb scale model of the city and a fibreglass replica of the famous hieroglyphic frieze around El Castillo, from which you get a good idea of its significance. The nearby original **museum** has several well-preserved stelae.

El Castillo, the tallest building at the site, dominates the countryside for miles around – you'll see it as you approach from San Ignacio. Pronounced "Shun-an-tun-ich", the site's name means "the stone maiden" in Mopan Maya – though this is

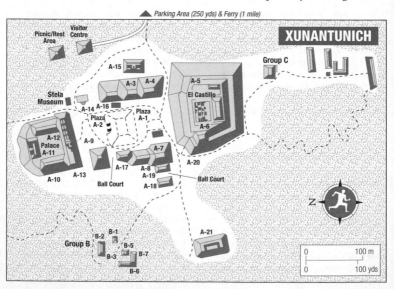

not what the ancient Maya called it. In fact, one of the most significant finds here was a chunk of stone frieze bearing the site's original name: **Kat Witz**, or "clay mountain". Xunantunich was first explored in the 1890s by Dr Thomas Gann, a British medical officer; in 1904, Teobalt Maler of Harvard's Peabody Museum took photographs and drew up a plan. Gann returned in 1924 and unearthed (looted, in modern terminology) numerous artefacts, including the carved glyphs of Altar 1, whose whereabouts are unknown. In 1938, British archeologist J. Eric S. Thompson found pottery, obsidian, jade, stingray spines and more, while recent excavations offer evidence of Xunantunich's role in power politics: it was probably allied as a subordinate, like Caracol, with the regional superpower Calakmul, against Tikal (see p.170). By the Terminal Classic it was in decline, though still apparently populated until around 1000 AD, shortly after the Classic Maya collapse.

Built on top of an artificially flattened hill, Xunantunich incorporates five plazas, although the remaining structures are grouped around just three. The entrance road brings you to Plaza A–2, while to the left, Plaza A–1 is dominated by **El Castillo** (structure A–6), the tallest building at forty yards high and a prominent symbol for Belize. The building is layered, with later versions built on top. It's ringed by a restored **stucco frieze** decorated with abstract carvings, human faces, jaguar heads and a king performing authority rituals. The climb up El Castillo is a challenge, but the views from the top are superb, with the forest stretching out all around and the rest of the city clearly laid out. To your right as you enter the site, Plaza A–3 is almost completely enclosed by an acropolis-like collection of buildings, known as the **Palace**. Artefacts found here in 2003 suggest that this was the place where the ruler met important officials. Human sacrificial remains found in a lower room may be connected with ceremonies conducted while the structure was being deliberately filled-in in the Late Classic – but well before the entire site was abandoned.

Benque Viejo and the border

The last town on the Western Highway before the Guatemalan border is **BENQUE VIEJO DEL CARMEN**, eight miles from San Ignacio. Culturally, Belize and Guatemala merge here with almost equal potency, and Spanish is certainly the dominant language, despite English street names such as Elizabeth and Victoria. Benque, as it's usually known, is a pleasant, quiet town, home to many artists, musicians and writers, and it's undergoing a fascinating cultural revival. Several villagers produce excellent **wood and slate carvings** which are on sale at Xunantunich.

If you're interested in mestizo tradition, visit the **Benque House of Culture** in the old police station (Mon–Fri 8am–5pm, Sat 9am–noon; ☏823-2697). Inside are displays of old photos and documents on the town, as well as logging and chicle-gathering equipment, paintings and musical instruments. Visiting exhibitions, films and local performances take place, and the managers, the Ruiz brothers, also organize a lively biennial **Festival of Mestizo and Maya Culture**, held in November. Ask here about another manifestation of local artistic spirit: the **Poustinia** sculpture park (see box, opposite). For nightlife in Benque, the hotspot is *Benque Rock*, a nightclub on Baron Bliss Road uphill next to the cemetery; it's a large place which attracts people from all over Belize at weekends for reggae dancehall, soca and punta rock.

Crossing the border, 1.5 miles beyond Benque, is straightforward – there's a constant stream of taxis (Bz$2–3 per person); see box, p.162.

Well south of Benque, the **Mopan River** begins in the Maya Mountains, first flowing into Guatemala before it re-enters Belize at the village of **Arenal**, three miles south of the Benque Viejo border post along the Arenal/Mollejon Hydro Road. The **international boundary** runs right through the middle of this Maya-mestizo village of stick-and-thatch houses, bisecting a football pitch with a goal in each country. The river then leaves Belize briefly again, rushes under a bridge, before returning for its

Poustinia Land-Sculpture Park

It's hard to imagine a more atmospheric venue for artwork than this thirty-acre rainforest setting. The brainchild of local architect Luis Ruiz, the extraordinary **Poustinia Land-Sculpture Park** holds a collection of thirty sculptures by both Belizean and foreign artists, all provoking and portraying contemporary Belize. It seeks to build awareness of the **natural environment**, reforestation and land beautification following human abuse, and many sculptures are themselves organic, in time disappearing to be replaced by new works. *Returned Parquet*, by Tim Davies, is a fine example: reclaimed mahogany parquet flooring, laid as a path through a forest glade, which will eventually biodegrade and return to whence it came. Other excellent works include installations by David and Luis Ruiz and the schoolchildren of Benque Viejo, and a recent glass "apparition" door; even its hinges are glass.

Given their thought-provoking mission, it's hard to see why Poustinia is not better known – but its location three miles south of Benque on the Arenal Road ensures that it's not on the tourist trail – it remains firmly forest property. You're likely to have the park to yourself, an opportunity for peaceful reflection a million miles from a city art gallery. Walking the park is best enjoyed in sunny weather and at leisure; allow three daylight hours to complete the route, and bring water. The **entry fee** (Bz$20) is paid at the entrance and visitors are given a map for a self-guided tour; guided tours also available (Bz$50; book in advance at the Benque House of Culture ☎822-1574; see also above), and visit ⊛www.poustiniaonline.org. Taxis ply the route from Benque Viejo to Arenal, so transport shouldn't be a problem unless you're returning late in the day – even then, the one-hour walk back to town is enjoyable.

most picturesque final fifteen-mile stretch north and eastwards to its confluence with the Macal River at pretty Branch Mouth, just north of San Ignacio.

Further along the Arenal/Mollejon Hydro Road, about five miles from Poustinia, is **Che Chem Ha Cave** (daily tours at 9.30am and 1.30pm; 90min; ☎820-4065). Maya for "running water", Che Chem Ha boasts a huge collection of intact ceremonial Maya pottery, scattered throughout its chambers – some two thousand years old. Primarily used for food storage and ceremonies, it remains just as it was found in 1989, when William Morales stumbled upon it during a hunt with his father. William now leads tours here, and will pick groups up from Benque; be sure to bring sturdy shoes, insect repellent and water, and the will to get muddy – you can rinse off in a waterfall at the site, and Vaca Falls is an easy, thirty-minute hike away.

Travel details

Various bus companies run along the western and southern routes. A shared taxi to the border costs Bz$3 per person from Benque, though it's often quicker to take a shared taxi (Bz$5–6 per person) from the market area in San Ignacio.

Belize City to: Destinations along the Western Highway, terminating in Benque Viejo (for the Guatemalan border; 3hr 30min), are served by at-least-hourly buses (5am–9pm). An express service stops only in Belmopan, every 2 hours, saving an hour on journey times.
Belmopan to: Dangriga (roughly hourly 5am–7pm; 1hr 40min); Independence (for Placencia) and Punta Gorda (10 daily 6.30am–4.30pm; 4hr); San Ignacio and Benque Viejo (hourly Mon–Fri 6.30am–10pm, fewer on weekends; first bus each day continues to Melchor, Guatemala).
Benque Viejo to: Belize City, calling at San Ignacio and Belmopan (half-hourly daily 4am–5pm, express service every 3–4hr).
San Ignacio to: Belmopan and Belize City (half-hourly & some express 3.30am–6pm); Benque Viejo (half-hourly until 11.30pm; 20min); Cristo Rey and San Antonio (4 daily Mon–Sat 10.30am–5.15pm; 1hr); Guatemalan border (usually once daily at 7.30am).

Tikal and Flores

CHAPTER 5

Highlights

✳ **Yaxhá** The impressive, restored ruins of Yaxhá tower above the shores of a lovely lake. **See p.168**

✳ **El Remate** Stay overnight in this relaxed little village on the eastern edge of Lago Petén Itzá and get an early start for Tikal the next day. **See p.169**

✳ **Tikal** Explore this enormous, ancient Maya metropolis, amid protected rainforest teeming with wildlife. **See p.170**

✳ **Flores** Stroll the cobbled streets of this tiny colonial capital set on an island, then enjoy cocktails at a lakeside bar. **See p.177**

▲ Tikal

Tikal and Flores

Guatemala's vast northern department of **Petén** reveals spectacular nature reserves and hundreds of Maya ruins, many completely buried in the jungle. The jewel of the region is **Tikal**, arguably the most magnificent of all Maya sites. It towers impressively over the rainforest less than two hours from the Belize border, making for an accessible – and unmissable – side-trip, and it can be done independently or on an organized tour. Tikal's monumental temple-pyramids are testament to the fact that Petén was the heartland of ancient Maya civilization during the Preclassic and Classic periods (around 300 BC–900 AD), and that here Maya culture reached the height of its architectural achievement.

En route to Tikal, there are other Maya sites worth stopping for, and you'll see signs for several as you head west along the road from the bustling yet nondescript border town of **Melchor de Mencos**. The first major sites are **Yaxhá**, the third largest in Petén, and the much smaller **Topoxté**. Both occupy beautiful settings on opposite shores of Laguna Yaxhá, about nineteen miles from the border, and there's camping and cabaña accommodation nearby. If you're travelling directly to Tikal by bus from the Belizean border, you'll need to change buses at the village of **Ixlú**, from where it's only about a mile to the peaceful community of **El Remate** – a good base if you plan to spend more than a day exploring the area. Those with the time for a more extended trip could make for the village and ruins of **Uaxactún**, to the north of Tikal, which also serves as a jumping-off point for expeditions to El Zotz and the remote northern sites of Río Azul and El Mirador.

But archeology isn't the only thing to tempt you over the border. Petén is a huge, rolling expanse of tropical forest, swamps, lakes and dry savannahs, stretching into the Lacandón forest of southern Mexico. Tikal itself lies at the centre of a large national park, which forms part of the **Maya Biosphere Reserve**, covering six thousand square miles of northern Petén. As one of the largest tropical forest reserves in Central America, it's extraordinarily rich in **wildlife**, particularly birds, though you're also virtually guaranteed to see **howler** or **spider monkeys**. One

Guatemala accommodation price codes

Accommodation in this chapter has been given a **price code** according to the scale below, which represents the cost of **a double room in high season**. The scale is in US$, due to possible fluctuation in the exchange rate of the quetzal.

① US$10 and under   ④ US$26–40   ⑦ US$76–100
② US$11–15   ⑤ US$41–55   ⑧ US$101–125
③ US$16–25   ⑥ US$56–75   ⑨ US$126 and over

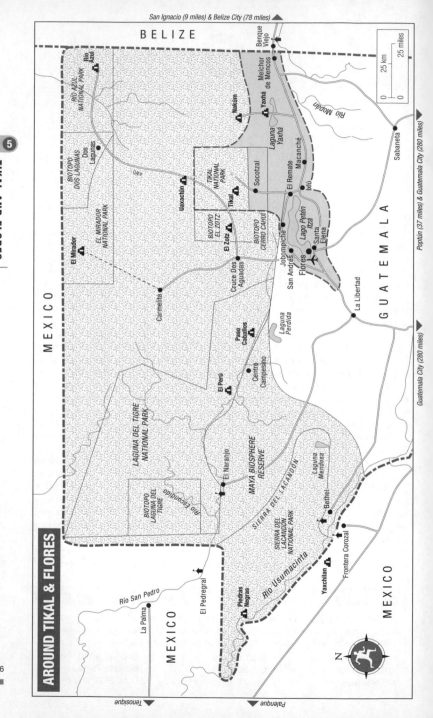

AROUND TIKAL & FLORES

BELIZE

San Ignacio (9 miles) & Belize City (78 miles)

Benque Viejo

Melchor de Mencos

Río Azul

RÍO AZUL NATIONAL PARK

BIOTOPO DOS LAGUNAS

Dos Lagunas

Nakúm

Yaxhá

Laguna Yaxhá

Rio Mopan

Macanché

Socotzal

TIKAL NATIONAL PARK

El Remate

Ixlú

EL MIRADOR NATIONAL PARK

Uaxactún

Tikal

BIOTOPO EL ZOTZ

BIOTOPO CERRO CAHUÍ

Lago Petén Itzá

El Mirador

El Zotz

Jobompiche

Santa Elena

San Andrés

Flores

Cruce Dos Aguadas

Carmelita

Laguna Perdida

La Libertad

Paso Caballos

Sabaneta

GUATEMALA

Poptún (37 miles) & Guatemala City (280 miles)

Laguna Mendosa

LAGUNA DEL TIGRE NATIONAL PARK

El Perú

Centro Campesino

MAYA BIOSPHERE RESERVE

BIOTOPO LAGUNA DEL TIGRE

Río Escondido

El Naranjo

SIERRA DEL LACANDÓN

SIERRA DEL LACANDÓN NATIONAL PARK

Bethel

Frontera Corozal

Guatemala City (280 miles)

MEXICO

La Palma

Río San Pedro

El Pedregral

Piedras Negras

Yaxchilán

Río Usumacinta

MEXICO

Tenosique

Palenque

MEXICO

25 km

25 miles

0

0

N

Getting there

From Belize City, **buses** leave regularly for Benque Viejo (all stopping at San Ignacio; see p.145), just over a mile from the Guatemalan border. After you disembark at Benque Viejo, you'll need to take a *colectivo* taxi (around US$2 per person) the rest of the way to the border. Alternatively, the Linea Dorada bus line will take you directly from Belize City to Flores or Tikal, with a stop at the border for formalities. Belize's two domestic airlines discontinued service to Flores, but it's worth checking with Maya Island Air (see p.21) to get the latest update.

On the Guatemalan side of the border, you can take a minibus (known locally as microbuses) to **El Remate** or **Flores** (prices depend on the number of people, and your final destination) or **taxi** (around US$15–20 per person, depending on the number of people); this is generally the quickest and most comfortable way to travel. You can also take a taxi to **Tikal** from the border (around US$15 per person, with four people in the taxi). Public buses also run to **Flores/Santa Elena** (every couple of hours from 5am to 7pm), which can be picked up from Melchor – take a shared taxi from the border to Melchor for a couple of quetzales. You can also take a public bus to Tikal; catch a bus from Melchor to Ixlú and get another from there. Renting a car is also an option for getting to Tikal from Belize; note, though, that some companies don't allow you to take a rental vehicle into Guatemala. Crystal Auto Rental (see p.68), in Belize City, is one of the few that does.

Border practicalities

Both the Belizean and Guatemalan border posts are on the eastern bank of the Mopan River, nine miles west of San Ignacio. Even if you're leaving Belize for just one day, you'll have to pay the **exit tax** of Bz$30 and the PACT conservation fee of around Bz$7.50; keep your receipt, as it could reduce your next exit tax. Although **visas** are not needed by most nationalities, and most visitors aren't required to pay an entry fee, everyone must fill in the immigration form. As for changing money: it's sometimes easier to use the moneychangers who'll pester you on either side of the border; bargain with a couple and you'll get a fair rate.

Phones

The international dialling code for Guatemala is **502**.

Language

Guatemala is a **Spanish**-speaking country and you'd be wise to acquire at least some knowledge of the language; overcharging foreigners is routine, and the better you are at getting by, the less likely you are to be ripped off. See p.278 for a brief Spanish-language guide.

Money and costs

The Guatemalan unit of **currency** is the quetzal (Q). **Costs** are generally far cheaper than in Belize; for transport, accommodation and food they can be as much as forty or fifty percent less. El Remate (roughly on the way to Tikal) and Flores have some of the best budget accommodation in the country.

Crime and safety

In Guatemala you'll need to take even greater **safety precautions** than in Belize. The border crossing (and indeed travel to Tikal) is best undertaken in daylight. In the past, violent robberies and assaults on tourists have taken place in and around El Remate and within Tikal itself, though **Tourism Police** patrols in vehicles and on foot have successfully driven most violent criminals elsewhere.

of the best places to get an understanding of the forest (apart from Tikal itself) is to visit the **Biotopo Cerro Cahuí** reserve near El Remate.

Finally, the departmental capital, **Flores**, is a picturesque town set on an island in Lago Petén Itzá, while close by, on the mainland, the town of **Santa Elena** is its transport hub.

Melchor de Mencos to El Remate

The 27 miles from the **Belize border** to the **Ixlú junction** takes you through rolling countryside and farmland, past a series of small villages and the Maya sites of **Yaxhá** and **Topoxté**. The road from Melchor de Mencos is in reasonable condition, though the first section beyond the border is still unpaved. It runs roughly parallel to a chain of lakes – the largest of which is **Lago Petén Itzá** – used in Maya times as the main route across the region. Other lakes along the way include Macanché, with more ruins and a nature reserve, and Sal Petén, where there's another major Maya site. Near the shore of Lago Petén Itzá, the Melchor road meets the Flores–Tikal road at the village of **Ixlú**, from where you can continue west to Flores, or north, through **El Remate**, to Tikal.

Yaxhá and Topoxté

Nineteen miles from Melchor the road passes about five miles to the south of **lagunas Yaxhá and Sacnab**, beautiful bodies of water ringed by dense rainforest. Laguna Yaxhá is home to two Maya ruins that are worth a visit: **Yaxhá**, on a hill overlooking the northern shore, and **Topoxté**, on an island near the southern shore. The turn-off is clearly signposted and the bus driver will stop if you ask. If you haven't arranged for a tour it can be tough to reach without your own vehicle; you could hitch from the main Flores–Belize road to La Máquina, about a mile from the lakes. You can inquire about a taxi at the border or El Remate.

Yaxhá (Q80 entry fee), a huge ruin covering a couple of square miles of a ridge overlooking the lake, is primarily a Classic-period city. The site is open daily; if you're not on a guided trip, one of the knowledgeable guards will show you around for a small fee. The scale model of the site near the entrance is another good source of information. The ruins are spread out over nine plazas and more than five hundred structures have been mapped so far, including several huge pyramids and large acropolis complexes. The tallest and most impressive pyramid, **Structure 216**, northeast of the entrance, rises in tiers to a height of over 98ft; the restoration enables you to climb to the top for spectacular views over the forest and lake.

Topoxté, a much smaller site on the easternmost of three small islands, is best reached by boat from *El Sombrero*. There is a four-kilometre trail to a spot opposite the islands, but you still have to get over to them – and large crocodiles inhabit the lake. The structures you see are not on the scale of those at Yaxhá, and date mainly from the Late Postclassic, though the site was occupied since Preclassic times.

If you want to **stay** nearby, the wonderful, solar-powered *Campamento El Sombrero* (☎7861-1687, ⊕www.ecosombrero.com; ❸–❺), on the south side of the lake, has thatched wooden cabañas and a campsite. The restaurant and lounge overlooking the lake, outfitted with low couches and hammocks, is a peaceful spot to stop for lunch even if you're not staying. The Italian-born owner is a great source of information about Yaxhá, and can arrange boat trips on the lake and horseback trips to other sites; she'll pick you up from the bus stop if you call in advance.

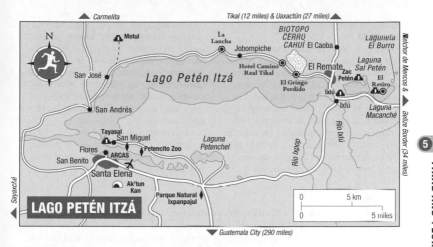

El Remate and around

EL REMATE, on the shore of Lago Petén Itzá, is a small, friendly village that's a convenient base for visiting Tikal, making for a relaxing alternative to Flores. The accommodation here is cheaper and nicer than at the site itself, and all buses and **minibuses** to and from Tikal pass through the village.

One mile further west along the lake, an unpaved road passes the **Biotopo Cerro Cahuí** (daily 7am–4pm; Q20), a 2.5-square-mile **nature reserve** with a lakeshore, ponds and trails leading through the forest to hilltop Maya ruins. Beyond here is the village of **Jobompiche**, served by buses from Santa Elena, and the road continues on to circle the entire lake – good for exploring by mountain bike. A few hotels have bikes for guests to borrow or rent. There are plenty of **guides** in El Remate who can lead you on multi-day trips to remote Maya sites; to find a good guide, ask a hotel for a recommendation.

Accommodation

Accommodation in El Remate is dotted along the main road and the one that runs along the northern shore of the lake. Though few, if any, have exact addresses, most are clearly signposted from the road, and El Remate is small enough that you'll pass many of them on a stroll through the village.

La Casa de Don David At the junction with the road to Biotopo Cerro Cahuí ☎7928-8469 or 5306-2190, ⓦwww.lacasadedon david.com. Comfortable and secure wooden bungalows and rooms with private hot-water bath set in extensive, lovely plant-filled grounds just back from the lakeshore. The popular restaurant serves *guatemalteca* home-cooking. The staff can arrange trips to Tikal and bus tickets for Belize and Guatemala City. Their website has lots of useful information on the area. ❸–❹

Las Gardenias On the main road ☎7928-8377 or 5992-3380, ⓔhotelasgardenias@yahoo.com. Decent a/c and fan rooms with private bath. The simple restaurant, with thatch-and-stick-style walls and a stone floor, serves local fare. ❸–❹

El Gringo Perdido On the north shore, 1.5 miles from *Don David's* ☎2334-2305, ⓔgringo_perdido @hotmail.com. Long-running, relaxed place on the tranquil shores of the lake. Simple rooms with wooden beds, with private and shared bath. You can also camp (Q25 per person). The open-air restaurant serves plenty of vegetarian options. Note that the hotel is opening up a small "eco-luxury" resort, *Pirámide Paraíso*; ask at reception. ❸–❺

Hotel Mon Ami Half a mile down road to Cerro Cahuí ☎7928-8143, ⓦwww.hotelmonami.com. Well-maintained and comfortable, this friendly spot includes ample adobe bungalows with breezy porches hung with hammocks, as well as clean, inviting dorms; the restaurant serves tasty

169

Guatemalan dishes – sometimes with a French twist. ❸–❹

La Lancha In Aldea Jobompiche, about nine miles west of El Remate along the north shore of the lake ☎7928-8331, ⓦwww.blancaneaux.com. For true lakeside comfort, head to Francis Ford Coppola's third resort in Central America. Winding paths lead through verdant grounds to plush *casitas* featuring Balinese headboards, bright red-and-orange Guatemalan fabrics, marble bathrooms and ample wooden decks overlooking the placid lake. Other than a shell phone to call reception, the *casitas* are decidedly gadget-free – no TVs or a/c. In keeping with Coppola's belief in environmental sustainability, the *casitas* are designed from local materials and benefit from natural ventilation. The rustic-chic restaurant – think wooden canoes as planters – serves top-notch *guatemalteca* fare. Breakfast included in the price. ❾

La Mansión del Pájaro Serpiente On the main road ☎5702-9434. Set in a tropical garden with a pool, these stone-built, two-storey cabañas offer lovely lake views. ❺

Sun Breeze Hotel On the main road ☎7928-8044 or 5898-2665. Clean, basic, fan-cooled rooms with lake views and comfortable beds equipped with mosquito nets. ❷–❸

Eating

El Remate is dotted with casual **restaurants**, many offering outdoor dining with lake views. A number of the hotels also have attached restaurants. The restaurant at *Don David* (see p.168), which features views of the leafy grounds and the lake in the distance, serves nightly Guatemalan dinner specials. At the thatched-roofed *Las Orchideas* (☎5701-9022), on the road to Biotopo Cerro Cahuí, you can dine on home-made Italian dishes, including fresh pastas.

Tikal

North of El Remate, the road climbs a limestone escarpment, and the settlements begin to thin out as you approach the entrance to **Tikal National Park**, a protected area of some 143 square miles that surrounds the archeological site. As you get closer, the sheer scale of Tikal as it rises above the forest canopy becomes overwhelming, and the atmosphere spellbinding. Dominating the ruins are five enormous **temples**: steep-sided pyramids that rise up nearly two hundred feet from the forest floor, and around which lie literally thousands of other structures, many still hidden beneath

▲ Tikal

mounds of earth and covered with jungle. As with most Maya sites, excavations are often ongoing; in the case of Tikal, active excavations take place for part of the year.

Some history: the rise and fall of Tikal

According to archeological evidence, the first occupants of Tikal had arrived by 900 BC, during the **Middle Preclassic**, making this amongst the oldest of Maya sites, though at that time it was little more than a village. Its inhabitants called it **Mutul**, or "knot of hair", an image depicted in the city's emblem glyph – a rear view of a head with what appears to be a knotted headband around it. The earliest definite evidence of buildings dates from 500 BC, and by about 200 BC ceremonial structures had emerged, including the first version of the **North Acropolis**. Two hundred years later the **Great Plaza** had begun to take shape, and Tikal by this point was established as a major site with a large permanent population. For the next two centuries, art and architecture became increasingly ornate and sophisticated, though Tikal remained a secondary centre to **El Mirador**, a massive city about forty miles to the north.

The closing years of the Preclassic (250–300 AD) saw trade routes disrupted, culminating in the decline and abandonment of El Mirador. In the resulting power vacuum, the two sites of **Tikal** and **Uaxactún** emerged as substantial centres of trade, science and religion. Less than a day's walk apart, the expanding cities grappled for control of the region. A winner emerged in 378 AD, when, under the inspired leadership of **Great Jaguar Paw (Toh Chac Ich'ak)**, Tikal's warriors overran Uaxactún, securing its dominance over central Petén for much of the next five hundred years.

This extended period of prosperity saw the city's population grow to somewhere between fifty thousand and one hundred thousand, spreading to cover an area of around eleven square miles. Crucial to this success were Tikal's alliances with the powerful cities of Kaminaljuyú (in present-day Guatemala City) and Teotihuacán (to the north of modern Mexico City); stelae and paintings from the period show that Tikal's elite adopted Teotihuacán styles of clothing, pottery and weaponry. In the middle of the sixth century, however, Tikal suffered a huge setback. Already weakened by upheavals in central Mexico, where Teotihuacán was in decline, the city now faced major challenges from the east, where the city of **Caracol** (see p.142) was emerging as a significant regional power, and from the north, where **Calakmul** (see Contexts, p.239) was becoming a Maya "superstate". In an apparent pre-emptive strike against a potential rival, **Double Bird**, the ruler of Tikal, launched an "axe war" against Caracol and its ambitious leader, **Lord Water (Yahaw-te)**, in 556 AD. Despite capturing and sacrificing a noble from Caracol, Double Bird's strategy was only temporarily successful; in 562 AD Lord Water hit back in a devastating attack which crushed Tikal and almost certainly sacrificed Double Bird. The victors stamped their authority on the humiliated nobles of Tikal, smashing stelae, desecrating tombs and destroying written records, ushering in a 130-year **"hiatus"** during which no inscribed monuments were erected and Tikal was overshadowed by Caracol and its powerful ally, Calakmul. When research from more recent discoveries at Temple V (see p.176) is published, however, the "hiatus" may come to be viewed in a new light.

Towards the end of the seventh century, however, Caracol's stranglehold had begun to weaken and Tikal gradually started to recover its lost power. Under the formidable leadership of **Heavenly Standard-bearer (Hasaw Chan K'awil)**, who reigned from 682 to 723 AD, the main ceremonial areas were reclaimed from the desecration suffered at the hands of Caracol. By 695 AD, Tikal was powerful enough to launch an attack against Calakmul, capturing and executing its king, **Fiery Claw/ Jaguar Paw (Ich'ak K'ak)**, and severely weakening the alliance against Tikal. The following year, Heavenly Standard-bearer repeated his astonishing coup by capturing **Split Earth**, the new king of Calakmul, and Tikal regained its position among the most important of Petén cities. Heavenly Standard-bearer's leadership gave birth to

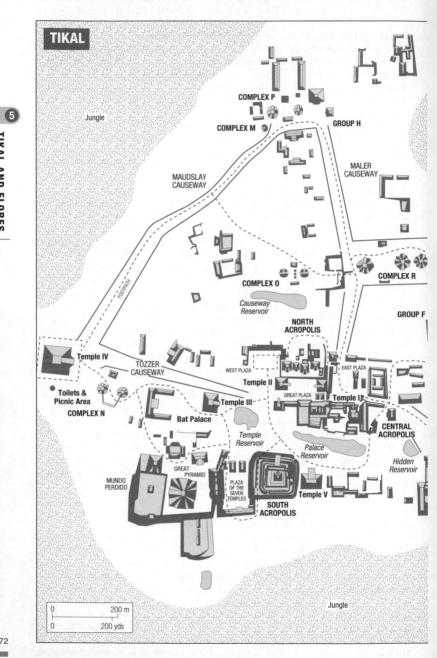

TIKAL

Jungle

COMPLEX P

COMPLEX M

GROUP H

MALER
CAUSEWAY

MAUDSLAY
CAUSEWAY

FOOTPATH

COMPLEX O

COMPLEX R

Causeway
Reservoir

GROUP F

NORTH
ACROPOLIS

Temple IV

TOZZER
CAUSEWAY

WEST PLAZA

EAST PLAZA

Temple II

Toilets &
Picnic Area

COMPLEX N

GREAT PLAZA

Temple I

Temple III

Bat Palace

CENTRAL
ACROPOLIS

Temple
Reservoir

Palace
Reservoir

Hidden
Reservoir

GREAT
PYRAMID

MUNDO
PERDIDO

PLAZA
OF THE
SEVEN
TEMPLES

Temple V

SOUTH
ACROPOLIS

Jungle

| 0 | 200 m |
| 0 | 200 yds |

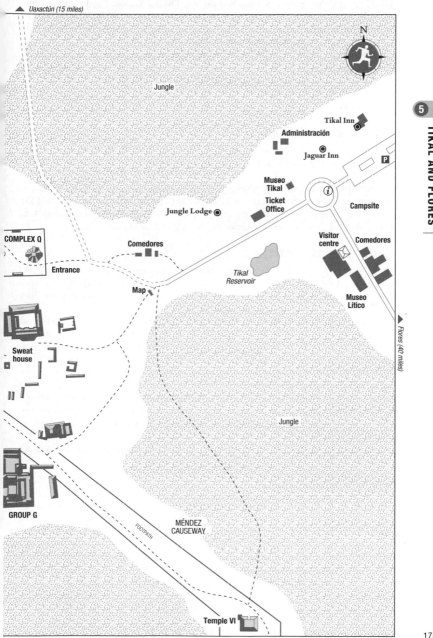

Uaxactún (15 miles)

Jungle

Tikal Inn

Administración

Jaguar Inn

Museo
Tikal

Ticket
Office

Jungle Lodge

COMPLEX Q

Comedores

Entrance

Map

Tikal
Reservoir

Campsite

Visitor
centre

Comedores

Museo
Lítico

Flores (40 miles)

Sweat
house

Jungle

GROUP G

MÉNDEZ
CAUSEWAY

FOOTPATH

Temple VI

N

a revitalized and powerful ruling dynasty: in the hundred years following his death, Tikal's five main temples were built and his son, **Divine Sunset Lord (Yik'in Chan K'awil)**, who ascended the throne in 734 AD, had his father's body entombed in the magnificent **Temple I**. Temples and monuments were still under construction until at least 869 AD, the last recorded date in Tikal, inscribed on Stela 24.

What brought about Tikal's final **downfall** remains a mystery, but it's certain that around 900 AD, almost the entire lowland Maya civilization collapsed, and that by the end of the tenth century, Tikal had been abandoned. Afterwards, the site was used from time to time by other groups, who worshipped here and repositioned many of the stelae, but it was never formally occupied again.

Getting to Tikal

Coming by bus **from the Belize border**, you may need to change buses at **Ixlú** (see p.168). At the junction, you can take local buses to El Remate or a *colectivo* minibus to Tikal.

From Flores, any hotel or travel agent will arrange transport to Tikal in one of the many minibuses leaving at least hourly from around 4am; tickets start at Q55 return. At the **airport**, you can also catch minibuses to Tikal (via El Remate). **Car rental** is available from the airport or in Santa Elena (see Listings, p.180).

Site practicalities

At the national park entrance barrier, nine miles before the site itself, you pay a Q150 **entrance fee** (due every day you stay at the site). If you arrive after 3pm you'll be given a ticket for the next day, which you can also use the day you buy it. The ruins are open from 6am to 6pm.

At the entrance to the ruins is a **visitor centre** with a café and gift shop (with a good selection of books) and post office. The highlights are the **Museo Tikal** (see opposite; Q10) and the **Lithic Museum** (Museo Lítico; Mon–Fri 9am–5pm, Sat & Sun 9am–4pm; Q10), containing a selection of the finest stelae and carvings from the site.

Near the entrance, you can hire a **licensed guide** (many speak English) who can show you the site starting at around US$48 for four hours for groups of four. A number of tour companies and guides in El Remate and Flores also offer sunrise tours of Tikal, which involve a departure time of 3.30am and offer the chance to observe the jungle waking up around the towering temples; most hotels and guesthouses in El Remate and Flores can set you up with the tour. Do note, though, that it's rare to actually witness an impressive sunrise over the ruins because the sun's appearance is often obscured and delayed by thick mist.

Accommodation

There are three **hotels** (all with restaurants) near the entrance. Although you can comfortably see the main Tikal temples and sights in one day, these park hotels can be convenient if you plan on spending several days exploring the site, and want a chance to wake up to the jungle coming to life around you. They are fairly expensive by local standards though (you'll find much better deals in Flores and El Remate); electricity can be sporadic, and service can be lacking.

Jungle Lodge (☎2476-0570 or 7861-0446, ⓦwww.junglelodgetikal.com), has large, private bungalows on shady grounds (❺–❽) and a few basic rooms with shared bath. The decent restaurant and bar features international and local fare. *Tikal Inn* (☎7926-1917, ⓦwww.tikalinn.com; ❻–❼) has attractive, thatched bungalows around a pool. *Jaguar Inn* (☎7926-0002, ⓦwww.jaguartikal.com) offers comfortable bungalows (❻–❼) and camping (Q70 per person). The cheery restaurant serves up simple fare of grilled chicken, pastas, burgers and omelettes.

There are several **comedores** at the park entrance, offering a limited menu of traditional Guatemalan specialities – eggs, beans, grilled meat and a few "tourist" dishes; a decent value is *Comedor Tikal*. Otherwise, for longer (and pricier) menus, try the hotel restaurants.

Museo Tikal

At the entrance, between *Jungle Lodge* and *Jaguar Inn*, the one-room Museo Tikal (Mon–Fri 9am–5pm, Sat & Sun 9am–4pm; Q10) houses some of the stelae found here, including the remains of **Stela 29**, Tikal's oldest carved monument (dating from 292 AD), as well as many artefacts: tools, jewellery, pottery and obsidian and jade objects. There's a spectacular reconstruction of **Hasaw Chan K'awil's tomb**, one of the richest ever found in the Maya world, with beautiful polychrome ceramics, jade ornaments, including bracelets, anklets, necklaces and earplugs, and delicately incised bones, among them a famous, carved human bone depicting deities paddling the dead to the underworld in canoes.

The site

The sheer size of Tikal can at first be daunting, and the site is certain to exhaust you before you exhaust it. However, even if you only make it to the main plaza, and spend an hour relaxing atop a temple, you won't be disappointed. The **central area**, with its five main temples, forms by far the most impressive section and should be your priority. Outside the main area are countless smaller, unrestored structures, and though they pale beside the scale and magnificence of the main temples, these rarely visited sections can be exciting if you're armed with a good map (check the visitor center).

You should take great care **climbing the temples**: the steps are narrow and can be slippery after rain, and getting down is always more difficult than getting up. Visitors have been injured (and one killed) by falling from great heights, so the authorities close the taller structures from time to time, especially in the rainy season.

From the entrance to the Great Plaza

As you walk into the site, the first structures that you come to are the rather unevocatively named **Complex Q** and **Complex R**. Dating from the reign of Hasaw Chan K'awil, these are two of the seven sets of twin pyramids built to mark the passing of a *katun* (a period of twenty 360-day years). Only one of the pyramids (in Complex Q) is restored, with the stelae and altars re-erected in front of it. The carvings on the copy of **Stela 22** (the original is in the Museo Lítico), in the small enclosure set to one side, record the ascension to the throne in 768 AD of Tikal's last known ruler, **Chitam**, portrayed in full regalia, complete with enormous, sweeping headdress and staff of authority.

Following the path as it bears to the left, you approach the back of the restored **Temple I**, a steep pyramid topped by a three-room building and a hollow roof comb that was originally brightly painted. Unfortunately, the stairway is roped off and you're strictly forbidden to climb. The temple towers above the **Great Plaza**, the heart of the ancient city; surrounded by four massive structures, this plaza was the focus of ceremonial activity at Tikal for around a thousand years. Now the celebrated symbol of the entire site, Temple I was built as a burial monument to contain the magnificent **tomb of Hasaw Chan K'awil**. Within the tomb at the temple's core, the ruler's skeleton was found facing north, surrounded by an assortment of jade, pearls, seashells and stingray spines – a traditional symbol of human sacrifice. A few pieces of magnificent pottery was also discovered here, depicting a journey to the underworld made in a canoe rowed by mythical animals.

Standing opposite, like a slightly shorter, wider version of Temple I, **Temple II** rises 125ft, although when its roof comb was intact it would have been the same height as Temple I. When open, it's a fairly easy climb to the top, and the view, almost level with the forest canopy, is incredible, with the Great Plaza spread out below. As an added bonus, you'll almost certainly see toucans in the nearby branches.

The North Acropolis, the Central Acropolis and Temple V

The **North Acropolis**, which fills the whole north side of the plaza, is one of the most complex structures in the entire Maya world. In traditional Maya style, it was built and rebuilt on top of itself; beneath the twelve temples visible today are the remains of about a hundred other structures, some of which, along with two large **masks**, have been uncovered by archeologists. One of the masks, facing the plaza and protected by a thatched roof, remains quite distinct. In front of the North Acropolis are two lines of **stelae** carved with images of Tikal's ruling elite, with circular altars at their bases. These and other stelae throughout the site bear the marks of **ritual defacement**, carried out by newly enthroned rulers to erase any latent powers that the image of a predecessor may have retained.

On the other side of the plaza, the **Central Acropolis** is a maze of tiny, interconnecting rooms and stairways built around six smallish courtyards. The buildings here are usually referred to as palaces rather than temples, although their precise use remains a mystery. The large, two-storey building in Court 2 is known as **Maler's Palace**, named after the archeologist Teobert Maler, who made it his home during expeditions in 1895 and 1904.

Further behind the Central Acropolis, a wide path leads to **Temple V**, though the best approach is from the Plaza of the Seven Temples, where you'll catch a particularly good view of the creamy limestone of the restored monumental staircase. An extremely steep wooden stairway to the left of the stone one is what's open to visitors, and the view from the top is superb. Temple V has been the focus of intensive research (funded by the Spanish government) for much of the past two decades. It was once thought to be among the last of the great temples to be built, but findings from the many burials here indicate that it was in fact the earliest, dating from around 600 AD and almost certainly constructed by **Kinich Wayna**, Tikal's governor at the time. This discovery alone overturns most previous views of this era of Tikal's history, as it was built early in the Mid-Classic "hiatus", which followed Tikal's defeat by Lord Water of Caracol in 562 AD; experts previously thought that no new monuments were erected at Tikal during this period.

From the West Plaza to Temple IV

The **West Plaza**, behind Temple II, is dominated by a large, Late Classic temple on its north side, and scattered with various altars and stelae. From here, the **Tozzer Causeway** – one of the raised routes that connected the main parts of the city – leads west to **Temple III**, covered in jungle vegetation. Around the back of the temple is a huge palace complex, of which only the **Bat Palace** has been restored, while further down the causeway, on the left-hand side, is **Complex N**, another set of twin pyramids. In the northern enclosure of the complex, the superbly carved **Stela 16** depicts Hasaw Chan K'awil.

Looming at the end of the Tozzer Causeway, the massive **Temple IV**, at 210ft, is the tallest of all the Tikal structures. Built in 741 AD, it is thought by some archeologists to be the resting place of the ruler **Yik'in Chan K'awil**, whose image was depicted on wooden lintels built into the top of the temple. To reach the top you have to ascend secure wooden ladders (one to go up and another to come down). Slow and exhausting as this is, it's always worth it, offering one of the finest views of the whole site. All around you the green carpet of canopy stretches to the horizon, interrupted only by the great roof combs of other temples.

The Plaza of the Seven Temples and Mundo Perdido

The other main buildings in the centre of Tikal lie to the south of the Central Acropolis. Here, reached by a trail from Temple III, you'll find the **Plaza of the Seven Temples**, which forms part of a complex dating back to before Christ. There's an unusual triple ball-court on the north side of the plaza, and to the east, the unexcavated South Acropolis. **Mundo Perdido**, or Lost World, lies immediately to the west, another magical and very distinct section of the site with its own atmosphere and architecture. The main feature of this area, the **Great Pyramid**, is a 105ft-high structure whose surface conceals four earlier versions, the first dating from 700 BC. From the top of the pyramid you'll get incredible views toward Temple IV and the Great Plaza, and it's another excellent place to watch the dramatic sunrise or sunset.

Flores

Although it's the capital of Petén, **FLORES** is an easy-going, sedate place with an old-fashioned atmosphere – quite different from the rough, bustling commercialism of other towns in the region. A cluster of cobbled streets and ageing houses built around the white, twin-domed church of Nuestra Señora de Los Remedios,

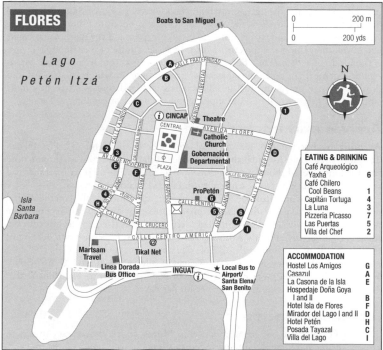

FLORES

Boats to San Miguel

| 0 | 200 m |
| 0 | 200 yds |

Lago Petén Itzá

N

CALLE FRATERNIDAD

CALLE LA LIBERTAD

(i) CINCAP

Theatre

CENTRAL

AVENIDA FLORES

Catholic Church

AVENIDA 10 DE NOVIEMBRE

Gobernación Departmental

CALLE 15 DE SEPTIEMBRE

PLAZA

CALLE EL ROSARIO

ProPetén

AVENIDA SANTA ANA

CALLEJON PEDRITO

AVENIDA REFORMA

CALLE CENTRAL

Isla Santa Barbara

CALLE BARRIOS

CALLEJON EL CRUCERO

CALLE CENTRO AMERICA

Martsam Travel

Tikal Net

Linea Dorada Bus Office

INGUAT (i)

★ Local Bus to Airport/ Santa Elena/ San Benito

EATING & DRINKING

Café Arqueológico Yaxhá	6
Café Chilero Cool Beans	1
Capitán Tortuga	4
La Luna	3
Pizzeria Picasso	7
Las Puertas	5
Villa del Chef	2

ACCOMMODATION

Hostel Los Amigos	G
Casazul	A
La Casona de la Isla	E
Hospedaje Doña Goya I and II	B
Hotel Isla de Flores	F
Mirador del Lago I and II	D
Hotel Petén	H
Posada Tayazal	C
Villa del Lago	I

▼ *Causeway to Santa Elena (approx. 750 yds)*

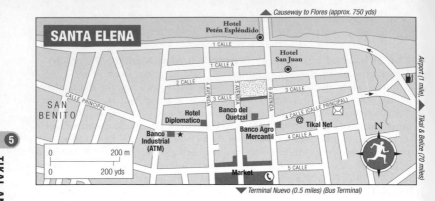

Causeway to Flores (approx. 750 yds)

Hotel
Petén Espléndido

1 CALLE

1 CALLE A

Hotel
San Juan

2 CALLE

CALLE PRINCIPAL

SAN
BENITO

2 AVENIDA

3 CALLE

3 AVENIDA

5 AVENIDA

6 AVENIDA

3 CALLE

Hotel
Diplomatico

Banco del
Quetzal

4 CALLE (CALLE PRINCIPAL)

@ Tikal Net

Banco
Industrial
(ATM) ★

Banco Agro
Mercantil

4 CALLE A

Airport (1 mile), ▲ Tikal & Belize (70 miles)

0 ___ 200 m
0 ___ 200 yds

Market

5 CALLE

N

▼ Terminal Nuevo (0.5 miles) (Bus Terminal)

it sits beautifully on an island in Lago Petén Itzá, connected to the mainland by a causeway; even if you're heading back to Belize after visiting Tikal, it's worth making a detour here on the way.

The **lake** is a natural choice for settlement and its shores were heavily populated in Maya times. **Noh Petén** ("great island"), which would become modern Flores, was the capital of the Itzá – the last independent Maya kingdom to succumb to Spain, which conquered and destroyed it in 1697. Cortés, the conqueror of Mexico, passed through here in 1525, and once in a while Spanish friars would visit, though they were rarely welcome. For the entire colonial period (and indeed up to the 1960s), the town languished in virtual isolation, having more contact with neighbouring Belize than the Guatemalan capital. Eventually Flores acquired its modern elements, the ugly, sprawling, chaotic twin towns of **Santa Elena** and **San Benito**, which lie across the water. Santa Elena, opposite Flores at the other end of the causeway and strung out between the airport and the market, has banks and buses; there's no need to venture into the chaotic mire of San Benito.

Today, despite the steady flow of tourists passing through for Tikal, Flores retains a genteel air, and offers pleasant surroundings in which to stay, eat and drink. If you're not going to the Guatemalan highlands but want to buy *típica* clothing and **gifts**, you'll find the shops here have better prices than at Tikal.

Arrival and information

Arriving by bus from Belize or Tikal, you'll be dropped off at Santa Elena's Termina Nuevo on 6 Avenida, about one mile south of the causeway (though note that the Linea Dorada buses will continue on to Flores). The **airport** is on the road to Tikal, 1.5 miles east of the causeway, and a US$3 **taxi** from town.

Inguat has an **information** booth at the airport, and another office on the central plaza in Flores (usually daily 8am–noon & 3:30–6pm; ☎7926-0533). For more detailed information and maps on Petén, try CINCAP (Centro de Información sobre la Naturaleza, Cultura y Artesanías de Petén; Mon–Fri 9am–noon & 2–8pm; ☎7926-0718), on the north side of Flores' plaza.

A good travel agency is **Martsam Travel**, Calle 30 de Junio (☎7867-5093, Ⓦwww.martsam.com), which runs a range of trips, including to Tikal and Yaxhá. Tours start at around US$35–55 per person per day.

Accommodation

There is a great range of accommodation in **Flores**, so it's unnecessary to stay in noisier, dirtier and increasingly unsafe **Santa Elena**.

Casazul Calle Fraternidad ☎2366-2841, ⓦwww.corpetur.com. This colonial-style house is tastefully done up in shades of blue. All rooms have private bath, hot water, fridge, a/c and TV, some have balcony and the lobby is decorated with old photographs of Flores. Relax in a blue wicker chair on the upstairs terrace that juts over the lake. ❺

La Casona de la Isla Calle 30 de Junio ☎&℻7926-0593, ⓦwww.corpetur.com. An attractive mid-range hotel; modern rooms have clean, tiled bath, a/c, telephone and cable TV. There's also a swimming pool and lovely sunset views from the terrace restaurant/bar. ❺

Hospedaje Doña Goya 2 Calle la Unión ☎7926-3538. Friendly, family-run budget guesthouse with spare but decent rooms, some with private bath and balcony. At the end of a long day, kick back on the rooftop terrace with hammocks. They also run the similar, adjacent *Doña Goya 1*. ❷–❹

Hostel Los Amigos Calle Central ☎7867-5075, ⓦwww.amigoshostel.com. The island's backpacker hangout, this sociable, brightly painted hostel has dorm beds, simple private rooms and a courtyard restaurant/bar with couches, hammocks and a vegetarian-friendly menu. If you're looking to meet up with other travellers or pick up local info, this is the spot. They also offer internet and can book a variety of tours. ❷

Hotel Isla de Flores Ave de la Reforma ☎7926-0614, ⓦwww.hotelisladeflores.com. A lobby with white wicker furniture gives way to clean, a/c rooms with TV, private bath and bright bedspreads; about half the rooms feature lake views. A skylight and hanging plants liven up each floor. ❺

Hotel Petén Calle 30 de Junio ☎7926-0692, ⓦwww.corpetur.com. Modern hotel with well-maintained rooms with TV and a/c, and many with lake views. The restaurant, with a menu of grilled fish, pastas and burritos, sits on a terrace overlooking the lake for fiery sunset views. Internet access for guests. ❺

Mirador del Lago I and II Calle 15 de Septiembre ☎7926-3276. Basic, well-furnished rooms with private bath and fan, some with lake views. Friendly, well-priced restaurant and internet. *Number I* is on the lakeshore and *Number 2* is across the street. ❷

Posada Tayazal Calle la Unión ☎&℻7926-0568. Decent budget rooms, some with private bath and balcony. Prices and views increase as you head upstairs. Internet available. ❷–❸

Villa del Lago Calle 15 de Septiembre ☎7926-0508, ⓦwww.hotelvilladelago.com. Modern, well-run hotel with comfortable, occasionally faded, rooms with private bath, a/c and TV – and many with great lake vistas. ❺

Eating and drinking

You'll find plenty of good, reasonably priced **restaurants** in Flores, serving everything from local Guatemalan fare to Italian pastas.

Café Arqueológico Yaxhá Calle 15 de Septiembre ⓦwww.cafeyaxha.com. True to its motto – "the meeting point for the Maya World" – this is a great spot to get your fill of Mayan history – and cuisine. The menu features both basic, international fare and traditional Mayan cuisine, like yucca and *filete pescado*, a fish filet.

Café Chilero Cool Beans Calle 15 de Septiembre. Pleasant restaurant-café with wicker lamps overlooking a coconut-strewn garden and the lake beyond. Come for the reasonably priced breakfasts, plus sandwiches and salads, served with whole wheat bread. Closed Tues.

Capitán Tortuga Calle 30 de Junio ☎7926-0247. Large restaurant with a lakeside terrace. Good grills and salads, chicken burritos and fine cocktails.

La Luna At the far end of Calle 30 de Junio ☎7926-3346. Pleasant, colourful, plant-filled restaurant, popular with locals and visitors. The international menu includes grilled fish, garlic shrimp over rice, pastas, chicken and vegetarian choices like falafel.

Pizzeria Picasso Calle 15 de Septiembre ☎7926-0673. Good pizzas and pastas; they also deliver.

Las Puertas Signposted off Ave Santa Ana ☎7926-1061. Cheery restaurant-bar with six *puertas* (doors), hanging rattan lamps and health offerings like generous salads, grilled shrimp and vegetarian omelettes. Occasional live music.

Villa del Chef Calle La Unión. A quiet, even romantic, restaurant serving Guatemalan and Arab cuisine, like grilled meats and chicken shish kebab, along with a range of vegetarian choices, including ratatouille. The tables on the lakeshore terrace are candlelit in the evenings.

Around Flores

On the peninsula opposite Flores, the **Petencito Zoo** (daily 8am–5pm; Q25) houses a collection of regional wildlife, in a hilly, jungle setting on the lakeshore.

Moving on from Flores

Flores is well served by buses and planes to and from Guatemala City, and there are also buses from Cancún and Belize (for more on buses to Belize, see box, p.167.) Nearly all buses use Santa Elena's Terminal Nuevo bus station (see p.178); only a couple of bus services depart from the market area. You'll find about thirty bus departures daily to Guatemala City (8–9hr), from non-direct chicken buses to luxury air-conditioned coaches. Linea Dorada (℡7926-1788, ⓦwww.tikalmayanworld.com) and Fuente del Norte (℡7926-0666) offer luxury buses, and ADN (℡5414-2668, ⓦwww.adnautobusesdelnorte.com) has standard buses.

Numerous daily planes fly the Guatemala City–Flores route (4 daily; from US$220–250; 1hr). There are also flights to Cancún (1 daily; US$475; 1hr 45min). Note that Belize's two domestic airlines had discontinued services to Flores/Santa Elena, but it's worth checking with Maya Island Air (see p.21) to get the latest update.

For another view of local fauna, drop by the animal rescue centre of **ARCAS**, about two miles east of San Miguel. Note that though there's no public access to the rescue area itself, there is an environmental education centre (generally open during daylight hours) and botanical trail here. Boats depart to both from behind the *Hotel Santana*, in the southwestern part of Flores.

The **Parque Natural Ixpanpajul**, six miles from Santa Elena, just off the road to Guatemala City (daily; US$25 per activity; ℡4146-7557, ⓦwww.ixpanpajul .com) features a system of suspension bridges and stone paths connecting forested hilltops. From the middle of the bridges you can enjoy a monkey's eye view of the canopy, and on top of the highest hill there's a *mirador* with views of virtually the whole of the Petén Itzá basin. Get your thrills from a variety of activities, including zip-lining, horseriding and heading out on a night safari. You can get there from Flores by bike (45min) or any Poptún-bound microbus, which will drop you at the entrance.

Listings

Banks In Flores, you'll find an ATM on Calle 30 de Junio; Santa Elena has plenty of banks, with ATMs, on Calle Principal.

Car rental Budget, Hertz and Tabarini (which has the widest choice; ℡7926-0253, ⓦwww.tabarini .com) operate from the airport, and there are some offices in Santa Elena. Rates (usually including insurance) start at around US$50/day for a small car.

Internet You'll find a number of internet centres in Flores, particularly on Calle Centro América, where you can also make phone calls, including Tikal Net.

Doctor Centro Médico Maya, 4 Ave near 3 Calle in Santa Elena (℡7926-0180), is helpful and professional, though no English is spoken.

Post office In Flores, on Ave Barrios.

The south

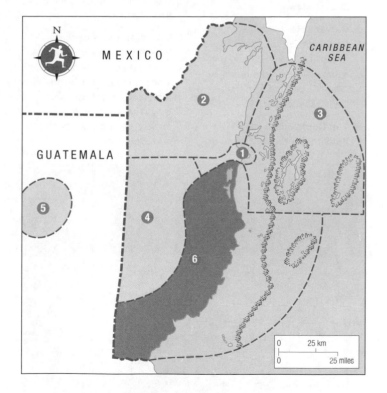

CHAPTER 6

Highlights

✱ **The Hummingbird Highway** Take the most scenic drive in the country, heading south to Dangriga. **See p.186**

✱ **Gales Point** Stay in this tiny Creole village, where you can listen to drums in the evening, then rise early to spot manatees and wading birds at dawn. **See p.187**

✱ **Glover's Reef** Indulge your Robinson Crusoe "desert island" fantasy in a beach cabin on the most stunningly beautiful coral atoll in the Caribbean. **See p.195**

✱ **The Cockscomb Basin Wildlife Sanctuary** Spend a night or two in the world's first jaguar reserve, following the tracks of the largest cat in the Americas. **See p.202**

✱ **Placencia** Stroll along the best beaches in the country, or head out to sea for snorkelling off Laughing Bird Caye and swimming with whale sharks at Gladden Spit. **See p.207**

✱ **Lubaantun** Admire the beautifully restored buildings of the "place of fallen stones" – and ponder whether the famous Crystal Skull was truly discovered in this ancient city nearly a century ago. **See p.227**

▲ The Hummingbird Highway

The south

Belize's southern half contains its wildest terrain, from mangrove swamp, lagoon and savannah to sandy bays, river-hewn valleys and forested ridges. In the far south, the estuaries of the slow-moving Temash and Sarstoon rivers, lined by the tallest **mangrove forest** in Belize, form **Sarstoon–Temash National Park**, adjoining protected land in Guatemala. **Inland** from the coast, the Maya Mountains remain unpenetrated by roads, with practically the entire massif under national park protection. The most accessible area is **Cockscomb Basin Wildlife Sanctuary**, preserving a sizeable jaguar population and a perfect base for exploring the rainforest. You'll come across plenty of jaguar tracks here, but don't count on seeing what's left of them.

Southern Belize's population is low, with most towns located on the coast. **Dangriga** is the headquarters of the **Garifuna** people – descended from Carib Indians and shipwrecked African slaves (see box, p.190) – and allows access to a number of idyllic cayes, sitting right on top of the barrier reef. **Gales Point**, north of Dangriga, and **Hopkins**, on the coast to the south, are worth visiting to experience a truly tranquil way of life. Further south along the Southern Highway, the **Placencia peninsula** is the focus of coastal tourism, from where you can visit **a variety of marine reserves**, one established specifically to protect **whale sharks** – the world's largest fish. The highway reaches its terminus in **Punta Gorda**, an access point to Guatemala, with **ancient Maya sites** and modern **Maya villages** nearby, as well as excellent hiking.

South to Dangriga

Two routes traverse their way through mountains, pine and citrus into southern Belize. Southeast from Belmopan, the **Hummingbird Highway** offers the most beautiful drive in the country, the **Maya Mountains** rising up until you're suddenly amongst them, with citrus plantations on the flatter plains all around. For years much of the region's rainforest lay untouched, but here and there Salvadoran or Guatemalan refugees have hacked down a swath of jungle to plant maize and beans. Near Belmopan, the **Caves Branch River** and **Blue Hole National Park** are covered in Chapter 4 (see p.125), while beyond, just past the highest point on

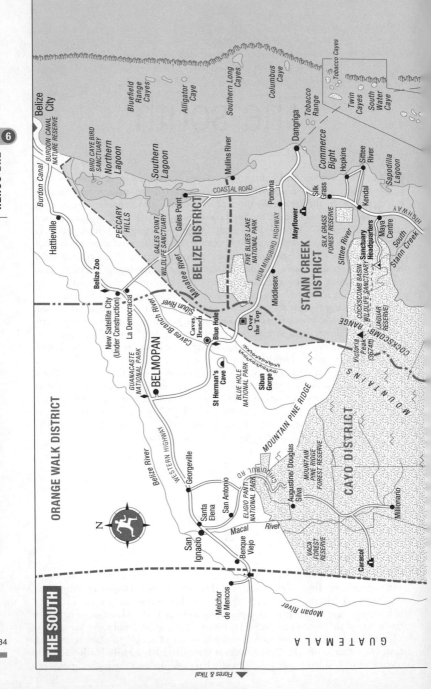

6

THE SOUTH

THE SOUTH

ORANGE WALK DISTRICT

GUATEMALA

BELIZE DISTRICT

STANN CREEK DISTRICT

CAYO DISTRICT

N

Belize City

Burdon Canal

BURDON CANAL NATURE RESERVE

BIRD CAVE BIRD SANCTUARY

Bluefield Range Cayes

Alligator Caye

Southern Long Cayes

Columbus Caye

Tobacco Range

Tobacco Cayes

Twin Cayes

South Water Caye

Northern Lagoon

Southern Lagoon

Dangriga

Commerce Bight

Hopkins

Sittee River

Sapodilla Lagoon

PECCARY HILLS

Hattieville

GALES POINT WILDLIFE SANCTUARY

Gales Point

Mullins River

COASTAL ROAD

Pomona

Silk Grass

SILK GRASS FOREST RESERVE

Kendal

HIGHWAY

Belize Zoo

New Satellite City (Under Construction)

La Democracia

GUANACASTE NATIONAL PARK

BELMOPAN

Manatee River

Sibun River

FIVE BLUES LAKE NATIONAL PARK

HUMMINGBIRD HIGHWAY

Middlesex

Mayflower

Sittee River

Maya Centre

South Stann Creek

COCKSCOMB BASIN WILDLIFE SANCTUARY (JAGUAR RESERVE)

Sanctuary Headquarters

Caves Branch

Blue Hole

Over the Top

St Herman's Cave

BLUE HOLE NATIONAL PARK

Sibun Gorge

Victoria Peak (3674ft)

COCKSCOMB RANGE

MOUNTAINS

Georgeville

San Antonio

MOUNTAIN PINE RIDGE

CHIQUIBUL RD

ELIGIO PANTI NATIONAL PARK

Augustine/ Douglas Silva

MOUNTAIN PINE RIDGE FOREST RESERVE

San Ignacio

Santa Elena

Benque Viejo

Macal River

Mopan River

Melchor de Mencos

VACA FOREST RESERVE

Caracol

Millonario

Western Highway

Belize River

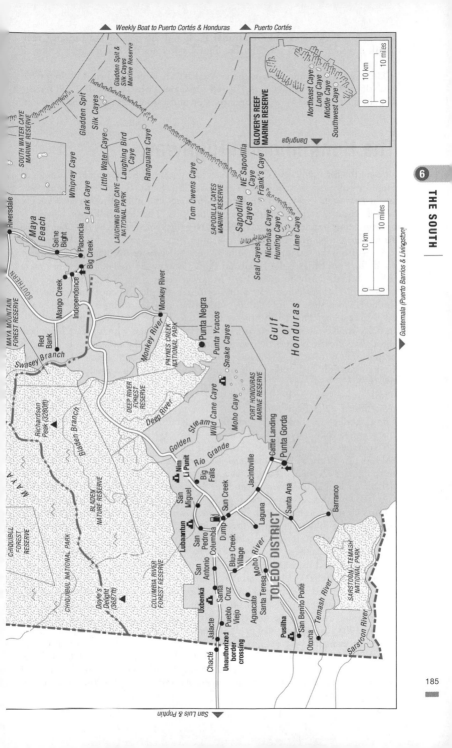

the road, is **Five Blues Lake National Park** and the start of the **Indian Creek Trail**. Descending from the hills, the highway follows the Stann Creek valley all the way to Dangriga.

The alternative route south is the Coastal Road, an unpaved road leading from near Belize City to Stann Creek District via **Gales Point**, a beautiful and remote Creole village with low-key accommodation and a stunning natural environment.

The Hummingbird Highway

Beyond the Blue Hole and Caves Branch (see p.130), the stunning Hummingbird Highway traverses a makeshift bridge over the Sibun River (the original was washed away in heavy rains) before undulating smoothly through increasingly hilly landscape, eventually mounting a low pass. The downhill slope beyond is appropriately, if unimaginatively, called Over the Top, marked by the *Over the Top Restaurant*, a good rest-stop on the trip south.

Across from the restaurant, at Mile 32 near St Margaret's Village, is the turnoff to idyllic **Five Blues Lake National Park** (Ⓦwww.5blueslake.org), ten square miles of luxuriantly forested karst scenery, centred on a beautiful lake that constantly changes colour. In a mysterious geological phenomenon, the lake drained like a sink in July 2006, with fishermen reporting a noise like 'the lake was crying'. Thankfully, the water miraculously reappeared in June 2007; initially baffled scientists determined that the blockage which created the lake must have dissolved with the water exiting through the limestone below, and reappearing only as the blockage reassembled itself. There are no rangers, and though you can visit under your own steam, a visit with a guide such as from Maya Guide Adventures (see p.147) enables you to follow the **Indian Creek Trail**, co-managed by local communities, which ends here after snaking its way over fifteen miles from Monkey Bay. The trail winds through dense riparian forest, perfect for observing rare flora and fauna, cave systems and a so-far unexcavated Maya city.

Two miles from Over the Top, you'll see the red, gold and green Rasta colours of 🌴 *Palacio's Restaurant and Mountain Retreat* (Mile 31; buses stop right outside; ☎802-3683, Ⓦwww.palaciosretreat.com; ❹, camping Bz$20 per person, including breakfast). Proud of their Garifuna heritage (see p.190), the family owners serve very good food, including vegetarian and vegan options, while two simple cabañas with hot shower overlook a beautiful river lined with beaches and boulders; it's great for swimming, and you can hike upstream to a thirty-foot jungle waterfall. Emphasis is on natural living, with medicinal gardens and massage available.

As you descend from the mountains, the flat **Stann Creek valley** begins: the centre of the Belizean **citrus** industry. Bananas were grown here initially, with half a million stems exported annually through Stann Creek (now Dangriga) by 1891. However, the banana boom came to an abrupt end in 1906 due to disease, and fostering the growth of **citrus fruits**, a small railway was built here in 1908 – many highway bridges were originally rail bridges. Today, citrus comprises a major part of agricultural exports and is heralded as one of the nation's great success stories – though for the largely Guatemalan labour force, housed in rows of scruffy huts, conditions are poor. The presence of tropical parasites like the leaf-cutter ant has forced planters to use powerful insecticides, including DDT.

Further along, at Mile 25, signs appear for **Billy Barquedier National Park**, a 1500-acre expanse whose highlight is a 100m hike up to a refreshing waterfall. There are two entrances to the park, but if you're travelling by bus be sure to use the northern one as the walk is much shorter. The park is officially open only on weekends (Bz$10), but you can arrange a weekday guided tour with a ranger (call the Stedfast village community phone; ☎509-2011).

The petrol station six miles before Dangriga is a useful place to refuel without heading into town; just beyond this is the junction with the **Southern Highway**, heading to Hopkins, Placencia and Punta Gorda.

The Coastal Road and Gales Point

Alternatively known as the Manatee Road, the **Coastal Road** heads southeast from Mile 30 of the Western Highway, skirting the village of La Democracia and eventually meeting the Hummingbird Highway at Melinda, nine miles from Dangriga. The government has been threatening to pave the route for years – creating a very useful shortcut from Belize City to Dangriga – but for now it remains unpaved and undeveloped, a rough route served by just three buses a week from Belize City to its one community of size, **Gales Point**. The scenery along the way is typical of southern Belize: citrus plantations, pine ridges and steep limestone hills covered in broadleaf forest.

The tranquil Creole village of **GALES POINT** is the ideal place to explore the area, straggling a narrow peninsula into the lagoon. The community was originally settled over two hundred years ago by runaway slaves – "maroons" (from the Spanish *cimarron*, meaning wild or untamed) – from Belize City, who found solace among the mangrove-cloaked creeks and shallow lagoons. A rich wetland area comprising the **Northern and Southern lagoons**, the area is protected as part of the Burdon Canal Nature Reserve, the largest manatee breeding ground in the entire Caribbean basin, and Belize's main nesting beaches of the endangered **hawksbill** and **loggerhead turtles**, which lie on either side of the mouth of the Manatee River. Wildlife is certainly the main attraction here, with other rare animals including jabiru storks and crocodiles, and numerous bird species. Declared by the government as a Manatee Special Development Area to encourage conservation and low-key tourism, several villagers are licensed **tour guides** – ask around for John Moore, Kevin Andrewin, or for birding, Raymond Gentle – and with help from international conservation organizations, they guard the turtles' nesting beaches and have installed signs and buoys warning boatmen to slow down to avoid harming manatees. You can **volunteer** here for a longer stay. Wading through mosquito-infested mangroves in search of turtles can be uncomfortable, but it's infinitely rewarding to see adult females laying their eggs or to cheer on newly hatched babies as they race for the sea.

Gales Point is also a centre of **traditional drum-making**; you can learn how at ♣ **Maroon Creole Drum School** (☎603-6051, ⓦwww.maroondrumschool .com), for around Bz$250, including materials and instruction, and it's Bz$20 per hour to learn to play (group rates available). You'll also absorb much about local history and culture, and sip owner Emmeth's home-produced cashew or berry wine in the evenings. With your newly acquired skills, you may be able to participate in a **sambai**, a Creole fertility dance ritual. The drummers here, playing in a circle around a fire, are supremely talented, and dancers take turns interpreting their rhythms.

Practicalities

Gales Point is served by three NTSL **buses** weekly, usually leaving Belize City at 5pm on Monday, Friday and Saturday; confirm times in advance. There are no scheduled services onwards to Dangriga. Hitching from Democracia is also relatively easy, and it's a pleasant 2.5 miles from the junction into the village if you're not carrying too much luggage. Another way to get here is **by boat** from Belize City along amazing mangrove-lined **inland waterways** – Haulover Creek, Burdon Canal and Sibun River – ask around at the harbour or arrange with your accommodation in advance.

There are several **accommodation** options. For basic bed-and-breakfast, Ionie Samuels at Martha's Store and Giftshop (☎220-8066; ❶) has a room and can arrange meals and tours; *Gentle's Cool Spot* (☎609-4991; ❶–❷), a small bar and restaurant where the buses turn around, also has a few clean, basic rooms in a wooden house, one with private bath; or you can **camp** at *Metho's Coconut Camping* (Bz$12 per person), in a sandy spot north of the village centre. The best accommodation within the village is ⌖ *Manatee Lodge* (☎220-8040, ⓦwww .manateelodge.com; ❺), a white-painted, colonial-style building set amid lush lawns and coconut trees surrounded by a lagoon at the peninsula's tip – the ideal spot to take in the sunset. Rooms are spacious and comfortable (choose one on the upper floor with veranda), and there's good food too (US$35 for three meals/day). **Internet** is free, there's a book and video library, and canoes and small sailing boats are available (free for guests; otherwise Bz$20 for a canoe and Bz$100 per day for a sailing boat). Call ahead for boat transport from Belize City (Bz$350, 1–4 people) or Dangriga (Bz$300, 1–4 people).

For **eating**, book in advance at *Manatee Lodge* for delicious Creole/international food, featuring game and wonderful coconut crisps. Cheaper Creole fare (and home-made wine) is available at *Gentle's Cool Spot* or the *Sugar Shack*, which amazingly also serves **cappuccinos** and cakes. Raymond Gentle, owner of the *Cool Spot*, leads trips in his large, motorized dory to **Ben Lomond's Cave**, on the north shore of the lagoon, and other guides (mentioned above) will take you fishing or hiking.

Dangriga

DANGRIGA is the capital of Stann Creek District and the largest town in southern Belize. It's also the cultural centre of the **Garifuna**, a people of mixed indigenous Caribbean and African descent, who make up eleven percent of the country's population (see box, p.190). Since the early 1980s Garifuna culture has undergone a tremendous revival, including the renaming of the town to Dangriga (from Stann Creek), a Garifuna word meaning "sweet (or standing) waters", in reference to the North Stann Creek flowing through the town centre. Be sure to visit the **Gulusi Garifuna Museum** at the entrance to town on Stann Creek Valley Road (Chuluhadiwa Park; Bz$10; ☎669-0639, ⓦwww.ngcbelize.org; Mon–Fri 10am–5pm, Sat 8am–noon), for fascinating exhibits on the migration of the Garifuna from St Vincent to Roatán and on to Belize, as well as artwork, clothing, food and music.

Dangriga is home to some of the country's most popular **artists**, some of whom have small galleries. Best of these is Studio Gallery Pen Cayetano (3 Aranda Crescent off Ecumenical Drive, ☎628-6807, ⓦwww.cayetano.de). Pen's striking deep-coloured oils on canvas aim to depict Garifuna culture as well as wider Belize, with numerous portraits. Elsewhere, fine **crafts** are easy to

DANGRIGA

| 0 | | 200 m |
| 0 | | 200 yds |

N

Airstrip ▲ ⓐ

1ST STREET
2ND STREET
3RD STREET
4TH STREET — **Benguche Park**
5TH STREET
6TH STREET
7TH STREET — **Football Field**
8TH STREET
9TH STREET
10TH STREET

①

Thomas Vincent Ramos statue

PEN ROAD

◀ *Marie Sharp's Factory (8 miles)*

MELINDA ROAD

Marie Sharp's Office

CHURCH STREET

FRONT STREET

Carl Ramos Stadium

School

GRAPEFRUIT RD
COCONUT RD
CITRON STREET
GIBNUT STREET
LEMON STREET
PLUM STREET
ORANGE ST

KUYLEN'S ALLEY

COURT HOUSE ROAD

Police Station ☎

RECTORY RD

★ **James Bus Stop**

Town Hall

RAMOS ROAD

WEST ST

North Stann Creek

DOCTOR'S ALLEY

Market

Princess Royal Park

② ③ ⓑ

NORTH RIVERSIDE DRIVE

COMMERCE STREET

Boat to Puerto Cortés

Boats to Tobacco Caye
★ **Bus to Hopkins**

ⓒ

④

⑤

Gulf of Honduras

BLUEFIELD ROAD

ⓓ

CASTILLO ALLEY
REAR PINE ST
PINE STREET

CANAL STREET

CEDAR STREET

OAK STREET

MAGOON ST

KNOPP'S STREET

CHATUYE ST

SOUTHERN FORESHORE

ALEJO BENI AVENUE

MOHO ROAD

ECUMENICAL DRIVE

ⓔ

ST VINCENT STREET

ⓕ

MADRE CACAO RD

MAHOGANY ST

GANEY STREET

HOWARD STREET

SALMWOOD ROAD

ⓖ

TUBROSE STREET

SHARP STREET

Studio Gallery Pen Cayetano ■

POLACK STREET

YEMERI ROAD

ⓗ

◀ *Hummingbird & Southern Highways & Gulisi Garifuna Museum*

ZERICOTE STREET

MANGROVE ROAD

Wadani Shed Community Center

⑦

ⓘ

Stann Creek Ecumenical College ■ ■

ISLA ROAD

Havana *Creek*

SAMPSON'S ST
DANIEL'S ST
UNITY STREET

STANN CREEK VALLEY ROAD

Bus depot ★

CABBAGE ROAD

HAVANA STREET

Drums Monument ⑧ ⊙

EATING & DRINKING

Garden of Eating	C
Ilaguleu	8
J&D's Culture Kitchen	6
King Burger	3
Malibu Beach Club	1
Riverside Restaurant	4
Riviera Club	5
Roots Kitchen	7
Starlight	2

ACCOMMODATION

Bluefield Lodge	D
Bonefish Hotel	F
Chaleanor Hotel	E
Jungle Huts Hotel	C
Pal's Guest House	I
Pelican Beach Resort	A
Riverside Hotel	B
Ruthie's Cabañas	H
Val's Backpacker Hostel	G

A Garifuna history

The **Garifuna** (or Garinagu) trace their history back to the island of **St Vincent** in the eastern Caribbean. Recently settled by people from South America, who subdued the previous Arawaks, the new arrivals called themselves Kalipuna or Kwaib, from which the names Garifuna, meaning cassava-eating people, and Carib probably evolved. When Columbus's contemporaries came ashore, they encountered descendants of Carib men and Arawak women.

In 1635, two Spanish ships, carrying **slaves** from Nigeria to Spanish colonies in America, were wrecked off St Vincent and the survivors took refuge on the island. The Caribs and Africans initially clashed, but the former had been weakened by war and disease, and the foothold the Africans gained eventually led to the rise of the **Black Caribs** or Garifuna. Though the British nominally controlled St Vincent for most of the seventeenth and eighteenth centuries, vying for control with France and the Nether-lands, for all practical purposes it belonged to the Garifuna. In the mid-1700s, the British attempted to gain full control, but were driven off by the Caribs, with French assistance. Another attempt twenty years later was more successful, and in 1783 the British imposed a treaty on the Garifuna, granting themselves ownership of over half the island. Rejecting the treaty, the Garifuna continued to defy British rule through frequent uprisings, consistently supported by the French. From 1795, a year of bitter fighting aimed at establishing Garifuna independence inflicted horrendous casualties and led to the loss of their leader, Chief Joseph Chatoyer. The Garifuna and French finally surrendered on June 10, 1796.

Since Britain could not countenance free blacks living amongst slave-owning European settlers, they decided to **deport** the Garifuna, whom they hunted down, destroying homes, uprooting culture and causing hundreds of deaths. The survivors – around 4300 Black Caribs and one hundred Yellow Caribs, as designated by the British – were transported to the nearby island of Balliceaux; within six months over half died, many of yellow fever. In March 1797, the remainder were shipped to **Roatán**, one of the Bay Islands off Honduras. The Spanish commandeered one of the ships and redirected it to the mainland at Trujillo; barely two thousand Garifuna lived to see Roatán. A few years later, the Spanish *comandante* of Trujillo arrived

find – distinctive basketware, woven palm-leaf hats and Garifuna dolls – while the bronze **"Drums of Our Fathers" monument**, on the roundabout at the southern end of town, is Nigerian artist Stephen Okeke's ode to the centrality of **drumming** in Garifuna culture.

This musical tradition plays an important role in the most important local celebration, **Garifuna Settlement Day**, on November 19, when the town erupts into wild celebration, packed with expatriate Dangrigans returning to their roots. The party begins the evening before, with drumming, sound systems and punta dancing all night. In the morning there's a re-enactment of the Garifuna's original arrival from Honduras, with people landing on the beach in dugout canoes decorated with palm leaves. Similar exuberance goes into Christmas and New Year, when you might see the *wanaragu* or *Jonkunu* (John Canoe) dances, with **masked and costumed performers** representing a cast of eighteenth-century naval officers and Amerindian tribal chiefs.

At quieter times the atmosphere is enjoyably laidback, though there's little to do during the day and not much nightlife outside weekends. However, Dangriga is increasingly used as a base for visiting offshore cayes, and the mountains, Maya ruins and Jaguar Reserve inland.

and took possession of the island, shipping survivors to his jurisdiction to augment his labour force. The Spanish hadn't succeeded in agriculture, and the proficient Garifuna benefited the colony considerably. Boys and men were conscripted into the army and proved to be effective soldiers and mercenaries. As their renown spread, they were brought to other areas along the coast, and in 1802, 150 arrived in Stann Creek and Punta Gorda to be woodcutters. The understanding they gained of the coastline made them expert **smugglers**, able to evade Spanish enforcement that forbade trade with the British.

In spite of this economic relationship with the British, the Garifuna's incursion into Belize did not please its colonizers, and in 1811 Superintendent Barrow ordered their expulsion – to little effect. When European settlers arrived in Stann Creek in 1823, the Garifuna were continuing to flow in. **Methodist missionaries**, who found their mix of Catholicism, ancestor worship and polygamy outrageous, attempted to completely Christianize the Garifuna, but this met with little success. The largest single Garifuna migration to Belize took place in 1832 under the leadership of Alejo Benji. Several hundred fled Honduras (by then the Central American Republic) after supporting government opposition. This arrival is still celebrated as **Garifuna Settlement Day,** each November 19.

Through the **twentieth century**, Stann Creek (later Dangriga) was a stable community, its women employed in bagging and stacking cohune nuts and men working in agriculture. The Garifuna continued to travel widely for work, however, initially confining themselves to Central America (they can now be found right along the Caribbean coast from Belize to Nicaragua), but in World War II they joined the crews of British and US merchant ships. Since then, trips abroad have become an important part of the local economy, and there are small Garifuna communities in New York, New Orleans, Los Angeles and London. Today, Belize has a National Garifuna Council (@www.ngcbelize.org), who have refined a written language, publishing *The People's Garifuna Dictionary* and school textbooks, and opened a museum in Dangriga (see opposite). *The First Primer on a People Called Garifuna*, by Myrtle Palacio, is in English and available throughout the country.

Arrival, orientation and information

In addition to **buses** heading just for Dangriga, all services between Belize City (via Belmopan, 90min away) and Punta Gorda call here: both destinations are around three hours away. In general, there should be either a James or NTSL bus passing by every hour from 5am to 7pm (Mon–Sat) going both north and south, with a reduced Sunday service. Buses enter Dangriga at the southern end of town and stop by the drums monument by the petrol station, with James continuing to their terminal off Commerce Street; buses for Hopkins (two daily Mon–Sat, currently 10am and 1pm; 30min) leave from the dock near the *Riverside Restaurant*. There are usually four daily buses between Dangriga and **Placencia** (2hr), between 10am and 5 pm, though you can also hop on any Punta Gorda bus, alight at **Independence** (1.5hr), and take the fast boat to Placencia (see p.188). Dangriga's **airstrip**, served by at least eight daily flights in each direction on the Belize City–Punta Gorda run (fares Bz$80–150), is by the shore, just north of the *Pelican Beach Resort*; you'll need a taxi (at least Bz$8) into town. A **fast skiff** runs to/from Puerto Cortés, Honduras each Tuesday, Thursday and Saturday at 8.30am (3hr; US$50) from the north bank of the creek; be there at 7.30am with your passport so that the skipper (@522-3277 or 608-5515) can take care of the formalities.

▲ North Stann Creek, Dangriga

Almost everything you're likely to need in town, including **hotels**, **restaurants**, **banks** and **transport**, is on or very near the central thoroughfare either side of the **bridge** over North Stann Creek; north is Commerce Street and south St Vincent Street. There's no tourist office, but the town hall has a visitor's **map**; you can also download it and find other information at Ⓦwww.dangrigalive.com. The *Riverside Restaurant*, just south of the bridge in the centre of town, may also provide some information – especially if you need a **boat to the cayes**. Belize Bank and First Caribbean, both close to the bridge, have ATMs that accept foreign cards. The **post office** is on the corner of Mahogany and Ganey streets, and the **Immigration** office (for visa extensions) lies nearby on St Vincent Street – unlike others in Belize, it rarely has a queue. High-speed **internet** access is available at *Val's Hostel* on Mahogany Street, which also does **laundry**.

For **bookings and tours**, contact C&G Tours (Ⓣ522-3641, Ⓔcgtours@btl.net), who run to sights inland with a fleet of comfortable vehicles. You can rent high-quality **sea kayaks** from Island Expeditions (next to *Ruthie's Cabañas*; Ⓦwww .belizekayaking.com); a double costs US$55/day or US$350/week, and expedition leaders can shuttle you out to the cayes along with everything else you'll need for an extended outing. Just outside of town, fans of Belize's ubiquitous hot sauce can take a tour of **Marie Sharp's Factory** (Mon–Fri; Ⓣ520-2087, Ⓦwww .mariesharps-bz.com), with history and samplings available from the "Fiery Lady" herself – or buy them from Marie's downtown office on Pier Road.

Accommodation

Bluefield Lodge 6 Bluefield Rd
Ⓣ522-2742, Ⓦwww.toucantrail.com.
A clean, secure and well-run small hotel –

everything a budget place should be. Welcoming, with comfortable beds, bedside lights, some rooms with private bath and TV. Large veranda, payphone and excellent information board. ❷–❸

Bonefish Hotel 15 Mahogany St ☏522-2243, ✉bonefishhotel@yahoo.com. Good hotel with spacious rooms featuring TV, private bath and a/c, in a quiet, seafront location. Specializes in fishing trips and is the office for *Blue Marlin Lodge* on South Water Caye (see p.195). Wi-fi and great restaurant. ❺–❻

Chaleanor Hotel 35 Magoon St ☏522-2587, ⓦwww.toucantrail.com. Friendly, hospitable, value option with a variety of clean, spacious rooms, most with private bath, some have a/c. Free coffee, fruit and purified water available. The owner's son Elihue is a skilled guide. ❶ & ❹

Jungle Huts Hotel 4 Ecumenical Drive ☏522-0185. Sixteen pleasant rooms and cabañas alongside North Stann Creek with private bath and some with a/c or kitchenette, set around a peaceful, flowered courtyard. The amiable family owners serve great food; an unlimited American/Belizean breakfast Bz$18. Also good for groups. The hotel have packages with a stay on Glover's Reef. ❷–❹

Pelican Beach Resort On the beach, one mile north of town ☏522-2044, ⓦwww.pelicanbeachbelize.

com. A well-managed large hotel with the best beachfront location. Rooms and suites (economy rooms have no balcony) are in a wooden, colonial-style structure or a modern concrete building; most have TV, a/c and sea view. Frequently used by tour and conservation groups and scientists. Wonderful accommodation also available on South Water Caye (see p.195). Discounts in low season; it's worth asking. Best restaurant in Dangriga. ❼

Ruthie's Cabañas 31 Southern Foreshore ☏502-3184. Two bargain, thatched cabañas right on the sand, sleeping up to four, with private bath and porch with hammocks, plus even cheaper rooms, one with bunkbeds. Ruthie cooks delicious meals by arrangement. ❷–❸

Val's Backpacker Hostel 1 Sharp St, corner of Mahogany St ☏502-3324, ⓦwww.valsbackpackerhostel.com. A one-stop shop for budget travellers, with dorm beds (Bz$22) and private rooms available, and breakfast for Bz$5. Hot water, lockers, laundry service and bike hire are available, along with an internet café with ice cream and Val's delicious banana bread while you browse. ❶–❷

Eating, drinking and nightlife

There are surprisingly few restaurants here specializing in Garifuna food (you'll find more options in Hopkins – see p.198), though if you do happen upon them, **Garifuna dishes** feature fish and vegetables like yam, plantain, okra and cassava, often served in *sere*, a rich, thick, coconut-milk sauce similar in consistency to a chowder, accompanied by rice or the Garifuna staple of thin, crispy **cassava bread**, baked on a metal sheet over an open fire. The restaurant at *Pelican Beach* (see above) is the best in town, with skilled staff specializing in all of Belize's cultural specialities. Good Chinese food is to be found at *Starlight*, just north of *King Burger*. For fruits and picnic supplies, try the **market** on the north bank of the creek near the seashore; other groceries are available at the supermarket just south of the bridge.

There's no shortage of **bars** in Dangriga, though some, particularly those calling themselves clubs, like *Kennedy Club*, *Roxy* and *Harlem Club*, are rather dubious. Slightly more reputable is *Riviera Club*, right in the centre of town, with karaoke and a local scene. The best nightspots are *The Beach Place* and *Malibu Beach Club*, just before *Pelican Beach Resort*, north of the centre on the sand (weekends only), while *Ilaguleu* is a new nightspot by the roundabout. Live music and drumming can be found at the *Wadanani Shed* on St Vincent Street.

Garden of Eating *Jungle Huts Hotel* ☏522-0185. Serves a great American breakfast (Bz$18), and affordable set menu dinner (order in advance) of Latin and Creole foods, like tamales, *garnachos* (corn tortilla wraps), shrimp and vegetable dishes (Bz$25).

J&D's Culture Kitchen Canal St at Madre Cacao Rd. Daily specials and hearty, home-style portions

of traditional Creole and Garifuna dishes (around Bz$12). Mon–Sat 8am–9pm.

King Burger Commerce St, north of the creek. Serves good rice, chicken, burgers, fish, fruit juices and conch soup, a Belizean delicacy. Mon–Sat 7am–3pm & 6–10pm.

Riverside Restaurant South bank of the creek. Meeting place for boats to the cayes, serving tasty

Creole and Garifuna food (Bz$15–25), including great breakfasts and seafood, and fresh juices. Good for local information. Open 7am–9pm, Sun 8.30am–3pm.
Roots Kitchen Ecumenical Drive and Yemeri Rd. Best for traditional Garifuna dishes like *hudut* (mashed, half-ripe plantain with fish) and *bundiga* (savoury dish made from fish and banana), and very affordable (Bz$12–20), under a thatched roof. Open weekends 6am–9pm, breakfast/lunch at other times.

Offshore from Dangriga: The Cayes

The **Tobacco Range** is a group of mangrove cayes ten miles east of Dangriga. The largest in the range, **Man-O'-War Caye**, is a **bird sanctuary** named after the frigate (or man-o'-war) birds you'll see hanging on the breeze with outstretched wings. In the breeding season the males develop an immense, bright red balloon on their throats and the island fills with nesting birds; watching them is permitted, but you can't land on the caye. Tiny **Tobacco Caye**, together with the slightly larger **South Water Caye**, have a number of delightful places to stay, and sunsets out here can be breathtaking, outlining the distant Maya Mountains with a purple and orange aura. Beyond, thirty miles from Dangriga, is the coral atoll of Glover's Reef, one of the Caribbean's hidden treasures, with an assortment of excellent lodges and adventure oufits.

Tobacco Caye

Tobacco Caye, ideally situated right on the reef, is the easiest to reach in the area and has a range of cheaper accommodation on its sands. **Boats** leave from near the bridge in Dangriga, but there are no regular departures; check at the *Riverside Restaurant* in Dangriga, where you can meet the skippers. Captain Buck runs a reliable daily service leaving the caye at 9am and returning later, though any of the island lodge owners will take you if they're in town. It's a thirty-minute trip and the one-way fare is Bz$35 per person.

The cayes of Columbus Reef were originally visited by turtle fishermen; Tobacco Caye was a trading post where passing boats could pick up supplies, including the tobacco that gave the island its name. At just five acres, the island is tiny, and if you stand in the centre you're only one minute from the shore in any direction, with unbroken reef stretching north for miles. Since the reef is within wading distance of the shore, you don't even need a boat for some superb **snorkelling and diving**, saving precious time to eat, drink or relax in a hammock. Some lodges have dive shops, and Tobacco Caye Dive Center (☎670-3919 or 522-2419) offers trips to Glover's Reef atoll. A two-tank dive just off the island (including equipment) costs US$95, and there's plenty to see, since the caye is part of the **South Water Marine Reserve**, one of the best-protected areas for snorkelling and diving. The entrance fee is Bz$10 per day or Bz$30 per week, usually collected at the hotels by rangers.

Accommodation

Accommodation here is simple but comfortable, and generally of good value as prices include all meals. Bargaining is possible at slack periods, but make sure you check what you're paying for — and whether the price is in US or Belize dollars. Rates are charged per person per night, unless you've arranged a package in advance. All lodges can arrange scuba, snorkelling and fishing trips.

Gaviota Coral Reef Resort ☎509-5032 or 666-8699. Choose from basic and well-run cabins on the sand and rooms in a main wooden building, with shared or private bath. Most of the hotel is run by solar power, and there's a thatched shelter with hammocks and snorkel equipment for rent. ❺

Lana's on the Reef ☏ 520-5036, Four simple, neat rooms in a lovely wooden house; upstairs quarters, with private bath and communal balcony, are more expensive. Great food and good coffee. ❺–❻

Reef's End Lodge ☏ 522-2419 or 670-3919, ⓦ www.reefsendlodge.com. Stay right on the shore in the large wooden building, in spacious, private cabañas, all with private bathroom and deck, or in a smarter honeymoon suite with a/c. The restaurant and bar hover over the sea, a fantastic place to enjoy the sunset. Delicious food, dive shop and discounts for *Rough Guides* readers. ❸ & ❽

Tobacco Caye Lodge ☏ 520-5033, ⓦ www.tclodgebelize.com. Holds the most private land on the island, with a good beach bar by the dock, and three spacious, comfortable duplexes with hot-water bath, deck with hammocks and solar lights. Great seafood, bbq and fresh fruit. ❼

Tobacco Caye Paradise ☏ 520-5101, ⓔ bluefield@btl.net. Simple rooms in a wooden house (Bz$30 per person) and basic yet attractive thatched, stilted cabañas with private bath and verandas with hammocks over the sea (Bz$85 per person); all within a well cared-for property. ❸–❻

South Water Caye

Five miles south of Tobacco Caye and about three times larger, **South Water Caye** is one of the most beautiful and exclusive islands in Belize. It takes its name from a well at its centre, still in existence, which provided fresh water for passing ships. Like Tobacco Caye, the island sits right on the reef and offers fantastic, very accessible snorkelling and scuba diving in crystal-clear water; it's also the centre of the **South Water Marine Reserve** – a World Heritage Site – and its southern end is part of a small nature reserve. Turtles nest in the sand here, and the reef curves around offshore, protecting the pristine beach. Most of the resorts have their own very good **dive shops** and can arrange trips to **Glover's Reef** (see below). The tiny island off the caye's south end is **Carrie Bow Caye**, where the Smithsonian Institute has a research station; you can ask your hotel to arrange a visit, but there's no overnight accommodation.

Accommodation

Accommodation here is mainly upmarket and must be booked in advance; rates are typically either for groups or all-inclusive packages including the US$125 skiff from Dangriga.

Blue Marlin Lodge ☏ 520-5104, in the US ☏ 1-800/798-1558, ⓦ www.bluemarlinlodge.com. Luxurious, Belizean-owned property on raked white sand under coconut trees. A variety of carpeted a/c cabins with beautiful bathrooms, some dome-shaped and others with a deck over the sea, and rooms in a traditional "caye house". A thatched dining room serves delicious meals, and there's diving and fishing from a fleet of boats. Starts at US$2500 for two to four nights, including transfers and meals. ❾

Leslie Cottages ☏ 670-5030, in the US ☏ 1-800/548-5843, ⓦ www.ize2belize.com. Very comfortable private-bath cabins with wraparound decks and shared-bath dorm rooms, all fan-cooled, in a tropical field research station.

Two are right over the reef. Many guests come on study trips – the manager is a biologist focusing on reef ecology – but it's a wonderful place for anyone. Packages include transport, meals and boat tours, from US$1500/week per person. Internet access. ❾

Pelican's Pouch Resort ☏ 522-2024, ⓦ www .pelicanbeachbelize.com. A range of idyllic accommodation in a stunning location. Seven private cabañas and five sea-view rooms, some in a former colonial convent; rates (starting at US$270 for a double) include meals and snorkel gear. Solar electricity and composting toilets. *The Pelican's University*, on the west side of the island, has a bunk-and shared-bath design ideal for groups (ten or more) of students or travellers. ❽

Glover's Reef

The southernmost of Belize's three coral atolls, **Glover's Reef** lies twenty miles east of the Tobacco range. Named after British pirate John Glover, the reef is about twenty miles from north to south, and is physically the best-developed atoll in the Caribbean, rising from depths of 3000ft, with the reef wall beginning less than ten yards offshore. It offers some of the most spectacular **wall diving** in the world – the fantastic Long Caye Wall is less than 300ft offshore – with visibility of over 300yd. Glover's Reef is home to rare seabirds such as the white-capped noddy, all its cayes have nesting ospreys, and Belize's **marine turtles** lay their eggs on the beaches. The vitally important snapper spawning grounds on the atoll attract dozens of immense **whale sharks**, which congregate during the late spring full moons to feast on snapper eggs. Within the aquamarine lagoon are hundreds of smaller **patch reefs** – a snorkelling wonderland. These unique features informed the declaration of the atoll as a protected area in 1993 – the **Glover's Reef Marine Reserve**, further enhanced by its designation as a World Heritage Site in 1996. No fishing is allowed from the cayes themselves, but you can fish in special zones shown marked on the map you should receive when you pay the Bz$20 **entry fee**.

The main cayes lie in the atoll's southeastern section. **Northeast Caye**, covered in thick coconut and broadleaf forest and with evidence of Maya fishing camps, lies just across the channel from **Long Caye**. Four kilometres southwest, **Middle Caye** is a wilderness zone, with a marine research and monitoring station run by the Wildlife Conservation Society (ⓦwww.wcsgloversreef.org; see also Contexts, p.265). Fisheries Department **conservation officers** are based here, rigorously patrolling the reserve. Only staff, scientists and students stay on the caye, but you can usually visit with permission; the ecology of the atoll is explained in interesting displays, and you may see research in progress. Contribute to conservation efforts by purchasing an excellent T-shirt here, found only on the caye. **Southwest Caye**, 5km beyond Middle Caye, was sliced into two distinct islands by Hurricane Hattie in 1961, with a swimable narrow channel between them.

Since a chartered boat from Dangriga or Hopkins/Sittee River will cost you US$350 each way, package transport from your hotel is the best way to arrive and depart. For charters, ask at your hotel or try Michael Jackson (☏620-8913), who may be inclined to give a *Rough Guides* discount.

Accommodation and outdoor activities

Glover's Reef is unusual among Belize's remote atolls in that it offers accommodation within the reach of budget travellers. All options offer **package accommodation**, mostly in purpose-built camps and cabins, used by **sea kayaking** and diving groups; you can easily hop between the four cayes by boat or kayak. Most accommodation include weekly shuttles to and from the mainland in their packages.

Glover's Atoll Resort Northeast Caye ☏614-7177 or 520-2016, ⓦwww .glovers.com.bz. Indulge your Robinson Crusoe "desert island" fantasy right here, overlooking sea and reef. Prices are per person per week, and include transport from Sittee River on the resort's catamaran – leaving Sun morning and returning Sat. Twelve simple stilted wood-and-thatch beach cabins, some ideal for families and over the water (US$249–299), a wooden dorm room (US$199), and space for camping (US$149, including tent and bedding); if you stay for a month the fourth week is free. Meals not included, but there are bbqs and cabins have kerosene stoves; one evening each week features a potluck supper. Bring food/drink (fish, lobster, bread and basics available to buy) or eat at the excellent restaurant. Drinking water is provided free (as well as coconuts), and shower-water is drawn from a well. Activities like sea kayaking, fishing, snorkelling and scuba diving (with bargain PADI certification) available with expert guides, some born and raised on the atoll. Owned by long-time French-American residents, the resort often closes Sept–Oct. ❷–❸

Isla Marisol Resort ☏520-2056 or 610-4204, ⓦwww.islamarisolresort.com. Eleven attractive wooden cabañas on the beach, each with queen-sized bed, ceiling fan, private hot-water shower and a shady veranda with hammocks. The food is excellent and the bar is built on a deck over the water. A PADI dive centre offers beginner to Advanced Open Water courses; a week's package in high season, including transport, meals and seventeen dives (two night dives) is US$1795; you'll dive on all three of Belize's atolls, depending on weather conditions, and April to June you can dive with whale sharks. A week's fly-fishing is US$2395, or just relax and swim off the gorgeous beach for US$1295; three- or four-day packages also available. ❾

Island Expeditions Southwest Caye ⓦwww .islandexpeditions.com (see also Basics, p.21). A Vancouver-based, experienced sea kayaking and snorkelling outfitter with superb guides and an exemplary environmental record. You fly into Dangriga and are taken by fast skiff to the caye, where you sleep in spacious, comfortable white tents with proper beds and eat gourmet meals in the screened dining room. Beginners receive kayak training, and veterans can visit the other cayes or take part in overnight camping expeditions to uninhabited islands. Also offers excellent, biologist-led educational trips. Two- to eight-night packages available, starting at US$449 per person all-inclusive. ❾

Off the Wall Dive Center and Resort
Long Caye ☎614-6348, ⓦwww .offthewallbelize.com. A well-managed dive resort offering a full range of responsible and professional PADI courses, snorkelling and fishing packages for around US$1400–2000/week per person, depending on the activity, including all meals and boat transfer from Dangriga. Guests stay in charming wooden cabañas with separate showers, and the only gift shop on the atoll sells souvenirs. ❾

Slickrock Adventures Long Caye US ☎1-800-390 5715, ⓦwww.slickrock.com (see also Basics p.22). Wonderful sea kayaking expeditions and multi-sport adventures including kite- and paddle-boarding, surf kayaking, fishing and windsurfing. Guests are transported from Belize City by fast launch to their sturdy, comfortable stilted cabins, with a deck and hammock overlooking the reef, or in tents under a thatched roof. Varied, filling meals are served in the spacious dining room. Eco-friendly, the base camp uses composting toilets and wind and solar power. An experienced adventure outfitter, they also offer packages with inland sights and jungle trips. Four- to nine-night all-inclusive packages start at US$900 per person. ❾

The Southern Highway to Placencia

South of Dangriga the country becomes more mountainous, with settlements mainly restricted to the coastal lowlands. The only road heading in this direction is the **Southern Highway**, spanning 105 miles from Dangriga to Punta Gorda. For its entire length the highway is set back from the coast, running beneath the jagged peaks and dense rainforest of the **Maya Mountains**, itself often passing through pine forest and citrus and banana plantations on the lower plains. The tallest summits are those of the Cockscomb range, which includes Victoria Peak, at 3365ft the second-highest mountain in Belize and a dramatic sight on a clear day. Several branch roads lead off to settlements such as **Hopkins**, a Garifuna village on the coast, and the nearby Creole village of **Sittee River**. From the village of **Maya Centre**, 36km south of Dangriga, a road leads west into the Cockscomb Basin Wildlife Sanctuary (generally referred to as the **Jaguar Reserve**); your first reason to pull off the highway, however, might be to visit the Maya site of **Mayflower**.

South to Hopkins and the Jaguar Reserve

Six miles south of the junction with the Stann Creek Valley Road, an unpaved, four-mile branch road twists through citrus groves and forest to the foothills of the Maya Mountains and the Late Classic site of **Mayflower**. There are really three Maya sites here: Mayflower, near the end of the branch road, and Maintzunun ("hummingbird") and T'au Witz ("dwelling-place of the mountain god"), both a short distance through the forest. Apart from a few stone mounds and open plazas, the sites have not yet been fully cleared. The location on a creek, however, is sublime, and rich in bird and animal life. The sites are being excavated by the Mayflower Archaeology Project (see Contexts, p.258, for details of how to participate), and the area around them is now protected in the 7000-acre **Mayflower Bocawina National Park** (Bz$10), whose hiking trails lead to waterfalls tumbling into Silk Grass Creek.

You can stay in the midst of this natural beauty at family-run **Mama Noots Backabush** (☎670-8019, ⓦwww.mamanoots.com; ❺), in fifty acres of forest and hillside. Solar and wind power add to the tranquillity, along with occasional visits by a jaguar. Accommodation is in a family-sized cabaña, a two-room thatched house or a wheelchair-accessible lodge; all are large, with private bath, fan, electricity and balconies; internet is available. The **restaurant** serves delicious food (open to non-guests) using organic vegetables, while a short trail has descriptions of plants' medicinal properties, en route to nearby waterfalls: there's also excellent early-morning guided birding. Buses heading south pass the resort; call ahead for a pickup from the junction, four miles away.

Hopkins

Stretching for two miles along a shallow, gently curving bay, **HOPKINS** is home to around 1200 Garifuna, traditionally living from small-scale farming, and fishing with baited handlines or paddling dugout canoes to pull up fish traps. Their traditional wood-and-thatch houses have now largely been replaced by less visually appealing, but more secure, concrete. The village, named for a Catholic bishop who drowned nearby in 1923, was first settled in 1942 after a hurricane levelled its predecessor, Newtown, just to the north. People are proud of their culture here – most speak Garifuna as a first language – and **Garifuna Settlement Day** on November 19 is celebrated enthusiastically with singing, dancing and the beating of drums – an integral custom. Now firmly inducted into the tourist circuit, you'll be made to feel welcome by the exuberant friendliness of Hopkins' villagers, particularly the children.

Great beaches and delicious food and accommodation in all price ranges makes Hopkins a pleasant place to spend a few days relaxing, but it's also well equipped for numerous outdoor activities, from diving and snorkelling to kayaking and windsurfing (see tours, below). Just north of the village, a narrow creek gives way to a large, peaceful lagoon – great for kayaking – but construction of timeshares and condominiums threaten its accessibility. Still, the view inland from here, with the village and the high ridges of the Maya Mountains behind, is breathtaking.

The Drumming Center at Lebeha (ⓦwww.lebeha.com) showcases **Garifuna drumming and dancing** by local young people every Friday night at around 8pm. Drumming lessons are available here for Bz$30 per hour; if you would like to purchase a drum, visit drum-maker Mr Coleman (☎523-7217) on the north side of the village.

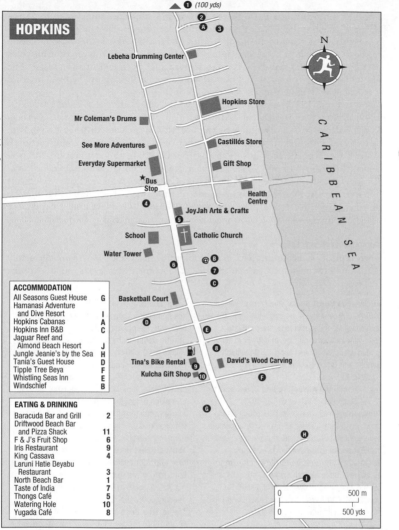

HOPKINS

▲ ● *(100 yds)*
②
Ⓐ ③

Lebeha Drumming Center

Hopkins Store

Mr Coleman's Drums

See More Adventures

Everyday Supermarket

Castillós Store

Gift Shop

★ Bus Stop

Health Centre

④

JoyJah Arts & Crafts
⑤

School   ✝ Catholic Church

Water Tower

⑥   @ Ⓑ
⑦
Ⓒ

Basketball Court

Ⓓ   Ⓔ
⑧

Tina's Bike Rental   David's Wood Carving
⑨
Kulcha Gift Shop ⑩   Ⓕ

Ⓖ

Ⓗ

Ⓘ

C A R I B B E A N   S E A

N

Southern Highway (4 miles)

ACCOMMODATION	
All Seasons Guest House	G
Hamanasi Adventure and Dive Resort	I
Hopkins Cabanas	A
Hopkins Inn B&B	C
Jaguar Reef and Almond Beach Resort	J
Jungle Jeanie's by the Sea	H
Tania's Guest House	D
Tipple Tree Beya	F
Whistling Seas Inn	E
Windschief	B

EATING & DRINKING	
Baracuda Bar and Grill	2
Driftwood Beach Bar and Pizza Shack	11
F & J's Fruit Shop	6
Iris Restaurant	9
King Cassava	4
Laruni Hatie Beyabu Restaurant	3
North Beach Bar	1
Taste of India	7
Thongs Café	5
Watering Hole	10
Yugada Café	8

| 0 | 500 m |
| 0 | 500 yds |

Sittee River (2 miles) ▼ ● *(100 yds)*, ⑪ *(350 yds)* & ▼ *Sittee River Marina (2 miles)*

Arrival, information and tours

The **bus** service from Dangriga to Hopkins is reliable; KC's Bus leaves from the dock outside the *Riverside Restaurant* (Mon–Sat 10.30am and 1pm, returning from Hopkins at 7am via Sittee River and 2pm, no Sun service; Bz$5). Note that at the time of writing there is no service onwards to the Jaguar Reserve or Placencia; you could choose to change at Dangriga or wait on the Southern Highway intersection for the next James Bus service south.

As there are no street names in Hopkins, the best way to locate anything is in relation to the point where the road from the Southern Highway enters the village centre. The main road through the village is paved, but asphalt gives way to sand at the southern end; this road passes a number of luxury resorts along a beautiful beach called **False Sittee Point**, and continues three miles to **Sittee River**. Cycling is the mode of transport for most guests (though golf buggies *a la* San Pedro are starting to creep in) – quite useful as Hopkins extends so far along the beach - with most hotels providing these free of charge. You can **rent bicycles** (Bz$25/day) from Tina's Bike Rental, toward the south end of the village. The Health Centre, (with nurse and occasional doctor) is located by the pier. Internet is available at *Windschief* and at *Thongs Café*.

You can rent kayaks at Tipple Tree Beya and windsurfers at *Windschief* (☎523-7249). Diving here is excellent and uncrowded. If you're not staying at *Hamanasi Resort*, visit See More Adventures by the Everyday supermarket (☎666-6658). Run by two local PADI registered instructors, they offer snorkelling and diving on South Water Caye, Turneffe and Glovers atolls (from US$100), plus certification. Bullfrog Tours (☎669-0046 or 667-7431, ✉ssymcm@yahoo.com), based at *Driftwood Beach Bar* (see opposite) also uses local PADI-certified guides who are expert freedivers (often to harvest lobster and conch) and spearfishermen. The outfit offers a range of other boat trips around the cayes plus a traditional Garifuna fishing experience using handlines. Otherwise, most local hotels can arrange trips to the reef and cayes.

Accommodation

There is plenty of **accommodation** in Hopkins, with advance booking not generally needed unless you want a particular place at Christmas, Easter or around Garifuna Settlement Day.

All Seasons Guest House South end of village ☎523-7209, ⓦwww.allseasonsbelize.com. Three beautifully decorated rooms with a/c, private bath, coffeemaker and fridge, in a lovely, tranquil garden with patio. Dune buggy rental available; German and Dutch spoken; long term rentals are possible. ❸

Hamanasi Adventure and Dive Resort South end of village ☎520-7073, ⓦwww.hamanasi.com. One of the country's top dive resorts, with a range of luxuriously appointed beachfront suites and rooms, plus six "treehouse" cabañas on stilts; all have a/c, fans, king- or queen-size beds, Belizean hardwood furniture, attractive bathrooms and private porches. Excellent service, fast, modern dive boats and superb equipment. *Hamanasi* offers tours around reef and atolls plus inland adventures. ❽–❾

Hopkins Inn B&B On the beach, near village centre ☎523-7283, ⓦwww.hopkins inn.com. Friendly place with four immaculate, whitewashed cabañas each sleeping up to four, with veranda, private bath, fridge and coffeemaker. Local guides available. Large continental breakfast included. German spoken. ❺

Jaguar Reef and Almond Beach Resort False Sittee Point, 1.3 miles south ☎520-7040, ⓦwww.jaguarreef.com. A fifty-room luxury resort with large, thatched, family cabañas and a modern resort building, within beautifully landscaped grounds by the beach. The restaurant, under a huge, thatched roof overlooking the

beach and pool, is highly rated. There is also a spa and coffee shop, and kayaks and bikes are available free of charge. ❽

Jungle Jeanie's by the Sea South end of the village ☎523-7047, ⓦwww.junglebythesea.com. Eight hardwood cabañas sleeping up to four, some on stilts, one wonderful treehouse; all have private bath, some a fridge. Located at the edge of a patch of jungle by the beach in a shady, relaxed setting. The friendly owners serve international food (stir frys, crêpes) and rent kayaks. Camping available. ❸–❹

Tania's Guest House South of centre, west side of road ☎523-7058. A small, friendly option, basic but a bargain. All rooms have private shower (most hot water); some have fridge and cable TV. Complimentary coffee. ❶–❷

Tipple Tree Beya Near south end of village ☎520-7006, ⓦwww.tippletree.com. Good-value, clean beachside rooms in a wooden building with deck, hammocks, coffeemaker and either hot or cold-water bathrooms. The friendly owner is a good source of information, ensuring you have an enjoyable stay. There's also a furnished wooden cabin, sleeping four, with fridge and microwave. ❸ & ❺

Whistling Seas Inn Towards south of village ☎661-3013, ✉marcello@whistlingseas.com. Five brightly painted beachside cabañas with hot-water bathrooms, fridge, a/c and veranda, sleeping up to four. Friendly Belizean owners. Great value, and the restaurant/beach bar serves good local food. ❸

Windschief On the beach, close to the centre ☎523-7249, 𝕎www.windschief.com. Two simple, clean cabins sleep up to four. Both have coffee-maker, fridge, cold shower, and great beachfront view. External hot shower, bar and internet café. Windsurfing lessons are available. ❷–❸

Eating and Drinking

Though your choice may be limited outside of the tourist season, Hopkins has a good selection of **restaurants**. You'll always find delicious Garifuna and Creole meals, and usually very good seafood. Service can be slow at inexpensive places, so be prepared to wait – at least you'll know it's fresh. Most reliable Chinese food can be found at *Rainbow* by *Whistling Seas Inn*. For more upmarket dining, sample the restaurants in resorts at False Sittee Point. Fresh **fruit and vegetables** can be found at F&J's Fruit Shop, and there's a good grocery right opposite. Many businesses and restaurants close from 2 to 4pm, then remain open until around 9 or 10pm at night.

For a drink with the locals head to *King Cassava* (see below); most locals' bars open until midnight. Some resorts, as well as *Lebeha* (see p.198), also feature live drumming, but it's best to check with your hotel what's going on in the community. Oliver's *palapa* bar/internet café at the *Windshief* is also a popular gathering place in the evenings (closed Thurs; later at weekends).

🏃 **Baracuda Bar and Grill** *Beaches and Dreams Hotel*, False Sittee Point. Superb, creative, and moderately priced Mediterranean and Caribbean food at this beachside restaurant/lounge bar run by Alaskan chef Tony. Try the pesto-baked snapper, tenderloin topped with lobster and heart of palm, or the jerk/black bean pork. The chocolate pecan pie is to die for.

Driftwood Beach Bar and Pizza Shack North End of the village. Brand new rustic chill-out beach bar serving really good thin-crust pizza and fresh fish.

Iris Restaurant Near the southern edge of the village. Good Belizean mains and burgers at great prices, served from 8am to 9pm (closed Sun).

King Cassava In the centre at the junction. Full Belizean and international menu with bar service in an open-air dining space. Daily specials may include fresh, local game like gibnut. Nightly entertainment (at weekends live music or drumming); this was the last place award-winning musician Andy Palacio (see p.269) played in before he died in 2009. Open late, closed Mon.

🏃 **Laruni Hatie Beyabu Restaurant** On the beach, north of the centre. The only Belizean-owned eatery with a beachfront view,

serving delicious Garifuna specialities like *hudut*. A favourite among locals.

North Beach Bar North end of the village. This smartish Canadian/Belizean owned beach bar/restaurant has a reliable menu like pork and pineapple kebabs, burgers, quesadillas and fish with chutney/ginger sauce.

Taste of India Centre of the village. A surprising find – a cheap and reliable Indian-owned restaurant with a range of curries (seafood and chicken) and dahls.

Thongs Café Centre of the village. Smart and relaxed new café/restaurant with espressos, teas, smoothies and the like, alongside sandwiches, salads and light bite mains (spaghetti, fajitas). Owner/DJ spins dance/chillout tunes in the evenings. Wi-fi access. Daily 8am–2pm, 6pm–late.

Watering Hole South of the centre, near the edge of the village. One of the best restaurants in town, serving great seafood and daily specials.

🏃 **Yugada Café** Main street, south of the centre. The Nuñez sisters serve tasty international fare, fresh juices and great desserts in a pleasant, warm and friendly dining room. Serves breakfast; closed Wed. Occasional entertainment.

Sittee River

A few miles along a dirt road south of Hopkins, with its own turnoff (5m) from the Southern Highway, is the pleasant village of **SITTEE RIVER**. Sitting prettily on the north bank of the community's namesake, the river is a wildlife hotspot, with excellent birding and a number of creeks and pristine lagoons revealing freshwater crocodiles and turtles basking along the riverbanks; a new marina at the river mouth (☎520-7887, 𝕎www.sitteerivermarina.com) offers boat trips (Bz$200) and charters, while kayak rental is available at just Bz$30 per day from basic *Glover's Guest House* (☎520-5016, 𝕎www.glovers.com.bz; ❶), where you check in for

Sunday morning trips to *Glover's Atoll Resort* on Glover's Reef (see p.195) – one of Belize's best budget accommodations. With dorm beds and double rooms in elevated cabins, two nights here earns you a third free, while there's a **restaurant** right on the riverbank. The best **accommodation** in Sittee River, however, is *Sir Thomas at Toucan Sittee* (℡523-7039, Ⓦwww.sir-thomas-at-toucan-sittee.com; ◑), signposted at the entrance to the village from the Hopkins road, and set on the riverbank, graced by toucans most mornings. Five solidly built raised cabañas have innovative thatch and bamboo ceilings and exquisite hardwood furniture – two king-size beds in each – plus fan, hot-water bathroom and fridge. Complete with its own twenty-acre nature reserve, birding (a previous guest recorded 97 species in an hour), fishing and river trips are a highlight, with a choice of salt- or freshwater lagoons, mangroves, tropical forest and offshore cayes to explore (tours around US$300 per group per day). Excellent local guide Udell Foreman can take you on an exciting night paddle, while inland caving is also available. The food here includes lots of fresh fruit (numerous mangos) and vegetables, alongside American and Belizean home cooking, like baked potatoes, quality burgers and vegetarian options; there's also a pizza oven.

Coming in from the highway, you'll see the ruins of the nineteenth-century **Serpon Sugar Mill**, now preserved as a local park with a small museum, wonderful trees and good birding. **Buses** are infrequent here; the morning bus from Hopkins passes through Sittee River on its way back to Dangriga, so without your own transport your best bet is to take a taxi (it's a 25min cycle ride) from Hopkins, or hitch in from the highway. Should you spend much time in the village, be warned that the sandflies can be atrocious; guesthouses provide screens and mosquito nets for good reason.

Check your **email** at Sittee River Internet (℡603-8358), and if you need to stock up on **supplies** before heading out to sea, Reynold's Store covers most groceries.

Maya Centre and the Cockscomb Basin Wildlife Sanctuary

Beneath the sharp ridges of the Maya Mountains is a sweeping bowl, part of which was declared a **jaguar reserve** in 1986 – since expanded to cover an area of over 250 square miles: the **Cockscomb Basin Wildlife Sanctuary**. The region was inhabited in Maya times, and the ruins of **Kuchil Balam**, a Classic-period ceremonial centre, still lie hidden in the forest. It was also exploited by mahogany loggers; the names of their abandoned camps, such as Leave If You Can and Go to Hell, illustrate how they felt about life in the forest. In more recent times the residents of Quam Bank, a Maya village, moved out of the Cockscomb when the reserve was established, relocating to **Maya Centre** on the Southern Highway. The sanctuary is managed by the Belize Audubon Society, with financial assistance from international conservation organizations. It's possible to **volunteer** here, maintaining trails, working on displays in the visitor centre or even tracking howler monkeys; contact BAS in Belize City for more information (see p.58).

All buses heading south from Dangriga pass tiny **MAYA CENTRE** (35min), from where a rough six-mile track leads to the sanctuary headquarters. You need to sign in and pay the reserve entrance fee at the Craft Centre (daily 7.30am–5pm; Bz$10; ℡666-3495); it's run by the village women's group, and there's information here about accommodation as well as inexpensive wood and slate carvings and embroidery. The Mopan Maya families living in Maya Centre are enthusiastic proponents of eco-tourism, and staying here before entering the reserve is a perfect way to learn about forest life and Maya culture.

Although many tour operators will tell you that you can't get into the Jaguar Reserve without going on a tour, you can easily walk in from Maya Centre (a two-hour gentle uphill slope; leave excess luggage at Julio's Store, see p.204). If you've come by bus and don't fancy walking, a taxi or truck to the headquarters will cost about Bz$40 for up to five people – ask at the Craft Centre. You'll have a better experience, though, if you go with a guide from Maya Centre, all of whom know the reserve intimately. Greg Sho is amongst the best bush and river kayaking

The Victoria Peak Trail

Viewed from the sea, the jagged granite peaks of the Cockscomb range take on the appearance of a colossal, recumbent head, whose sloping forehead, eyebrows, nose, mouth and chin have earned the range the nickname of "The Sleeping Maya". The first recorded successful attempt to the summit of **Victoria Peak was in 1888**, though it's reasonably certain that the ancient Maya were first to make it to the top. The highest point in the Cockscomb at 3675ft, and the second-highest mountain in Belize after Doyle's Delight (3687ft), it's no giant by world standards, but the trek should not be undertaken lightly. You'll need to find a guide in Maya Centre (see p.204; guides cost around Bz$800 per group, normally including a porter to help carry supplies); or contact Maya Guide Adventures (see p.147), since it involves scaling some of the rock faces below the peak using climbing equipment, and being able to carry supplies for three to five days. You'll begin each day's walk at first light to minimise the danger of **heat exhaustion** later in the day. Creeks cross the trail regularly and the water is generally safe to drink, though you may prefer to purify it. Simple **shelters** along the way mean it's not necessary to bring a tent, but they do offer protection from biting insects. There's no charge for using the trail – you just pay the Jaguar Reserve entrance fee and backcountry campsite charges.

The trail (which is marked in kilometres) begins at the Jaguar Reserve headquarters, following a level, abandoned logging road through secondary forest for 12km to the first rest point, where the **Sittee Branch River** beckons with the chance of a cooling swim. On the far bank, a thatched shelter with kitchen and pit toilets provides the first **campsite**. Beyond, the trail climbs and descends steeply in a series of energy-sapping undulations until you reach km 17, where you walk along a steep ridge before descending to the second campsite, at km 19. A **helipad** hacked out of the forest at km 18 offers the first real views of the peak. If you've set off early and are fit you can reach this campsite in one day, but be warned that the 7km from the first campsite are extremely rigorous. Here, you can hang hammocks in an open-sided wooden shelter; your shower is a small waterfall cascading over smooth rocks. The final stretch to the peak is four relentless uphill hours, with much of the trail along a steep, rocky creek bed – too dangerous to attempt in heavy rain. As the ascent becomes ever more vertical and you rise above the forest canopy, the views increase in splendour. Closer to the ground, wildflowers cling to rock crevices. Just below the peak, you haul yourself up through a narrow gully on a rope; above here the track along the final ridge passes though elfin **cloud forest**, with gnarled tree limbs draped in filmy moss and tiny ferns, before reaching the summit. Low, waxy-leaved bushes offer only scraps of shade, and the Belize flag flutters in the breeze. Tethered to the rock that marks the peak is an exercise book for recording the names of successful climbers. Spread beneath you are a series of deep green, thickly forested ridges and valleys – on a very clear day you can see to the Caribbean – and not a sign of humanity's impact. The trek down is almost as arduous, taking about an hour less to reach the campsite. With an early start, you can walk all the way out to the sanctuary headquarters the following day.

6

▲ Cockscomb Basin Wildlife Sanctuary

guides in the country, but if he's booked up, ask for Gregorio Chun, Raul Balona or William Sho. William also has a **butterfly exhibit** (daily 6am–5pm; Bz$5) across the creek from the Craft Centre. Nearby, **Julio's Store** sells basic supplies and cold drinks (there's no restaurant or shop in the reserve) and has a **bar** and **internet access**. Owner Julio Saqui runs Cockscomb Maya Tours (☎520-3042, ⓦwww.cocks combmayatours.com) and can also arrange **guides and transport**.

Maya Centre: accommodation and eating

Maya Centre has several simple **places to stay**, generally with electricity and sometimes a private bathroom. You can also **camp** at any of these (Bz$10 per person) if you have your own tent. Accommodation is also available within the sanctuary.

On the main highway, *Tutzil Nah Cottages* (☎520-3044, ⓦwww.mayacenter .com; ❶–❷) has two neat, clean cabins, one with private bath. Run by the Chun family, brothers Gregorio, Julian and Ouscal are excellent guides and arrange superb **kayak trips** along South Stann Creek; the family also manages a store and gift shop. Set in lovely gardens behind the Craft Centre, *Mejen Tz'il Lodge* (☎520-3032, ⓔlsaqui@btl.net; ❶–❷) has a thatched cabaña with private bathroom, as well as dorm rooms in a wooden cabin (Bz$20 per person). Co-owner Yoli serves great **meals**, and you can rent **tents** here for use on the Victoria Peak Trail. Some 500yd up the track to the reserve, *Nu'uk Che'il Cottages* (☎520-3033 or 615-2091, ⓦwww.mayacottages.com; ❷–❸) offer simple but delightful rooms, some with private hot-water bathroom, as well as dorm beds (Bz$20) and **homestays** with Maya families (Bz$50 per person, including dinner and breakfast). The **restaurant**, serving Maya and Belizean food, is great for a filling meal on your way to or from the reserve. Aurora is one of the Garcia sisters from San Antonio in Cayo (see p.137), and has developed a medicinal trail (Bz$5) and makes **herbal medicines** (for sale in the H'men Herbal Center), and also arranges Maya cultural events featuring *marimba* music.

The Jaguar Reserve

The road from Maya Centre fords streams and crosses the Cabbage Haul Gap before reaching the sanctuary headquarters, in a grassy area surrounded by beautiful foliage. Technically, this is a **tropical moist forest**, with an annual rainfall of up to 118in that feeds a network of wonderfully clear streams. A sizeable percentage of Belize's plant and animal species live in this verdant habitat; mammals include tapirs, otters, coatis, deer, anteaters, armadillos and, of course, jaguars, as well as other cat species. Three hundred bird species have also been recorded, including endangered scarlet macaws, great curassows, keel-billed toucans and king vultures, while it serves as a refuge for large raptors like harpy, solitary and white hawk eagles. Reptiles and amphibians abound, including red-eyed tree frogs, boa constrictors and the deadly fer-de-lance snake, known in Belize as "yellow-jaw tommy-goff". The forest is made up of a range of plant species, including orchids, giant tree ferns, air plants (epiphytes) and trees like banak, cohune, mahogany and ceiba.

At the headquarters, the excellent **visitor's centre** has a relief model of the Cockscomb Basin, displays on the area's ecology and trail maps. You can pick up a copy of Louise Emmons's *Cockscomb Basin Wildlife Sanctuary* here, a superb guide to the reserve's history, flora and fauna, and the shop sells drinks and snacks. **Accommodation** is available if you want to fully experience Cockscomb by listening to its night-time sounds; it's aimed at students and researchers, but anyone can stay – there are a range of cabins and dorm rooms, as well as an entire house (❶–❹). No food is served, but cabins have a basic kitchen; local cooks can be arranged. **Camping** is allowed at designated sites along the trails (Bz$20 per person); get a permit from the rangers.

Although roughly sixty of Belize's seven hundred **jaguars** live in the sanctuary, your chances of seeing one are slim. It's nonetheless an ideal environment for plant-spotting, birding or seeking out other evasive wildlife, and the trails are the best of any of Belize's protected areas. Short trails lead through the forest to the riverbank or to **Tiger Fern Falls**, a picturesque, two-tiered waterfall with a pool at the upper level. **Ben's Bluff Trail** is a more strenuous 2.5-mile hike to a forested ridge, with a great view of the entire Cockscomb Basin and a chance to cool off in a rocky pool. **Inner tube and kayak** rental is available; follow the marked trail upstream and tube down South Stann Creek for a soothing, tranquil view. For a longer (or overnight) trip using inflatable kayaks, contact the Chuns at *Tutzil Nah* (see opposite). If you're prepared, you can climb **Victoria Peak** (see box, p.203); two miles along the route, a trail leads to Outlier Overlook – a great challenging day-hike or overnight camp.

Kanantik Reef and Jungle Resort

About four miles south of Maya Centre a side road heads east to the sea, ending at **Kanantik Reef and Jungle Resort** (☎520-8048, ⓦ www.kanantik.com; ❾), one of Belize's all-inclusive luxury resorts. The brainchild of Italian investors, the property has 25 elevated cabañas with elegant conical thatched roofs. Composed of the finest local materials, Guatemalan textiles and four-poster beds, and surrounded by tropical gardens, the resort fuses rustic simplicity with sophistication more successfully than anywhere else in the country. *Kanantik* means "to take care" in Mopan Maya, and you're certainly well cared for; the meals and service are superb, but thankfully without any fussy formality. With three hundred acres of beach, jungle, pine forest and wetlands just south of Sapodilla Lagoon, the area abounds with wildlife, including jaguars, crocodiles and birds, which can be spotted from two towers. The pool is metres from the sea, and expertly guided activities include scuba diving, snorkelling, sailing, canoeing, horseback riding, fishing and expeditions to Maya sites and the Jaguar Reserve. Most guests arrive on Tropic Air flights (Fri–Mon), landing at the resort's own paved airstrip, but a pickup from Dangriga can also be arranged.

The Placencia peninsula

6

Ten miles south of Maya Centre, a new paved road cuts east from the Southern Highway, heading through pine forest and banana plantations and eventually reaching the sea at the tiny settlement of **Riversdale** – a community rudely awakened by the recent construction of Belize's second international airport, scheduled for completion in late 2010. This marks the start of the **Placencia peninsula**, a narrow, sandy finger of land sheltering Placencia Lagoon from the sea. Sixteen miles in length, the road passes through a beautiful stretch of coast called **Maya Beach** before ending at **Placencia**, a small, laidback fishing village just coming to terms with its status as Belize's second tourist honeypot (after San Pedro). Lined with sandy beaches, a mangrove lagoon and with a reef a little way offshore, the peninsula's development may come as no surprise, but the speed with which current constructions are being approved has shocked even those most familiar with Belize – used to fast talk and slow action. Alongside the airport, a brand new resort and casino, *The Placencia*, is located at the northern end of Maya beach, and marinas holding over six hundred yachts will shortly open. Remaining undeveloped land is selling at a premium – and fast. Concerns over local ecology remain paramount: residents have banded together and formed the Placencia Citizens for Sustainable Development (PCSD; Ⓦwww .saveourpeninsula.org), an effort to counterbalance stealthy and unplanned construction. With a fragile marine environment containing rays, manatees and dolphins, a reef largely dependent on preservation of coastal mangroves, and a local population pushed out of the job market by a surge in migrant labour from across Central America, they're right to be worried.

The entire peninsula is served by four daily **buses** from Dangriga (see box, p.211); hitching is relatively easy and the road is ideal for cycling.

Maya Beach

Larger construction is currently taking place at the northern end of Maya Beach; about halfway down its length, however, are a smattering of really good laidback accommodations and restaurants. In addition to the pleasures of a sandy Caribbean beach, most resorts also have access to Placencia Lagoon and can arrange fishing and diving trips, as well as tours inland. Many have bikes and kayaks for guests, and it's a relatively easy paddle to False Caye. Some hotels offer self-catering (groceries are delivered by van), with incidentals purchased from the Maya Point Market – a local **grocery store** – or the *Hungry Gecko*, run by a friendly Honduran family, which also has a cheap upstairs restaurant serving tasty Belizean **breakfasts** and Central American snacks, plus sandwiches and seafood (closed Wed). The superb *Maya Beach Hotel and Bistro* (closed Mon; see p.212) is the best place to eat on the whole peninsula; this and other resort restaurants are listed on p.212. A **taxi** to or from Placencia costs around Bz$30. A laundry service on Maya Beach is available from Boston's Suds (℡520-8003). For more information, visit Maya Beach's **website** (Ⓦwww.gotobelize.com).

Accommodation

Maya Beach accommodation tends to be boutique-style upmarket, and some places give worthwhile *Rough Guides* discounts. All-inclusive packages are available or you can self-cater. More accommodation, for all budgets, is available at Placencia village. Hotels are listed in the order you approach them from the north, and all are right by the road.

Maya Beach Hotel and Bistro Eight miles north of Placencia village ℡520-8040, Ⓦwww.mayabeachhotel.com. Eco-sensitive and quiet resort with a range of rooms and apartments, some single, private units and others around an infinity pool yards from the sea. There are stylish soft colours, wooden furniture and atmospheric artwork. All rooms have a/c, private bath and queen beds. Excellent restaurant. Online booking (at last minute) can yield good discounts. ❻–❽

Green Parrot Beach Houses 50yd south of the *Maya Beach Hotel* ☎ 523-2488, ⓦ www .greenparrot-belize.com. Choose from six wooden houses (sleeping up to five) raised on stilts, and two thatched "honeymoon" cabins on the beach. Each house has a living room, a loft with queen and single bed, kitchen and deck with hammock. Great restaurant. Rates include transport from Placencia airstrip, breakfast and kayaks. ❻

Maya Breeze Inn Immediately south of *Green Parrot* ☎ 523-8012, ⓦ www.mayabreezeinn.com. Beautifully furnished wooden cabins and suites on a gorgeous beach, plus four comfortable hotel rooms on the roadside. All have a/c, private bathroom, fridge and balcony or deck; suites have a full kitchen. Pool, beach bar and *Monarch Café*, serving breakfast only. ❻

Barnacle Bill's Beach Bungalows 400m south of *Maya Breeze* ☎ 523-8110, ⓦ www.barnacle bills-belize.com. Two well-equipped wooden houses on stilts on a beautiful sandy beach. Each house has a double bedroom, bathroom with tub, living room with sofa bed and kitchenette with microwave, grill, coffeemaker and fridge; call ahead and they'll stock you up with groceries. Kayaks and bikes included for guests. ❻

Singing Sands Inn 200yd south of *Barnacle Bill's* ☎ 520-8022, ⓦ www.singingsands.com. Very stylish mahogany and thatch cabañas with queen-sized bed, porch, hammock and in-room bathrooms with mosaic washbasins. There's also a good-value family-sized bungalow overlooking a wonderful pool with fountain. It's extremely romantic at night, when the whole property is lit up. Very good Asian restaurant. Snorkel from the bar on the pier. Kayaks and fishing charters available. ❼

Maya Playa 250yd south of *Singing Sands* ☎ 523-8121, ⓦ www.mayaplayaresort.com. Three palmetto-and-thatch, A-frame family-sized cabañas in a beautiful, beachfront location. Each has a queen-sized bed, small balcony, fridge and semi-circular bathroom with jungle plants; ground-floor living rooms have a couch and extra bed. Friendly owner Chuck Meares has built a tall *palapa* on the beach for his kitchen/diner, where guests can cook and eat their meals. Free bikes, kayaks, coffee and fruit, and your 7th night free. ❹

Seine Bight to Placencia

Two miles beyond Maya Beach the Garifuna village of **SEINE BIGHT** has several resorts and hotels, some looking out of place alongside the settlement's often dilapidated shacks. Reputed to have been founded by privateers in 1629, Seine Bight was possibly given its present name by French fishermen deported from

▲ Placencia beach

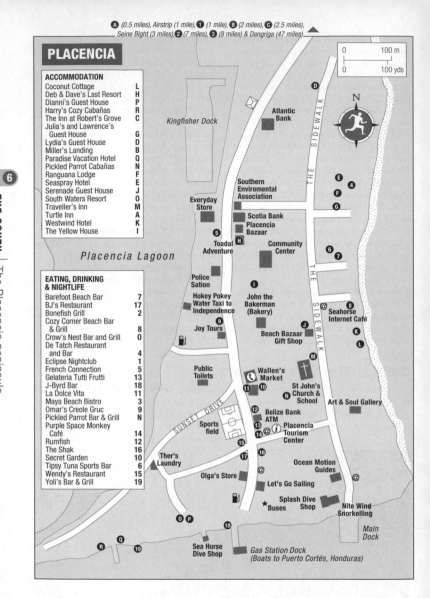

PLACENCIA

ACCOMMODATION

Coconut Cottage	L
Deb & Dave's Last Resort	H
Dianni's Guest House	P
Harry's Cozy Cabañas	R
The Inn at Robert's Grove	C
Julia's and Lawrence's Guest House	G
Lydia's Guest House	D
Miller's Landing	B
Paradise Vacation Hotel	Q
Pickled Parrot Cabañas	N
Ranguana Lodge	F
Seaspray Hotel	E
Serenade Guest House	J
South Waters Resort	O
Traveller's Inn	M
Turtle Inn	A
Westwind Hotel	K
The Yellow House	I

EATING, DRINKING & NIGHTLIFE

Barefoot Beach Bar	7
BJ's Restaurant	17
Bonefish Grill	2
Cozy Corner Beach Bar & Grill	8
Crow's Nest Bar and Grill	O
De Tatch Restaurant and Bar	4
Eclipse Nightclub	1
French Connection	5
Gelateria Tutti Frutti	13
J-Byrd Bar	18
La Dolce Vita	11
Maya Beach Bistro	3
Omar's Creole Gruc	N
Pickled Parrot Bar & Grill	N
Purple Space Monkey Café	14
Rumfish	12
The Shak	16
Secret Garden	10
Tipsy Tuna Sports Bar	6
Wendy's Restaurant	15
Yoli's Bar & Grill	19

Placencia Lagoon

Newfoundland after Britain gained control of Canada. The present inhabitants are descendants of the Garifuna settlers who arrived in Seine Bight around 1869. The village is certainly worth a visit even if you're not staying: Seine Bight has various **Garifuna musicians**, many of them experts in powerful, evocative drumbeats – contact drum maker Bobby for lessons (☎601-5096). Make sure you check out Lola Delgado's superb (and affordable) oil and acrylic paintings of village life at 🏠Lola's Art Gallery (☎601-1913, ⓦwww.jcasadart.com), just behind the soccer field. Specializing in beach scenes, flora and fauna, and (faceless) portraits of the Garifuna, she also does overnight commissions. Seine Bight's other claim to fame is its Goss Chocolate factory (☎523-3544, ⓦwww.gosschocolate.com), based at *Blue Crab Resort* just north of the village, which produces superb organic dark, white and milk chocolate. Truffles, bars and boxes are available to buy.

Perched on the tip of the peninsula, shaded by palm trees and cooled by the sea breeze, **PLACENCIA** has some of the country's most beautiful **beaches**, and these, together with the abundant accommodation for all budgets, make it a great place to relax. The villagers enjoy the easy life as much as visitors – as you'll find out during **Lobster-Fest**, celebrated over a fun-filled weekend in late June. You could also try to visit during the **Sidewalk Arts Festival**, held around Valentine's Day in early February, on Placencia's tiny pavement street, once listed in the *Guinness Book of Records* as the narrowest in the world. At the festival, you can meet some of the artists and musicians of Belize's vibrant arts scene. If Placencia has one drawback, it might be that its distance from the reef puts some tours out of the reach of budget travellers – but more options are becoming available.

Arrival, transport and information

The easiest way to reach Placencia is by the regular Maya Island or Tropic Air **flights** from Belize City (about 45min); **taxis** (Bz$10) wait to take you into the village. (Local taxi numbers are Kingfisher ☎523-3323; Percy's ☎614-7831; or Noel's ☎600-6047.) **Flights** from Placencia to Dangriga are Bz$95 (20min), and Bz$164 to Belize Municipal (45min). Direct **buses** ply the route from **Dangriga**, leaving mid-morning and late afternoon, ending up at the beachfront petrol station at the end of the peninsula; they return at 6am, 7am, 1.15pm and 2pm, but check locally as times change (1hr 30min; Bz$10); all connect with departures to Belmopan and Belize City. You can also hop over easily on the *Hokey Pokey* **boat service** from **Independence/ Mango Creek** (20min; Bz$12), the small town just across the lagoon, where residents buy supplies and older children go to school. It arrives at the small lagoon dock south of the police station. Independence is on the Dangriga–Punta Gorda bus route and the ferry meets most arriving buses; see box on p.211 for full details.

A fast sixty-seat skiff, *D'Express*, leaves Placencia for **Puerto Cortés**, Honduras, every Friday at 9.30am (4hr; US$55; ☎523-4045), going first across the lagoon to Big Creek (where there's a delay to clear immigration); the onward journey is only 2hr 30min. It returns to Placencia on Mondays, arriving around 2pm. Additional information is available at the **Placencia Tourism Center** (Mon–Fri 9–11.30am & 1–5pm; ☎523-4045, ⓦwww.placencia.com), the best tourist information office in the country, located near the end of the main road; call in to find out what's going on locally or to call hotels. The Center also produces the excellent free *Placencia Breeze* **newspaper**, with full local listings, transport schedules and a good map. The **post office** is located at the village's north end near Atlantic Bank; there are several payphones around town, including at the **BTL office** by the soccer field. Best for **internet** is Placencia Office Supply near the end of the main road, at *De Tatch Café* and *The Shack*. Three **banks** with currency exchange and 24-hour ATMs are easily found along the main road.

If you're self-catering, **groceries** can be found at Wallen's Market, by the sports field, and Olga's, just before the petrol station, in the heart of the village. If your hotel doesn't offer **laundry service**, then find Julia's Laundry (☎503-3478) along The Sidewalk, or Ther's Laundry southwest of the sports field. Numerous tour operators around town can book **domestic flights**, and Maya Island Air and Tropic Air both have offices at the airstrip. Several **gift shops** sell souvenirs: The Placencia Bazaar, on the main road next to Scotiabank has the best selection, and both Art 'n' Soul Gallery and Denyses's Originals along The Sidewalk showcase local arts and crafts. Leo's gift shop, near Tipsy Tuna on The Sidewalk, has a good selection of Belizean wood carvings.

Accommodation

You should have no problem finding a room here when you arrive (book ahead at Christmas, New Year or Easter). Budget options are scattered throughout the village, while upscale resorts line the road north to the airstrip and Seine Bight – most have top **restaurants**.

If you want to **rent a house** for a longer period, check with resorts along the peninsula; with Merlene at *Yoli's* (see p.212; ☎503-3153, ⓔyolandaestephan @hotmail.com); or for best value, *Colibrí House* (☎523-4046, ⓔcatalina@btl.net), a beautiful, fully furnished studio in an octagonal wooden house. The Tourism Center's website (ⓦwww.placencia.com) has a range of other options.

Inexpensive to mid-range

Coconut Cottage On the beach south of the centre ☎523-3234, ⓔkwplacencia@yahoo.com. A comfortable, well-decorated and deservedly popular wooden cabin on the beach, with full kitchen; very popular, so you'll need to book in advance. ❺

Deb & Dave's Last Resort Main Rd, near Scotiabank (buses stop outside) ☎523-3207, ⓔdebanddave@btl.net. The nicest budget place in the village; homely and comfortable wooden rooms with clean, shared bathrooms and set in lovely gardens with pool and veranda with hammocks. The owners also rent a house with two apartments. Kayaks for rent; Dave Vernon, who runs Toadal Adventure (see p.214), is a great tour guide. ❷

Dianni's Guest House On the south beach ☎523-3519, ⓦwww.diannisplacencia.com. A very comfortable two-storey hotel with clean, well-furnished rooms, all with private bathroom, a/c, fridge and coffeemaker. The wide, breezy verandas with hammocks are great for relaxing and you can borrow a cooler to take to the beach. Internet access, laundry service and kayaks and bikes for rent. ❹–❺

Harry's Cozy Cabañas 300yd west from the south dock ☎523-3155, ⓔharbaks@yahoo.com. Spacious wooden cabins on stilts on the beach, with a screened porch, double and single bed, fridge and coffeemaker; one has a small kitchen. The plant-filled gardens are an iguana sanctuary. According to Harry, kicking back with a Belikin beer under his "Tree of Knowledge" imparts wisdom. Three-night minimum stay. ❹

Julia's and Lawrence's Guest House In the centre of the village, south of the *Seaspray* ☎503-3478. Choose from simple, comfortable rooms in a wooden building near The Sidewalk and cabins nearer the beach, all with private hot-water bath, TV and porch. There's also a small furnished house for rent, Bz$130/night. ❸

Lydia's Guest House Near the north end of The Sidewalk ☎523-3117, ⓔlydias@btl.net. No-frills budget option; simple, clean and secure, in a quiet location. Expect shared bathrooms, veranda, plus fridge and kitchen for guests' use. Wi-fi available. ❷

Pickled Parrot Cabañas Signposted just past Wallen's Market, towards the south end of the village ☎604-0278, ⓦwww.pickledparrotbelize .com. Two varnished wooden cabins with double beds, private bath, fridge and coffeemaker, and a deck with lounge chairs and a hammock, set in an attractive garden. The bar and restaurant here (see p.212) is a great place for local information. *Rough Guides* discount. ❹–❺

Ranguana Lodge On the beach in the centre of the village ☎523-3112, ⓦwww.ranguanabelize.com. Set in a beautiful tropical garden, five white cabañas have porches with hammocks (optional a/c), all close to or on the beach. Comfortably furnished with hardwood floors and fittings, fridge and coffeemaker; bathrooms have tubs. Beach *palapas* for relaxing. ❺

Seaspray Hotel On the beach near village centre ☎&ⓕ523-3148, ⓦwww.seaspray hotel.com. Placencia's first hotel, built in 1964 and still run by the same family, the Leslies. Popular and well-run, with budget rooms and a beach cabin, all with private bathroom, some with fridge, kitchenette, TV and balcony. Tours and internet access available. Don't miss *De Tatch* restaurant on the beach. ❷–❺

Serenade Guest House On The Sidewalk just south of the centre ☎523-3380, ⓔhotelserenade @btl.net. Very good-value rooms with private bath and a/c in a large, white-painted concrete building. Great restaurant. ❸

Traveller's Inn Towards southern end of The Sidewalk ☎523-3190, ⓦwww.toucantrail.com. Five basic rooms with shared bath and a communal porch for relaxing. Owner Lucille also has some comfortable rooms with private bath in a separate building. ❶–❸

Westwind Hotel Across from the Beach Bazaar gift shop ☎523-3255, ⓦwww.westwindhotel.com. An eccentric but attractive wooden hotel offering bright rooms with private bath and decks with a beachfront view. You can "crack back" in one of many hammocks arranged around a large and spacious *palapa* out on the beach. Wi-fi access. ❺

The Yellow House In the centre of the village, east side of the road ☎ 523 3401, ✉ veronique @ctbelize.com. Bargain rooms with comfortable beds and private bathrooms (two also have kitchenette) in a bright yellow wooden building with balcony and hammocks. French spoken. **❸**

Expensive

🏃 The Inn at Robert's Grove Half a mile south of Seine Bight ☎ 523-3565, ⓦ www .robertsgrove.com. Well-managed luxury resort with spacious, elegant, a/c rooms and suites, all with cable TV and sea balcony. Three pools, several rooftop jacuzzis and an oceanfront spa. The *Seaside Restaurant*, with tables on a wooden deck on the beach, serves superb international and local dishes. *Habañeros Mexican Café* is great for snacks and drinks by the lagoon. On site there's also a dive centre, plus snorkelling, fishing, sailing, kayaking, windsurfing and tennis. Three tiny cayes for guests to visit are offshore, with an overnight stay possible. **❽**
Miller's Landing 300yd south of *Robert's Grove* ☎ 523-3010, ⓦ www.millerslanding.net. Small, secluded resort set amid original vegetation just off a quiet beach. It's very laidback and a bit more rustic than many of the places here, with comfortable

rooms in wooden cabins, all with private bathroom, ceiling fans and a porch; also two "economy" rooms with shared bathroom. There's a good bar and restaurant, locally famous for its pizza. Complimentary kayaks and bikes for guests. **❻–❼**
South Waters Resort On the south beach, 100yd west of the south dock ☎ 523-3308, ⓦ www.south watersresort.com. Spacious and comfortable, with pastel-painted cement cabañas on the beach, each with fridge, microwave, coffeemaker, and private patio. There are also two storey a/c suites with full kitchen, living room and wide verandas. Excellent open-air *Crow's Nest Bar and Grill*. **❻–❼**
Turtle Inn Just north of the village ☎ 523-3244 or 824-4912, ⓦ www.turtleinn.com. Francis Ford Coppola's resort on the Caribbean is just as sumptuous as his *Blancaneaux Lodge* in Cayo (see p.142) and *La Lancha* in Guatemala (see p.170). The thatched seafront "cottages" (US$415) have lots of varnished wood and Indonesian art, plus fabulous bathrooms and a screened deck. Garden cottages are just as comfortable and less expensive, and a two-bedroom, two-bathroom beachfront villa is US$650. The atmosphere is more relaxed than *Blancaneaux*, and there's a soothing spa as well as a pool and dive shop; complimentary kayaks and bikes. **❾**

Eating, drinking and nightlife

There is a great range of **restaurants** along the peninsula, though places here move or change hands fast, so it's always worth asking a resident's advice. For upscale dining, most options are higher up the peninsula – take a cab to try one out if you're without transport. Most places close early; you'll certainly have more options if you aim to eat by 8pm.

Independence travel connections

Just across the lagoon from Placencia, **Independence**, though of little intrinsic interest, is a useful travel hub, served by all **buses** between Dangriga and Punta Gorda (see p.188 & p.217). Although some maps show **Mango Creek** and Independence as separate places, the creek just lends its name to one end of town; Independence begins at the road junction, a kilometre or so away. There's a regular fast **boat to Placencia** from here – the ironically named *Hokey Pokey* (20min; Bz$12 one way) – and the boatman usually meets arriving buses, often with a truck to carry your luggage. The *Hokey Pokey* leaves Independence/Mango Creek at 6.30am, 7.30am, 8am, 11am, 12.15pm, 2.30pm, 4.30pm and 5.30pm, returning from Placencia at 6.30am, 10am, 4pm and 5pm, sometimes even more frequently. Alternatively, a charter costs Bz$45 which is good if you're in a group.
    James **bus** has at least twelve departures daily in each direction along the Southern Highway (some are express services), heading **north to Dangriga** (under 2hr), Belmopan and Belize City between 6am and 4pm, and **south to Punta Gorda** (2hr) from 9am to 7pm. Catch James buses where the crews take their meal break: *Sherl's Restaurant*, which also serves inexpensive Belizean dishes and snacks. With good transport connections, you should avoid getting stuck overnight in Independence. If you do, clean, simple *Ursula's Guest House* on Gran Main Street (☎ 608-7109; **❷**) is reliable.

Evenings in Placencia are as relaxed as the days, but a few places have a lively atmosphere – ideal for drinking rum and watching the sun set. Some places in the village and many resorts along the peninsula have regular evening entertainment – happy hours, bar games, music and drumming, or a special dinner or barbecue; check the *Placencia Breeze* for what's on where. Both *Tipsy Tuna Sports Bar* and *Barefoot Beach Bar* on The Sidewalk are popular evening spots and open late; the latter has live music at weekends. *J-Byrd Bar*, by the south dock and open all day, is a great place to meet local characters. *Eclipse Nightclub* (☎ 602-2148) by the airstrip is Placencia's only proper nightclub, with a young, up for it crowd dancing to Caribbean sounds from 11pm at weekends.

Inexpensive to mid-range

BJ's Restaurant By the road junction just past the sports field. Some of the best Belizean food in the village at genuine local prices, with friendly service in clean surroundings. Mon–Sat 7am–10pm, Sun 7am–3pm.

Cozy Corner Beach Bar & Grill On the beach just south of the centre. A heavily trafficked open-air restaurant and bar serving an array of blended drinks and large portions of international fare such as burgers, seafood and steaks. The daily specials are a deal here. Open 11am–11pm (later at weekends).

🏃 **De Tatch Restaurant and Bar** On the beach, just north of the centre ☎ 503-3385. The best Belizean-owned restaurant in town, with a lovely, thatched open-air dining room and a scenic view of the ocean. *De Tatch* serves Caribbean cuisine at very affordable rates and delicious seafood mains at all hours; the fry-jacks are especially good at breakfast. There are also computers with high-speed internet access. 7am–10pm.

La Dolce Vita In the centre above Wallen's Market. A charming restaurant serving a good variety of Italian food and imported wines. The a/c dining room is tastefully adorned with scenes from Fellini's movie, and dinner is served nightly. Open from 5.30pm until late.

🏃 **Gelateria Tutti Frutti** Near the end of the road. Genuine Italian ice cream, quite simply the best in Belize; it's available in dozens of flavours and you should try at least one every day you're in town. Daily until 9.30pm.

Omar's Creole Grub On The Sidewalk, across from Beach Bazaar. Inexpensive joint for rice and beans, great, filling burritos, seafood and daily specials. Closed Sun.

Pickled Parrot Bar & Grill At *Pickled Parrot Cabañas* (see p.210). Friendly place under a big thatched roof. The *Pickled Parrot* is consistently the best restaurant in the village and deservedly popular, serving fresh seafood, great pizza, pastas, salads with a daily special. The bar has wonderful blended tropical drinks and a 5–6pm happy hour. Open Mon–Sat 11am–9.30pm.

Purple Space Monkey Café Opposite the sports field. Serving good coffees and great American/Belizean-style breakfast, lunch and dinner under a huge thatched roof. Also has a paperback exchange and wireless internet. Opens early, closes late.

The Shak Opposite the south end of the sports field. Serves a variety of smoothie combinations using the freshest fruits and juices around. Healthy eats and vegetarian-friendly menu.

Wendy's Restaurant Near the south end of the main road. A comfortable, a/c diner serving fresh juices and delicious Spanish and Creole dishes. Open daily 7am–10pm.

Yoli's Bar & Grill On the south beach ☎ 503-3153. Great for breakfast, serving good coffee and home-made bread and fry-jacks. Try the fish at lunch or dinner, though you may have to wait for a table. Exuberant Yoli is renowned for her cakes – if it's your birthday, ask if she can make one for you. Closed Sun.

Higher end dining

Bonefish Grille Singing Sands, Maya Beach. Superb, creative Southeast Asian food at this intimate beachside restaurant with exceptionally romantic lighting. Try the Korean beef, Thai fish or rice noodles with shrimp. The breakfast menu is also good.

French Connection Main St, opposite Scotia Bank. Placencia village is surely going upmarket with the addition of this excellent French restaurant, using only the freshest local ingredients. Choose from a menu that changes weekly but always features imaginative fish dishes and delectable salads; dine before 6pm to make the most of the great-value set menu.

🏃 **Maya Beach Bistro** Maya Beach (see also p.206). Deservedly popular and expensive, the menu features top-end Belizean food with an international twist – try the lobster bread pudding or pumpkin coconut soup – though there's also burgers and a range of succulent pork dishes.

Entirely unpretentious, and also great for breakfast or evening cocktails.

Rumfish Opposite the sports field. Attractive and upmarket tapas bar in a new, though traditional, wooden building. Extensive wine list and small plates: ceviche, seafood, chicken, pastas and Thai options. Dine indoors or on the veranda.

Secret Garden Opposite the sports field near Wallen's Market. As the name implies, this café/restaurant's location makes for a peaceful respite, also serving as a massage and spa centre and wi-fi hotspot. Great for coffee or Sun brunch; expect anything from falafel, risotto, curried shrimp or chicken pasta. Closed Mon.

Around Placencia, offshore and inland

Trips from Placencia can include anything from a day on the water to a week of camping, fishing, snorkelling or sailing around any number of idyllic islands. Diving or snorkelling along the reef is excellent, with shallow **fringing and patch reefs**, and some fantastic **wall diving**. You can visit several virtually pristine protected areas, including **Laughing Bird Caye National Park** and **Gladden Spit and Silk Cayes Marine Reserve**. **Placencia lagoon** is ideal for exploring in a **canoe or kayak**; you may even spot a manatee, though it's more likely to be a series of ripples as the shy giant swims for cover. The reefs and shallows off Placencia are rich **fishing** grounds too, and the village is home to a number of renowned fly-fishing guides.

It's also worth **heading inland** from Placencia – up the thickly forested banks of the **Monkey River** (see p.215) or to the **Jaguar Reserve** (p.205). Many tour operators offer day-trips to the latter (around Bz$140), but it's quite feasible to go independently by bus, leaving Placencia in the early morning and returning on the afternoon bus from Dangriga as it passes Maya Centre. **Car rental** is another option: Barefoot Rentals (near Placencia airstrip, ☎523-3438 or 610-3214, ⓦwww.barefootrentalsbelize.com) has a good selection of 4WD vehicles from US$75 per day. If high petrol prices turn you off car rental, explore the peninsula on a **bike**, which you can rent from *Dianni's Guest House* for around Bz$25 per day.

After a long day of outdoor activity, you'll certainly need some pampering: Z-Touch (☎523-3513) has a **massage**, spa and beauty parlour, and Secret Garden (☎523-3420) also offers massage services.

Laughing Bird Caye and Ranguana Caye

The Bugle Cayes, with a good section of reef, are only a few miles from Placencia, though most operators prefer to take you to uninhabited **Laughing Bird Caye National Park** (Bz$20), about eleven miles away. The caye itself (named for the laughing gull) is under 1.5 acres, and gulls no longer nest here, but the national park protects over ten thousand acres of sea as a "no take zone" (no fishing), and it's a World Heritage Site. The caye sits on top of a "faro", a limestone reef rising steeply from the sea bed, with an outer rim enclosing a lagoon, and thus similar to an atoll. There's a ranger station, and many tours stop for lunch on the beach. The northern tip of the caye protects native vegetation and nesting birds and turtles, and is off-limits.

Ranguana Caye, twenty miles southeast of Placencia and visited by some snorkel trips, is a jewel of an island just 120yd long by 25yd wide, surrounded by perfect patch reefs. For divers, the 2400ft drop-off begins 750yd offshore. The sand on Ranguana is softer than in Placencia, the palm trees taller and the sunsets glorious, silhouetting mountain ranges in the distance. It's owned by *Robert's Grove* at Placencia (see p.211), and you can stay here in beautiful wooden cabins facing into the breeze, with meals served in a *palapa*-covered dining area (US$345 per person per night, including transport, meals, drinks, use of kayaks and snorkel gear).

Gladden Spit and Silk Cayes Marine Reserve

Twelve miles beyond Laughing Bird Caye, the exquisitely beautiful Silk Cayes form part of the **Gladden Spit and Silk Cayes Marine Reserve** (Bz$10), a large protected

The Barrier Reef is wider here than in the north of Belize, and it breaks into several smaller reefs and cayes that create even more coral canyons and drop-offs. Because it lies about eighteen miles offshore, **snorkelling and diving** trips are more expensive here than elsewhere; the upside is that there are mangrove islands and coral heads closer to the coast, and you can still see a lot of fish and some coral by snorkelling just offshore. For more detailed information on local ecology visit the **Southern Environmental Association (SEA)** office (☎523-3377, ⓦwww.seabelize.org) above Scotiabank in the village; SEA co-manages the area's marine reserves – support their work by becoming a "Friend".

Day-trips to the cayes (including visits to see **whale sharks** in season) are offered by several operators, and the choice of dive sites is so wide that during a month-long stay you need never visit the same one twice. PADI Open Water Certification costs around Bz$700, and a two-tank dive trip roughly Bz$150–200. Snorkelling trips cost from Bz$65 to $85, depending on the location; they usually include lunch and sometimes equipment. If not, you can rent snorkels, masks and fins for around Bz$15. Several resorts have their own **dive shops**; in the village, go to Splash Dive Shop at the end of The Sidewalk (☎523-3345 or 661-8160, ⓦwww.splashbelize .com), or Brian Young at Sea Horse Dive Shop on the south dock (☎523-3166, ⓦwww .belizescuba.com), for the best instruction, excursions and equipment rental. For **snorkelling** or **manatee-watching**, check with Toadal Adventure (see below), Nite Wind Guides by the south dock (☎523-3847), or Ocean Motion Guides (☎523-3363), located nearby.

Sailing among the cayes off Placencia is, if anything, even more beautiful than the northern cayes, and the village is a base for top-tier catamaran charters. For a week's sailing you'll need to book well in advance; see p.25 in Basics for contact details. Some resorts have Hobie Cats (small catamarans) for rent; other than these, regular **sailing trips** are offered by Let's Go Sailing (☎523-3138,ⓦwww.belize-sailing-charters .com), who have day sails to the cayes (9am–3pm; US$125 per person, including buffet lunch and open bar), with snorkelling and kayaking or sunset cruises (4–7pm; US$85 including snacks and wine). The company has been around for thirty years and brokers for the Belize charter fleet, with overnight packages on fully crewed yachts from US$500 to over $1000, and they can also arrange sailing certification.

Several places rent **canoes** and sit-on-top kayaks for around Bz$35 per day, and some resorts have free ones for guests. For top-quality double **sea kayaks** (Bz$70/ day) and tours (Bz$120 per person) contact Dave Vernon at Toadal Adventure (☎523-3207, ⓦwww.toadaladventure.com), one of the best tour guides in Belize, a great natural historian as well as river and kayaking guide.

World-class **fishing** draws anglers eager to catch permit, tarpon, snook and bonefish that abound here. A day out with a boat and guide will set you back around US$300; any of the dive or snorkel places can arrange this – you could go with Trip 'n' Travel's Earl Godfrey, an excellent fly-fishing guide (☎523-3614, ✉lgodfrey@btl.net), or Bernard Leslie (not fly) at Ocean Motion Guides (see above). Rods, flies and tackle are available from Fred's Fishing Gear (next to *Dianni's*; ☎523-3304 or 601-1914).

area designated to safeguard the seasonal visitation of the enormous yet graceful **whale shark**. These migratory fish, found throughout tropical waters, are attracted to Gladden Spit during the full moons of April, May and June by huge numbers of spawning snapper. The sharks are filter-feeders, so it's the protein-rich spawn they're after, not the fish themselves. Research conducted by the University of York and the Nature Conservancy indicates that this is one of the largest and most predictable aggregations of whale sharks in the world; radio-tracking shows that they travel as far as Cancún in Mexico and down to Honduras – and probably further. All guides

THE SOUTH | The Placencia peninsula

6

taking you to see the sharks will have undergone training not to disturb their feeding; boats should stay 15yd away, and snorkellers and divers at least 3yd away. *Isla Marisol* on Glover's Reef also runs trips here (see p.196).

French Louie Caye and Whipray Caye

Kitty Fox and Ran Villanueva offer a great **sea kayaking** or overnight trip to beautiful **French Louie Caye** (ⓦ www.frenchlouiecayebelize.com), a tiny island fringed with mangroves just eight miles offshore. There's fantastic snorkelling with hard and soft corals, sea anemones and schools of tiny fish among the mangrove; you can also visit half a dozen uninhabited cayes nearby. French Louie has a resident pair of ospreys who successfully rear chicks every year. Staying here, you sleep in a wooden cabin with delicious meals served by a resident cook – or you can self-cater. This simple paradise costs US$450 per night for two people, including transport (in a skiff, or you can paddle a kayak), use of a double kayak, a dory and snorkelling gear, and all food; camping is half price. Mosquitoes are not a problem; drinking (rain) water is available, and there are composting toilets. Inquire in Placencia on ⓣ 523-3636.

Whipray Caye (shown on some maps as Wippari Caye), eight miles northeast of Placencia, is another small, idyllic island, surrounded by reef and coral heads, and it also has some fine cabin accommodation. *Whipray Caye Lodge* (ⓣ 608-8130, ⓦ www .whipraycayelodge.com; ❺, meals US$50/day per person and transport US$40 per person each way) has two comfortable wooden cabins with private bathrooms, fans and windows on all sides so you can enjoy the view and the breeze. Run by expert fishing guide Julian Cabral and his wife Beverley, it's an ideal base for serious angling, or just relaxing, and you'll be eating plenty of fresh fish.

Monkey River

One of the best inland day-trips from Placencia takes you by boat twelve miles southwest to **Monkey River**, teeming with fish, birdlife and **howler monkeys**. Monkey River Magic, in Placencia, runs the best **tours** (US$60, minimum four people; contact Trip 'n' Travel ⓣ 523-3614), led by Evaristo Muschamp, an experienced local guide. Tours set off by 8am from the petrol station dock, and a thirty-minute dash through the waves is followed by a leisurely glide up the river and a walk along forest trails. Binoculars are essential to make the most of amazing **birding** and the chance to see turtles, crocodiles and howler monkeys. The area was badly hit by Hurricane Iris in 2001 – as was Placencia – and the forest is only now fully recovering. The monkeys survived the ordeal, however, and continue to breed successfully.

If you've brought a picnic, lunch is taken on a sandbank in the river, or you can get a meal in *Alice's Restaurant* in **MONKEY RIVER TOWN** – in reality a small village. There's also time to enjoy a stroll and have a drink at one of the **bars**: *Ivan's Cool Spot*, where the river meets the sea, is probably the best. The community was one of the last villages in the country to get grid electricity, finally hooking up in December 2009. If you want **to stay**, *Enna's Guest House* (ⓣ 720-2033 or call community phone ⓣ 709-2069; ❶) has a nice river view with shared bath, and Enna's brothers are tour guides. You can also find the *Sunset Inn* (ⓣ 720-2028, ⓔ sunsetinn@btl.net; ❷) on a tiny bay at the back of the village; rooms are in a two-storey wooden building with comfortable beds and private bath, while a wide veranda overlooks the river and there's tasty Creole food. Owner Clive Garbutt is an excellent guide (contact him on the village's community telephone, see above). Eloy Cuevas, also from the village, is one of the best **fly-fishing guides** in Belize; contact him at ⓣ 523-2014. A higher-level option, *Steppingstones*, is a specialist fishing resort (ⓦ www.steppingstonesbelize .com; ❼), a little way along the coast.

If you'd rather **drive** to Monkey River, take the fourteen-mile dirt road that connects the village to the Southern Highway, south of Independence. The road ends on the opposite bank of the river from the village, but just call out and someone will give you a ride over in a boat.

The far south: Toledo

South of the Placencia and Independence junctions, the well-maintained **Southern Highway** twists through pine forests, neat ranks of citrus and crosses numerous creeks through **Toledo District** – with only a few villages along the way. The highway ends at **Punta Gorda**, the southernmost town in Belize, and the base for rewarding visits both to inland **Maya villages** – with a way of life far removed from that of greater Belize – and the little-visited southern **cayes and marine reserves**, as well as offering daily skiffs to **Puerto Barrios** in Guatemala and **Livingston** in Honduras. If you're driving south and looking for a refreshment stop en route, try *Coleman's Café* at Big Falls (see p.226).

Although the Maya of Belize are a fairly small minority within the country, in Toledo the two main groups – Mopan and Kekchí – make up about half the population. For the most part they live in simple villages, very similar in appearance to their Guatemalan counterparts in the Alta Verapaz and southern Petén, where the ancestors of most of Toledo's Maya came from. Despite this, very few people here speak Spanish, maintaining instead their indigenous languages and Belizean Kriol. The largest villages are **San Antonio** and **San Pedro Columbia**, reached by a good road west from the highway. Simple guesthouses and Maya homestays are available in the rural areas, though a few **lodges** have opened their doors in recent years, most

---

Confederates and Methodists in Punta Gorda

To the north of Punta Gorda are the remains of the **Toledo settlement**, founded in 1867 by **Confederate** emigrants from the US who chose Belize (then British Honduras) as a location to recreate the antebellum South. Since **slavery** had been abolished in Belize decades before (and resident Garifuna and Creoles had no inclination to work for former slave owners), the settlers brought over indentured labourers from India. They called these labourers "coolies", and their descendants still live in Punta Gorda and along the Southern Highway; though long since fully assimilated into Belizean culture, they're still referred to as "coolies" by other ethnic groups, though rarely in a derogatory way. A fascinating **book**, *Confederate Settlements in British Honduras*, by Donald C. Simmons, Jr, can be found online and in Belizean libraries. Many Confederate settlers drifted home, discouraged by the torrential downpours and the rigours of frontier life, but those who stayed were soon joined by Methodists from Mississippi. The Methodists were deeply committed to the settlement and, despite a cholera epidemic in 1868, managed to clear 160 acres. Between 1870 and 1890 sugar became the main product, with twelve separate estates running their own mills. After this, falling sugar prices ensured that farmers moved into alcohol production, but this was out of the question for the Methodists, who preferred to feed their molasses to their cattle. By 1910 their community was destitute, although it was largely as a result of their struggle that Toledo was permanently settled.

The Maya world

**Belize and neighboring Guatemala boast an impressive range
of Maya sites, from Lamanai and Caracol to Tikal, where
you can immerse yourself in ancient history, surrounded
by the mist-shrouded rainforest. And, what a history: from
1500 BC to 1000 AD, the Maya dominated Central America,
developing an advanced society that left behind a magnificent
and mysterious legacy. Their cities were far larger and more
elaborate than anything in Europe at the time, a feat made
all the more remarkable without the aid of wheeled transport
or metal tools. The Maya also showcased their brilliance by
producing highly accurate calendars, sophisticated counting
and writing systems and intricate jade jewellery,**

Ceramic figure, Lamanai ▲

Stone carving of Altar 12, Caracol ▲

Tikal ▼

The mysterious collapse

The ancient Maya still fascinate archeologists, not least because of the civilization's sudden and inexplicable decline in the tenth century, when its grand cities were emptied and abandoned in the jungle. The enigma of the Maya's "collapse" remains unsolved to this day, though lengthy droughts, overpopulation, exhaustion of arable land, social revolution, disease and extended warfare have all been proposed as possible explanations.

The Maya legacy

Whatever the reason for their fall, the Maya left behind a treasure trove of **remains**, visible at most sites throughout the country. Closely observing the glyphs and **stelae**, fine jade artwork and stone and ceramic vessels, you'll find scenes depicting mythology, science, politics and warfare – as well as the events of everyday life. Some sites are littered with **pottery shards**, and by examining the colour and consistency of the clay, you can estimate the time of their origin. Murals on temple walls provide a wealth of information about community life, especially aspects of work and trade. Etchings chronicle the births, coronations, marriages, conquests and deaths of Maya kings.

Many Maya structures are incredibly tall – **Tikal**, especially – and climbing their steep stairs will make you breathless, but you'll be greeted at the top by outstanding panoramas of ruins and forest. In most cases you'll be in the midst of deep jungle, revealing just how hidden these sites were before excavation. The layout of many structures was carefully aligned with the stars to draw upon their perceived powers, and often designed to mirror other elements of the natural world. An interesting feature that most sites share is the **"ball-court"**, the venue for a violent game that symbolized the epic battle between the Hero Twins and the Lords of Death as depicted in the **Popol Vuh**, the Maya creation story.

The modern Maya

Although their glorious past now lies in ruins, the Maya themselves did not disappear – nine million still live throughout Central America, and another million in the US – and most have retained their pre-Hispanic traditions and customs. Just as their ancestors did, contemporary Maya regard **corn** as the key to their existence; in fact, Maya belief holds that the first man was made from corn kernels. Modern Maya generally make their living from **subsistence farming**, producing corn, cacao and beans and raising cows, pigs and chickens, and some along the Caribbean coast rely on **fishing**. With the rapid rise of Belize's tourism industry, however, many Maya have turned to hospitality work, and you'll likely interact with them on a daily basis during your visit to the country.

▲ Mayan calendar

▼ Indian Creek, Maya village

▼ Maya woman, Toledo

Stay with the Maya

The best way to understand the Maya of today is to venture south to **Toledo District**, where most reside; incidentally, it's also home to some remarkably remote and unspoilt landscapes. Villages here are rich in tradition, and many inhabitants still speak **Maya dialects**, such as Mopan, Kekchí and some Yucatec. Several villages have a **homestay** or guesthouse programme (see p.224), allowing you to interact with the Maya and gain insight into their past.

Rio Frio cave, Cayo ▲

Ceramic artefact, Lamanai ▼

Barton Creek cave, Cayo ▼

Exploring the Maya underworld

Though most evidence of the Maya is above ground, the culture was fascinated by the subterranean, and **caves** held sacred status. They were considered entrances to the underworld, called **Xibalba**, the "place of fright", but despite their fearsome nature they also provided privileged access to the dwelling of gods, ancestors and spirits. Almost every cave in Belize – thanks to the country's porous karst limestone, there are plenty – has revealed unique findings, including wall paintings, pottery shards and the remains of fires. Because the Maya gods had to be appeased with **sacrifices**, you'll also see weapons, altars and skeletons, typically left as archeologists first discovered them.

In addition to their attraction as Maya sites, caves also invite a slew of adventure activities, heavily promoted by tour organizers. **Cave tubing**, **abseiling** (or rappelling) and **canoeing** are some of the most popular activities and run the gamut from relaxing to exhilarating.

Maya caves

▶▶ **Actun Tunichil Muknal** (or ATM) in Cayo District is perhaps the best cave to visit for its cache of Maya artefacts. Visiting involves a short swim and, depending on the water level, a forty-minute hike through waist-deep water. See p.127

▶▶ **Che Chem Ha** in Cayo District is another highlight, with some of the most intact artefacts in the country. See p.162

▶▶ **Crystal Cave** in the Blue Hole National Park features crystal formations, and you can explore the nearby caves and artefacts around **Caves Branch River** by rock-climbing, rappelling and floating on inner tubes. See p.129 & p.130

of them superb accommodation. Of course the ancient Maya lived here too, with ruins scattered throughout. The best-known sites are **Lubaantun**, where the famous Crystal Skull was "discovered" and **Nim Li Punit**, with some impressive stelae. Near the Guatemalan border, **Pusilhá** is a little harder to reach, but contains the best example anywhere of a Maya bridge.

Punta Gorda

The Southern Highway comes to an end at **PUNTA GORDA** (commonly known as "PG"), the heart of **Toledo District**. Cooling sea breezes here reduce the worst of the heat and, though this is undeniably the **wettest** part of Belize, most of the extra rain falls at night, leaving the daytime no wetter than Cayo District. PG has a population of around eight thousand, including Garifuna, Maya, East

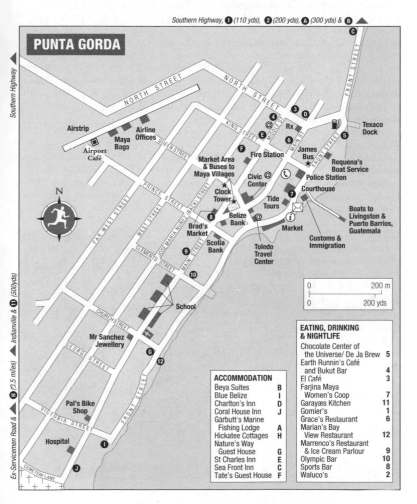

Southern Highway, ❶ (110 yds), ❷ (200 yds), ❹ (300 yds) & ❸ ▲

PUNTA GORDA

Southern Highway ◀

NORTH STREET
NORTH STREET
KING STREET
FRONT STREET
MIDDLE ST
MAIN ST

Airstrip
Airline Offices
Maya Bags
Airport Café
QUEEN STREET
PRINCE STREET
WEST STREET
FAR WEST STREET
JOSE MARIA NUÑEZ (BACK) STREET
MAIN STREET
CLEMENS STREET
CHURCH STREET
GEORGE STREET
VICTORIA STREET
CEMETERY LANE

@ Moses
Rx
Fire Station
James Bus
Market Area & Buses to Maya Villages
Civic Center @
Clock Tower
Belize Bank
Brad's Market
Scotia Bank
Toledo Travel Center
Market @
School
Mr Sanchez Jewellery
Pal's Bike Shop
Hospital

Texaco Dock
Requena's Boat Service
Police Station
Courthouse
Tide Tours
Customs & Immigration
Boats to Livingston & Puerto Barrios, Guatemala

N

Ex-Servicemen Road & ❶ (0.5 miles) ◀ Indianville & ⓫ (500yds)

| 0 | 200 m |
| 0 | 200 yds |

EATING, DRINKING & NIGHTLIFE
Chocolate Center of the Universe/ De Ja Brew 5
Earth Runnin's Café and Bukut Bar 4
El Café 3
Farjina Maya Women's Coop 7
Garayæs Kitchen 11
Gomier's 1
Grace's Restaurant 6
Marian's Bay View Restaurant 12
Marrenco's Restaurant & Ice Cream Parlour 9
Olympic Bar 10
Sports Bar 8
Waluco's 2

ACCOMMODATION
Beya Suites B
Blue Belize I
Charlton's Inn D
Coral House Inn J
Garbutt's Marine Fishing Lodge A
Hickatee Cottages H
Nature's Way Guest House G
St Charles Inn E
Sea Front Inn C
Tate's Guest House F

Indians, Creoles and some Lebanese and Chinese, but it's also the business centre for nearby villages and farming settlements, with Saturday the busiest market day. Despite a minor building boom, Punta Gorda remains a small, unhurried and hassle-free town – though as a tourist (here and in the villages) you'll constantly be approached by polite Maya women and girls, imploring you to buy the small and undeniably attractive **decorative baskets** they make from a local vine.

Arrival, information, tours and shopping

James Buses from Belize City (all via Belmopan, Dangriga and Independence) take around six hours to reach Punta Gorda, though express services cut an hour off the journey time. Buses stop at the main bus office near the dock on King Street. **Flights** to and from Belize City, Placencia and Dangriga land at the small airstrip five blocks west of the main dock. **Skiffs** to and from **Puerto Barrios** (see box opposite) and **Lívingston** in Guatemala use the main dock, roughly in the centre of the seafront; the **immigration** office is nearby. See the box opposite for more details on transport.

Despite PG's relatively few visitors, the Belize Tourism Industry Association (BTIA) has an excellent **information** office, just south of the dock (☎722-2531), able to help with local transportation schedules and information on staying in the Maya villages. Across the street is Tide Tours (see p.221; ☎722-2129), which offers trips to the cayes and marine reserves, while a block south is the Toledo Travel Center (☎665-6778 or 604-2124; see also *Sun Creek Lodge*, p.223), home to IBTM tours, which offers expert trips around inland Toledo, including the Cacao trail and to Maya ruins.

For **car rental**, call former PG mayor Carlos Galvez Taxi & Auto Rental (☎722-2402 or 722-0088), or contact Bruno Kuppinger at *Sun Creek Lodge* (see p.223; ☎722-0112). For a reliable **taxi**, call Allan Hines (☎607-5337). **Bike rental** is available from Mr Pops at Pal's Bike Shop, 5 Victoria St (☎625-3923).

PG's two **banks**, the Belize Bank and Scotia Bank (both Mon–Thurs 8am–3pm, Fri 8am–4.30pm) are located along Main Street near the main square, both with 24-hour ATMs. There's usually a **moneychanger** outside the immigration office

▲ Arriving in Punta Gorda

Transport from Punta Gorda

James buses leave for **Dangriga** (around 3hr), **Belmopan** (4–5hr), and **Belize City,** (5–6hr) roughly hourly between 4am and 4pm. **Express services** normally leave at 6am and 10am, though check all times in advance.

Buses for the **Maya villages** and **Barranco** leave around noon on market days (Mon, Wed, Fri & Sat) from the streets behind the Civic Center; the BTIA office (see opposite) has full details. Most village bus companies are literally one-man operations and Sunday is their day off. **Pop's bus** leaves for **Indian Creek** (near **Nim Li Punit**, see p.232) Monday through Saturday at 5pm, while **San Antonio** – the biggest Maya village – also has a (sometimes twice) daily service, continuing on demand to **Jalacte** on the Guatemalan border (not yet a legal crossing). If you're heading for **Lubaantun** (see p.227) you'll need the bus for **San Pedro Columbia**, though you can also usually get there any day with rides in pickup trucks. If you're heading for **Uxbenka**, **Río Blanco** or **Pueblo Viejo Falls** (see p.232), take the **Pueblo Viejo** or **Jalacte** bus; for **Pusilhá**, take the **San Benito Poité** bus. Returning from the villages, all buses leave early, around 3–6am.

There are three regular daily **skiffs** to **Puerto Barrios** in Guatemala (1hr in good weather; Bz$35–38). Placida Requena's *Mariestela* leaves at 9.30am (☏722-2070, ⊚watertaxi@btl.net), Carlos Carcamo's *Pichilingo* leaves at 2pm and Rigoberto James's ferry *Marisol* leaves at 4pm (☏722-2870). Rigoberto James also runs a ferry to **Lívingston**, departing Tuesday and Friday at 10am (1hr; Bz$38). There's no need to buy your ticket in advance; just turn up at the dock half an hour before departure. You'll also have to pay the PACT **tourist exit tax** of Bz$37.50. Beware of less reliable boat operators touting on the street; go with an experienced skipper.

Domestic airlines have five daily **flights** from 7am to 4pm to Belize City Municipal Airport (1hr; Bz$220), calling at Placencia and Dangriga; check at the offices at the airstrip.

when international boats are coming and going, and you can also change money in *Grace's Restaurant*, a block from the dock. If you're leaving Belize, get rid of your Belize dollars before you cross the border. The **post office** is located right on the sea front, and the **BTL office** (for phone calls) is behind the courthouse near the dock. **Internet access** is available at V-Comp on Main Street (Mon–Sat 8am–8pm), Dreamlight, next to nearby *Emery's Restaurant*, or at Toledo Travel Center. **Laundry** can be dropped off at PG Laundry across from the Belize Bank (☏722-2273).

For the best local souvenirs go to Mr Sanchez Jewellery, a shack at Main and Church streets, which sells silver Maya and black coral earrings, while at the western end of the airstrip, Maya Bags stocks high-quality hand-embroidered bags of all varieties, expensive due their intricate labour-intensive designs.

Accommodation

Punta Gorda has a range of options for most budgets (more luxury accommodation is located out of town, and there are plenty of bargains. For **longer stays**, *Casa Bonita Apartments* (☏722-2270) at the northern end of town have full kitchens, face the sea and cost Bz$90–170 per week.

Beya Suites Front St, 0.5 mile north of the centre ☏722-2188 or 621-0140, ⊛www.beyasuites.com. Belize's 2006 "Small Hotel of the Year" is a good Belizean-owned option. On the seafront, all rooms offer a/c, TV, wi-fi and private bath. Most have balconies, and there's a rooftop sun deck. Internet, laundry and breakfast available. Bar downstairs. ⑤

Blue Belize 139 Front St ☏722-2678, ⊛www .bluebelize.com. An impressive, friendly new option set amid flowering gardens on the seafront, with rooms and apartments with imaginative artwork within two buildings joined by a raised boardwalk. With plenty of breeze, a/c is not needed, though is available in the upstairs apartments, which also have kitchens and a stunning veranda. Wi-fi, breakfast and bicycles included. ⑤–⑥

Charlton's Inn 9 Main St ☎722-2197, ⓦwww .charltonsinn.com. Principally good for groups on a budget, rooms have 1-5 beds, hot-water showers and most with a/c. *Charlton's* often houses Peace Corps members. There's safe parking; owner Duwane Wagner can arrange car rental. ❶–❷

Coral House Inn 151 Main St ☎722-2878, ⓦwww.coralhouseinn.com. This smart and attractive guesthouse makes you feel truly at home, in comfortable a/c rooms or a self-contained cottage, featuring decor from local artisans. Gorgeous pool with thatched bar, hammocks and verandas. Complimentary wi-fi, breakfast and bicycles. ⑥

🏃 **Hickatee Cottages** Ex-Servicemen Rd, two miles from Punta Gorda ☎662-4475, ⓦwww.hickatee.com. Among the very best value accommodation in Belize, with four smart and charming cottages set amid twenty acres of peaceful jungle, drawing numerous butterflies, birds and monkeys each day. The property is full of nice thoughtful touches, and the owners strive for minimal environmental impact. Kate serves excellent meals using fresh ingredients grown on their farm. Bicycles, internet, a pickup from town, continental breakfast and a visit to the owner's

butterfly farm are all included, and there's a small pool on-site. ⑤–⑥

Nature's Way Guest House 65 Front St ☎702-2119, ⓔnatureswayguesthouse@hotmail .com. Rustic and ramshackle yet clean and safe dorms and private rooms around an overgrown garden. Great breakfast. The owner promotes eco-tourism and can arrange trips to Maya villages. ❶

St Charles Inn 23 King St ☎722-2149, ⓦwww .toucantrail.com. A smarter budget option, with clean rooms offering TV, private tiled bathrooms, fan or a/c, in a charming wooden building with hammocks on the balcony. It's in the centre of town and close to all main activity. ❷–❸

Sea Front Inn Front St, 600yd north of the centre ☎722-2300, ⓦwww.seafrontinn.com. A four-storey, imposing yet eccentric building with steep Alpine-style eaves. Spacious rooms have tiled floors, a/c, TV; some have balcony. Furnished apartments for longer stays (Bz$750/two weeks). Wi-fi, breakfast and tours available. ⑥

🏃 **Tate's Guest House** 34 José María Nuñez St ☎722-0147, ⓔtatesguesthouse@yahoo .com. A quiet and very friendly family-run guest-house close to the centre. Rooms are simple but have a/c, TV, private tiled bathroom; one has a kitchen. Wi-fi and computer available. ❷–❸

Eating, drinking and nightlife

Good, cheap **eating options** abound in Punta Gorda; if you're looking for superb, higher end dining, make a reservation for dinner at *Hickatee Cottages* (see above). PG's **nightlife** heats up when a band is playing at the *Sports Bar* opposite Scotia Bank, or at *Waluco's* – an otherwise laidback seafront bar a mile from the centre along Front Street, north across the metal bridge over Joe Taylor Creek. A few other **bars** around town are good for meeting locals and fellow travellers; a warm welcome is to be had from Olympia Vernon at her *Olympic Bar*, by the corner of Main and Clements streets, and reggae vibes are to be found at *Earth Runnin's* (see below), popular with the US NGO crowd (surprisingly large in PG). Chocolate treats can be found at the Chocolate Center of the Universe, on Front Street at the north end of town; its tiny *De Ja Brew* café offers accompanying espressos.

El Café North St, beside *Charlton's Inn*. Good, inexpensive Belizean dishes, often using organic produce; opens for good breakfasts and coffee at 6am; Belizean lunches and burgers.

🏃 **Earth Runnin's Café and Bukut Bar** North and Middle streets. A bit pricier than PG's other options, with a sophisticated menu always featuring good breakfasts, fresh seafood, pasta and delicious vegetarian meals. Also a popular bar, serving creative cocktails.

Farjina Maya Women's Coop Front St, opposite immigration, upstairs. Small lunchtime joint serving tasty and cheap traditional food, including an excellent chicken *caldo* with corn tortillas.

Garay's Kitchen Behind the town, three blocks beyond Far West St. A little far to go on foot, but nonetheless a great-value little lunchtime diner, selling out by 1pm of standard Belizean meals plus East Indian dahl and curry, including heart of palm.

Gomier's Front St, 100yd north of *Sea Front Inn*. A tiny place serving delicious, organic vegetarian, soy and seafood meals, with a daily special. Eat inside or at a table beneath a thatched roof and enjoy the sea breeze.

Grace's Restaurant 19 Main St, opposite the BTL office. Inexpensive, tasty Belizean and East Indian dishes served in clean surroundings. You can change money here, and all buses heading north stop across the road. 6am–10pm.

Marian's Bay View Restaurant Front St, across from *Nature's Way*. Daily menu serving fresh food for breakfast, lunch and dinner. Enjoy a delicious meal while gazing at the magnificent ocean from your table. Vegetarians welcome.

Marrenco's Restaurant & Ice Cream Parlour Main St, a block south of the square. Burgers, fish and fries, and Belizean dishes, with a good variety of desserts, ice cream and milkshakes. Open till 10pm.

Out to sea: the cayes and the coast

The cayes and reefs off Punta Gorda mark the southern tip of Belize's Barrier Reef and get relatively little attention from visitors. Roughly 130 low-lying mangrove cayes cluster in the mouth of a large bay to the north of PG, a part of the 370 square miles of coastline protected in the **Port Honduras Marine Reserve**, partly there to safeguard **manatees** living in the shallow water. **Fly-fishing** is particularly good here; the best guides are the Garbutt Brothers – Scully, Oliver or Dennis (☎722-0070 or 604-3548, 🌐www.garbuttsfishinglodge.com). Toledo NGO **TIDE** (see box below) offers a range of tours and specialist knowledge of the reserve and cayes, while tours of coast and cayes are also available from Dan Castellanos of Blue Belize, at 139 Front St (☎722-2678, 🌐www.bluebelize.com). Dan is a traditional fisherman-turned-tour guide and PADI Divemaster, offering an array of expert marine tours, from fishing to snorkelling.

The cayes and coastline here were once home to ancient **Maya sea traders** and salt works. Since 1981, archeological fieldwork by Heather McKillop (through Louisiana State University) has documented sea-level rises since the end of the Classic period (900 AD), which submerged ancient sites and created the modern mangrove landscape. The ancient Maya port of **Wild Cane Caye**, a mangrove-covered caye twelve miles north, was once responsible for the salt trade (produced in nearby Punta Ycacos Lagoon) – a necessity for the inhabitants of the great inland cities. The works were abandoned with the Classic Maya collapse, but Wild Cane Caye continued to participate in sea trade with Postclassic cities as far away as Chichén Itzá in Yucatán. McKillop's project also documented unique **coral architecture**, in which coral rock was mined from the sea to build platforms for structures of perishable material. The coastal area is managed by TIDE (see below), and before visiting the site visitors must check in at the **ranger station** on nearby **Abalone Caye**, which also has spectacular views.

Toledo Institute for Development and Environment

TIDE, the **Toledo Institute for Development and Environment** (☎722-2129, 🌐www.tidetours.org), is an excellent local NGO that manages **Payne's Creek National Park**, north of Punta Gorda, and **Port Honduras Marine Reserve** offshore, plus sixteen thousand acres of private land. These reserves form part of the continuous Maya Mountain Marine Corridor, protecting a wide swath of southern Belize and linked with other marine protected areas in Guatemala and Honduras under the umbrella of the **Tri-national Alliance for the Conservation of the Gulf of Honduras** (🌐www.trigoh.org), a group comprising prominent NGOs from the three countries involved in conservation and sustainable livelihoods. If you're interested in **volunteering** for these conservation programmes, contact Celia Mahung, TIDE's executive director.

TIDE's subsidiary, Tide Tours, offers a range of **tours** (☎722-2129, 🌐www.tidetours.org), including a full-day **kayak** trip along the lower Moho or Río Grande (up to four people, Bz$150), **snorkelling** at the manatee-rich Snake Cayes (min 4 people, Bz$85/person), boat trips to see whale sharks and overnight camping and fishing trips to Payne's Creek, staying at the tiny, isolated seaside community of **Punta Negra**, nineteen miles north of Punta Gorda.

The first real beaches north of Punta Gorda appear on the idyllic **Snake Cayes**, a group of four islands surrounded by glorious white coral sand beaches. Seventeen miles northeast of PG, they're quite easy to visit. Beyond here the main reef is fragmented into several clusters of cayes, each surrounded by a small independent reef.

The Sapodilla Cayes

The most easterly of the caye clusters at the southern end of the barrier reef are the stunningly beautiful **Sapodilla Cayes**, a chain of five main islands – each encircled by coral and with gorgeous soft-sand beaches. Some cayes have accommodation and others have even been used by refugees; the area faces increasing visitor pressure, though a management plan co-devised by the **Southern Environmental Association** (SEA; ☎722-0125, ⓦwww.seabelize.org), aims to limit damage. SEA is active in environmental education, taking boatloads of schoolchildren to the Sapodillas to learn about marine ecosystems and participate in beach clean-ups; committed **volunteers** can contact their office at Joe Taylor Creek in PG.

Now a part of the **Sapodilla Cayes Marine Reserve**, day-trippers from Guatemala and Honduras challenge the already thinly stretched conservation agencies. Uninhabited **Northeast Caye**, thickly covered with coconut trees and under government ownership, is the **core zone** of the reserve, to be left undeveloped. You'll pay the Bz$20 reserve entrance fee at **Hunting Caye**, an immigration post handling foreign visitors (and also has limited camping and picnicking facilities). The sand at stunning Crescent Moon Beach on the caye's east side attracts hawksbill turtles to nest. **Nicolas Caye** has an abandoned resort, and you could **camp** here or ask the caretaker for permission to sleep in a basic cabin. The most southerly main island, **Lime Caye**, is a fantastic place to savour glorious isolation, with rudimentary cabins available to rent from *Garbutt's Fishing Lodge* (see p.221; ❸), and snorkelling available on the reef just offshore.

Inland Toledo and the Maya Villages

Exploring inland Toledo is one of the highlights of a trip to Belize. Eco-tourism is a buzzword throughout the country, and several projects here are reaping the benefits, successfully achieving a balance between economic development and preserving the area's rich natural and cultural heritage. Tourism here is distinctly low-impact – providing additional income without destroying the communities' traditional ways of life. Many Maya villages are sited on **Indian Reservations**, designated as such in colonial times to protect the Maya's subsistence lands. Title, however, remained with the government (which leases logging concessions), not the Maya who actually occupied the reserves. Recent developments in forestry policy have alarmed community leaders, who fear that "conversion forestry", where all trees over a certain size are cut down for timber, will cause severe erosion and silt up previously clear streams used for drinking. In response, international conservation organizations have stepped up to better support policy initiatives.

Accommodation: Rural Toledo

Cotton Tree Lodge Moho River (Rd access from San Felipe village) ☎670-0557, ⓦwww.cottontreelodge.com. Impressive new property on the riverbank, with eleven smart thatched cabañas on stilts, connected by a raised boardwalk lined with cacao and mango trees. All rooms have a chic feel while offering varying levels of comfort; more expensive units have a veranda with hammocks, while the honeymoon suite has a jacuzzi and plunge slide straight into the river. The

Cacao and the Maya

It was the ancient Maya who first processed cacao into **chocolate**, assigning great value to the beans which could be used as money and traded over vast distances. Today, commercial production and eco-tourism also generates monetary value. You'll often see cacao beans drying on special concrete pads as you meander through the Toledo villages, an environment which provides ideal growing conditions. Almost all the crop Is organically produced and used to make the delicious **Maya Gold** chocolate sold abroad. The Toledo Cacao Growers' Association was established in conjunction with chocolate company *Green and Blacks*, and the UK's first Fair Trade product was born.

In 2007, the district inaugurated a **Cacao Festival** to be held each May, and it's now become an important part of the Toledo calendar (see Ⓦwww.toledochocolate .com) with events promoting cacao, childrens' activities, concerts and the Miss Cacao Pageant; check at the BTIA information centre in Punta Gorda for more details. New, local entrepreneurs have started up, too: *Goss Chocolate* bases its processing of delicious Toledo cocoa on the Placencia Peninsula, while *Cotton Tree Chocolate* is manufactured at the *Chocolate Center of the Universe* in Punta Gorda, who offer an interesting little tour of their processes. Cyrilla Cho in the village of San Felipe has also begun production and can offer you a tour of her small premises.

Of greater visitor interest are Toledo's day-long **Cacao Trail** tours such as those run by Bruno Kuppinger at IBTM (and Sun Creek Lodge, see below), who combines the trail with a visit to one of the region's Maya ruins. Offering a chance to see cacao growing and to understand more about the Maya culture from which chocolate came from, they start at one of the village cacao farms at San Antonio or San Pedro Columbia. You follow a trail through the farm: unlike conventional farming, cacao is planted amongst existing trees and many other crops like corn, avocado, beans, wild bananas, Jamaican limes and coffee, which gives these places a beautiful, wild feel, almost like the jungle itself. Farmers provide an excellent account of Maya methods, philosophy, and rainforest remedies, and afterwards you eat lunch with a Maya family, who demonstrate the grinding of the beans and making the chocolate. Several other resorts in Toledo, such as *Cotton Tree* and *Machaca Hill*, also run tours.

giant ten-sided *palapa*-restaurant flaunts imaginative local artwork, while the location is ideal for exploring sites inland. kayaking the river or sunset boat cruises straight out to the cayes. Chocolate tours a speciality. Room-only or all-inclusive packages available. ❼

The Lodge at Big Falls Big Falls, signposted half a mile west from the highway ☎671-7172 or 671-6677, Ⓦwww.thelodgeatbigfalls.com. Smart, comfortable and very spacious thatched cabañas, set in 29 landscaped and flower-filled acres on a meandering bend of the Río Grande. Fully screened, all have tiled floors, ceiling fans, roomy bathrooms, hardwood furniture and a large deck with hammocks. two hundred species of birds have been recorded here, and butterflies are everywhere along the trails by the riverbank; kayaks and inner tubes also available – put in at San Miguel, five miles upstream, for a wonderful float back to the *Lodge*. Fresh juices from the lodge's citrus trees are served in the restaurant, or at an outdoor grill by the swimming pool. ❼

Machaca Hill Lodge Laughing Falcon Reserve, turn-off four miles south of Jacintoville ☎722-0050, Ⓦ www.machacahill.com. Toledo's latest super-upscale resort, whose glorious hilltop setting on landscaped grounds high above the Río Grande offers wonderful views. Guests stay in spacious, beautifully furnished wooden cabañas, each with a private glass-screened deck shaded by trees, and enormous shower rooms. Meals are served in the main lodge building. Enjoy the spa, or take the on-site cable car down to the river, which must rate as Belize's most spectacular jungle setting. Spend time fishing or just relaxing at the hilltop pool, enjoy a breathtaking panorama from the main lodge or walk the nature trails through the forest. Packages available. ❾

🏃 **Sun Creek Lodge** ☎614-2080 or 662-0496, Ⓦwww.suncreeklodge.com. Five beautiful thatched cabañas (one is a four-bed dorm), all with electricity and two with double beds and private bathrooms. The lodge is a

Maya Village Homestays and Guesthouses

An innovative development in rural tourism in Toledo is Yvonne and Alfredo Villoria's aptly-named *Dem Dats Doin* (☎722-2470, ©demdatsdoin@btl.net), the **Maya Village Homestay Network**, which enables visitors to stay with a Mopan or Kekchí Maya family in any one of five villages. You'll learn about medicinal plants and ancient Maya myths, and it's an excellent way to find out about their life and culture without feeling like an intruder. You'll participate in village work – grinding corn, chopping firewood, cooking tortillas and the like – you'll learn some Maya words, and sometimes sleep in a hammock. There are few modern conveniences like electricity and flush toilets (though most villages have community telephones), and if you go with an open mind you'll have a fascinating and rewarding experience.

Another important initiative is a guesthouse programme initiated by the **Toledo Ecotourism Association (TEA)**, from which a representative is sporadically present at the BTIA office in Punta Gorda (☎722-2531). Ten villages in Toledo each have a basic but clean eight-bed guesthouse (Bz$25 per person), and you can take meals at different houses in the villages. Each location has its own attraction, be it a cave, waterfall, river or ruin, and there are guided walks (around Bz$10/hr) or perhaps canoes for rent. The programme has also raised awareness among villagers about both eco-tourism and the political process of protecting their forest. The guest houses covered in the villages in this chapter are part of the programme; in most cases you can just show up in the village and stay – it's highly unlikely the guesthouse will be booked out.

In 2009 villagers at remote San Benito Poité near the Maya ruin of **Pusilhá** (see p.229) also built and opened their own unique accommodation, the **Kehil Ha Jungle Lodge** (no phone, ⊛www.kehilha.com). It offers simple accommodation in traditional Maya buildings, sleeping up to twelve in bunk beds in one, while another has a traditional fire hearth kitchen – which can accommodate individuals, providing an experience of living like the Maya of 1000 years ago (though thankfully with modern composting toilets). Maya food such as spinach-like *callalou* and *jippi jappa* soup is served and numerous activities are available: farming, cooking, animal tracking, plus swimming and horseback riding. Rates are provided in response to individual requests.

naturalist's paradise, providing all necessary modern conveniences whilst maintaining a rustic feel. The innovative jungle bucket showers make you feel as though you're standing under a waterfall. Belizean/German owner Bruno knows Toledo District and the entire country exceptionally well and runs International Belize Tourism Marketing, which offers a range of hard-to-find services for visitors to southern Belize, including tours and jeep rental (US$65/day). Computer and wi-fi access. Includes breakfast. ❸
Tranquility Lodge Jacintoville, 300yd from the paved highway by the Barranco Rd ☎677-9921, ⊛www.tranquility-lodge.com. On the bank of

beautiful Jacinto Creek, this relaxing retreat offers a/c comfort in spacious, tiled, en-suite rooms with soft and earthy colours and iPod docks, or in thatched casitas, all surrounded by orchid-laden gardens. The wonderful large and fully screened thatched restaurant serves excellent meals, and gives great all-round views. The place is very popular with birders, with over two hundred species seen along the forested trails here, and the natural, rock-lined pool in the creek is perfect for a refreshing dip. An ideal base for visiting inland Maya villages and ruins or the southern coast. Full American breakfast included. ❺

Barranco and the southern coast

The Belizean coastline south of Punta Gorda is flat, with tidal rivers meandering across a coastal plain covered with thick tropical rainforest that receives over 11ft of rain a year, forming a unique ecosystem with numerous orchids and palms. The **Temash River** is lined with the tallest mangrove forest in the country, **black** mangroves towering more than 90ft above the riverbanks, while in the far south the **Sarstoon River**, navigable by small boats, forms the border with Guatemala; the land between is known as **Sarstoon–Temash National Park** (Ⓦ www.satiim .org.bz) – currently the controversial site for oil exploration. You can arrange tours from operators in Punta Gorda and the rivers are sometimes paddled by tour companies using inflatable river kayaks.

At **Jacintoville**, seven miles from Punta Gorda (stop at *Miss Flora's Beer Parlour* for drinks or snacks), a rough branch road heads south through the scattered Maya community of **San Felipe** to the small and traditional Garifuna village of **BARRANCO** (community phone ☎709-2010), Belize's southernmost coastal settlement. The only accommodation here is at the simple TEA guesthouse (see opposite), while buses run to Punta Gorda at 6am on Monday, Wednesday, Friday and Saturday, returning to the village at noon on the same days, crossing the Moho River over a high-level bridge. The village is set amongst forest and

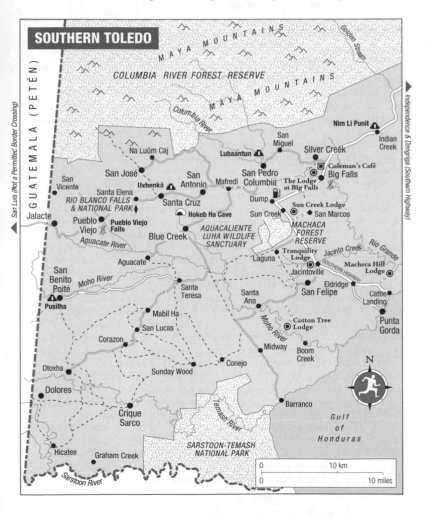

SOUTHERN TOLEDO

◀ Independence & Dangriga (Southern Highway)

MAYA MOUNTAINS
Golden Stream

COLUMBIA RIVER FOREST RESERVE

MAYA MOUNTAINS

Columbia River

◀ San Luis (Not a Permitted Border Crossing)

GUATEMALA (PETÉN)

Na Luûm Caj
San Miguel
Lubaantun
Silver Creek
Nim Li Punit
Indian Creek

San José
San Antonio
 Uxbenká
Mafredi
San Pedro Columbia
Coleman's Café
Big Falls
The Lodge at Big Falls

San Vicente
Santa Elena
RIO BLANCO FALLS & NATIONAL PARK
Santa Cruz
Dump
Sun Creek Lodge

Jalacte
Hokeb Ha Cave
Sun Creek
San Marcos

Pueblo Viejo
Pueblo Viejo Falls
Blue Creek
AQUACALIENTE LUHA WILDLIFE SANCTUARY
MACHACA FOREST RESERVE

Aguacate River
Aguacate
Laguna
Tranquility Lodge
Jacinto Creek
Rio Grande
Macheca Hill Lodge

San Benito Poité
Moho River
Santa Teresa
Jacintoville
SOUTHERN HIGHWAY
Eldridge
San Felipe

Pusilha
Santa Ana
Cattle Landing

Mabil Ha
San Lucas
Cotton Tree Lodge
Punta Gorda

Corazon
Conejo
Midway
Boom Creek

Otoxha
Sunday Wood

Dolores

N

Barranco

Gulf of Honduras

Crique Sarco

Temash River

SARSTOON-TEMASH NATIONAL PARK

Hicatee
Graham Creek

Sarstoon River

0   10 km
0   10 miles

savannah, with scattered houses shaded by trees. Several jungle trails can be explored on foot or horseback, and local **guides** can show you excellent birding spots; check with village chairman Alvin Lindo.

The birthplace of celebrated musician Andy Palacio (see Contexts, p.269), the world music award-winner was also buried here following his sudden death in 2008 following a heart attack. Home to around 150 people, most villagers of working age have left to seek opportunities elsewhere, leaving Barranco populated by children and the elderly, and Garifuna is regularly spoken here only by older people. The culture lives on, however: despite virtually all the villagers being Roman Catholics, the village boasts the largest *dabuyaba* (a traditional **Garifuna temple**, built of poles with a thatched roof) in the country. It's occasionally used for *dugu* rites, when family members honour the spirits of their ancestors. Preparation takes many months and the **ceremonies** – comprising prayers, drumming, singing, dancing and offerings of food – last four days. In the Garifuna belief system, ancestors have a direct influence on the world of the living.

North to Big Falls and the Maya villages and ruins

Heading northwards, you soon meet the unfortunately-named road junction at **Dump**; there's a **petrol station** here, selling beer and cold drinks, and if you're driving it's a good place to pick up information. Going straight ahead takes you into the Maya villages, while a right turn continues along the main Southern Highway a couple of miles into **BIG FALLS**, a village with petrol station, store, a couple of bars and major bridge over the Río Grande, as well as a luxury resort. It's not a particularly pretty village but it does boast Belize's only **hot spring**, a sumptuous spot for a warm bath. The spring feeds a creek that flows into the Río Grande, just upstream of the bridge in the village centre. Alongside the highway is ⅍ *Coleman's Café*, an excellent and delicious local spot for a Belizean (or Belizean-East Indian) **meal**, which also offers wine with dinner.

Heading west from Dump, you can explore the forested southern foothills of the Maya Mountains, dotted with ruins and some delightful riverside Maya villages. Paving of this road will lead to a **new border crossing** point at Jalacte into Guatemala, and it's always been controversial, with some Maya fearing marginalization as developers follow in the highway's wake. Until this happens, however, all the existing roads are unpaved and the crossing not a legal exit point. Numerous **Maya sites**, **caves** and **waterfalls** dot the surrounding countryside, and the area offers wonderful hiking (especially San José, p.230); you can usually find a guide to lead you on foot or horseback through lush valleys and over the hills.

All across the area, you'll encounter yet another uniquely Belizean culture: here **Mopan Maya** from Petén mix with **Kekchí** speakers from the Verapaz highlands of Guatemala. For the most part each group keeps to its own villages, language and traditions, although both are partially integrated into modern Belizean life and many people speak English (scarcely any Maya here speak Spanish). Guatemalan families have been arriving here for the last 130 years or so, escaping repression and land shortages; people still cross today along these well-used routes to settle in land-rich Belize. All villages have a basic bus service from Punta Gorda (see box, p.211), although moving around is far from easy and if you're not with a tour or your own jeep you'll have to rely on hitching – despite a distinct shortage of traffic. A good option is to **rent a bike** from Punta Gorda (see p.217) and put it on the bus, cycling between the villages in the **guesthouse** programmes (see p.224). The people here are, of course, used to walking, and the villages are connected by an intricate network of footpaths.

The Crystal Skull of Lubaantun

Lubaantun's most enigmatic find supposedly came in 1924, when the famous **Crystal Skull** was unearthed. Made from pure rock crystal, it was found beneath an altar by Anna Mitchell-Hedges, the adopted daughter of a British Museum expedition leader, F.A. Mitchell-Hedges. By a stroke of luck the find happened to coincide with her seventeenth birthday, and the skull was then given to the local Maya, who in turn presented it to Anna's father in gratitude for his assistance. It is possible that the "discovery" was a birthday gift, placed there by Anna's father after he'd acquired it on previous travels, although she strenuously denied this.

Mystery and controversy still surround the original skull; some people maintain that Mitchell-Hedges first laid eyes on it at Sotheby's in 1943 and that the whole story is an elaborate hoax. London's British Museum in fact has another crystal skull which – according to Dr G.M. Morant, an anthropologist who examined both skulls in 1936 (the Lubaantun skull was then in the possession of one Sydney Burney, either before or during Mitchell-Hedges ownership) – is a **copy** of the one found at Lubaantun. He also concluded that both life-size skulls are modelled on the same human head, but could give no answer as to their age and origin. The skull was displayed in the Museum of Mankind in London, but when this closed the British Museum decided not to exhibit it, as its origin could not be proved. At the Museum of Mankind, its label was suitably vague: "Possibly from Mexico, age uncertain...resembles in style the Mixtec carving of fifteenth-century Mexico, though some lines on the teeth appear to be cut with a jeweller's wheel. If so it may have been made after the Spanish Conquest." There is a similar, smaller crystal skull in the Musée de l'Homme in Paris, and others exist; all attract great interest from **New Age** mystics, who believe in their supernatural properties.

Anna herself died at 100 years old in 2007, leaving the Lubaantun crystal skull to a friend.

Lubaantun and San Pedro Columbia

The Maya site of **Lubaantun**, near the mainly Kekchí village of **San Pedro Columbia**, is an easy visit from Punta Gorda (bus daily except Sun), and you can also hitch a ride with a pickup truck from the Dump junction. To **get to the site**, cross the bridge over the Columbia River, just beyond which you'll see the track to the ruins, a few hundred yards ahead on the left. If you ask around in the village someone will show you the way; the ruins are about a twenty-minute walk from where the bus drops you. There are a couple of simple restaurants in the village, and you could get someone to paddle you to the **"source"** of the **Columbia River** – a gorgeous spot a mile or two from the village where the river re-emerges from an underground section, gushing forth among the rocks in an enormous, crystal-clear spring overhung with jungle foliage.

The TEA guesthouse is the only official place to stay in San Pedro Columbia (community phone ☎709-2484; there is also a TEA guesthouse at the nearby village of **San Miguel** – ask for Mr Ack), though you may also be able to find **accommodation** with a local family though the MVHN (see p.224). You can stay as a volunteer or student intern at the **Maya Mountain Research Farm** (☎630-4386, ⓦwww.mmrfbz.org), in a beautiful riverside setting on the outskirts of the village. Located on 150 acres of forest and farmland, the centre offers local training and guidance in installing photovoltaic lighting systems and community water systems. With study facilities and several miles of trails (you can walk to Lubaantun), **accommodation** is in private rooms, a dorm or camping, with shared bathrooms. Volunteer projects usually need to be planned well ahead.

Lubaantun (daily 8am–5pm; Bz$10) is a major Late Classic city which at one time covered a much larger area – impressive though it is – than you see today. The name means "place of the fallen stones" in modern Maya, though the site's original name is unknown, and it's thought to have been occupied only briefly, from 730 AD to sometime before 880 AD. The ruins sit on a high ridge, and though climbing the high pyramids is not allowed, the view over the forest is staggering. With eleven major structures, five plazas and three ball-courts, it's a very interesting site – essentially a single **acropolis**.

Lubaantun was brought to the attention of colonial authorities in 1903, and archeologist Thomas Gann was sent to investigate. A survey in 1915 revealed many structures, and three ball-court markers were removed and taken to the Peabody Museum at Harvard. The British Museum expedition of 1926 was joined in 1927 by J. Eric S. Thompson, who became a renowned Maya expert, though no further excavations took place until Norman Hammond mapped the site in 1970, showing trading links with communities on the coast and inland – relationships likely enhanced by Lubaantun's wealth of cacao.

To visit the site, sign in at the **visitor centre**, where glass cases display eccentric flints (symbols of a ruler's power) and ceramics. Wall panels give accounts of the site's excavation and depict life in a modern Maya village. The very knowledge-able head caretaker Santiago Coc, who's assisted with excavations here for forty years, or his son Kenan, may be able to give you a guided tour. Santiago also makes working replicas of *ocarinas* – clay whistles in the shape of animals – that have been found here; their evocative notes occasionally float through the ruins. Dozens of mass-produced ceramic figurines litter the site, often depicting ball-players – items found nowhere else in such quantities.

Buildings here were constructed by layering and fitting together precisely carved stone blocks, Inca-style, with nothing to bind them. This technique, and the fact that most of the main buildings have **rounded corners**, give Lubaantun an

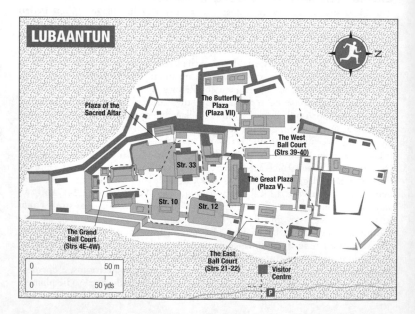

elegance sometimes missing from larger sites. Another anomaly is that no stelae were found; it's conjectured that Lubaantun was the regional administrative centre while Nim Li Punit, only eleven miles away and with numerous stelae, had a more ceremonial function. The plainness and monumentality of Lubaantun's architecture is also similar to the buildings at Quiriguá in Guatemala (which has numerous stelae), and there may have been a connection between them.

Blue Creek

At the tiny village of **Mafredi**, about 5.5 miles from San Pedro Columbia, a branch road (served by buses from Punta Gorda) heads south and west to **BLUE CREEK** (served by buses three times per week), where the main attraction is the village's namesake – a beautiful stretch of water that runs through magnificent rainforest. The Mafredi junction is marked by *Roy's Cool Spot*, a well-stocked shop where you can get a snack, a drink and possibly a meal, while a mile westwards along the track, *Marisol* sells excellent empanadas.

Another two miles brings you to Blue Creek itself, with the river flowing through the middle of the village. To get to the best **swimming** spot, walk upriver along the right-hand bank, and in ten minutes you'll come to a lovely turquoise pool and the wooden cabins of *Blue Creek Rainforest Lodge* (☎523-7076 or 722-2199, ⓦwww.ize2belize.com; US$55 per person, including meals; advance booking essential), set among the trees. The lodge, used by student and adventure groups, is the sister property of *Leslie Cottages* on South Water Caye (see p.195), and set in the **Blue Creek Rainforest Preserve**, a two hundred-acre private park. It's mainly used as a rainforest ecology study centre, though other visitors can arrange to stay (student packages with four nights here and five nights on the caye start at US$1450).

The **source of Blue Creek**, where the water gushes from beneath a mossy rock face, is about another fifteen minutes' walk upriver. Alongside is the entrance to **Hokeb Ha Cave**, fairly easy to explore, and often busy on Sundays with visitors and children trying to sell souvenirs. The entire area is made of limestone bedrock honeycombed with caves, many of which were sacred to the Maya, and plenty of others are doubtless waiting to be rediscovered. Ask at *Sho's Local Restaurant* (signposted, on left side of road) for a reliable **guide** in Blue Creek; they'll take you to Maya altars deep in Hokeb Ha Cave, as well as on to Pusilhá (see below) – where you should not venture without a guide. Delphina Sho serves simple, tasty meals, but not everyday.

Beyond the restaurant you come to the Blue Creek crossroads; four miles straight ahead (southwest) is the undeveloped yet sublimely pretty Kekchí village of **Aguacate**, home to a few families in the Maya Homestay programme, an ideal place to learn traditional cooking of wild meat and freshly caught river shrimp. A left turn takes you on the road to **Pusilhá**. Just to the right, you'll find the **Tumul K'in Center of Learning** (☎608-1070 or 666-1071, ⓦwww.tumulkinbelize .org), an active community development organization with programmes in Maya culture, philosophy, cultivation, food processing (try the papaya jam), plus a radio station. Eco-tourism activities are run by Rosemary Salam, including tours to Maya sites and cultural nights with food provided – book in advance.

Pusilhá

The road south of Blue Creek climbs a ridge to the valley of the Moho River, and through the community of **Santa Teresa**. Further up the valley, almost on the Guatemalan border, lies **Pusilhá**, the largest Maya site in southern Belize, where you can view the finest example of an **ancient bridge** anywhere in the Maya world. The site is located in and around the village of **San Benito Poité**, served by two or three buses per week from Punta Gorda (2hr; returning on market days). At the entrance to the village there's a bridge over the fast-flowing Pusilhá River, with a lovely **camping** spot nearby. Just downstream from here the Pusilhá (Machaca) and Poité rivers join to form the **Moho River**, the middle stretch of which has some of the best **whitewater rapids** in Central America – occasionally paddled by raft and kayak expedition groups from overseas (see Basics).

It's best to **visit the site** when archeologists from the **Pusilhá Project** (undertaken by the State University of New York) are working, usually in spring and summer, as the structures are all currently being excavated. Bear in mind also that this is a very traditional village (most speak only Kekchí and a little Spanish), and people may not be as immediately welcoming as you expect. You must **ask permission** from the *alcalde* (similar to a mayor) to visit as soon as you arrive, and you're strongly recommended to go only with a Kekchí-speaking guide – check at the BTIA office in Punta Gorda (see p.218) or go with Bruno Kuppinger at IBTM/*Sun Creek Lodge* (see p.223) – the latter usually has a copy of the **information sheet** written by the Pusilhá Project's director. If you haven't come with a guide, the *alcalde* will supply one from the village for a small fee; food and lodging is available.

The city, strategically built on high land between the confluence of the rivers, has yielded an astonishing number of carved monuments, including **zoomorphic altars** – great, rounded stone tablets carved with stylized animals – similar to those at Quiriguá in Guatemala. This initially led archeologists to suggest that Pusilhá was under Quiriguá's control, but recent studies indicate a closer connection with Copán in Honduras.

Although many monuments were removed to the British Museum during expeditions in the late 1920s, the **Stela Plaza** – the city's sacred centre – still has a few eroded stelae and three zoomorphic altars resembling frogs. Nearby you can see the remains of a **walled ball-court**. The highlight, however, is the **Maya bridge**, built at a narrow point over the Pusilhá River. Clearly visible are the remains of the main abutments, solid vertical walls of cut stones several yards high and supported by ramps of rock. In ancient times the bridge supports would have been spanned by beams of sapodilla wood, carrying the road to the **Gateway Hill Acropolis** – the residential palace of Pusilhá's rulers and the city's administrative centre. During construction a coffer dam would have held back the river upstream, and on either side of the main river are channels to take extra water during heavy rains.

The mystery is, why build a bridge at all? The ancient Maya built very few, and rivers were usually crossed by canoe. It would appear this feat of engineering was constructed solely as an impressive **processional route** to the **Acropolis**, Pusilhá's most imposing remains. Here, a series of pyramidal platforms, terraces and facades have created an awe-inspiring edifice rising 240ft above the river – almost twice the height of Belize's tallest Maya structure at Caracol.

San Antonio and San José

The Mopan Maya village of **SAN ANTONIO**, perched on a small hilltop, is the easiest of the villages to reach, as it's served by daily buses from Punta Gorda, twenty miles away. There is a TEA village guesthouse, a couple of shops and **meals** are cooked at the homes of residents Theodora or Clara. The area is rich in wildlife, surrounded by jungle-clad hills and swiftly flowing rivers. Further south and west are the villages of the Kekchí Maya, including many fairly recent immigrants who still retain strong links with Guatemala.

The founders of San Antonio came from the Guatemalan town of San Luis, and they maintain many traditions, including the worship of their patron saint. The beautiful **stone church** of San Luis Rey is currently looked after by an American Jesuit order. The third to stand here (two previous versions were destroyed by fire), the church features a set of **stained-glass windows** depicting the twelve apostles and other saints, donated by St Louis, Missouri. The villagers also observe pre-Columbian traditions, with a fiesta taking place on June 13, featuring *marimba* music, masked dances and much heavy drinking.

Nestled among the southern foothills of the Maya Mountains, **SAN JOSÉ** village is served by a bus from Punta Gorda at noon on market days (about 1hr); the turn-off is just over a mile east of San Antonio. To stay at the **guesthouse**, call the community phone on ☎702-2072. If you're fit, you can hike higher up into the mountains; ask in the village for Alfredo Sho or Emelino Cho, who will guide you as far as **Little Quartz Ridge**, a steep and isolated plateau with an ecosystem unique to Belize, or even to (at least) the lower slopes of **Doyle's Delight**, the highest peak in Belize. For either of these trips, you'll need camping gear and supplies for at least three days, plus a great deal of stamina. An even more adventurous hike is the arduous eight-day **Maya Mountain Divide Trail** from San José to **Las Cuevas**, at the end of the Chiquibul Road in Cayo; if you're interested in any of these, contact Marcos Cucul (see p.147) or Bruno Kuppinger (see p.223).

Uxbenká

Four miles west from San Antonio and 300yd before the village of **Santa Cruz**, the ruins of small **UXBENKÁ** ("ancient place") are superbly positioned on an exposed hilltop. Uxbenká only became known to archeologists in 1984 after reports of looting; though there's still no official site caretaker, the community of Santa Cruz is increasingly involved in developing the site. Inquire in the village about a guided tour – someone involved in the TEA guesthouse programme will gladly show you around. You're likely to encounter research in progress: currently, Dr Keith Prufer from University of New Mexico heads the **Uxbenká Archeological Project**, which began in the summer of 2005.

The core area consists of seven architectural plazas spread across three ridges. Appearing to contain the civic, ceremonial and elite residences of Maya society, it has been grouped into three clusters: the **Stela Plaza** (Group A), an **"acropolis"** residential group (Group G), located atop the highest hill, and a set of five conjoined **plazas** (Groups B–F), the site's main ceremonial groups. Uxbenká was an early Maya political centre from the Early Classic period, and it may even have existed in the Preclassic and had links to Tikal. An important discovery was the **Stela Plaza**, containing 22 monuments and stelae, and an intact, but collapsed, tomb in its floor.

Research currently underway has led to several intriguing discoveries. One is that Uxbenká was a major **agricultural centre** engaged in cacao, a theory supported by terraces on the surrounding hills, which hold rich soil. Excavations in the Stela Plaza and the discovery of an intact **ball-court marker** in Group D suggest that it was still operating in the Late Classic. The star finding, however, is an **ancient canoe** – likely the oldest discovered in Mesoamerica – dated to somewhere between 200 and 800 AD, though carbon testing will be more accurate. Archeologists hypothesize that the canoe was part of a funerary offering which, prior to looting, contained a cut-stone crypt. The canoe was found in a cliff-top cave, believed to have been used as a royal crypt and containing remains of an ancient tomb. The craft's placement was symbolic of the Maya's spiritual journey through the underworld, as caves, many with navigable waterways, were closely associated with the afterlife.

If you'd like to stay nearby to explore the area, there's a **guesthouse** at the entrance to Santa Cruz, and buses run on market days; some continue to the border village of **Jalacte** (see below). There are numerous forest and river **trails** here, and you can walk to **San José** in about three hours (see p.230).

On to Jalacte

Continuing west toward Guatemala, you can enjoy some wonderful **waterfalls** within easy reach of the road. Eight miles west of San Antonio, between Santa Cruz and Santa Elena, the **Rio Blanco Falls** tumble 15ft over a wide, rocky ledge into a deep pool, perfect for a dip. The falls form part of **Rio Blanco National Park**, and the bus passes right by; walk down the short trail at the side of the building to reach the falls. At **Pueblo Viejo**, four miles further, an impressive series of cascades on Pueblo Creek proves an even more spectacular sight. Above the falls, a steep trail leads through orchid-laden rainforest to a mountaintop overlook; ask in the village for a guide. Trucks and buses continue eight miles further west to **Jalacte**, at the border, used regularly as a crossing point by nationals, though it's not currently a legal entry or exit point.

Indian Creek and Nim Li Punit

Back on the Southern Highway heading north (five miles from Big Falls, and 35 miles from the Independence junction), near the Maya village of **Indian Creek**, you pass the entrance to **NIM LI PUNIT** (daily 9am–5pm; Bz$10), a Late Classic-period Maya site that was probably allied to nearby Lubaantun (see p.227). It occupies a commanding position on a ridge above Indian Creek, with views over the maize fields to the coastal plain – a scene largely unchanged since ancient times. Discovered only in 1976, it's home to the largest and one of the

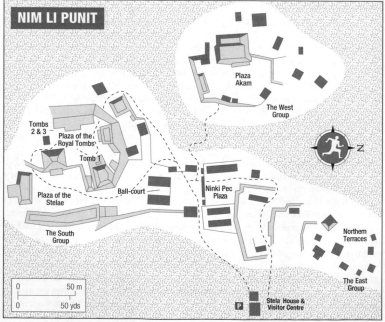

NIM LI PUNIT

Plaza Akam

The West Group

Tombs 2 & 3

Plaza of the Royal Tombs

Tomb 1

Plaza of the Stelae

Ball-court

Ninki Pec Plaza

The South Group

Northern Terraces

The East Group

0   50 m
0   50 yds

P   Stela House & Visitor Centre

▼ Southern Highway (0.5 miles)

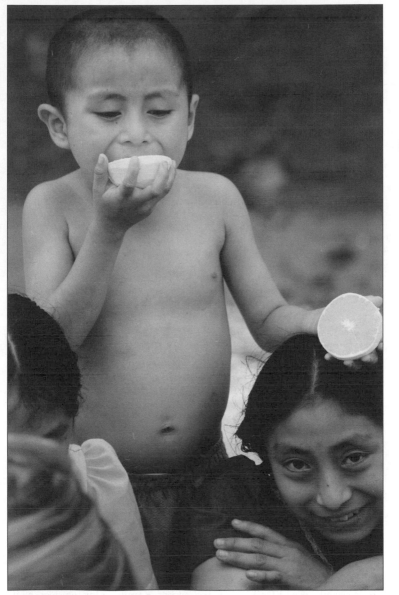

▲ Maya villagers, Indian Creek

best-preserved stelae in Belize, and recent restoration has revealed more features. **Getting here** is easy: all passing James buses go by the entrance road, making a day-trip possible. Leave luggage at the little shop by the roadside, where you can also find out the times of onward buses; Pop's, the village bus service, leaves for Punta Gorda Monday and Saturday at 11.00am, and Tuesday and Thursday at

10am. It's a well-signposted fifteen-minute walk west of the highway. The site is often included on tour itineraries, and nearby *The Lodge at Big Falls* provides upscale **accommodation** (see p.223). Six miles south of Indian Creek, the road to **Silver Creek** branches off to the left (west); with your own transport you can use this route to visit Maya villages and the site of Lubaantun (see p.227).

The **Stela House and Visitor Centre** has a good map of the site, and explanations of some of the stelae texts. The site caretaker, Adriano Mas, may be able to show you around. You enter through a plaza surrounded by walls and buildings of cut stones held together without mortar, and pass through the beautiful **walled ball-court** to the **South Group** – which may have functioned as an observatory to record the sunrise at the solstices and equinoxes. A total of 25 **stelae** were found here, eight of them carved. **Stela 14**, at almost 30ft high, is the tallest in Belize, and one of the tallest anywhere in the Maya world – although it was never erected. Unfortunately, the site was badly looted, and in 1997 several stelae were again damaged – by fire and machete.

Although Stela 14 lives in the Stela House, it's still an impressive sight, with panels of glyphs above and a richly attired ruler: it's his elaborate headgear that gives Nim Li Punit its name – Kekchí for "big hat". **Stela 15**, dated to 721 AD and the earliest here, is even more impressive. Carvings on this great slab depict a ruler in the act of dropping an offering – perhaps *copal* incense or corn kernels – into a burning brazier supported on the back of a monster, in order to conjure up a vision of **Waxaklahun Ubah Kan**, or "Mosaic War Serpent", the ruler's battle standard. To the right, a smaller figure also makes an offering, while on the left side a column of very clear glyphs separates the main figure from a guard.

Belize Foundation for Research and Environmental Education

Twenty-odd miles closer to Independence (four miles south of the Bladen River), a track heads west for six miles to the **Belize Foundation for Research and Environmental Education** ("Bfree"; ℡614-3896, ⓦwww.bfreebelize.net). Here you can stay in a **field station** on the riverbank in a comfortable, rustic bunkhouse (Bz$80 per person), **camping** (Bz$80 per person; tents available), or in private cabins. Wholesome meals using organic produce are included in the rates, and there's **internet** service. **Interns** (paying only Bz$40/day) are favoured to help with conservation and practical maintenance. All buses pass the turn-off (200 yards before the Gomez sawmill), which is signposted as **"Bladen Nature Reserve"**. It's a pleasant level (2hr) hike to the foundation through pine and broadleaf forest; call out at the riverbank and someone will paddle you across in a canoe. Alternatively, you can charter Bfree's 4x4 from the sawmill.

Surrounded by magnificent forest and mountain scenery, Bfree is a research facility founded in 1994 by biologists Jacob and Kelly Marlin. Set in over 1100 acres of private reserve at the meeting point of four protected areas (the Bladen Reserve is only accessible to accredited researchers), the jade-green Bladen River emerges from a steep-sided valley, with jungle-clad **Richardson Peak** – the country's third-highest peak (3000ft) rising to the west. You can climb it with a guide or hike over 30 miles of trails. Canoes are available for the river, while nearby a tranquil lagoon overhung by bromeliads is home to numerous fish, crocodiles, bathing tapirs and howling monkeys. Many definitive books on wildlife have been researched here, with 300 bird and 180 reptile/amphibian recorded species.

Contexts

Contexts

History

Belize is the youngest nation in Central America, only gaining independence from Britain in 1981, and its history has been markedly different from the surrounding republics since at least the mid-seventeenth century. Although the whole region was (to a greater or lesser degree) colonized by Spain in the sixteenth century, it was the entanglement with Britain that gave Belize its present cultural, social and political structures.

Delving far back into the past, prior to the advent of Maya civilization, scattered archeological remains and a handful of written texts provide very little concrete knowledge, and excavations could throw up new information at any time. It's generally thought that the region's first human inhabitants were **Stone Age hunter–gatherers** who crossed the Bering land bridge from Asia, beginning probably around 25,000 BC. They spread rapidly southwards, developing the **Clovis** culture (named after stone projectile points found in New Mexico) at least 11,000 years ago, and subsisted on hunting large mammals like mammoths, mastodons, deer and horses. By 9000 years ago, scarcity of game due to climatic change forced a different way of life, with more intensive use of plants. This **Archaic** period saw the cultivation of peppers, squash, beans and, importantly, maize, with more settled societies enabling an identifiable culture – broadly known as **Proto-Maya**. Archeological evidence suggests Archaic sequences in Belize until later than 2000 BC, and an early Proto-Maya language was also in use.

Belize is thought to have been an area of savannahs and broad-leaved woodland throughout this time, with tropical forests not appearing until the Classic period. The country was part of a vast region known to archeologists as **Mesoamerica**, stretching from north-central Mexico to El Salvador and Honduras. The cultures that developed throughout the region shared several characteristics, including a complex calendar, hieroglyphic writing, a similar cosmology and religion and a highly organized, stratified society – possibly having a common origin in the **Olmec** civilization of southern Mexico. For Belize, the most important group were the **Maya**, whose culture emerged here as early as 2500 BC and whose cities were at the height of their power between 250 and 900 AD.

The Maya in Belize

The development of the culture recognized as distinctly Maya began in what's known as the **Preclassic** (or Formative) period, from 2000 BC to 250 AD. The phase is subdivided into Early, Middle and Late periods, with boundaries not marked by exact dates, but understood as cultural and technological milestones; for example, when advances were made in architecture or administration. Current excavations appear to be pushing back the date when the earliest breakthroughs were made.

The **Early Preclassic** (roughly 2000 BC–1000 BC) marks the beginning of agriculture, notably the annual cutting and burning of forest in order to plant maize. Food needs were supplemented by hunting, fishing and foraging, and though there's no evidence of structures larger than dwellings during the period, ceramics were produced; pottery found at **Cuello**, near Orange Walk, dates from around 1000 BC – among the earliest in the Maya lowlands. Elsewhere in Mesoamerica, the emergence of the great Olmec civilization was to have a far-reaching impact, originating in the coastal plain of Veracruz. Often regarded as the true ancestors of Maya culture, the Olmecs developed a complex polytheistic religion, a writing system and a calendar known as the "long count", later adopted by the Maya.

By the **Middle Preclassic** (1000 BC–300 BC) there was a substantial increase in population – evidence of numerous settlements can be found from southern Guatemala to northern Yucatán, including almost all of Belize, in particular the main river valleys. All the settlements produced Mamóm style red and orange monochrome pottery and stone metates for grinding corn, and it's thought that a common Maya language was spoken throughout the area. A universal belief system, practised from a very early date, may have provided the stimulus and social cohesion to build bigger towns. As in all early agricultural communities, food surpluses would have eventually freed some people to become seers, priests and astronomers. By 750 BC Nakbé, in northern Petén, was a large city, perhaps the first one in the Maya world, evidence that the Maya had progressed far beyond a simple peasant society.

The explosion in Maya architecture, culture and population came in the **Late Preclassic** (300 BC–250 AD), when **Chicanel culture** dominated the Maya world. The famous Maya corbelled arch (without a keystone, but consisting of two sides, each with stones overlapping until they eventually met, thus able to span only a narrow gap) was developed, and hugely ambitious large pyramids with elaborate temples were built at Tikal, El Mirador and Río Azul in Petén. In northern Belize, Cuello, Nohmul, Lamanai and Cerros were the great centres, all featuring major examples of public architecture. Lamanai and Cerros controlled trade routes right through the Classic and into the Postclassic periods. The Belize River valley was fully settled, with local centres such as Cahal Pech, Pacbitún and El Pilar consolidating their power.

The question of what sparked this phase of rapid development is a subject of much debate. Most archeologists agree that the catalyst was the Olmec culture, which the Maya adopted and adapted, developing complex administrative mechanisms to feed and control the growing population. A hierarchical structure evolved, with ultimate military and spiritual power vested in Maya kings, who established ruling dynasties and communicated with the gods by spilling their own blood at propitious festivals.

Building the Maya cities

The start of the greatest phase of Maya achievement, the **Early Classic** period (250 AD–600 AD), is marked by the introduction of both the long count calendar and a recognizable form of writing, which took place before the fourth century AD. The cultural influence of the Olmecs was replaced by that of **Teotihuacán**, which dominated Central Mexico during the early Classic period. Armed merchants spread the power of Teotihuacán as far as Yucatán, Petén and Belize, bringing new styles of ceramics and alternative religious beliefs. While complete subjugation remained unlikely, in around 400 AD the overwhelming power of Teotihuacán did radically alter Maya life: in Petén, **Tikal**'s rise was helped by close links with Teotihuacán, and both cities prospered greatly; Tikal has a stela (a freestanding carved monument) depicting a Tikal lord on one side and a warrior from Teotihuacán on the other.

Most of the now ruined cities that we see today were built during the Classic period, almost always over earlier structures. Elaborately carved stelae, bearing dates and emblem-glyphs, tell of actual events in rulers' lives – battles, marriages, dynastic succession and so on. The deciphering of these dates has provided confirmation (or otherwise) of archeological evidence and offers major insights. Made up of independent city-states, the Maya region was bound together by religion, culture and sophisticated trade. The cities jostled for power and influence, occasionally erupting into warfare, with three or four main centres dominating through a process of alliances. **Calakmul**, in Campeche, Mexico, and Tikal were the nearest of these "superstates" to Belize, and in 562 AD an alliance of Calakmul and Caracol, in southern Cayo District, defeated Tikal, as shown by an inscription on Altar 21 at Caracol. Other detailed carvings on wooden lintels and stone monuments at the site depict costumed lords trampling on bound captives. Victory of the subordinate state over the dominant regional power may well have caused the major upheaval that followed.

The collapse of Teotihuacán in the seventh century caused shock waves throughout the civilizations of Mesoamerica in what is known as the **Middle Classic Hiatus**. No stelae were erected in the Maya cities, and many existing monuments were defaced. Warfare raged as rival lords strove to win political power in the dominant Maya centres. But as new kings established dynasties, free of Teotihuacán's political control, Maya cities flourished as never before. Architecture, astronomy and art reached degrees of sophistication unequalled by any other pre-Columbian society. Many centres were larger than their contemporary Western European cities, then in their "Dark Ages": Caracol had an estimated 150,000 people.

The prosperity and grandeur of the **Late Classic period** (600 AD–850 AD) reached all across the Maya lands: from Bonampak and Palenque in the west, to Calakmul and Uxmal in the north, Altun Ha and Cerros in the east, and Copán and Quiriguá in the south. Masterpieces of painted pottery and carved jade (the Maya's most precious material) were crafted, often to be used as funerary offerings, while exquisite works of shell, bone and (rarely) marble also appeared. Temples were painted in brilliant colours, and though most pigments have faded, enough vestiges remain to vividly reconstruct the ancient cities.

Collapse of the Classic Maya

Though it was abrupt when the end came for each Maya centre, it took around a century (**Terminal Classic**; 800 AD–c.1000 AD) for Classic Maya civilization to be extinguished in Belize. By 750 AD alliances and trade links were breaking down, warfare increased and stelae were carved less frequently. The sacking of Dos Pilas, in the Petexbatún region of southwest Petén, by nearby Tamandarito in 761 AD is regarded as the first phase of the **Classic Maya collapse**. Strife and disorder spread throughout Mesoamerica, cities became depopulated, and new construction ceased over much of Belize by 830 AD. Bonampak, in Chiapas, was abandoned before its famous murals could be completed, and many of the great sites along the River Usumacinta (now the border of Guatemala and Mexico) were occupied by militaristic outsiders.

The decline and subsequent collapse of Classic Maya civilization had several probable causes. Strong evidence suggests that a prolonged drought in central Yucatán caused competition for scarce resources, with the effects rippling outward. The massive increase in population may have put intolerable pressure on food production, ultimately exhausting the soil. But also, the growth and demands of an unproductive elite may well have led to a peasant revolt, leading to the abandonment of city life. By the tenth century, the Maya had largely abandoned their central cities and most of those that remained were reduced to a primitive state.

Not all Maya cities were deserted, however: many in northern Belize survived and even prospered, with Lamanai and others remaining occupied throughout the **Postclassic period** (c.900 AD–1540 AD). The Yucatán peninsula escaped the worst of the depopulation, and came under the influence (possibly by outright conquest) of the militaristic **Toltecs**, who came from central Mexico in 987 AD, creating a hybrid of Classic Maya culture.

From around 900 AD to the time of the Spanish Conquest the Yucatán peninsula and northern Belize consisted of over a dozen rival provinces, bound up in a cycle of competition and conflict. Northern Belize was part of the Maya province of **Chactemal** (later known as Chetumal), covering an area from around Maskall, near the site of Altun Ha, to Laguna Bacalar in southern Quintana Roo in Mexico, and with Santa Rita, near Corozal, as its likely capital. Chetumal was a wealthy province, producing cacao and honey; trade, alliances and wars kept it in contact with surrounding Maya states up to and beyond the Spanish conquest of Aztec Mexico. Further south, thick forests and the ridges of the Maya Mountains intruded, becoming known as **Dzuluinicob** to the Maya of Chetumal – "land of foreigners" – whose capital was Tipú, located at present-day Negroman on the Macal River. Here, the Maya controlled the upper Belize River valley, strenuously resisting attempts by the Spanish to subdue and convert them.

Arrival of the Europeans

The general assumption that Belize was practically deserted by the time Europeans arrived is now widely discredited. In 1500 AD the native population in the area which was to become Belize is estimated to have been around two hundred thousand – almost as high as it is today – and the Maya towns and provinces were still vigorously independent. **Spanish** sailors Pinzón and de Solis first set eyes on the mainland of Belize in the early sixteenth century, though a landing didn't occur until 1511, when a small group of shipwrecked Spanish sailors reached land on the southern coast of Yucatán: five were immediately sacrificed and the others became slaves. At least one of the slaves must have escaped and regained contact with his fellow countrymen, because when **Cortés** reached Cozumel in 1519 he knew of the existence of two other enslaved survivors, and sent gifts for their release. Geronimo de Aguilar immediately joined Cortés, but the other survivor, **Gonzalo Guerrero**, refused: Guerrero had married the daughter of Na Chan Kan, the chief of Chactemal, and preferred life among his former captors. Due to his knowledge of Spanish tactics he became a crucial military adviser to the Maya in their subsequent resistance to Spanish domination: the archeologist Eric Thompson calls him the first European to make Belize his home.

The Spanish made few reports of their early contact with the Maya in Belize, probably because they heard no stories of gold – their overriding obsession. In 1525 Cortés himself probably passed through southern Belize on his epic march from Veracruz in Mexico to punish a rebellious subordinate in San Gil de Buena Vista, near the mouth of the Río Dulce on the Bay of Honduras. One hundred and forty Spanish soldiers and three thousand Indians marched across the Maya heartland, which still contained many thriving towns and cities. At Tayasal on Lake Petén Itzá, he was welcomed by Can Ek, chief of the Itzá, who had heard of Cortés's cruelty in conquering Mexico and decided not to oppose him. At the valley of the Sarstoon River, the present boundary with Guatemala, Cortés pacified rebels before sailing north to Mexico, apparently without realizing that Yucatán was not an island.

Attempted conquest and Maya resistance

For the Spanish it proved relatively simple to capture and kill the "living god" leaders of such highly organized empires as the Aztecs and Incas. However, the Maya provinces of present-day Yucatán and Belize were not united, and their rulers were accustomed to dealing with enemies by fighting or by forming temporary alliances – one reason why the Spanish found this region so difficult to subdue.

In 1528 **Francisco de Montejo**, granted permission by the Spanish Crown to colonize the "islands" of Cozumel and Yucatán, established a settlement called Salamanca on the mainland coast south of Cozumel, and his lieutenant, **Alonso Dávila**, led an expedition south. Neither was successful: both groups encountered hostile Maya, and Dávila was forced to turn away from Chetumal by Maya under the command of Gonzalo Guerrero. A second attempt by Dávila in 1531 was marginally more successful but nevertheless short-lived. On the advice of Guerrero – who realized they could not defeat the Spanish outright – the Maya abandoned Chetumal. Dávila occupied the town, renaming it **Villa Real**, but the Maya continually harassed his troops and they were driven out eighteen months later, fleeing south along the coast of Belize to Omoa in Honduras. For some years after, the Maya in Belize remained free from Spanish interference; Chetumal regained its trading links and became a powerful military ally, sending fifty war canoes to Omoa in 1542 to assist the local chief fighting the Spanish.

Montejo's vision of ruling a vast province of the Spanish empire comprising Yucatán, Belize and Honduras was not to be fulfilled, though his son, Montejo the Younger did complete the conquest of Yucatán, establishing a capital at Mérida in 1542. Late the following year, however, **Gaspar Pacheco**, his son Melchor and nephew Alonso began another chapter in the sickeningly familiar tale of Spanish atrocities, advancing on Chetumal, destroying crops and food stores and ruthlessly slaughtering the inhabitants. By 1544 the Pachecos had founded a town on Lake Bacalar, and claimed *encomienda* (tribute) from villages surrounding Chetumal. To the south, however, Tipú maintained alliances with other Maya provinces and continued in armed resistance.

During the second half of the sixteenth century missions were established, including one at Lamanai in 1570, and the Spanish, with difficulty, strengthened their hold over northern Belize. In 1618, Spanish priests Fuensalida and Orbita visited **Tipú**, on the Macal River, and punished the Maya for worshipping "idols". Resentment was always present, however, and the Maya burnt the church in defiance, before boiling over into total rebellion in 1638, which forced Spain to abandon Chetumal and Tipú completely and more or less permanently.

In the mid-seventeenth century the nearest permanent Spanish settlements to Belize were Salamanca de Bacalar in southern Yucatán and Lago de Izabal in Guatemala. Records are scarce, but it seems the Maya of Belize were under some form of Spanish influence even if not under direct rule: perhaps the determination of Maya resistance deterred Spain from full colonization; or perhaps the Maya fled to inaccessible forests to retain their independence. Repeated **expeditions** were nonetheless mounted by Spanish friars in an attempt to bring the heathen Maya of Tipú into the fold of the Catholic Church, though these were never more than partially successful.

In 1695 a Spanish mission met leaders of the Itzá to discuss the **surrender of the Itzá**. The negotiations were fruitless, and in 1697 Spanish troops attacked Tayasal, the Itzá capital on Lake Petén Itzá (near modern Flores). At Tipú, the struggle was to continue with simmering resentment until 1707, when the population was forcibly removed to Lake Petén Itzá. This cruel act effectively ended Spanish attempts to settle the west of Belize, as without labourers it would be impossible to establish a successful colony.

In the late seventeenth century Bacalar was abandoned after years of **Maya and pirate attacks**. Spain's forces were simply too stretched to secure the vast (and relatively gold-free) territory from Campeche to Nicaragua. British territorial ambitions now focused on the Caribbean, too, resulting in continuous conflict. The capture of Jamaica in 1655, after 150 years of Spanish rule, gave England a base from which it could harass Spanish shipping.

British incursions

The failure of the Spanish to dominate southern Yucatán allowed British **bucca-neers** (or pirates) preying on Spanish treasure fleets to find refuge along the coastline, and in turn   much later – led to Guatemala's claim to British Honduras and refusal to recognize Belize's independence.

Some of the great Elizabethan sailors, such as Raleigh, Hawkins and Drake are known to have been in the Bay of Honduras, and they may have sought refuge on the coast of Belize after raids on Spanish ships, though there are no records to prove any kind of settlement or temporary camp until the 1700s. Certainly, there was no attempt by Britain to colonize Belize like it was doing elsewhere in the Caribbean, instead being content to let pirates like Blackbeard roam the region; he is though to have camped on Turneffe Atoll around 1718. Britain also competed with **France** and the **Netherlands** to establish a foothold in the Caribbean, each one setting up companies to equip privateers – really government-sanctioned pirates – to raid Spanish treasure fleets. In the periodic absences of bounty, they would plunder piles of **logwood**, ready cut and awaiting shipment to Spain. Hard and extremely heavy, it was worth £90–110 a ton back in Britain, where it helped to build up the textile industry as a black, red and grey dye for woollens. Such an abundance of convertible wealth attracted numerous British buccaneers, possibly as early as 1638, who settled along the Spanish Caribbean coastline, including at the mouth of the Belize river.

The various treaties signed between Britain and Spain from the late seventeenth to the mid-eighteenth century, attempted to first outlaw the buccaneers, but eventually allowed the British to establish logwood camps along the rivers in northern Belize. This was never intended to legitimize permanent British settle-ment of perceived Spanish imperial territory, thus the camps periodically came under attack. But the attention of European powers rarely rested long upon the humid and insect-ridden swamps where the logwood cutters, who were becoming known as **Baymen**, worked and lived. The British government, while profiting from the trade in logwood, preferred to avoid the question of whether or not the Baymen were British subjects and left them to their own devices.

Life in the logwood camps was uncomfortable. Though the wood was mainly cut in the dry season, it was too heavy to float, and the men had to build rafts to float it down to the river mouth in the rainy season, where it awaited shipment. The Baymen lived in rough huts thatched with palm leaves (known as "Bay leaf" – still used today in tourist cabañas), and survived on provisions brought from Jamaica. These ships also brought rum, which the Baymen drank with relish. An English merchant (writing in 1726) reported: "Rum Punch is their Drink, which they'll sometimes sit for several Days…for while the Liquor is moving they don't care to leave it." Though many of the woodcutters "voluntarily" gave up buccaneering, raiding of Spanish ships still occurred throughout the seventeenth century; punished by Spain whenever it had the opportunity. One such reprisal against British woodcutters in the Bay of Campeche left the survivors imprisoned in Mexico.

As gangs of woodcutters advanced further into the forests in search of valuable **mahogany** (which overtook logwood as principal export by the 1760s) for furniture making, they came into contact with the Maya. Although they had no wish to colonize or convert them, records show that early buccaneers took Maya captives to trade in the slave markets of Jamaica, and they also enslaved people to work in Belize. The Maya were so weakened by disease and depopulation that they only offered limited resistance.

Spanish attacks occurred throughout the eighteenth century, with the Baymen driven out on several occasions. Increasingly though, Britain – at war with both

Spain and France during the period 1739 to 1748 – began to admit a measure of responsibility for the protection of the settlers. In 1746, in response to requests, the governor of Jamaica sent troops to aid the Baymen, but this didn't stop the Spanish decimating the settlement in both 1747 and 1754. The **Paris Peace Treaty** of 1763 allowed the British to cut logwood, but since it did not define boundaries the governor of Yucatán sent troops from Bacalar to ensure that the cutters confined themselves to the Belize River. In 1765 Admiral Burnaby, the British commander-in-chief at Jamaica, visited Belize to ensure that the provisions of the treaty were upheld, finding them "in a state of Anarchy and Confusion". The admiral, recognizing that the Baymen would benefit from some form of regulation, drew up a simple set of laws concerning the maintenance of justice in what was a remote and uncouth area where the British government was only reluctantly involved. Known as **Burnaby's Code**, it gave authority to a bench of magistrates, supported by a jury, to hold quarterly courts with the power to impose fines. The Baymen attached a grand importance to the Code (though only sporadically obeyed it), and voted to increase its scope a year later.

A century of antagonism, boundary disputes and mutual suspicion between the Spanish and the Baymen meant that relations were never secure. The Spanish feared raids on their ships, while the Baymen fostered a spirit of defiance in the face of Spanish reprisals, leading to the realization that British rule was preferable – as long as they could choose which of its institutions to accept. Their tenure was nonetheless still very uncertain: in 1779 Spain (allied with France in the American War of Independence) sent a fleet and captured all the inhabitants of St George's Caye – the capital of the Baymen – imprisoning them in Mérida and Havana. The **Versailles Peace Treaty** (1783) did little to resolve matters, but a convention signed three years later allowed timber to be cut as far south as the Sibun River – also stipulating that no system of government could be established without approval from Madrid. True to their "turbulent and unsettled disposition", the Baymen ignored it, cutting wood where they pleased, and after 1791, the British governor of Jamaica also failed to add authority to the settlement.

The Battle of St George's Caye

The final showdown between the waning Spanish empire and the Bay settlers (supported this time by a British warship and troops), the **Battle of St George's Caye**, came as a result of the outbreak of war between Britain and Spain in 1796. Field Marshal **Arthur O'Neil**, an Irishman and the captain general of Yucatán (named **Don Arturo by the Spanish**), assembled ships and troops, determined to drive out the British settlers and this time to occupy Belize. Lord Balcarres, the governor of Jamaica, despatched **Lieutenant-Colonel Barrow** to command the settlers in the event of hostilities. At a vital Public Meeting held on June 1, 1797, the Baymen decided by 65 votes to 51 to defend the settlement rather than evacuate. A few companies of troops were sent from Jamaica, and slaves were released and armed. The sloop **HMS Merlin**, under the command of Captain John Moss, was stationed in the Bay, local vessels were armed, gun rafts were built and an attack was expected at any time. Throughout the next year the mood of the defenders vacillated between aggression and despair, preparing for war with scant resources under the martial law supervision of Colonel Barrow.

The **Spanish fleet**, reported to consist of 32 vessels, including sixteen heavily armed men-of-war and two thousand troops, arrived just north of St George's Caye in early September 1798. On September 3 and 4 several of the Spanish warships attempted to force a passage over Montego Caye Shoals, between Long Caye and St George's Caye, but were repulsed by the Baymen's sloops. Stakes put down by the Spanish to mark the channels were removed by the defenders, who knew these waters well. Barrow and Moss correctly guessed that the Spanish would then try to seize St George's Caye. The *Merlin* and part of the Baymen's tiny fleet sailed there on the evening of September 5, securing it just as twelve Spanish warships were attempting to do the same.

The next few days passed anxiously: the Spanish with their massive firepower severely restricted by the shallow water; and the Baymen with their small but highly manoeuvrable fleet awaiting attack – and slaves apparently at least as eager to fight the Spanish as their masters. On the morning of **September 10, 1798**, fourteen large Spanish ships sailed to within 1.5 miles of St George's Caye, keeping to the deep water to the east, and began firing. Captain Moss held his fire – the Spanish broadsides were falling short. At 1.30pm he gave the order to attack. Guns blazing, the *Merlin* and the Baymen's fleet swept forward, wreaking havoc among the heavy and crowded Spanish ships. The Spanish fleet, already weakened by desertions and yellow fever, suffered heavy losses and fled in disorder to Caye Chapel. There they remained for five days to bury their dead, and on the morning of September 16 they sailed for Bacalar, still harassed by the Baymen.

Though a victory was won against overwhelming odds, the Battle of St George's Caye was not by itself decisive as no one in Belize could be sure that the Spanish would not return. The territory remained as a timber-cutting settlement, but not within the British Empire. In practical terms the power of the Spanish was waning while the British was expanding, but in Belize the slaves were still slaves, and though they had fought valiantly, their owners expected them to go back to cutting mahogany. Indeed controversy still exists in Belize over the fact that the battle was fought between two European powers to establish rule, while also enabling slave owners to claim that the slaves were willing to fight on behalf of their masters. Whatever its legacy, 1798 was the last point at which Spain attempted to gain control; Britain gradually assumed a greater role in the government of Belize.

Settlers and slaves

A report by a Spanish missionary in 1724 mentions the ownership of **slaves** by English settlers, and it's possible that Africans were brought in (from Jamaica and Bermuda) even before that time. The British population in the Bay of Honduras had never been more than a few hundred, their livelihoods dependent on the attitude of authorities in the adjacent Spanish colonies. In order to gain concessions from Spain favourable to the Belize settlement, Britain agreed to relinquish claims to the Mosquito Coast (a British protectorate along the coasts of Honduras and Nicaragua) in the **Convention of London** in 1786. Many aggrieved displaced inhabitants settled in Belize, and by 1790 the population reached 2900, of whom over 2100 were slaves.

The often held view that slavery in Belize was somehow less harsh than elsewhere is a misconception that may have arisen due to the differences between plantation slavery in the West Indies and United States and the mainly forest labour that Africans in Belize were required to perform. The myth has been skilfully manipulated by apologists for colonialism, who maintain that during the pivotal Battle of St George's Caye black people voluntarily fought "shoulder to shoulder" with their white masters, and thus preferred slavery over the freedom offered by the Spanish authorities to any slave who escaped. Although some slaves did fight alongside their masters in 1798, they also continued to run away: in 1813 fifteen slaves belonging to Thomas Paslow, one of the heroes of the battle, escaped "because of ill-treatment and starvation", their desperation evidence enough to refute the myth. Many escaped slaves ended up in maroon settlements such as at **Gales Point** (see p.187). Records of **slave revolts** from 1745 to 1820 are further indication that relations were not as amicable as some would like to believe.

Belizean whites were always vastly outnumbered by blacks, and they feared rebellion at least as much as Spanish attack. The biggest (and arguably most successful) revolt occurred in 1773 when six white men were murdered and at least eleven slaves escaped across the Hondo River, where they received asylum from the Spanish authorities. This was not a display of altruism – moreover, encouraging slaves to flee was calculated to weaken the British settlement's economy.

The nature of slavery in Belize was, however, very different from that on the sugar plantations. The cutting of mahogany involved small gangs working in the forest on their own or on a fairly harmonious level with an overseer. The slaves were armed, with firearms in some cases, to hunt for food and for protection against the Maya. Skills developed in searching for the trees, cutting them down and transporting them to the coast involved a position of trust that slave masters depended on for the continuation of their own way of life. **Manumission**, whereby a slave would purchase freedom or be freed as a bequest in a will, or simply a gift, was much more frequent in Belize than in the Caribbean islands – perhaps an indication of the greater informality of Belizean society. However, treatment was still harsh, with no protection offered by the law. Owners could inflict up to 39 lashes or imprisonment, and if a slave was hanged for rebellion the owner could be compensated for financial loss.

Ironically, it was the **Abolition Act of 1807** – which made it illegal for British subjects to continue with the African slave trade but not illegal to transport slaves from one British colony to another – that gave the settlers in Belize recognition as **British subjects**. Belize was clearly not a colony, and therefore slaves could not be transported from Jamaica. Superintendent Arthur, the British government's representative in Belize, decided that the settlers were British subjects and therefore forbidden to engage in the slave trade. The **Abolition Act of 1833** ended slavery throughout the British empire, and contained a special clause to include Belize. The Act, however, did not end slavery immediately: "freed" Africans were to be called "apprentices", required to work for forty hours per week for free before being allowed to work for payment. This abuse continued until full freedom in 1838. Despite inherent immorality in the institution of slavery, the Act provided for **compensation** to be paid to the owners for the loss of property, rather than to former slaves for their suffering – and, at £53 per slave, the compensation paid in Belize was higher than in any British colony.

The Colony of British Honduras

The consolidation of British logging interests in the eighteenth century and the grudging steps towards recognition from Spain led to a form of **British colonial government** gradually becoming established in Belize. The **Public Meeting**, beginning in the early 1700s, was the settlers' initial efforts at a rudimentary form of government, assuming greater importance until the 1730s when they elected magistrates – though only property-owning white men could vote. Free black men could vote at the Public Meeting after 1808, though their franchise was limited through higher property requirements than that of whites. **Burnaby's Code** in 1765 had enlarged the jurisdiction of the magistrates and allowed laws passed at the Meeting to be enforced by a British naval captain, though officers' reports invariably commented on the lamentable inability of settlers to keep their own laws.

Britain's early acceptance of some form of responsibility to the settlers led to the arrival in 1786 of the first **superintendent**, Captain Despard. The office appears to have been difficult, often facing an unsupportive Public Meeting, which wanted to run the settlement without "interference" from London. But gradually, the powers of the superintendent grew, while the election of magistrates ceased altogether in 1832, when they were appointed by the superintendent. In 1854 an elected **Legislative Assembly** was formed, establishing the beginnings of colonial-rule parliamentary democracy. The assembly began petitioning for recognition as a colony, arguing that the settlement was in fact, if not in law, already a British colony. Earl Grey, at the Colonial Office, supported the assembly and Palmerston, the British prime minister, agreed. On May 12, 1862, the Belize settlements, with the boundaries that still exist today, became the **Colony of British Honduras**. In 1871 the British government established a **Crown Colony** assembly in line with colonial policy throughout the West Indies, under the control of a governor appointed by the Colonial Office.

Mexican and Guatemalan claims

After the Battle of St George's Caye in 1798 Spain maintained its claim to Belize, and the **Treaty of Amiens** in 1802 required Britain to hand back territory captured during the war, taken by Spain to include Belize. The Baymen, however, had no intention of leaving, and in the face of increasing difficulties throughout the Spanish empire, and Britain's willingness to assist the settlers, Spain's claim became insupportable.

Although **Mexico's independence**, achieved in 1821 and followed two years later by the colonies in Central America, marked the effective end of the Spanish empire, it didn't signal the end of external claims to Belize. The nineteenth century was filled with claims and counter-claims and treaties made and broken. Mexico's claim to the northern half of British Honduras as an extension of Yucatán was unacceptable to the British government, and after numerous diplomatic exchanges an **Anglo-Mexican Treaty** was ratified in 1897.

Guatemala's claim was the source of more belligerent disagreement with Britain, and there's no doubt that the British government shares much of the blame for the confusion. In treaty after treaty Britain regarded Belize as a territory under Spanish sovereignty, and long after Spain's expulsion, Britain maintained the fiction of Spanish sovereignty. Guatemala's assertion rested upon the acceptance in international law of *uti possidetis* – the right of a colony that successfully gains independence from a colonial authority to inherit the rights and territory of that authority. For this to be valid, however (even if Britain accepted its premise – which was doubtful), the entire territory of Belize would have had to have been under Spanish control in 1821. Since this was clearly not the case Britain asserted that Guatemala's claim was invalid.

In a vain attempt to reach a settlement, Britain and Guatemala signed the **Anglo-Guatemalan Treaty** in 1859: the interpretation of its various clauses has been the source of dispute ever since. The treaty, which in the British view settled the boundaries of Guatemala and Belize in their existing positions, was interpreted by Guatemala as a disguised treaty of cession of the territory – if Article 7 was not implemented. Under the provisions of this crucial article, Britain agreed to fund and build a road from Guatemala City to the Atlantic coast and in return Guatemala would drop its claim to Belize. If the road was not built then the territory would revert to Guatemala. Although a route was surveyed in 1859, Britain considered the estimated £100,000 cost of construction too high a price to pay to secure the territory of Belize, and the road was never built. The dispute was no nearer resolution when the settlement became British Honduras in 1862, and Article 7 remained a cause of rancour and disagreement for decades. Finally, in 1940, Guatemala repudiated the treaty on the grounds that the provisions of Article 7 were not fulfilled, and the new constitution of 1945 declared Belize – *Belice* in Spanish – to be the 23rd department of Guatemala. In 1948 Guatemala made the first of several **threats to invade** to "recover" the territory; Britain responded by sending cruisers and troops, the first of many military deployments over the next four decades. In hindsight, £100,000 in 1859 would have been a comparative bargain.

The Caste Wars of Yucatán

The terrible, bloody **Caste Wars** of Yucatán began with a riot by Maya troops at Valladolid in 1847. They sacked the town, killing whites, spreading terror and coming within a hair's breadth of capturing the peninsula's capital, Mérida, and throwing off white rule completely. From 1848, as Mexico sent troops to put down the rebellion, thousands of Maya and mestizo **refugees** fled to Belize, increasing the population of Orange Walk and Corozal districts. The superintendent in Belize encouraged them to stay as they cleared land for sugar cane and brought much-needed farming skills.

The rebellious **Cruzob Maya** (taking their name from a sacred "talking cross") occupied a virtually independent territory in the east of Yucatán. They established their capital at Chan Santa Cruz ("little holy cross" – they were also known as the **Santa Cruz Maya**), the modern town of Felipe Carillo Puerto, north of Belize. At this time, the border was not clearly defined, and Belizean woodcutters came into conflict with the Santa Cruz Maya, who attacked mahogany camps and took prisoners for ransom. Alarm spread and eventually a compromise was reached, with a ransom paid to secure the prisoners' release, and further royalties made for the right to cut wood in Maya territory. In fact British merchants profited by selling the Santa Cruz Maya arms, which provoked strong protests from Mexico.

In 1851, the **Icaiché Maya**, who were not in rebellion, were attacked by the Santa Cruz Maya, leading the Mexican government to propose an alliance between themselves and the Icaiché against the Santa Cruz. Icaiché leaders requested British help in their negotiations, and, wanting to enter Icaiché lands to log mahogany, the Belizean timber companies were also signatories to the treaty. In the **treaty of 1853** the Icaiché were granted virtual autonomy in return for recognizing the authority of Mexico, and the British were allowed to cut wood under licence in the Icaiché lands, in what was to become the northwest of Belize. British woodcutters viewed the agreement as a means to expand their territory at the expense of both the Icaiché and a weakened Mexico.

It was now the turn of the Icaiché to demand rent from the British loggers, which was only paid after further **Maya attacks**. British arms trading with the Santa Cruz Maya incensed the Icaiché, and the flames were fanned further after an attack by the Santa Cruz Maya. After years of broken agreements and betrayal the Icaiché, supported by Mexico and led by **Marcos Canul**, attacked mahogany camps on the Río Bravo and the New River in 1866, and captured dozens of prisoners. The lieutenant governor declared martial law and sent for reinforcements from Jamaica. Raids and counter-raids continued, with Belizean villages sacked and colonial troops retaliating. Canul briefly occupied Corozal in 1870, and after a battle at Orange Walk in 1872 Corozal became a fortified British base. Although the violence diminished, the danger of Maya attacks wasn't over until 1882 when the Icaiché leader, Santiago Pech, met the governor in Belize City to recognize British jurisdiction in the northwest.

The twentieth century onwards

By 1900 Belize was an integral, if minor, colony of the British empire. The population in the census of 1901 was 37,500, of whom 28,500 were born there. Comfortably complacent, white property owners could foresee no change to their rule, with workers in the forests and estates predominantly black, the descendants of former slaves, known as "Creoles". Wages were low and strict controls were maintained, stifling worker organization and with the power to imprison labourers for missing a day's work.

Belizeans rushed to defend the "mother country" in **World War I**, but black troops were not permitted to fight a white enemy and were instead placed in labour battalions in British-held Mesopotamia. On their return in 1919, humiliated and disillusioned, their bitterness exploded into violence, and the troops were joined by thousands of Belize City's population (including the police) in looting and rioting, an event which marked the onset of **black consciousness** and the beginnings of the independence movement. The ideas of **Marcus Garvey**, a phenomenally industrious and charismatic black Jamaican leader, and founder of the Universal Negro Improvement Association (UNIA), were already known in Belize – the government's ban on *Negro World*, the UNIA's magazine, contributed to the severity of the 1919 riot – and in 1920 a branch of the UNIA opened in Belize City. Garvey believed that the "Negro needs a nation and a country of his own" – a sentiment which found increasing support among all sectors of black society in Belize. Garvey himself visited Belize in 1921.

The status of workers had improved little over the previous century, and the Depression years of the 1930s brought extreme hardship, the disastrous hurricane of 1931 compounding the misery. The disaster prompted workers to organize in 1934 after an unemployment relief programme initiated by the governor was a dismal failure. **Antonio Soberanis** emerged as a leader, founding the Labourers and Unemployed Association (LUA), and holding regular meetings in the "Battlefield" – outside the colonial administration in Belize City. Soberanis was arrested in October 1934 while arranging bail for pickets at a sawmill who had been arrested. Released a month later, meetings resumed, but the government passed restrictive laws, banning marches and increasing the governor's power to deal with disturbances.

World War II gave a boost to forestry and the opportunity for Belizeans to work abroad, though conditions for returning soldiers and workers were no better than they had been following World War I. In 1946 political power still lay with the tiny wealthy elite and with the governor, a Foreign Office appointee, and the devaluation of the British Honduras dollar in 1949 caused even greater hardship. A new constitution emerged in 1951, and in 1954 a **general election** was held in which all literate adults over the age of 21 could vote. The election was won with an overwhelming majority by the **People's United Party** (PUP), led by **George Price**, ushering in a semblance of ministerial government. Belize became an **internally self-governing** colony in 1964, a step intended to lead to full independence after a relatively short time, as was the policy throughout the Caribbean. Until then, the British government, through the governor, remained responsible for defence, foreign affairs and security. The National Assembly became a bicameral system with an appointed Senate and an elected House of Representatives.

The delay in achieving independence was caused largely by the still unresolved **dispute with Guatemala**. Twice, in 1972 and 1977, Guatemala moved troops to the border and threatened to invade, but British reinforcements were an effective dissuasion. The situation remained tense but international opinion moved in favour of Belizean independence.

Belizean ethnic groups and languages

Belize today has a very mixed cultural background, with thirteen recognised ethnic groups - though the two largest, Creoles and mestizos, form 75 percent of the total population (currently around three hundred thousand).

The largest ethnic group (around fifty percent) are **mestizos**, descended from Amerindians and early Spanish settlers, most of whom speak Spanish as their first language. Mainly located in the north, Ambergris Caye and Caye Caulker, with a sizeable population in Cayo, many of their ancestors fled to Belize during the Caste Wars of Yucatán (see p.247). During the 1980s, the arrival of an estimated forty thousand mestizos – most referring to themselves as Ladinos – added permanently to Belize's Spanish-speaking population. The greatest shift in Belize's demography for centuries, most were fleeing conflicts and repression in El Salvador, Guatemala and Honduras. Those granted refugee status were settled in camps, mostly in Cayo, and allowed to farm small plots, though many, especially those undocumented, still provide convenient cheap labour. These immigrants are tolerated, if not exactly welcomed – few countries could absorb a sudden twenty percent population increase without a certain amount of turmoil – and many have integrated and learnt Kriol, if not English. Most original refugees have received Belizean nationality, and their children are Belizean citizens.

Creoles, descended from Africans brought to the West Indies as slaves and early white settlers, comprise just under a quarter of the population, though they make up a large proportion of Belize City, with scattered settlements elsewhere. Kriol (from "Creole') is the common language in Belize, a dialect of English similar to that spoken across the West Indies. Kriol underwent a recent formalization, with a more or less standardized written language. Controversy rages over whether or not Kriol should be taught in schools alongside English and become the country's official language.

The **Maya** in Belize are from three groups – Yucatec, Mopan and Kekchí – and make up around eleven percent of the population. The Yucatecan Maya also entered Belize to escape the fighting in the Caste Wars, and most were soon acculturated into the mestizo way of life as small-scale farmers. The Mopan Maya came to Belize in the 1880s and settled in the hills of Toledo and the area of Benque Viejo. The last and largest group, the Kekchí, came from the area around Cobán in Guatemala to work in cacao plantations in southern Belize. Small numbers still arrive in Belize each year, boosting villages in Toledo.

The **Garifuna** (see box, p.190) form just over six percent of the population and live mainly in Dangriga and the villages on the south coast. They are descended from shipwrecked and escaped African slaves who mingled with the last of the Caribs on the island of St Vincent and eventually settled in Belize in the years after 1832.

Another significant group are **East Indians**, established mainly in southern Toledo District, the descendants of indentured labourers brought over in the late 1860s by a small number of Confederate refugees seeking to re-establish the plantocracy following defeat in the American Civil War. More recent Indian immigration has occurred in Belize City. Though the white, German-speaking Mennonites (see box, p.81) form only around four percent of the population, they undertake the vast majority of agriculture in Belize. Their opposition to government interference in their religion, has over centuries forced them to move on, but in Belize they appear to have found a secure and permanent home. The **Chinese** are a small ethnic group, many arriving in the nineteenth century as labourers on sugar estates in the south. Many more (Taiwanese and Cantonese) arrived in the 1980s. While involved in agriculture, they are most evident in the lottery, retail and restaurant industries; most grocery stores are run by Chinese families.

An excellent TV **documentary series** entitled *Simply Belize* covers all thirteen ethnic groups, available on video in the Belize City Museum and some gift shops (see Ⓦ www.simplybelize.org).

C

CONTEXTS

Independence and the border dispute

The **UN resolution** of 1980 unequivocally endorsed Belize's right to self-determination, with all territory intact, before the next session. Further negotiations with Guatemala began but Belize's neighbour still insisted on territorial concessions. In March 1981, Britain, Guatemala and Belize released the "Heads of Agreement", which, they hoped, would result in a peaceful solution; accordingly, on September 21, 1981, Belize became an independent country within the British Commonwealth, with Queen Elizabeth II as head of state. British troops remained in Belize to ensure its territorial integrity.

The new government of Belize, formed by the PUP with George Price as premier, continued in power until 1984, when the United Democratic Party (UDP), led by **Manuel Esquivel**, won Belize's first general election. The new government encouraged private enterprise and foreign investment, and began a programme of neo-liberal economic reforms which privatized much of the public sector – unpopular changes that assured the PUP's return to power in 1989.

In 1988 Guatemala and Belize established a joint commission to work towards a "just and honourable" solution to the **border dispute**, and in 1990 Guatemala agreed in principle to accept the existing border. The only sticking point was the common boundary of the territorial waters between Belize and Honduras, making it theoretically possible for Guatemalan ships to be excluded from their own Caribbean ports. The PUP's response was to draft the **Maritime Areas Bill** in 1991, which allowed Guatemala access to the sea by restricting Belize's territory between the Sarstoon River and Ranguana Caye, sixty miles to the northeast. This measure proved acceptable to Guatemala's President Serrano, and on September 11, with just ten days to go before Belize's tenth anniversary celebrations, Guatemala and Belize established full diplomatic relations for the first time.

The air of euphoria soured somewhat during 1992 as domestic opposition to Serrano's recognition of Belize became more vocal and was challenged in Guatemala's Constitutional Court, though eventually Congress (albeit with thirteen abstentions) conditionally approved Serrano's actions. Nonetheless, in 1993 the unpopular President was overthrown and exiled; George Price hoped to gain from the uncertainty this caused in Belize and, with the UDP deeply divided, he called a snap general election. To his astonishment the gamble failed, and Manuel Esquivel's UDP was returned to office.

Negotiations were back on the table in 2002, with Belize finally agreeing to cede a sliver of land in the far northwest and to establish a joint-use area in the southern waters. The agreement also set up an **adjacency zone** either side of the border, where frontier disputes could be referred to the Organization of American States. Most Belizeans saw this as a golden opportunity to end the Guatemalan claim, for just a few square miles of unoccupied land and joint use of sea lanes – and neither country would lose face. The only problem is that in order to ratify the agreement a **referendum** has to be held in each country, with the electorate voting in favour. This would not be difficult to arrange in Belize, but most Guatemalans have only a vague idea of the border dispute, and it would require a massive education programme. The reality today is that though both countries are committed to **negotiation**, the failure to reach a watertight agreement means that the issue could resurface at any time.

Belize in the twenty-first century

The one major twenty-first century event that has the potential to dramatically alter the course of Belize's future was the discovery of **oil** at Spanish Lookout in Cayo District (see also p.134). Modest extraction began in 2005, but the country has now granted eight-year concessions for petroleum research to eighteen other companies, with the Taiwanese state *Chinese Petroleum Corporation* (OPIC) pursuing drilling exploration offshore, and US Capital undertaking seismic testing in Sarstoon Temash National Park (STNP) in coastal Toledo. A further oil field at Never Delay near Belmopan was declared commercial in January 2010, so there's clearly a good chance of more finds. Should greater oil extraction take off, it certainly puts into question Belize's position as a major centre of conservation, with much of its barrier reef declared a World Heritage Site in 1996. But there are also other pressing concerns. Commentators are rightly suggesting that the Belizean government's tiny administration does not have the resources to either monitor a domestic oil industry or to ensure that its revenues are used in the country's best interests. Furthermore, explorations in sensitive areas like Toledo risk disrupting sensitive agreements brokered over **Maya land rights**. Licences for logging and resource extraction in the 1990s were deemed to have adversely affected both local environment and culture, and a further dispute over land use will open up old wounds and divisions.

Tensions still simmer on with Guatemala, too. Peasant farmers regularly clear land just inside Belize's western border: regarded as illegal immigrants, the official policy is expulsion, while small groups of soldiers from each country also occasionally stray across the other's border. More aggravating to Belize are the numerous robberies of tourists (thankfully now vastly reduced) by Guatemalan *bandidos* around Caracol and the Mountain Pine Ridge. But in the future, it's not to be forgotten that Spanish Lookout lies squarely within border territory; with a long history of frontier disputes it remains to be seen how happy Guatemala would be to see its neighbour profiting (or not) from an oil boom.

Politically, Belize today is firmly **democratic,** with voters kicking out the incumbent government at almost every general election since independence. The nominally left-of-centre **People's United Party (PUP)** has alternated with the perceived-to-be more market-led **United Democratic Party (UDP)**. In 2003, the PUP under Prime Minister **Said Musa** proved an exception to the rule by winning an unprecedented second term in a landslide victory – though following a storm of corruption allegations including over government misuse of pension funds, the UDP were returned to power in 2008 under **Dean Barrow**. Belizean politics are both lively and divisive: the only national newspaper independent of political affiliation, the *Reporter*, regularly notes a lack of media transparency on political issues, and even intimidation of more outspoken journalists by the respective parties. In general, Belizeans are subject to a system of **political patronage** to either PUP or UDP, and while expressing discontent is allowed to a certain level, contesting your constituency party line could feasibly find you without land or services. Police shootings at a peaceful protest in **Benque Viejo** in 2003 against an increase in bus fares, together with government failure to condemn the action, demonstrated to many that while thirty percent of Belizeans live in abject poverty, human rights remain the preserve of the rich and powerful.

The booming **tourist industry**, bringing in over US$400 million a year out of Belize's US$2.3 billion GDP and employing almost a third of the country's workforce, is now the mainstay of Belize's **economy**, pushing agriculture and fisheries into a close second place. Annual growth hovers around three percent, with inflation at four percent, and unemployment a steady ten percent, while the high level of **external debt** stands at around US$1.9 billion or eighty percent of GDP. **Per capita** income is high for Central America, at about US$8400, boosted by remittances many Belizeans receive from relatives abroad. This apparent advantage is offset by the fact that many of the brightest and most highly trained citizens leave, fitting in well in English-speaking North America, though some graduates do return.

A flip side to increased tourism has been ex-pat immigration to Belize from North America and Europe. Though bringing in much needed capital, you'll hear Belizeans raise concerns about the domination of business by foreigners.

Figures are obviously not available for Belize's income from the lucrative drug trans-shipment business, but this illicit economy is certainly a sizeable fraction of the country's official income. Drug-related crime has been on the rise in Belize for thirty years – particularly in Belize City, which since 2000 has seen robberies and murders reach out-of-hand proportions, especially gang-on-gang ghetto violence. The government response has been to join Belize Defence Force (BDF) personnel with police on the city streets, and to introduce **checkpoints** on roads across the country. This increased **militarization** has yet to have an impact on crime levels, though accusations of abuse of power are commonplace – while not affecting tourists. A high murder rate also means that the **death penalty** remains popular, even though no one has been executed since 1985. The campaign to replace the British-based **Privy Council** with the **Caribbean Court of Justice** (established in 2005) as the highest court of appeal owes itself to the perception that more executions will be approved. While on the face of it removing this bastion of direct colonial authority seems a positive step, the fear in some quarters is of a lower standard of justice and an inability to uphold democratic principles.

Though Belize's traditional links with Britain and the Commonwealth countries in the West Indies remain strong, the **United States** is by far its largest trading partner and supplies much of the **foreign aid** on which Belize still depends – though multilateral organizations like the EU have also funded significant infra-structural projects. Belize has also joined the **Free Trade Area of the Americas** (FTAA), aimed at establishing the largest free trade area in the world. Concerns over a depression in agricultural prices and a manufacturing base unable to compete with imports are commonplace, though the idea that the agreement might signal an end to the **fixed rate of exchange** with the US$ has yet to be realized. The reality is that Belize is firmly linked to US designs for the region and may well have to face increasing challenges from global competition.

Chronology of the Maya

25,000 BC ▶ **Paleo-Indian** First waves of nomadic hunters from Siberia.

10,000 BC ▶ **Clovis culture** Worked stone tools found at many sites in North and Central America.

7500 BC ▶ **Archaic period** Beginnings of settled agricultural communities throughout Mesoamerica; maize and other food crops cultivated.

4500 BC ▶ **Proto-Maya period** First Maya-speaking groups settle in western Guatemala; Proto-Maya speakers probably spread throughout extent of Maya area.

2000 BC ▶ **Preclassic** or **Formative period** Early: 2000–1000 BC; Middle: 1000–300 BC; Late: 300 BC–250 AD. The Maya begin building centres which will later develop into great cities. Trade increases, and contact with the **Olmec** on the Gulf coast of Mexico brings cultural developments like the calendar and new gods. **Kaminaljuyú** dominates highland Guatemala, **El Mirador** in Petén and by 1000 BC **Lamanai** is a large city.

200 BC ▶ Earliest carved stela found in Belize: Stela 9 at Cahal Pech.

250 AD ▶ **Classic period** Early: 250–600 AD; Late: 600–850 AD. Maya culture reaches its height, with **the long count calendar** used to mark important dates on stelae and monuments. The central lowlands are thickly populated, with almost all sites flourishing. Monumental architecture develops; **Caracol** is the largest Maya city in Belize.

800 AD ▶ **Terminal Classic period** Decline (some say collapse) of Classic Maya civilization for reasons that remain unclear. Population diminishes and cities are abandoned, though some in Belize – notably **Lamanai** – survive.

987 AD ▶ Yucatán sites show strong evidence of **Toltec culture**, possibly a result of invasion. Toltec culture grafted onto Maya culture, probably extending into Belize.

1000 AD ▶ **Early Postclassic period** Re-focus of populations. Some centres, such as **Xunantunich**, which survived the Terminal Classic, are now abandoned, but many centres in Belize continue to thrive. Toltec domination of the Guatemalan highlands.

1250 ▶ Rivalry and trade among the city-states of Petén, Yucatán and Belize. New, competitive power structures formed along trade routes. **Tayasal** (near Flores) rises to dominance in Petén. Cities in the river valleys of Belize grow rich controlling trade.

1511 ▶ First **Spanish contact with Maya** in Yucatán; Spanish sailors are captured.

1521 ▶ Aztec capital Tenochtitlán falls to Spanish troops commanded by **Cortés**.

1531 ▶ **Alonso Dávila** makes first attempt to capture and settle at Chetumal.

1543 & 1544 ▶ Gaspar and Melchor **Pacheco** brutally conquer southern Yucatán and northern Belize.

1570 ▶ **Spanish mission** established at Lamanai; eight others built in northern Belize.

1697 ▶ **Conquest of the Itzá Maya** of Noh Petén (present-day Flores), the last independent Maya kingdom.

Maya life and society

For some three thousand years before the arrival of the Spanish, Maya civilization dominated Central America, with a complex and sophisticated culture. While remains of the great Maya centres, which tower above the forest roof, are testament to the scale and sophistication of Maya civilization, they offer little insight into daily life. Archeologists have instead turned to the **residential groups** that surround each site, littered with the remains of household utensils, pottery, bones and farming tools. These wattle-and-daub structures were each home to a single family, within a larger group housing the extended family who farmed and hunted together and specialized in some trade or craft. Dependent on **agriculture**, they farmed maize, beans, cacao, squash, chillies and fruit trees in raised and irrigated fields, while wild fruits were also harvested from the forest. Much of the land was communally owned and groups of around twenty men worked in the fields together. The early practice of slash-and-burn was soon replaced by more intensive farming methods to meet the needs of a growing population. Sophisticated processes of terracing, drainage and irrigation improved soil fertility, with each large city – today hemmed in by forest – once surrounded by open fields, canals and residential compounds. Most people would have bought some of their food in markets, though all households had a kitchen garden where they grew herbs and fruit.

Maize has always been the basis of the Maya **diet**, in ancient times as much as it is today. It was made into *saka*, a corn-meal gruel, which was eaten with chilli as the first meal of the day. Labourers ate a mixture of corn dough and water, and we know that *tamales* were a popular speciality. The main meal, eaten in the evenings, was similarly maize-based, probably including vegetables, and occasionally meat. As a supplement, deer, peccary, wild turkey, duck, pigeon and quail were all hunted with bows and arrows or blowguns. The Maya also made use of dogs, both for **hunting** and eating. Fish were eaten too, as the remains of fish hooks and nets have been found, and those living on the coast probably traded dried fish far inland. As well as food, the forest provided firewood, and cotton was cultivated to be dyed with natural colours and then spun into cloth.

The main sites represent larger versions of the basic residential groups, housing the most powerful families and their assorted retainers. They took on larger political, religious and administrative roles, becoming large cities. Members of royal families and nobility were accompanied by bureaucrats, merchants, warriors, architects and assorted craftsmen – an emerging **middle class**. The hierarchy was controlled by a series of hereditary positions, with a **king** (occasionally a queen) at its head, who also occupied the role of religious leader. At certain times in the calendar kings (and probably other members of the ruling class) communicated with gods and illustrious ancestors by performing ritual **blood-letting** upon themselves, as well as the sacrifice of important captives kept alive for these ceremonial celebrations.

The relationship between the cities and the land, drawn up along feudal lines, was at the heart of Maya life. **Peasant farmers** supported the ruling class by providing labour and food, and in return the elite provided leadership, direction, protection and above all else the security of their knowledge of calendrics and supernatural prophecy. This knowledge was thought to be the basis of successful agriculture, and the ruler-priests were relied upon to divine the appropriate time to plant and harvest.

In turn, the cities themselves became organized into a hierarchy, with at times a single city, such as El Mirador, Tikal or Calakmul controlling smaller sites across a vast area. A complex structure of **alliances** and rivalries bound the various sites together in an endless round of competition and conflict, and there were frequent outbursts of **open warfare**. The structure of the alliances can be traced through emblem-glyphs.

Only those of the main centres are used in isolation, while the names of smaller sites are used in conjunction with those of their larger patrons.

The Maya calendar

For both practical and mystical reasons the Maya developed a highly sophisticated understanding of arithmetic, calendrics and astronomy, all of which they believed gave them the power to predict events. Great occasions were interpreted on the basis of the **Maya calendar**, and it was this precise understanding of time that gave the ruling elite its authority. The majority of carving, on temples and stelae, records the date at which rulers were born, ascended to power, sacrificed captives and died.

The basis of all Maya **calculation** was the vigesimal counting system, which used multiples of twenty. Just three symbols were used in writing – a shell to denote zero, a dot for one and a bar for five – which you can still see on many stelae. In calculations the Maya used a slightly different notation known as the head-variant system, in which each number from one to twenty was represented by the head of a deity.

When it comes to the Maya **calendar** things start to get more complex. The basic unit of the Maya calendar was the day, or *kin*, followed by the *winal*, a group of twenty *kins* roughly equivalent to our month. In an ideal vigesimal system (as Maya arithmetic was) the next level would be four hundred *kins* – but for marking the passing of a period approximating a year the Maya used the *tun*, comprising eighteen (rather than twenty) *winals*, plus a closing month of five days, the *Uayeb*, a total of 365 days. This so-called "**vague year**", or *haab*, made it a very close approximation of the annual cycle, though of course the Maya elite knew that the solar year was a fraction over 365 days. Beyond this unit however, the passing of time was ordered in multiples of twenty, with the *katun* being twenty *tuns*.

The 260-day **sacred almanac** was used to calculate the timing of ceremonial events and as a basis for prophecy. Each day (*kin*) was associated with a particular deity that had strong influence over those born on that particular day. This calendar wasn't divided into months but had 260 distinct day names. (This system is still in use among the Cakchiquel in the highlands of Guatemala, who name their children according to its structure and celebrate fiestas according to its dictates.) These first two calendars operated in parallel so that once every 52 years the new day of the solar year coincided with the same day in the 260-day almanac, a powerful meeting that marked the end of one "**calendar round**" and the beginning of the next.

Finally, the Maya had another system for marking the passing of history, which is used on dedicatory monuments. Known as the **long count**, it's based on the "great cycle" of 13 *baktuns* (a period of 5128 years). The dates in this system simply record the number of days that have elapsed since the start of the current great cycle – dating from 3114 BC and destined to come to an end on December 21, 2012. The task

Maya time – the units

1 *kin* = 24 hours
20 *kins* = 1 *winal*, or 20 days
18 *winals* = 1 *tun*, or 360 days
20 *tuns* = 1 *katun*, or 7200 days
20 *katuns* = 1 *baktun*, or 144,000 days
20 *baktun* = 1 *pictun*, or 2,880,000 days
20 *pictuns* = 1 *calabtun*, or 57,600,000 days
20 *calabtuns* = 1 *kinchiltun*, or 1,152,000,000 days
20 *kinchiltuns* = 1 *alautun*, or 23,040,000,000 days

calls for ten different numbers, recording the equivalent of months, years, decades, centuries, etc, though in later years Maya sculptors tired of this exhaustive process and opted for an abbreviated **short count** version.

Astronomy and Religion

Alongside their fascination with time, the Maya showed a great interest in **astronomy** and devoted much energy to unravelling its patterns. Several large sites such as Copán, Uaxactún and Chichén Itzá have **observatories** carefully aligned with solar and lunar sequences; in all probability, a building or buildings in each city was dedicated to this role. With their 365-day "vague year", the Maya were just a quarter of a day out in their calculations of the solar year, while at Copán, towards the end of the seventh century AD, Maya astronomers had calculated the lunar cycle at 29.53020 days, just slightly off from our current estimate of 29.53059. In the Dresden Codex their calculations extend to the 405 lunations over a period of 11,960 days, which set out to predict eclipses. They also calculated with astonishing accuracy the movements of Venus and Mars. Venus was important as a link to success in war; there are several stelae that record the appearance of Venus prompting the decision to attack.

Maya **cosmology** is by no means straightforward; at every stage an idea is balanced by its opposite and the universe is made up of many complex layers. To the Maya, this is the third version of the earth, the previous two having been destroyed by deluges. The current version is a flat surface, with four corners, each associated with a certain colour; white for north, red for east, yellow for south and black for west, with green at the centre. Above this the sky is supported by four trees, each a different colour and species, which are also depicted as *Bacabs* – gods. At its centre the sky is supported by a ceiba tree. Above the sky is a heaven of thirteen layers, each with its own god, and the top layer overseen by an owl. However, it was the underworld, *Xibalba*, "the place of fright", which was of greatest importance, as this was where they passed after death, on the way to the place of rest. Nine layers of "hell" were guarded by "lords of the night", and deep caves were thought to connect with the underworld.

The Maya's incredible array of **gods** each had four manifestations based upon colour and direction, and many had counterparts in the underworld and consorts of the opposite sex. There were also extensive patron deities, each associated with a particular trade or class. Every activity from suicide to sex had its representative in the Maya pantheon.

The combined complexity of the Maya pantheon and calendar gave every day a particular significance, and the ancient Maya were bound up in a demanding **cycle of religious ritual**, upon which success depended. As every event, from planting to childbirth, was associated with a particular divinity, most daily events demanded some kind of religious ritual. For the most important, there were elaborate ceremonies, with the correct day carefully chosen by priests and fasting and abstinence maintained for several days beforehand. Ceremonies were dominated by the expulsion of evil spirits, the burning of incense before idols, an animal or human sacrifice and blood-letting.

In divination rituals, used to foretell the pattern of future events or to account for the cause of past events, the elite used various **drugs** to achieve altered states of consciousness. The most obvious of these was alcohol, made from fermented maize or a combination of honey and the bark of the balche tree. Wild tobacco, stronger than the modern domesticated version, was smoked. The Maya also used a range of hallucinogenic mushrooms, most importantly the *xibalbaj obox*, "underworld mushroom", and the *k'aizalah obox*, "lost judgement mushroom".

Archeology in Belize

A wealth of new material on the Maya has been unveiled by archeologists in Belize over the last couple of decades. As it emerged from siege by foreign expeditions and looters, the country has now taken control of its own archeological heritage. At least sixteen archeological teams visit Belize annually, some studying the extensive raised-field agriculture and irrigation canals in northern Belize, as well as the oldest known site so far found in the Maya world, at Cuello, near Orange Walk. Even Tikal in Guatemala, once thought to have been the centre of power of the lowland Maya, is now known to have been toppled by Caracol, the largest Maya city in Belize.

The ancient Maya sites of Belize began to be studied in the late nineteenth century, when British amateur archeologists and both British and American **museums** kept up a lively interest in artefacts. Preservation of monuments was not yet "in", and techniques were far from subtle. In some cases dynamite was used, and Belizean artefacts often found their way, unmonitored, into museums and private collections worldwide.

Since 1894 Belize's ancient monuments and antiquities have had loose legislation to protect them, but it was not until 1957 that the Belize Department of Archaeology (now called the **Institute of Archaeology**) was formed to excavate, protect and preserve these remains. Since then, excavation of hundreds of sites has been carried out by universities, museums and other institutions from the US, Canada and, to a lesser extent, Britain, always with permission from the institute. Permits are only issued to those whose proposals conform to the institute's policies and will be of benefit to the country, while the institute also now trains Belizeans to carry out archeological work, and it performs small-scale salvage excavations. The institute is also in charge of all **non-Maya historical and colonial remains**, with immovable man-made structures over one hundred years old and movable man-made items over 150 years old considered ancient monuments and artefacts respectively, under Belizean law. The responsibility of maintaining archeological sites falls to the institute, as does the safekeeping of the vast national collections. To try to stimulate the Belizean public's interest, an educational programme is also carried out, including lectures, slide shows and travelling exhibitions. The **Belize Archaeology Symposium**, held annually in July, offers the chance for all archeological teams to present their latest findings – a fascinating and well-organized event which anyone can attend; email @ia@nich belize.org for details.

With the wealth of Maya remains, it's extremely unfortunate that **looting** and the black market sale of antiquities is still prevalent. In Belize, all ancient monuments and antiquities are owned by the state, whether on private or government land or under water – residents are allowed to keep registered collections under licence, but the sale, purchase, import or export of antiquities is illegal. The law is aimed at keeping remains intact so that Belizeans and visitors alike can see the evidence of this splendid heritage.

Extensive **cave systems** form a vast network under much of inland Belize, and the Chiquibul Cave System (see p.144) contains the largest cave room in the western hemisphere. All caves discovered so far contain Maya artefacts, making them archeological sites only visitable with prior permission from the Institute of Archaeology or with a licensed tour guide. Cave tourism in Belize increases every year, and the **caves visitation policy** sets out regulations for both tourists and guides. Ancient Maya **maritime trade routes** are also a focus of recent research, with coastal sites and those on the cayes receiving more attention.

Many sites in Belize accept paying students (and often non-students): the average two- to four-week stint at a field school costs US$1100–2600. It's fascinating work, but be prepared for often arduous conditions. In addition to the projects listed below it's worth looking at the Archaeological Institute of America's website (Ⓦwww .archaeological.org), or check out *Archaeology Magazine* (Ⓦwww.archaeology.org). Earthwatch (see p.41 for details) also frequently has archeological projects in Belize. *Lamanai Outpost Lodge* (see p.85) has a field study centre. Finally, the websites Ⓦwww.mesoweb.com and www.famsi.org (Foundation for the Advancement of Mesoamerican Studies) have useful links.

Belize Fieldwork Program of Boston University Undertakes research at La Milpa, in the northwest (see p.86) and Xibun, in Cayo. Highly regarded programmes directed by Maya scholars Norman Hammond and Patricia McAnany. See Ⓦwww .bu.edu/archaeology.

Belize Postclassic Project at SUNY-Albany, New York. Long-term programme to understand social transformation of Maya populations in northern Belize after the Classic "collapse", from 1000 AD until the Spanish era. Research at the Freshwater Creek Forest Reserve. Contact Robert Rosenswig at SUNY-Albany, Ⓦwww.albany .edu/anthro/belize/belize.htm.

Belize River Archaeological Settlement Survey (BRASS) Working in the Belize River valley since 1983 and at El Pilar (see p.152) since 1993. Focuses on the new El Pilar Archaeological Reserve for Maya Flora and Fauna, emphasizing forest gardens, ceramics, drafting, computers and photography. Contact Dr Anabel Ford, MesoAmerican Research Center, University of California, Santa Barbara (Ⓦwww .marc.ucsb.edu/elpilar).

Belize Valley Archaeological Reconnaissance Project (BVAR) Conducting long-term research in the Belize River valley, particularly Baking Pot and Pook's Hill (see p.132). Students are involved in all aspects of excavation, including Maya architecture and artefact illustration. No previous experience required. See Ⓦwww.bvar.org.

Blue Creek Archaeological Project of the Maya Research Program (MRP) Conducting excavations at Blue Creek in northwestern Belize for twenty years, to better understand its role in the region. Contact Tom Guderjan (Ⓦwww.maya researchprogram.org).

Mayflower Archaeology Project Stann Creek District. Covers three Late Classic sites: Mayflower, Maintzunun and T'au Witz (see p.198). Still covered in tropical forest, much of the site is still to be excavated. Students stay in Hopkins (see p.198). Contact Wendy Brown, Social Sciences Division, College of Lake County, Grayslake, IL ☏847/543-2608, Ⓦclcpages.clcillinois.edu/home/soc050.

Minanha Archaeology Project Social Archaeology Research Program (SARP), Trent University, Canada. Focuses on ancient Maya sociopolitical interaction at Minanha, on the Vaca plateau in Cayo – between Caracol and Naranjo; students stay at *Martz Farm*. Contact Dr Gyles Iannone, Dept of Anthropology, Trent University (☏705/748-1011 ext. 1453, Ⓦwww.trentu.ca/anthropology/belize.php).

University of Texas Archaeological Field School Undertakes research at Rio Bravo, including La Milpa and Dos Hombres, where a royal tomb has been discovered. Volunteer for a minimum of one week (US$640) or enrol as a student. Contact Dr Fred Valdez, Dept of Anthropology, University of Texas at Austin, Ⓦuts.cc.utexas.edu/~marl.

Western Belize Regional Cave Project Undertakes research in Cayo, including at Actun Tunichil Muknal (see p.127), Actun Chapat ("the cave of the centipede") and other recently discovered caves. Volunteers/students must be fit and healthy and prior archeological/caving experience is preferred. Under direction of Jaime Awe of the Belize Institute. Contact Cameron Griffith, Ⓦwww.indiana.edu/~belize.

Nature and conservation

For its size, Belize has a diverse range of environments: from the coral reefs and atolls of the Caribbean coast, through lowland swamps and lagoons, up the valleys of pristine tropical rivers, to the exposed ridges of the Maya Mountains. Physically, the land increases in elevation as you head south and west; the main rivers rise in the west and flow north and east to the Caribbean.

Away from the coast, which is covered by marine sediments for 10–20km inland, the country can be roughly divided into three **geological regions**: the **northern lowlands**, a continuation of the Yucatán Platform, with Cretaceous limestone overlaid by deposits of alluvial sand; the **Maya Mountains**, where Santa Rosa quartz with granite intrusions rises to high peaks over 1000m; and **southern Belize**, where more Cretaceous limestone hills with wonderfully developed **karst features** – including caverns, natural arches and sinkholes – give way to foothills and the coastal plain. The **wildlife** is correspondingly varied; undisturbed forests provide a home to both temperate species from the north and tropical species from the south, including indigenous species unique to Belize. In winter, hundreds of native birds are joined by dozens of migrant species from the eastern seaboard of North America. The variety of land and marine ecosystems makes Belize a focus of scientific research.

Belize's impressive network of national parks, nature reserves and wildlife sanctuaries makes up over 42 percent of its land area, a feat made possible by a low population density. It's an amazing accomplishment for a developing country, and with such enlightened strategies to safeguard biodiversity, Belize has gained recognition as the most conservation-conscious country in the Americas. The success of these protected areas is due as much to the efforts of local communities as it is to governmental decisions.

The tropical forest

Belize still has over fifty percent of its **primary forest**, and across most of the country the natural vegetation is technically **tropical moist forest**, classified by average temperatures of 25°C and annual rainfall of 2000–4000mm; the only true **rainforest** lies in a small belt in the extreme southwest. More than four thousand flowering plant species can be found, including seven hundred species of tree (about the same as the whole of the US and Canada) and over two hundred varieties of orchid. Scientists have identified seventy different types of forest: thirteen percent **pine savannah** (known in Belize as "pine ridge", regardless of the elevation); nineteen percent **mangrove and coastal forest** (which includes rare **caye littoral forest**); with the remaining 68 percent **broadleaf forest** and cohune palm – commonly referred to as rainforest.

Diversity characterizes tropical forest, with each species specifically adapted to fit a particular ecological niche. This biological storehouse has yet to be fully explored, though it has already yielded some astonishing discoveries. Steroid hormones, such as cortisone, and diosgenin, the active ingredient in birth control pills, were developed from wild yams found here, while tetrodoxin, derived from a species of Central American frog, is an anaesthetic 160,000 times stronger than cocaine. But despite its size and diversity the forest is surprisingly **fragile**, forming a closed system in which nutrients are continuously recycled and decaying plant matter fuels new growth. The forest floor is a spongy mass of roots, fungi, mosses, bacteria and micro-organisms, in which nutrients are stored, broken down with the assistance of insects and chemical decay, and gradually released to the waiting roots and fresh

Conservation Strategy

In 1928 the southern tip of Half Moon Caye was established as a Crown Reserve to protect the rare red-footed booby (*Sula sula*); other bird sanctuaries were established in the 1960s and 1970s. The **Forestry Act** of 1960 focused on forest reserves, and passed primarily to protect the country's timber industry rather than for conservation. In the period since independence, the government has taken numerous measures to increase the area of land and sea under protection, including the **Wildlife Protection Act** of 1981 (amended 1991), which created closed seasons or total protection for endangered species like turtles, dolphins and manatees.

Hunting, which has long been a means of supplementing diet and income, remains a real problem in almost all reserves and protected lands; the most popular species include iguana, armadillo, hicatee (freshwater turtle), deer and the gibnut, or tepescuintle, a large rodent sometimes seen on menus.

Belize has also ratified and actively implements twenty **international environmental** agreements. Seven reserves on the Belize Barrier Reef, totalling 55 square miles, were declared World Heritage Sites in 1996: Bacalar Chico National Park, Blue Hole and Half Moon Caye Natural Monuments, South Water Caye, Glover's Reef, Sapodilla Cayes and Laughing Bird Caye. These and other protected areas form the **Belize Barrier Reef Reserve System**, which has the ultimate aim of forming a corridor of reserves from Mexico to Honduras, an aim aided by the Tulum Declaration between all four coastal countries, promoting conservation and sustainable use of the coral reef system. An even more ambitious project: the **Mesoamerican Biological Corridor** aims for an unbroken corridor of parks and wildlife refuges stretching from southern Mexico to Panama. It is hoped that international cooperation in linking the reserves will create a network of protected areas safeguarding the entire region's biodiversity.

Three government ministries in Belize shoulder most of the responsibility for conservation legislation, and ensuring compliance. The **Department of the Environment** has overall responsibility for management of the country's natural resources, while the **Fisheries Authority** monitors and enforces fishing regulations, and also manages the

seedlings. The thick canopy prevents much light from reaching the floor, ensuring that the soil remains damp but warm, a hotbed of chemical activity. The death of a large tree prompts a flurry of growth as seedlings struggle towards the sunlight. But once a number of trees are removed the soil is highly vulnerable – exposed to the harsh tropical sun and direct rainfall, an area of cleared forest becomes prone to flooding and drought. Recently cleared land contains enough nutrients for three or four years of crop growth, but soon afterwards its usefulness declines rapidly and within twenty years can become completely barren. If the trees are stripped from a large area soil erosion will silt the rivers and disrupt rainfall patterns.

Belize's forests are home to abundant **birdlife** – 574 species (260 resident) – the most visible of the country's wildlife and a huge draw for visitors. You'll be astonished by the sheer number of birds you can see just by sitting by a cabin in any one of the jungle lodges in Belize. Parrots, such as the **Aztec** and **green parakeets**, are seen every day, and you might catch a glimpse of rare species from the tiny **orange-breasted falcon** to the massive **harpy eagle**, the largest of Belize's raptors. Jewel-like **hummingbirds** feed by dipping their long bills into heliconia flowers, and their names are as fascinating as their colours: the rufous-tailed, the white-bellied emerald and the violet sabrewing, to mention just a few.

Although Belize has sixty species of **snakes**, only nine are venomous and you're unlikely to see any at all. One of the commonest is the **boa constrictor**, which is also the largest, growing up to 4m, and it poses no threat to humans. Others you might see are (venomous) **coral snakes** and (non-venomous) **false coral snakes**; you'd need to be quite skilled to tell them apart. **Frogs and toads** (collectively country's marine reserves and responsible exploitation of commercially viable species. The **Coastal Zone Management Authority and Institute** is responsible for implementing all policies that affect the use of the coastal zone and for fostering regional collaboration.

Belize's timber reserves (including all mangroves) have always been under the compass of the **Forest Department** (under the Ministry of Natural Resources and the Environment). The department's **Protected Areas Management Division** has responsibility for terrestrial protected areas and the coordination of biodiversity management. Its **Wildlife Management Programme** enforces the Wildlife Protection Act, and conservation officers have been appointed to all the country's forest reserves.

Apart from attracting tourists to Belize and providing them with information, the **Ministry of Tourism** licenses and trains the country's tour guides; you'll find the guides in Belize are highly motivated guardians of the environment. The **National Institute of Culture and History (NICH)** manages all cultural and historical features, including all **archeological sites** (which are also reserves), and has responsibility for developing appropriate tourism packages.

Government agencies have proved extremely successful in coordinating protection of the reserves, almost always with the cooperation of the private sector and a range of local and international NGOs. The dramatic increase in protected land has nonetheless posed the question of financing. The **Protected Areas Conservation Trust (PACT)** was established in 1996 and has since become an international model. The primary source of income is a conservation exit fee of Bz$ 7.50 per person, payable at all departure points. PACT also receives twenty percent of entrance fees to protected areas and fees from cruise ship passengers; a percentage is also invested in a trust fund as a long-term buffer against the vicissitudes of government funding. Other revenue is shared between government departments and voluntary organizations, but cannot be used for salaries or recurrent expenses. For more information visit PACT's excellent website, ⓦ www.pactbelize.org.

anurans) are plentiful, and at night in the forest you'll hear a chorus of mating calls. You'll also frequently find the **red-eyed tree frog** – a beautiful, pale green creature about 2–3cm long – in your shower in any rustic cabin. Giant **marine toads**, the largest in the Americas, weigh in at up to 1kg and grow to 20cm. These are infamous as the "cane toad", which caused havoc when introduced into Australia; it eats anything it can get into its capacious mouth. Like most frogs and toads it has toxic glands – a characteristic the ancient Maya employed in their ceremonies by licking these glands and interpreting the resultant hallucinations.

One thing you'll realize pretty quickly in Belize is that you're never far from an **insect**. Mostly you'll be trying to avoid or destroy them, particularly mosquitoes and sandflies. But the **butterflies** are beautiful, and you'll see clouds of them feeding at the edges of puddles on trails; the caterpillars are sometimes enormous. The largest and most spectacular are the gorgeous, electric-blue **blue morpho** and the **owl butterfly**, and you can see many more on a visit to one of a number of **butterfly exhibits**. Perhaps the most impressive of the numerous ant species are **army ants**, called the "marchin' army" in Belize, as the whole colony ranges through the forest in a narrow column voraciously hunting for insects. **Leafcutter ants** ("wee-wee ants" in Kriol) have regular trails along which they carry bits of leaves much larger than themselves – which is how they get the name "parasol ants". The leaves themselves aren't food, but they help in the growth of a fungus that the ants do eat. **Spiders** are also very common: take a walk at night with a torch and you'll see the beam reflected back by the eyes of dozens of **wolf spiders**. **Tarantulas**, too, are found everywhere – the fangs may look dangerous but tarantulas won't bite unless they're severely provoked.

The Maya Mountains

The **Maya Mountains** run southwest to northeast across south-central Belize and straddle the border with Guatemala. This wild region, covered in dense forest and riddled with caves and underground rivers, has few permanent residents. The most accessible areas are within the **Mountain Pine Ridge** (see p.138) and the **Cockscomb Basin Wildlife Sanctuary** (see p.202), home to the world's only **jaguar reserve**.

The flora and fauna, though similar to those found in the tropical forests of Guatemala, are often more prolific here as there's much less pressure on the land. Though rarely seen, the **scarlet macaw** is found in large flocks in the southern Maya Mountains and the Cockscomb Basin. All of Belize's cat species are found here, too: **Jaguars** ("tigers") range widely over the whole country, but the densest population is found in the lower elevation forests of the west; **pumas** ("red tigers") usually keep to remote ridges; **ocelots** and smaller **margays** (both spotted and called "tiger cat" in Belize, slightly larger than a domestic cat); and **jaguarundis**, the smallest and commonest – you might spot one on a trail since it hunts during the day. Belize's largest land animal, **Baird's tapir** ("mountain cow"), weighing up to 300kg, is found near water. Tapirs are endangered but not that rare in Belize, though you're unlikely to see one without a guide.

On the northern flank of the Maya Mountains, the **Mountain Pine Ridge** is a granite massif intruded into sedimentary quartz, resulting in a ring of metamorphic rock. Many of the rivers rising here fall away to the Macal and Belize river valleys, in spectacular waterfalls. On this nutrient-poor soil the **Caribbean pine** is dominant, covering sixty percent of the area; bromeliads and orchids adorn the trunks and branches, and it's a unique habitat with endemic species including frogs and a fish known only by its Latin name; trees are recovering from a severe outbreak of **pine bark beetles**.

Lowland Belize

The forests of Petén, Guatemala, extend into northwestern Belize, where low-lying topography is broken by a series of roughly parallel **limestone escarpments**. The Booth's River and Rio Bravo escarpments each have rivers that drain north to the Río Hondo. Here the **Rio Bravo Conservation and Management Area** (see p.85) protects a huge area of forest. Further east, the plain is more open; pine savannah is interspersed with slow-flowing rivers and lagoons, wetland habitats that continue to the coast. In the centre, **Crooked Tree Wildlife Sanctuary** (see p.78) covers several freshwater lagoons holding three hundred bird species, including the nesting sites of the rare jabiru stork. The tiny village of Sarteneja is the only settlement between Belize City and Corozal on the coast – holding wading birds, crocodiles (Morelet's and American) and several species of turtle, protected in **Shipstern Nature Reserve** (see p.89). Almost all the mammals of Belize – with the exception of monkeys but including jaguar, ocelot and tapir – can be found in this mosaic of coastal lagoons, hardwood forest and mangrove swamp. You might also see signs of collared and white-lipped peccaries ("warries"), brocket and white-tailed deer, opossums, weasels, porcupines and armadillos. At the **Community Baboon Sanctuary** in the lower Belize River valley (see p.75), visitors are almost guaranteed to see troops of black howler monkeys ("baboons"), or hear the male's deep-throated roar.

In the south there's only a relatively narrow stretch of lowland between the Maya Mountains and the coast. Along the navigable rivers much of the original forest has been selectively logged for mahogany and is in varying stages of regrowth after hurricane damage; other patches have been replaced by agricultural land and citrus A boat journey in **Burdon Canal Nature Reserve**, which connects the Belize and Sibun rivers to the Northern and Southern lagoons, and on into **Gales Point Wildlife Sanctuary** (see p.187), where manatees congregate, is a wonderfully rich wildlife, mangrove forest and lagoon experience.

Green **iguanas** (along with their similar cousin the spiny-tailed iguana - "wishwilly") are the most prominent of Belize's reptiles; despite protection they're still hunted for their meat and eggs. Rarer, but still fairly frequently seen, the Central American river otter is much larger than its European cousin. Along the New River and in many lagoons you'll see **Morelet's crocodiles**, which can be found in almost any body of water, and are of no danger to humans unless they're very large – at least 3m long. Previously hunted to the brink of extinction, they've made a remarkable comeback; now frequently spotted in the mangroves of Haulover Creek west of Belize City. Rivers offer great birdwatching, with several species of kingfisher alongside the tri-coloured heron, the boat-billed heron, the great egret and occasionally the two-metre tall jabiru stork.

Coastline and Barrier Reef

Belize's most exceptional environment is its **Caribbean coastline** and offshore barrier reef, dotted with hundreds of small islands and three atolls. Much of the shoreline is still covered with mangroves, which play an important role in the economy, not merely as nurseries for commercial fish species but also for their stabilization of the shoreline and their ability to absorb the force of hurricanes. Red mangrove dominates, although in due course it consolidates the seabed until it becomes more suitable for less salt-tolerant black and white mangroves. The cutting down of mangroves, particularly on the cayes, exposes the land to the full force of the sea and can mean the end of a small and unstable island.

Just inland from mangrove usually lies salt-tolerant **littoral forest**, many plants characterized by tough, waxy leaves which help conserve water. Species include red and white gumbo limbo, black poisonwood, zericote, sea grape, palmetto and of course the coconut palm, though it's not actually native and is now threatened by lethal yellowing disease. The littoral forest supports a high density of migrating birds, due to the succession of fruits and seeds, yet it also faces the highest development pressure in Belize due to its slightly higher coastal elevation; **caye littoral forest** is the most endangered habitat in the country.

The basis of the shoreline food chain is nutrient-rich mud, held in place by mangrove, while the roots themselves are home to oysters and sponges. Young stingrays cruise through the shallows adjacent to mangrove roots, accompanied by juvenile snappers, bonefish and small barracudas; you'll see the adult versions on the reef and around the cayes. The tallest mangrove forests in Belize are found along the Temash River, in **Sarstoon–Temash National Park**, with black mangroves reaching heights of 30m. From a canoe among the mangrove cayes and lagoons you can easily spot the brown pelican, white ibis or roseate spoonbill. American saltwater crocodiles are also here, rarer and larger than the Morelet's crocodile.

The mangrove lagoons are also home to the West Indian manatee. Belize has the largest manatee population in the Caribbean, estimated to be between three hundred and seven hundred, and are protected at **Corozal Bay**, **Gales Point** and **Swallow Caye** wildlife sanctuaries. Manatees can grow up to 4m in length and 450kg in weight, but are placid and shy, moving between freshwater lagoons and the open sea. Once hunted for their meat, the places where they congregate are now tourist attractions. In shallows offshore, "meadows" of seagrass beds provide nurseries for many fish and invertebrates and pasture for conch, manatees and turtles. The seagrass root system protects beaches from erosion by holding together fragments of sand and coral.

The **Western Caribbean Barrier Reef** is the longest in the western hemisphere, an almost continuous chain of coral that stretches over 350 miles from northern Quintana Roo in Mexico to the far south of Belize. For centuries the reef has been

Conservation organizations

Numerous nongovernmental **organizations** (NGOs) are active in conservation in Belize, most members of the **Belize Association of Conservation NGOs** (BACONGO), though lately differing attitudes over divisive developments like the Chalillo Dam have unfortunately opened a rift. Co-management agreements between government departments, national NGOs and local organizations play an important role in involving local communities in managing protected areas. The **Belize Audubon Society** (see below) already manages several reserves, and other reserves at the Sapodilla Cayes, Port Honduras, Gales Point and Laughing Bird Caye have co-management agreements in place. The tourism industry also plays a part. The **Belize Eco-Tourism Association** (BETA, ⓦwww.bzecotourism.org) is a small band of hotels and other businesses whose members agree to a code of ethics aiming to eliminate the use of disposable products and introduce a **"Green Listing"**, rating the environmental credentials of members.

NGOs also undertake scrutiny of government proposals, such as discussions leading to the **Lamanai Room Declaration** (Aug 1997). Signed by thirty NGOs, it sent a strong message to the government that it could not ignore their concerns over proposed developments, including damage to the reef by cruise ships and the sale of logging concessions on Maya lands in Toledo. A proposal by a Mexican company to build a "dolphin park attraction" near San Pedro caused most alarm, being a protected species in Belize, and in the end the government did not issue the necessary licence.

Organizations welcoming volunteers and students

Volunteers are often used to help carry out work, from constructing trails and camping facilities to undertaking wildlife surveys. If you're interested, contact the organizations directly, but have a look first at the general information on volunteering in Belize given on p.40. Many other organizations offer study opportunities, particularly in marine biology and conservation.

The Belize Audubon Society (BAS), founded in 1969, is the country's pre-eminent conservation organization and extremely well-respected both in Belize and internationally. While the name might suggest birdwatching as its main focus of activity, BAS is active in all aspects of nature conservation and manages nine of the country's protected areas. It also publishes a range of books, guides and fact sheets. Call in at the office to find out how to get to the various nature reserves. For details write to BAS, 12 Fort St, Belize City, call ⓣ223-5004 or visit ⓦwww.belizeaudubon.org.

The Belize Foundation for Research and Environmental Education (Bfree) was formed in 1995 by professional biologists to assist the government of Belize in the management and conservation of the rainforests as well as to coordinate and facilitate scientific research in the Bladen Nature Reserve and other protected areas in the south. Bfree welcomes interested volunteers. Contact Judy Dourson, General Manager, at ⓣ614-3896, ⓦwww.bfreebz.org.

Green Reef is dedicated to the promotion of sustainable use and conservation of Belize's marine and coastal resources. It's actively involved in implementing management plans for bird sanctuaries on the leeward side of Ambergris Caye. The organization also provides educational programmes for schools in Belize, and accepts volunteers to help with many aspects of its work. Contact Mito Paz, 100 Coconut Drive, San Pedro, Ambergris Caye (ⓣ226-2833, ⓦwww.ambergriscaye.com/greenreef).

The Programme for Belize (PFB), launched in Britain in 1989, manages over 260,000 acres in the Rio Bravo Conservation and Management Area. The programme has harvested by fishermen, in the past for manatees and turtles, but these days spiny lobsters and queen conch are the main catch; declining numbers mean they are both now protected during the breeding season.

bought land to be held in trust for the people of Belize, now managed entirely by Belizeans. For information on visiting the sites in Belize contact the PFB in Belize City (☎227-5616, ⓦwww.pfbelize.org). In the UK, the former PFB is now the **World Land Trust** (ⓦwww.worldlandtrust.org), raising funds for conservation in Belize under the title Friends of Belize and has volunteer opportunities.

The Smithsonian Institute operates a marine research station on Carrie Bow Caye, in South Water Caye Marine Reserve. It is primarily a base for marine scientists and supports the institute's Caribbean Coral Reef Ecosystems (CCRE) programme. Some of the ongoing research involves species interactions and behaviour and processes linking species and environment. Contact the Pelican Beach Resort in Dangriga for a visit. Scientists can contact the institute at the Arts and Industries Building 1163, Washington, DC 20560 (ⓔeducation@soe.si.edu, ⓦwww.si.edu/marinescience/msn) for study opportunities.

Southern Environmental Alliance co-manages Laughing Bird Caye National Park and Gladden Spit and Silk Cayes Marine Reserve, off Placencia (see p.206), and provides an environmental education programme for students from the village and four other local communities. The Friends of Nuture (FoN) office is at the south end of The Sidewalk in Placencia; call ☎523-3377 or visit ⓦwww.friendsofnaturebelize. org for volunteer opportunities.

The Toledo Institute for Development and Environment (TIDE) was formed in 1997 to focus resources and attention on the conservation of a network of protected areas in southern Toledo District, linking the Maya Mountains to the Sapodilla Cayes. TIDE, with support from The Nature Conservancy, also promotes Integrated Conservation and Development Projects (ICDPs), providing alternative sources of income for local people through tour-guiding activities such as fly-fishing and kayaking. TIDE co-manages Paynes Creek National Park and the Port Honduras Marine Reserve. Visit ⓦwww .tidebelize.org for more information and internship opportunities.

The Wildlife Care Center of Belize (WCCB), established in 1998, operates a holding facility for confiscated and rescued native wildlife, many of which have been kept illegally as pets. WCCB works in collaboration with the Forest Department's Conservation Division to raise public awareness of Belize's wildlife protection laws and to discourage the acquisition of wild animals. The WCCB is not open to the public but there are opportunities for volunteers; you'll need zoo experience, be self-funded and be able to commit for at least three months. If you're interested, email the director, Robin Brockett, see ⓦwww.wildlifebelize.com.

The Wildlife Conservation Society (WCS) works with all the countries involved in the Mesoamerican Biological Corridor to improve management of conservation lands, and to restore degraded habitat for migratory wildlife. Instrumental in establishing marine reserves throughout the barrier reef, it maintains a research station on Middle Caye, Glover's Reef, working closely with the Belize government. Visit ⓦwww.wcsgloversreef .org for volunter and research opportunities.

The Ya'axché Conservation Trust (YCT), an NGO established in 1997 and based in Toledo District, aims to promote biodiversity and sustainable economic opportunities for the Maya communities bordering the Golden Stream watershed, including furniture making. With financial and technical support from Flora and Fauna International (ⓦwww.fauna-flora.org), YCT co-manages the Golden Stream Corridor Reserve. For volunteer opportunities call ☎722-0108, or email ⓔyct_ffi@btl.net.

East of the reef are the **atolls**, roughly oval-shaped reefs rising from the seabed surrounding central lagoons. **Glover's Reef** atoll is considered to be one of the most pristine and important coral reefs in the Caribbean. Whale sharks, the largest fish in the world, are sometimes found here, gathering in large numbers to gorge on snapper eggs at **Gladden Spit**, offshore from Placencia. Beneath the water is a world of astounding colourful beauty, resembling a brilliant underwater forest. Each coral is in fact composed of colonies of individual polyps feeding off plankton. There are basically two types: hard, calcareous, reef-building corals, such as brain and elkhorn (hydrocorals), and soft corals such as sea fans and feather plumes (ococorals). You'll also find garish-pink chalice sponges, appropriately named fire corals, delicate feather-star crinoids and apartment sponges, a tall thin tube with lots of small holes.

Coral habitats are very easily damaged; human interference and increasing toxic runoff and sediment from coastal development adversely affect the already slow growth. "Coral bleaching", a symptom of extensive damage, occurs when the polyp loses some or all of the symbiotic microalgae (zooxanthellae) that live in its cells, usually in response to stress. Bleaching is often caused by above-average sea temperatures – such as that which occurred throughout the Caribbean in 1995, during the hottest decade on record. Temperatures continue to be above average, a sign of **global warming**. Recent discovery of oil and its export through Belize's maze of marine protected waters only furthers the dilemma.

The reef teems with bright **fish**, including **angel** and **parrot fish**, several species of **stingrays** and **sharks** (the most common the relatively harmless **nurse shark**), **conger** and **moray eels**, **spotted goatfish** and the striped **sergeant-major**. The sea and islands are also home to **grouper**, **barracuda**, **marlin** and the magnificent **sailfish**. Dolphins are frequently seen just offshore, mostly Atlantic **bottle-nosed**, though further out large schools of **spotted dolphins** are sometimes found. Belize's three species of **marine turtles**, the loggerhead, the green and the hawksbill, occur throughout the reef, nesting on isolated beaches. These are infrequently seen, and still hunted for food during a limited open season.

Above the water, the cayes have a wealth of birdlife, providing protection from predators and surrounded by an inexhaustible food supply. At **Half Moon Caye**, right out on the eastern edge of the reef, there's a reserve protecting a breeding colony of four thousand **red-footed boobies**, and you'll also see frigate birds, ospreys and mangrove warblers, among 98 species.

Current conservation issues

One of the most vociferous and contentious "conservation or development" debates has focused on the **Chalillo Dam project**, where a hydro-electric dam on the upper Macal River has flooded a beautiful valley that's not only ideal habitat for Baird's tapirs and a threatened subspecies of the scarlet macaw, but also contains unexcavated and undocumented Maya sites. The flooding has damaged legally designated protected areas and may also contravene international conservation conventions to which Belize is a signatory. After years of determined and often bitter opposition by environmentalists and activists, the dam proposal was given the go-ahead in 2004, despite the developers, Fortis, having been shown in court to have erased geological fault lines on a map submitted as part of the Environmental Impact Assessment (EIA). Recently, the dam that was built to save Belizeans money on their energy bills has done anything but: Fortis raised rates twelve percent in 2005 and another thirteen percent in 2006. The dam controversy highlights the perpetual problem in Belize of balancing conservation with improving infrastructure. For the latest news visit ⊛www.stopfortis.org.

Today the hottest topic on the conservation agenda is opposition to the meteoric rise in the number of **cruise ships** and their passengers to Belize's shores. The scale of increase in these arrivals is staggering: from just a few hundred passengers per year in the late 1990s to a peak of over 850,000 in 2004. Although the government's **Cruise Ship Policy Document** states a recommended upper limit of eight thousand cruise ship visitors per day, this limit is regularly exceeded with impunity. Visitor pressure at many archeological sites and certain cayes already exceeds carrying capacity many times over, leading to destructive trampling and environmental degradation. Other current issues include the **de-reservation** of protected areas, and the proposal to build a large tourism facility on Tom Owen's Caye, a tiny outcrop of rock in the Sapodilla Cayes Marine Reserve. The government has also allowed **oil exploration** in several protected areas, such as Sarstoon-Temash National Park, which encompasses fourteen rare and diverse ecosystems and supports indigenous Maya communities. BETA, BACONGO and several other conservation and tourism organizations are joining forces to resist these and other potentially damaging and unsustainable developments which may hurt Belize's world-renowned record of sound environmental stewardship.

Further undermining its country's natural splendour, the government actively sells remote cayes and other lands to foreign investors and Belizeans returning from overseas. **Mangrove-cutting** by resort developers is technically illegal, though fines are rarely imposed, and construction continues at an unprecedented rate all over the country. Currently, the rapid development of the Placencia Peninsula, including a new international airport and numerous resorts and marinas, threatens the whole area's ecology.

Music

For such a tiny country, Belize enjoys an exceptional range of musical styles and traditions. Whether your tastes run to the wind melodies and percussion of the Maya, the up-tempo punta rock of the Garifuna or to calypso, *marimba*, brukdown, soca or steel pan, Belize is sure to have something to suit. Some visitors still complain about the noisiness of Belizean society and the volume at which the music is played, but if you can get into it, it's one of the quickest ways to the heart of Belizeans and their culture. For a current list of the best of Belize's recorded music, check out **Stonetree's website**, ®www.stonetreerecords.com.

Roots and Kriol sounds

Until the demise of the Maya civilization and the arrival of the Spanish, the indigenous **Maya** of Belize played a range of instruments drawn almost entirely from the flute and percussion families. Drums were usually made from hollowed logs covered in deerskin, with rattles, gourd drums and turtle shells providing further rhythmic accompaniment. Trumpets, bells, shells and whistles completed the instrumentation. However, as befits a nation of immigrants, each new group arriving – the Europeans, the Creoles, the mestizos and the Garifuna – brought with them new styles, vigour and variety which today inform and influence popular culture.

Mestizo music combined elements of its two constituent cultures: Maya ceremonial music and new instruments from Spain, such as the classical guitar and violin, and later brass band music. Mestizo communities (including the Mopan Maya) in the north and west of the country continue to favour **marimba** bands: half-a-dozen men playing two large, multi-keyed wooden xylophones, perhaps supported by a double bass and a drum kit. Up to half-a-dozen bands play regularly in Cayo District: famed healer Eligio Panti presided over the nation's pre-eminent *marimba* group, **Alma Beliceña**, while leading *marimba* bands frequently pop over from Flores in Guatemala, and Mexican **mariachi** bands occasionally make an appearance, too. Nonetheless, traditional mestizo music remains under threat as the youth turn to rock, rap and punta. Traditional artists to look out for include **Pablo Collado**, a Maya-mestizo master flautist/guitarist, and **Florencio Mess**, a harpist maintaining a centuries-old Maya tradition; his *Maya K'ekchi' Strings* (Stonetree) is an essential album.

Europeans introduced much of the hardware and software for playing music: "western" musical instruments and sheet music, and, much later, record players, compact discs and massive sound systems. From the mid-nineteenth century onwards, British colonial culture, through church music, military bands and the popular music of the time, was able to exert a dominant influence over what was acceptable music in Belize.

An exciting melange of **West African rhythms** and melodies, as well as drums and stringed instruments, arrived in Belize as a result of the slave trade during the eighteenth century. However, given that the Baymen purchased slaves from **Jamaica** rather than directly from Africa it should be remembered that African influences arrived indirectly.

A new, syncretic style, nurtured in the logging camps and combining Western instrumentation with specifically African musical inflections, emerged in the late nineteenth century to create a specifically Belizean musical tradition known as "**brukdown**". Featuring a modern line-up of guitar, banjo, accordion, drums and the jawbone of an ass (rattling a stick up and down the teeth!), brukdown remains a potent reminder of past **Creole** culture. Although the style is slowly fading, as Creole society itself changes, there are a few active practitioners. The style's most prominent figure,

Andy Palacio

For over two decades **Andy Palacio** influenced, dominated and even helped produce the modern Belizean sound. The country's only truly professional star and music ambassador, his sudden death, due to a heart condition, en route to a show in the US in 2008 shocked and saddened the entire nation. Over the years Palacio succeeded in incorporating a diversity of national and regional styles into a unique popular sound, a consummate performer who established an enviable reputation for producing catchy melodies accompanied by articulate, astute and entertaining lyrics, underpinned by unique Garifuna rhythms. Named "UNESCO Artist for Peace" in 2007, it was his pre-eminent final album, *Watina*, firmly based on his Garifuna roots, that catapulted him into the annals of "World Music" stardom, winning him World Music Album of the Year as well as the BBC Radio 3 award in January 2008, shortly before he died.

Born in Barranco, he grew up in the rural cosmopolitanism of Garifuna, Maya and mestizo communities, integrating a diversity of linguistic and cultural influences from an early age. As a teenager in the 1970s he experienced first-hand the new Belizean cultural nationalism of the PUP party, which brought the country to independence, introducing a broader ideological dimension to his inevitable cultural affinity with the Garifuna musical tradition. The break came in 1987 when, on an exchange visit to London, he spent a year picking up the latest recording techniques and honing his compositional skills. He returned triumphantly to Belize a year later with enough equipment to open a studio, also bringing with him several London recordings of the songs that would become huge hits back home and transform the music scene.

The biggest song was undoubtedly the 1988 hit **Bikini Panti** – an English-Garifuna, punta-rock satire on Belize's burgeoning tourist business – which set a new musical and lyrical standard. But if *Bikini Panti* was the dancefloor killer, it was **Me Goin' Back** that provided the clear ideological expression of the new national sensitivity, as the almost calypsonian lyrics demonstrate:

> Now don't buss your brains wonderin what me goin' back to: Rice 'n Beans and a Belikin, Friends FM and a dollar chicken, Pine Ridge and a Swing Bridge, Brukdown, Punta Rock, Sunshine and a cashew wine, Belize Times and Amandala, Maya, Creole and the Garifuna

Palacio's longstanding collaboration with Ivan Duran at Stonetree Records saw three other major releases: *Keimoun* and *Til Da Mawnin* are two great danceable albums displaying a mastery of punta and incorporating Latin and Anglophone Caribbean sounds. *Watina*, recorded with the **Garifuna Collective**, is a more thoughtful and melodic recollection of his origins, featuring master *parranderos* Aurelio and **Paul Nabor**. For more information, visit ⓦwww.stonetree.com.

master accordionist **Wilfred Peters** (now in his late seventies and still playing), is the founder of the nationally celebrated **Mr. Peters and his Boom and Chime**, and has composed countless classics and performed to audiences in festivals around the world; any of his albums represent a musical journey through Creole culture. Generally, though, brukdown is recreational music best enjoyed in the Creole villages of Burrell Boom, Hattieville, Bermudian Landing and Isabella Bank.

Brad Patico, an accomplished guitarist and singer-songwriter, similarly does his best to keep the Creole folksong tradition alive from his base in Burrell Boom – his recordings can still be found in Belizean record stores. Originating from the same cultural roots, and equally conscious of a disappearing musical past, is Brother David Obi, better known as **Bredda David**, the creator of **kungo music**, a mixture of musical styles that includes the traditional Creole music of Belize and the pulsating drum rhythms of Africa. A skilful musician and songwriter, David still plays occasionally in Belize City with his **Tribal Vibes** band; look out for album *Raw*

(Stonetree), where rock guitars are overlaid on new-generation Belizean rhythm with lyrical kungo wit.

Currently the best-known singer seen to preserve traditional Creole folksong is **Leela Vernon** from Punta Gorda, who plays to highly appreciative audiences at national festivals, often appearing with long standing pop bands, including **Youth Connection**, **Gilharry 7** and **Santino's Messengers**. Her most famous song, "Who say Creole gat no culture?" is a national favourite amongst older people and a reminder of pride in Belizean society. Two recordings containing some of these artists are: **Various Artists** *Belize City Boil Up* (Stonetree/Contemporary Electronic Systems/Numero Group) – a sample of pre-Independence Belize, featuring remastered recordings from the 50s, 60s and 70s, alive with cool jazz, smooth rhythm and blues and even some psychedelic funk – and **Various Artists** *Celebration Belize* (Belize Arts Council), including contributions from Andy Palacio, Mr. Peters, Leela Vernon, Florencio Mess and many others.

More recently, the African elements in Creole music have been expressed through wider **pan-Caribbean** styles like calypso, reggae, soca and rap. **Calypso** enjoyed a brief period of pre-eminence – Belize's most famous calypsonian **Lord Rhaburn** is still occasionally to be seen as a special guest at official functions, increasingly rare performances that shouldn't be missed. In terms of today's popular music, California-based Belizean conscious-reggae outfit **Caribbean Pulse** (ⓦ www.caribbeanpulse .com) is making good headway with recent collaborations featuring reggae luminaries Tony Rebel and Damian Marley. Proving that Belizean musicians are breaking boundaries beyond drums and roots is Belize City-born **MKL**, alias Michael Lopez, a New York touring DJ and producer whose sound encompasses soul, jazz, dub and laidback electronics. Back in Belize City, dub poet **Leroy Young the Grandmaster** offers a powerful commentary and new Creole style featuring a wide range of roots rhythms and strings; look out for the album *Just Like That* (Stonetree).

Punta and the Garifuna

If traditional Maya, mestizo and Creole styles retain only a fragile hold on popular musical consciousness, it is the Garifuna who have been catapulted to centre-stage over the last two decades with the invention and development of **punta rock**. The key musical developments that led to punta rock were the amplification of several traditional **drum rhythms** originally associated with courtship dances, while keeping faith with other traditional instruments such as the turtle shell – and initially the almost universal aversion to singing in anything but Garifuna. Although many master musicians and cultural nationalists (both from Belize and the other Garifuna communities across Central America) pushed Garifuna culture forward, particular recognition must go to master drummer and drum-maker **Isabel Flores** and the enigmatic singer, guitarist and artist **Pen Cayetano** in Dangriga. Pen pioneered popular Garifuna music, widening the scope of punta with the introduction of electric guitars and helping to spark a new cultural assertiveness that saw dozens of younger musicians take up the challenge. His **Turtle Shell Band** set the standard (*Beginning*, the first-ever punta rock recording in 1982), and within a few years other electric bands – including **Sounds Incorporated**, **Black Coral**, **Jeff Zuniga**, **Mohubub**, **Aziatic** and **Titiman Flores** consolidated punta's popularity. Titiman's album *Fedu* (Stonetree), is a punta rock party album to control the dancefloor from beginning to end. Above all, however, **Andy Palacio** (see box, p.269) developed to become Punta Rock's most famous star; the seminal compilation *Punta Rockers* (1988) featured recordings by Andy and several other pioneers. Credit should also be given to Dangriga-based **Al Obando** in the development of the punta rock sound. As Belize's pre-eminent sound engineer, Obando produced the hugely popular band the **Punta Rebels** through the 1990s and is still relied upon for studio recordings today.

Guardians of more orthodox arrangements, **Lugua and the Larubeya Drummers** marked their debut with the release of *Bumari* (Stonetree, 1997), covering the full range of roots Garifuna drumming styles alongside powerful call and response vocals – a telling reminder of the African influence in Garifuna history. Recently there has also been a resurgence of the traditional Garifuna style of **parranda**, performed with acoustic guitars, drums and shakers. This was marked by the international release of the eponymous album, recorded by various *parranderos* living in Belize, Honduras and Guatemala. It is recognized as being one of the best collections to come out of Central America. This movement grows stronger with recent releases – one by Belize-produced Honduran **Aurelio Martínez** (*Garifuna Soul*), demonstrating soulful vocals over a rich blend of Latin, punta and *parranda* rhythms, and another by **The Garifuna Women's Project**, featuring wonderful soulful voices from coastal villages in Belize, Guatemala and Honduras. Another record to look for is **Various Artists** *PARRANDA: Africa in Central America* (Stonetree/Warner Classics) – three generations of Garifuna incorporating drumming, American blues, Cuban *son* and West African guitar.

Additionally, several young Garifuna stars from Dangriga have emerged to take the nation by storm, combining fast infectious punta with reggae dancehall and soca in highly energized performances. This is punta rock for the young generation, relying largely on **sound systems**, often at the expense of live musicians. Former Punta Rebel **Super G** is the main exponent and can be found performing regularly. Showing an awareness of the wider market potential in Guatemala and Mexico, Super G now also sings in Spanish and includes **cumbia** numbers on his albums – a Latin style highly popular amongst young mestizos. Increasingly often these punta rock stars make the trip across the borders to rapturous audiences in Chetumal and Flores, demonstrating the position of Belize both as a major regional music producer and as a bridge between Caribbean and Latin America.

Special events

Perhaps the best times to hear and see the full panoply of Belizean musical culture are the various national events that regularly punctuate the social calendar. Biggest and best are **National Day/St George's Caye Day** (Sept 10) and **Independence Day** (Sept 21) – dates that mark almost two weeks of festivities as Belize City comes close to the spirit and atmosphere of Caribbean carnival. In fact, between these dates there's a genuine **Carnival**, established only since independence but a hugely popular event, with an enormous street parade, floats, a carnival queen attended by a bevy of princesses and, of course, bands and sound systems. Block parties, "jump-ups" and late-night revelry characterize what are popularly known as the "**September Celebrations**". On Independence Day, Eve Street (leading to the BTL Park) is closed to traffic and the country's top bands and sound systems line the parade route and perform on stages in the park.

The **Costa Maya Festival**, held in San Pedro during the third week of August, is a celebration of dance, music and culture that attracts performers from Mexico and throughout Central America. **Garifuna Settlement Day** (Nov 19) brings huge crowds to Dangriga, where **Puntafest** – a long weekend of late nights, rum and rhythm – is a must-attend event. The **National Agricultural Show**, held just outside Belmopan in May, gathers together up to fifty thousand people over three days for all things agricultural and recreational. Almost all the country's top artists, bands and sound systems will appear at some stage during the weekend.

Mestizo communities celebrate with a number of Latin-type **fiestas**: bands, funfairs, sports and competitions, usually held around Easter. The week-long **Flores Fiesta**, held in mid-January across the border in Guatemala, is also great fun, with many Belizean artists performing alongside Guatemalan acts.

Books

The Belize Audubon Society (see p.264) offers a mail-order service for environmental titles, while Cubola Productions is Belize's pre-eminent publisher, with a wide range of specialist books; see ⓦwww.cubola.com. Angelus Press in Belize City also offers a mail-order service; see ⓦwww .angeluspress.com. Many books are published only in Belize; o/p means out of print, though these are still available online.

Travel, literature, society and environment

Rosita Arvigo with Nadia Epstein *Sastun: My Apprenticeship with a Maya Healer.* A rare glimpse into the indigenous wisdom of Maya *Curandero* Eligio Panti, which ensures the survival of generations of healing knowledge. *Rainforest Remedies: One Hundred Healing Herbs of Belize* was co-authored with Michael Balick of the New York Botanical Garden.

🏃 **If Di Pin Neva Ben: Folktales and Legends of Belize** (Cubola, Belize). A vibrant collection of traditional Belizean folklore, capturing a rich society that fluidly blends its different ethnic cultures. Other Cubola anthologies include *Snapshots of Belize* and *Ping Wing Juk Me*, six short plays which revive the Kriol theatrical tradition.

Les Beletsky *Belize and Northern Guatemala – The Ecotraveller's Wildlife Guide.* A reasonably comprehensive single-volume guide to mammals, birds, reptiles, amphibians and marine life, with illustrations.

Zee Edgell *Beka Lamb.* A girl's account of growing up in 1950s Belize alongside the problems of the independence movement. Explores everyday life, matriarchal society and the influence of the Catholic Church. Edgell's *In Times Like These* is an autobiographical account of the intrigues leading up to independence.

Byron Foster *Heart Drum and Spirit Possession in the Garifuna Community of Belize* (Cubola, Belize). Two slim volumes focusing on Garifuna

spirituality and the experience of spirit possession, as described to Foster, an anthropologist. Foster's *The Baymen's Legacy: A Portrait of Belize City* is approachable and interesting, while *Warlords and Maize Men – A Guide to the Maya Sites of Belize* is an excellent handbook to fifteen of the country's most accessible archeological sites.

H. Lee Jones *Birds of Belize.* Comprehensive guide to all 574 species so far recorded in Belize. Highly praised by the experts, this excellent book is written by a resident biologist. It includes 234 range maps and superb colour illustrations by Dana Gardner.

🏃 **Emory King** *Belize 1798, The Road to Glory* (Tropical Books, Belize). Rip-roaring historical novel on the Battle of St George's Caye, King's (see p.57) enthusiasm is supported by meticulous research. Also by the author: *Hey Dad, This Is Belize* is a hilarious account of family life; *I Spent It All In Belize*, an anthology of satirical articles on the pomposity of officialdom; and *The Great Story of Belize*, four slim volumes full of larger-than-life characters present a vivid account of Belize's history.

Carlos Ledson Miller *Belize – A Novel.* Fast-paced historical saga of a Central American father and his two sons – one American and one Belizean. From the eve of Hurricane Hattie in 1961, the reader is transported forty years through colonial unrest to present-day turbulence.

Jeremy Paxman *Through the Volcanoes* (o/p). A political travel account investigating the turmoil of Central America and finding solace in the calm of Costa Rica. Takes in seven countries including Belize, and offers a good overview of the region's politics and history in the mid-1980s.

Alan Rabinowitz *Jaguar*. A personal account of studying jaguars for the New York Zoological Society in the 1980s, living with a Maya family at Cockscomb. Rabinowitz was instrumental in the establishment of the Jaguar Reserve in 1984.

John Lloyd Stephens *Incidents of Travel in Central America, Chiapas, and Yucatán*. A classic nineteenth-century traveller, Stephens was American ambassador to Central America: while republics fought it out he was wading through the jungle stumbling across ancient cities. Written with superb Victorian pomposity and great illustrations of Maya sites.

Ronald Wright *Time Among the Maya*. A vivid, sympathetic and humorous account of travels in the late 1980s from Belize through Guatemala, Chiapas and Yucatán, meeting the Maya and exploring their obsession with time. Also investigates the violence that occurred throughout the 1980s. Superb historical insights.

Colville Young *Creole Proverbs of Belize* (Cubola, Belize). A wonderful compilation of oral folk-wisdom, written by the distinguished linguist and present governor general. Sayings and proverbs are written in Kriol and English, and then explained. See also *Pataki Full*, an anthology of Belizean short stories.

History and archeology

The Popol Vuh. The great creation myth poem of the K'iche' (Quiche) Maya of the Guatemalan highlands, written shortly after the conquest and intended to preserve the K'iche' people's knowledge of their history. It's an amazing swirl of fantastic gods and mortals who become gods. The best version is translated by Dennis Tedlock.

Readings in Belizean History (various authors; St John's College Press, Belize). Updated version of a highly acclaimed textbook, with essays by Belizean scholars offering deep insights.

O. Nigel Bolland *Colonialism and Resistance in Belize: Essays in Historical Sociology* (Cubola, Belize/UWI Press) The 2003 edition is a comprehensive academic study of Belize, covering colonization, slavery and the progress of Creole culture and nationalism with an emphasis on labour. A compelling and convincing analysis.

Michael Coe *The Maya*. Now in its seventh edition, this clear and comprehensive guide to Maya archeology is the best on offer.

David Drew *The Lost Chronicles of the Maya Kings*. Readable and engaging; an up-to-date account of ancient Maya political history with alliances and rivalries skilfully unravelled, and a revealing analysis of late Classic Maya power struggles.

Joyce Kelly *An Archaeological Guide to Northern Central America*. Practical guide to Maya sites and museums in four countries; an essential companion for travelling the Maya world. Still the most detailed guide available to the Maya sites of Belize, if slightly dated.

Simon Martin and Nikolai Grube *Chronicle of the Maya Kings and Queens*. Highly acclaimed work based on new epigraphic studies and re-readings of glyphs. Historical records of key Maya cities like Tikal and

Caracol, plus biographies of 152 kings and four queens, and all the key battles.

Heather McKillop *Salt: White Gold of the Ancient Maya*. A groundbreaking work demonstrating that the salt traded throughout the great lowland Maya cities was produced on the coast of Belize, at previously unknown underwater sites.

John Montgomery *Tikal: An Illustrated History of the Ancient Maya Capital*. The most readable book on Tikal, packed with fascinating history and general information, with a chronology of major Maya events. His other books include *A Dictionary of Maya Hieroglyphs*.

Assad Shoman *Thirteen Chapters of a History of Belize* (Angelus Press, Belize). A treatment of the country's history by a Belizean who's not afraid to engagingly examine colonial myths. Active in party politics, the author has written a number of other political titles.

Language

Language

Language

English is the official language of Belize and naturally enough it's spoken everywhere. However, it's really the first language of only a small percentage of Belize's population, since seven main languages are spoken here, including the Mopan, Yucatec and Kekchí Maya dialects. For at least half the population, mainly the mestizos in the north and the west, **Spanish** is the language spoken at home and in the workplace. The last thirty years have seen a large increase in spoken Spanish due to immigration from neighbouring countries. If you plan to cross the border into **Guatemala** to visit Tikal, some Spanish will be essential.

The first language of one third of the population – mainly the Creole people – is **Kriol** (the modern favoured spelling, though still often spelt "Creole"), a language partly derived from English and similar to the languages spoken in other parts of the Caribbean colonized by the British. Kriol is the **most widely spoken** language in Belize. English and Kriol are the languages used in public or official situations and for speaking to outsiders. That said, listening to conversations can be confusing, as people switch from, say, English to Kriol to Spanish to Garifuna and back – often in the same sentence.

Many **Garifuna** continue to speak their own tongue as their first language, although the only village where *everyone* does this is Hopkins (see p.198). The **Mennonites** add to the linguistic cocktail with their old form of High German, and the jigsaw puzzle is completed by recent immigrants from Asia speaking Chinese and south Asian languages.

Kriol

Kriol is the *lingua franca* of Belize: whether someone's first language is Maya, Spanish, Garifuna or English, they'll almost always be able to communicate in Kriol. It may sound like English from a distance and as you listen to a few words you'll think that their meaning is clear, but as things proceed you'll soon realize that complete comprehension is out of reach; though those familiar with other English dialects may find understanding easier. It's a beautifully warm, expressive and relaxed language, typically Caribbean, with a vocabulary loosely based on English but with significant differences in pronunciation and a grammatical structure that is distinctly West African in origin. One characteristic is the heavy nasalization of some vowels, for example *waahn* (want) and *frahn* (from).

Written Kriol, which you'll see in some newspaper columns and booklets, is a little easier to come to grips with, though you'll need to study it hard at first. A dictionary is available from some bookstores (Crosbie, Paul, editor, 2007, a Kriol-Inglish dikshineri), which also explains the grammar, though Kriol will always be much more of a spoken language than a written one.

Only in recent years has Kriol begun to be **recognized** as a distinct language, though there is still much debate as to whether it is just a dialect of English. In **colonial times** Kriol was not accepted as a legitimate language and its use was prohibited in schools, although in practice teachers often lapsed into it. But Kriol always remained the language of the people at home and at work, an integral part of culture and identity. **Independence** brought a growing pride in the language and today a movement is formalizing Kriol, aiming to recognize it as one of Belize's national languages.

For a long time Kriol was solely an **oral language**, but by the 1970s some writers and poets were writing it using ad hoc spelling. In 1980 Sir Colville Young – at that time a school principal and today Governor General of Belize – published his *Creole Proverbs of Belize*, and in 1993 a group of educators and enthusiasts started the **Belize Kriol Project** to work on developing it into a written language. The **National Kriol Council** was formed in 1995 with the aim of promoting the culture and language of the Creole people of Belize. A standardized writing system using a phonemic structure has since been developed and, despite some controversy, is gradually gaining acceptance. Some tips on spoken and written Kriol are available at Ⓦwww.belizeanjourneys.com (Kriol section supplied by John Stewart).

Useful phrases and proverbs

Excuse me, where is the post office?	Eksyooz mi, weh di poas aafis deh?
Where do I catch the bus to Dangriga?	Weh fu kech di bos tu Dangriga?
Do you have any rooms free?	Yu gat eni room fu rent?
How much is a single room?	How moch wahn singl room kaas?
I have some dirty laundry for washing.	Ah gat sohn doti kloaz fu wash.
Is there a restaurant near here serving Creole food?	Weh sel Kriol food kloas tu ya?

Proverb	Literal translation	Meaning
Mek di man weh loos taiga tai ahn bak.	*Let the man who loosed the tiger tie it back.*	Let the man who created a dangerous situation deal with it.
Fish geh kech bai ih own mowt.	*A fish gets caught by its own mouth.*	Guilt often gives itself away.
Kyaahn kech Hari, kech ih shot.	*If you can't catch Harry, catch his shirt.*	If you can't get what you want, get the next best thing.

Spanish

The **Spanish** spoken in both Guatemala and Belize has a strong Latin American flavour; if you're used to the intonation of Madrid or Granada then it may be a surprise to hear the soft "s" replaced by a crisp and clear version. If you're new to Spanish it's a lot easier to pick up than the Iberian version.

The rules of **pronunciation** are straightforward and strictly observed. Unless there's an accent, words ending in d, l, r and z are **stressed** on the last syllable, all others on the second last. All **vowels** are pure and short.

A somewhere between the "a" sound of back and that of father.

E as in get.

I as in police.

O as in hot.

U as in rule.

C is soft before "e" and "i", hard otherwise: *cerca* is pronounced serka.

G works the same way, a guttural "h" sound (like the *ch* in loch) before "e" or "i", a hard "g" elsewhere: *gigante* becomes higante.

H always silent.

J the same sound as a guttural "g": *jamón* is pronounced hamon.

LL sounds like an English "y": *tortilla* is pronounced torteeya.

N as in English unless it has a tilde (accent) over it, when it becomes "ny": *mañana* sounds like manyana.

QU is pronounced like an English "k".

R is rolled, RR doubly so.

V sounds more like "b", *vino* becoming beano.

X is slightly softer than in English – sometimes almost "s" – except between vowels in place names where it has an "h" sound – ie Mexico (Meh-hee-ko) or Oaxaca (Wa-ha-ka). Note: in Maya the English letter "x" is pronounced "*sh*", thus *Xunantunich* is Shunan-tun-eech.

Z is the same as a soft "c", so *cerveza* becomes servesa.

Although we've listed a few essential words and phrases, some kind of dictionary or **phrasebook** is a worthwhile investment: the *Rough Guide to Mexican Spanish* is the best practical guide, correct and colloquial, and certainly acceptable for most purposes when travelling in Guatemala. One of the best small Latin American Spanish dictionaries is the University of Chicago version (Pocket Books); the Collins series (published by HarperCollins) of pocket grammars and dictionaries is also excellent.

Basics

please, thank you	por favor, gracias
where...?	¿dónde...?
when...?	¿cuando...?
what...?	¿qué...?
how much is it?	¿cuánto cuesta?
here, there	aquí, allí
this, that	esto, eso
now, later	ahora, más tarde
open, closed	abierto/a, cerrado/a
with, without	con, sin
good, bad	buen(o)/a, mal(o)/a
big, small	gran(de), pequeño/a
more, less	más, menos
today, tomorrow	hoy, mañana
yesterday	ayer

Greetings and responses

hello, goodbye	hola, adios
Good morning	Buenos días
Good afternoon/night	Buenas tardes/noches
How do you do?	¿Qué tal?
See you later	Hasta luego
Sorry	Lo siento/disculpeme
Excuse me	Con permiso/perdón
How are you?	¿Cómo está (usted)?
Not at all/You're welcome	De nada
I (don't) understand	(No) Entiendo
Do you speak English?	¿Habla (usted) inglés?

I (don't) speak Spanish	(No) Hablo español
What (did you say)?	¿Mande?
My name is...	Me llamo...
What's your name?	¿Cómo se llama?
I am English	Soy inglés(a)
...American	...americano(a)
...Australian	...australiano(a)
...Canadian	...canadiense(a)
...Irish	...irlandés(a)
...Scottish	...escosés(a)
...Welsh	...galés(a)
...New Zealander	...neozelandés(a)

Needs, accommodation and transport

I want...	Quiero...
Do you know...?	¿Sabe...?
I'd like...	Quisiera... por favor
I don't know	No sé
There is (is there?)	Hay (?)
(one like that)	(uno así)
Do you have...?	¿Tiene...?
...the time	...la hora
...a room	...un cuarto
...with two beds	...con dos camas
...with a double bed	...con cama matrimonial
It's for one person (two people)	Es para una persona (dos personas)
...for one night (one week)	...para una noche (una semana)

279

It's fine, how much is it?	¿Está bien, cuánto es?
It's too expensive	Es demasiado caro
Don't you have anything cheaper?	¿No tiene algo más barato?
Can one...?	¿Se puede...?
...camp (near) here?	¿...acampar aquí (cerca)?
Is there a hotel nearby?	¿Hay un hotel aquí cerca?
How do I get to...?	¿Por dónde se va a...?
Left, right, straight on	Izquierda, derecha, derecho
Where is...?	¿Dónde está...?
...the nearest bank	...el banco más cercano (*ATM is cajero automático*)
...the post office	...el correo
...the toilet	...el baño/sanitario
Where does the bus to...leave from?	¿De dónde sale el camión para...?
What time does it leave (arrive in)...?	¿A qué hora sale (llega en)...?
What is there to eat?	¿Qué hay para comer?
What's that?	¿Qué es eso?
What's this called?	¿Cómo se llama?

Numbers

1	un/uno/una
2	dos
3	tres
4	cuatro
5	cinco
6	seis
7	siete
8	ocho
9	nueve
10	diez
11	once
12	doce
13	trece
14	catorce
15	quince
16	dieciséis
17	diecisiete
18	dieciocho
19	diecinueve
20	veinte
21	veintiuno
30	treinta
40	cuarenta
50	cincuenta
60	sesenta
70	setenta
80	ochenta
90	noventa
100	cien(to)
101	ciento uno/una
200	doscientos/as
500	quinientos/as
700	setecientos
1000	mil
1999	mil novecientos noventa y nueve
2000	dos mil
first	primero/a
second	segundo/a
third	tercero/a
fifth	quinto/a
tenth	décimo/a

Days

Monday	Lunes
Tuesday	Martes
Wednesday	Miércoles
Thursday	Jueves
Friday	Viernes
Saturday	Sábado
Sunday	Domingo

Travel store

Travel

Andorra The Pyrenees, Pyrenees & Andorra Map, Spain

Antigua The Caribbean

Argentina Argentina, Argentina Map, Buenos Aires, South America on a Budget

Aruba The Caribbean

Australia Australia, Australia Map, East Coast Australia, Melbourne, Sydney, Tasmania

Austria Austria, Europe on a Budget, Vienna

Bahamas The Bahamas, The Caribbean

Barbados Barbados DIR, The Caribbean

Belgium Belgium & Luxembourg, Bruges DIR, Brussels, Brussels Map, Europe on a Budget

Belize Belize, Central America on a Budget, Guatemala & Belize Map

Benin West Africa

Bolivia Bolivia, South America on a Budget

Brazil Brazil, Rio, South America on a Budget

British Virgin Islands The Caribbean

Brunei Malaysia, Singapore & Brunei [1 title], Southeast Asia on a Budget

Bulgaria Bulgaria, Europe on a Budget

Burkina Faso West Africa

Cambodia Cambodia, Southeast Asia on a Budget, Vietnam, Laos & Cambodia Map [1 Map]

Cameroon West Africa

Canada Canada, Pacific Northwest, Toronto, Toronto Map, Vancouver

Cape Verde West Africa

Cayman Islands The Caribbean

Chile Chile, Chile Map, South America on a Budget

China Beijing, China, Hong Kong & Macau, Hong Kong & Macau DIR, Shanghai

Colombia South America on a Budget

Costa Rica Central America on a Budget, Costa Rica, Costa Rica & Panama Map

Croatia Croatia, Croatia Map, Europe on a Budget

Cuba Cuba, Cuba Map, The Caribbean, Havana

Cyprus Cyprus, Cyprus Map

Czech Republic The Czech Republic, Czech & Slovak Republics, Europe on a Budget, Prague, Prague DIR, Prague Map

Denmark Copenhagen, Denmark, Europe on a Budget, Scandinavia

Dominica The Caribbean

Dominican Republic Dominican Republic, The Caribbean

Ecuador Ecuador, South America on a Budget

Egypt Egypt, Egypt Map

El Salvador Central America on a Budget

England Britain, Camping in Britain, Devon & Cornwall, Dorset, Hampshire and The Isle of Wight [1 title], England, Europe on a Budget, The Lake District, London, London DIR, London Map, London Mini Guide, Walks In London & Southeast England

Estonia The Baltic States, Europe on a Budget

Fiji Fiji

Finland Europe on a Budget, Finland, Scandinavia

France Brittany & Normandy, Corsica, Corsica Map, The Dordogne & the Lot, Europe on a Budget, France, France Map, Languedoc & Roussillon, The Loire, Paris, Paris DIR, Paris Map, Paris Mini Guide, Provence & the Côte d'Azur, The Pyrenees, Pyrenees & Andorra Map

French Guiana South America on a Budget

Gambia The Gambia, West Africa

Germany Berlin, Berlin Map, Europe on a Budget, Germany, Germany Map

Ghana West Africa

Gibraltar Spain

Greece Athens Map, Crete, Crete Map, Europe on a Budget, Greece, Greece Map, Greek Islands, Ionian Islands

Guadeloupe The Caribbean

Guatemala Central America on a Budget, Guatemala, Guatemala & Belize Map

Guinea West Africa

Guinea-Bissau West Africa

Guyana South America on a Budget

Holland see The Netherlands

Honduras Central America on a Budget

Hungary Budapest, Europe on a Budget, Hungary

Iceland Iceland, Iceland Map

India Goa, India, India Map, Kerala, Rajasthan, Delhi & Agra [1 title], South India, South India Map

Indonesia Bali & Lombok, Southeast Asia on a Budget

Ireland Dublin DIR, Dublin Map, Europe on a Budget, Ireland, Ireland Map

Israel Jerusalem

Italy Europe on a Budget, Florence DIR, Florence & Siena Map, Florence & the best of Tuscany, Italy, The Italian Lakes, Naples & the Amalfi Coast, Rome, Rome DIR, Rome Map, Sardinia, Sicily, Sicily Map, Tuscany & Umbria, Tuscany Map,

Venice, Venice DIR, Venice Map

Jamaica Jamaica, The Caribbean

Japan Japan, Tokyo

Jordan Jordan

Kenya Kenya, Kenya Map

Korea Korea

Laos Laos, Southeast Asia on a Budget, Vietnam, Laos & Cambodia Map [1 Map]

Latvia The Baltic States, Europe on a Budget

Lithuania The Baltic States, Europe on a Budget

Luxembourg Belgium & Luxembourg, Europe on a Budget

Malaysia Malaysia Map, Malaysia, Singapore & Brunei [1 title], Southeast Asia on a Budget

Mali West Africa

Malta Malta & Gozo DIR

Martinique The Caribbean

Mauritania West Africa

Mexico Baja California, Baja California, Cancún & Cozumel DIR, Mexico, Mexico Map, Yucatán, Yucatán Peninsula Map

Monaco France, Provence & the Côte d'Azur

Montenegro Montenegro

Morocco Europe on a Budget, Marrakesh DIR, Marrakesh Map, Morocco, Morocco Map,

Nepal Nepal

Netherlands Amsterdam, Amsterdam DIR, Amsterdam Map, Europe on a Budget, The Netherlands

Netherlands Antilles The Caribbean

New Zealand New Zealand, New Zealand Map

DIR: Rough Guide **DIRECTIONS** for short breaks

Available from all good bookstores

ROUGH GUIDES
Don't Just Travel

For more information go to www.roughguides.com

ROUGH GUIDE MAP

France

1:1,000,000 · 1 INCH: 15.8 MILES · 1CM: 10KM

"The most accurate maps in the world"

CITY MAPS 24 titles

Amsterdam · Athens · Barcelona · Berlin · Boston · Brussels
Chicago · Dublin · Florence & Siena · Frankfurt · Lisbon · London
Los Angeles · Madrid · Marrakesh · Miami · New York City · Paris
Prague · Rome · San Francisco · Toronto · Venice · Washington DC
US$8.99 Can$13.99 £4.99

COUNTRY & REGIONAL MAPS 50 titles

Algarve · Andalucía · Argentina · Australia · Baja California
Brittany · Crete · Croatia · Cuba · Cyprus · Czech Republic
Dominican Republic · Dubai · Egypt · Greece · Guatemala & Belize
Iceland · Ireland · India · Kenya · Mexico · Morocco · New Zealand
Northern Spain · Peru · Portugal · Sicily · South Africa · South India
Sri Lanka · Tenerife · Thailand · Trinidad & Tobago · Turkey
Tuscany · Yucatán Peninsula and more.
US$9.99 Can$13.99 £5.99

WATERPROOF • RIP-PROOF • AMAZING VALUE

Plastic waterproof map
ideal for planning and touring

Make the most of your time on Earth™

ROUGH GUIDES

CRYSTAL
AUTO RENTAL
Drive To TIKAL

PH: 223-1600

BZE Toll Free:
0-800-777-7777

BEST RATES   LARGEST SELECTION
BEST SERVICE   LARGEST INVENTORY

WWW.CRYSTAL-BELIZE.COM

UNFORGETABLE
BELIZE
ADVENTURES

**Sea Kayak & Snorkel
Remote Reefs
& Coral Atolls**

**Rainforest Rivers
Mayan Ruins
& Caves**

EXPEDITIONS.COM

www.islandexpeditions.com

FREE ADVENTURE GUIDE
1-800-667-1630

FREEPHONE UK 0800-404-9535

Small print and
Index

A Rough Guide to Rough Guides

Published in 1982, the first Rough Guide – to Greece – was a student scheme that became a publishing phenomenon. Mark Ellingham, a recent graduate in English from Bristol University, had been travelling in Greece the previous summer and couldn't find the right guidebook. With a small group of friends he wrote his own guide, combining a highly contemporary, journalistic style with a thoroughly practical approach to travellers' needs.

The immediate success of the book spawned a series that rapidly covered dozens of destinations. And, in addition to impecunious backpackers, Rough Guides soon acquired a much broader and older readership that relished the guides' wit and inquisitiveness as much as their enthusiastic, critical approach and value-for-money ethos.

These days, Rough Guides include recommendations from shoestring to luxury and cover more than 200 destinations around the globe, including almost every country in the Americas and Europe, more than half of Africa and most of Asia and Australasia. Our ever-growing team of authors and photographers is spread all over the world, particularly in Europe, the US and Australia.

In the early 1990s, Rough Guides branched out of travel, with the publication of Rough Guides to World Music, Classical Music and the Internet. All three have become benchmark titles in their fields, spearheading the publication of a wide range of books under the Rough Guide name.

Including the travel series, Rough Guides now number more than 350 titles, covering: phrasebooks, waterproof maps, music guides from Opera to Heavy Metal, reference works as diverse as Conspiracy Theories and Shakespeare, and popular culture books from iPods to Poker. Rough Guides also produce a series of more than 120 World Music CDs in partnership with World Music Network.

Visit www.roughguides.com to see our latest publications.

Rough Guide credits

Text editor: Lucy Cowie
Layout: Nikhil Agarwal
Cartography: JP Map Graphics Ltd
Picture editor: Nicole Newman
Production: Erika Pepe
Proofreader: Anita Sach
Cover design: Nicole Newman, Dan May,
Chloë Roberts
Photographer: Roger d'Olivere Mapp
Editorial: **London** Andy Turner, Keith Drew,
Edward Aves, Alice Park, Lucy White, Jo Kirby,
James Smart, Natasha Foges, Róisín Cameron,
James Rice, Lara Kavanagh, Emma Traynor,
Emma Gibbs, Kathryn Lane, Monica Woods, Mani
Ramaswamy, Harry Wilson, Alison Roberts, Eleanor
Aldridge, Ian Blenkinsop, Joe Staines, Matthew
Milton, Tracy Hopkins, Ruth Tidball; **Delhi** Madhavi
Singh, Lubna Shaheen, Jalpreen Kaur Chhatwal
Design & Pictures: **London** Scott Stickland, Dan
May, Diana Jarvis, Mark Thomas, Nicole Newman,
Sarah Cummins, Emily Taylor; **Delhi** Umesh
Aggarwal, Ajay Verma, Jessica Subramanian,
Ankur Guha, Pradeep Thapliyal, Sachin Tanwar,
Anita Singh, Sachin Gupta

Production: Rebecca Short, Liz Cherry,
Louise Daly,
Cartography: **London** Ed Wright, Katie Lloyd-
Jones; **Delhi** Rajesh Chhibber, Ashutosh Bharti,
Rajesh Mishra, Animesh Pathak, Jasbir Sandhu,
Karobi Gogoi, Swati Handoo, Deshpal Dabas,
Lokamata Sahu
Online. **London** Faye Hellon, Jeanette Angell,
Fergus Day, Justine Bright, Clare Bryson, Aine
Fearon, Adrian Low, Ezgi Celebi; **Delhi** Amit
Verma, Rahul Kumar, Narender Kumar, Ravi
Yadav, Debojit Borah, Rakesh Kumar, Ganesh
Sharma, Shisir Basumatari
Marketing & Publicity: **London** Liz Statham, Jess
Carter, Vivienne Watton, Anna Paynton, Rachel
Sprackett, Laura Vipond; **New York** Katy Ball;
Delhi Aman Arora
Digital Travel Publisher: Peter Buckley
Reference Director: Andrew Lockett
Operations Assistant: Becky Doyle
Operations Manager: Helen Atkinson
Publishing Director (Travel): Clare Currie
Commercial Manager: Gino Magnotta
Managing Director: John Duhigg

Publishing information

This fifth edition published November 2010 by
Rough Guides Ltd,
80 Strand, London WC2R 0RL
11, Community Centre, Panchsheel Park, New
Delhi 110017, India

Distributed by the Penguin Group
Penguin Books Ltd,
80 Strand, London WC2R 0RL
Penguin Group (USA)
375 Hudson Street, NY 10014, USA
Penguin Group (Australia)
250 Camberwell Road, Camberwell,
Victoria 3124, Australia
Penguin Group (NZ)
67 Apollo Drive, Mairangi Bay, Auckland 1310,
New Zealand
This paperback edition published in Canada in
2010. Rough Guides is represented in Canada by
Tourmaline Editions Inc., 662 King Street West,
Suite 304, Toronto, Ontario, M5V 1M7
Cover concept by Peter Dyer.

Typeset in Bembo and Helvetica to an original
design by Henry Iles.

Printed in Singapore
© Peter Eltringham 2010
Maps © Rough Guides
No part of this book may be reproduced in any
form without permission from the publisher except
for the quotation of brief passages in reviews.
296pp includes index
A catalogue record for this book is available from
the British Library
ISBN: 978-1-84836-512-4
The publishers and authors have done their
best to ensure the accuracy and currency of all
the information in **The Rough Guide to Belize**,
however, they can accept no responsibility for
any loss, injury, or inconvenience sustained by
any traveller as a result of information or advice
contained in the guide.

1   3   5   7   9   8   6   4   2

Help us update

We've gone to a lot of effort to ensure that the
fifth edition of **The Rough Guide to Belize** is
accurate and up-to-date. However, things change
– places get "discovered", opening hours are
notoriously fickle, restaurants and rooms raise
prices or lower standards. If you feel we've got it
wrong or left something out, we'd like to know,
and if you can remember the address, the price,
the hours, the phone number, so much the better.

Please send your comments with the subject
line "**Rough Guide Belize Update**" to ® mail
@roughguides.com. We'll credit all contributions
and send a copy of the next edition (or any other
Rough Guide if you prefer) for the very best
emails.
Have your questions answered and tell others
about your trip at ® www.roughguides.com

Acknowledgements

AnneLise Sorensen: In Belize, thanks to all who welcomed me in and shared information, advice, stories and lively evenings, including the wonderfully helpful team at the Belize Tourism Board; the staff at the superb, beachfront *Xanadu* on Ambergris Caye; the friendly *De Real Macaw Guest House*; the splendid *The Great House*; *Nerie's Restaurant* in Belize City, particularly for the grilled gibnut; tour guide extraordinaire Katie Valk; Mo and Irene Miller at the lovely *Lazy Iguana* on Caye Caulker; and the knowledgeable Charlie at *Las Palmas* hotel in Corozal. A big *gracias* to my co-author Robert Coates and, as always, we celebrate the dear memory of Peter Eltringham, who was a true lover of beautiful Belize. *Gracias* also to family, friends and *guapos* for all their cheery emails. And thanks to the top-notch Delhi team; to Katie Lloyd-Jones for maps; Nicole Newman for photo research; and Mani Ramaswamy and Lucy Cowie.

Robert Coates: Sincere thanks to my Dad John Stewart for all his help, contacts, and his company in the 4x4 to Placencia. In Belize City big thankyous to Jude and Delsie Lizama and family, plus Dominique Lizama at the Audobon Society for her assistance with environmental issues and the Cockscomb Basin, as well as Jeanie Shaw. In Belmopan, my gratitude to Gloria and Gean Cho for superb hospitality, in Cayo to the Juan family and Adrian Barton, in PG to Bruno and Melissa, and elsewhere to Sol and Adena Tucker, and Merrilie Ellis. Sincere thanks to Lucy Cowie, Christina Valhouli and AnneLise Sorensen

for all their hard work on this new edition, and of course to the inimitable Peter Eltringham for his phenomenal energy and for introducing me to Rough Guides at the outset – you're sadly missed.

The photographer **Roger d'Olivere Mapp** wishes to thank the following people for their wonderful hospitality and valuable local tips: Louise Belisle at Bluefield Lodge; Jessie Benner at *De Real Macaw*; Helwa Rosado at *Orchid Palm Inn*; Maria Preston, Michael Preston and Dorita Moralez at *Midas Resort*; Joan at *Conch Shell Inn*; and Verna at *Seaspray Hotel*. Thanks also to: Karina Cunil at BTB for her assistance with location permits; Elias Cambranes, tour operator at *Casa Blanca Guest House*, for his insightful and well organized trip to Tikal in Guatemala; Jan Meerman at the Green Hills Butterfly Ranch for showing us his spectacular butterfly farm and botanical garden; the keeper at Belize Zoo for sharing his knowledge of the wildlife he nurtures and protects, helping me to capture some amazing photographs; Isabella and her beautiful family, in San Pedro Columbia for a memorable afternoon; to all the people who shared with us local tips, delicious food, a friendly smile and your amazing country; and to my gorgeous travelling companion for her excellent navigation skills, enduring the endless giant potholes throughout our journey, especially along the infamous road to and from Placencia, for sharing the unforgettable heart-in-mouth experience of Shark Ray Alley and the convoyed trek into the lush otherworldly jungles of Caracol... nuff respect NMN!

Readers' letters

Thanks to all the readers who have taken the time to write in with comments and suggestions (and apologies if we've inadvertently omitted or misspelt anyone's name):

Linda Cox, Roy Fontaine, David Gobeil, Claudia Hardegger, Reinhard Illner, Noel D. Jacobs, Orla Keating, Stephen Lee, Dave Lindsay, Ann Llewellyn, Sheila McCaffrey, Allison Morris, Stefano Ragagnin, Dioniscio Rosalez, Nicoletta Sala, Dave Souza, Ruth Turner, Andrew Usher, Steve Willis.

Photo credits

All photography by Roger d'Olivere Mapp © Rough Guides except the following:

Things not to miss
05 The Blue Hole and Lighthouse Reef atoll
   © Ron Watts/Corbis
14 Carnival celebrations © Tony Rath/BTB

Underwater Belize colour section
Catching a barracuda © National Geographic/Getty
Gray angelfish © Getty
Whale shark © Norbert Wu/Corbis
Glover's Reef © Mark Lewis/Getty

Index

Map entries are in colour.

Map symbols

maps are listed in the full index using coloured text

– – – ·	International boundary	★	Bus/taxi stop
— – · ·	District boundary	✈	Airport
– – –	Chapter division boundary	✗	Airstrip
═══	Major road	◆	Place of interest
═══	Minor road	🅿	Parking
- - - - -	Path	ⓘ	Tourist information
———	River	@	Internet access
— —	Ferry route	ℂ	Telephone
ᒧᒧᒧ	Reef	✉	Post office
⌂	Mountain range	⛳	Golf course
▲	Mountain peak	⊙	Monument
⌇⌇	Gorge	♦	Museum
𝄞	Waterfall	⛽	Petrol station
⌒	Cave	✚	Church
⚒	Maya ruin	▮	Building
♦	Border crossing	⬭	Stadium
☨	Lighthouse	▦	Park
⚠	Campsite	⊞	Cemetery
◉	Accommodation	≈	Swamp
▣	Restaurant	▦	Beach

MAP SYMBOLS

295

So now we've told you about the things not to miss, the best places to stay, the top restaurants, the liveliest bars and the most spectacular sights, it only seems fair to tell you about the best travel insurance around

WorldNomads.com
keep travelling safely

Recommended by Rough Guides

www.roughguides.com
MAKE THE MOST OF YOUR TIME ON EARTH

ROUGH
GUIDE